Reagan's Disciple

ALSO BY LOU CANNON

Ronnie and Jesse: A Political Odyssey (1969)

The McCloskey Challenge (1972)

Reporting: An Inside View (1977)

Reagan (1982)

Official Negligence: How Rodney King and the Riots Changed Los Angeles and the LAPD (1998)

President Reagan: The Role of a Lifetime (1991, 2000)

Ronald Reagan: The Presidential Portfolio (2001)

Governor Reagan: His Rise to Power (2003)

ALSO BY CARL M. CANNON

The Pursuit of Happiness in Times of War (2003)

Boy Genius: Karl Rove, The Architect of George W. Bush's Remarkable Political Triumphs, co-author (2003, 2005)

Reagan's Disciple

George W. Bush's Troubled Quest

for a Presidential Legacy

Lou Cannon

and

Carl M. Cannon

PublicAffairs | *New York*

PublicAffairs books are available at special discounts for bulk purchases in the U.S. by corporations, institutions, and other organizations. For more information, please contact the Special Markets Department at the Perseus Books Group, 2300 Chestnut Street, Suite 200, Philadelphia, PA 19103, call (800) 255–1514, or email special.markets@perseusbooks.com.

Library of Congress Cataloging-in-Publication Data
Cannon, Lou.
    Reagan's disciple : George W. Bush's troubled quest for a presidential legacy / Lou Cannon and Carl M. Cannon.
        p. cm.
    Includes bibliographical references and index.
    ISBN 978-1-58648-448-4
    1. Bush, George W. (George Walker), 1946- 2. Reagan, Ronald—Influence. 3. Presidents—United States—Biography 4. Republican Party (U.S. : 1854-)—Biography. 5. United States—Politics and government—1981–1989. 6. United States—Politics and government—2001- I. Cannon, Carl M. II. Title.

E903.C36 207
973.931092—dc22
[B]
                                                                        2007040220

First Edition

10 9 8 7 6 5 4 3 2 1

To Mary and Sharon, with appreciation
And for David, Judy, and Jack
And Nicholas, Kelley, Grace, Tiffany, Stephanie, and Nathan
And Jenna

Contents

Preface

The idea for this book grew out of a joint presentation, "A Tale of Two Presidents," that the two of us gave March 27, 2006, at Stanford University where we were Hoover Media Fellows. The presidents were Ronald Reagan and George W. Bush. The two of us are Lou Cannon and Carl M. Cannon, father and son, who have occasionally worked together as reporters but are collaborating on a book for the first time. We were and remain fascinated by the degree to which George W. Bush, the son of President George H. W. Bush, modeled—or tried to model—his presidency not after his father's but after Ronald Reagan's. On matters of style and substance alike, the younger Bush and several of his aides and consultants evoked the Reagan model at every opportunity. Members of the Reagan team, at least when Bush was riding high in public approval, had welcomed the comparisons as ratification that their hero was the gold standard for presidents—and even more so for Republican presidential candidates.

In 1980 Reagan won the White House by easily besting the senior Bush and five other candidates for the Republican Party nomination and then defeating incumbent President Jimmy Carter. Four years later, under the gauzy slogan of "Morning Again in America," Reagan won reelection in an impressive forty-nine-state landslide. Reagan's vice president, George H. W. Bush, ascended to the Oval Office in 1988 in an election that was largely a referendum on Reagan and his policies. On his own in 1992, Bush lost to Bill Clinton in a three-way race. So it was not surprising that Team Bush relished Reagan comparisons in the 2000 presidential campaign. Ken

Khachigian, a premier speechwriter for Reagan, described Bush as lacking "artifice or contrivance," in supposed contrast to Democratic nominee Al Gore. "If nothing else, George W. Bush appears genuine," Khachigian said. "That's Ronald Reagan all over the place." Scott McClellan, campaign spokesman and later White House press secretary, would parry virtually any criticism by invoking Reagan's name. ("Like Ronald Reagan, Governor Bush understands that the role of a leader is to set a clear agenda," he would say. "Like Ronald Reagan, Governor Bush is setting up a positive, uplifting tone for the country.")

Even when the younger Bush was compared to his father, Reagan was part of the equation. When the voting ended on November 7, 2000, a key Bush adviser in Austin was asked by a British journalist what kind of president the Texas governor would make. "Truly, I think he will be a cross between his dad and Ronald Reagan," the aide replied. "He has the innate decency of his father and the ability of Reagan to set a broad course."[1] The "cross" Team Bush had in mind was the melding of Forty-One's "kinder and gentler" impulses with Reagan's conservatism on taxes, social policy, and America's place in the world. In this construct, taxes would be cut not only because government was insatiable and its programs counter-productive, but also because it was better for poor people. This was an echo of supply-side economics, which held that tax reductions spurred productivity and helped everyone.

Jack Kemp, a Republican House member representing a working-class district in Buffalo, had popularized supply-side in the late 1970s to attract Democrats who distrusted traditional Republican polices of balanced budgets and high interest rates. Kemp often quoted President John F. Kennedy, who had proposed tax cuts and famously said, "A rising tide lifts all boats." Reagan, also given to quoting JFK and attentive to measures that appealed to independent and Democratic voters, had embraced supply-side economics during the 1980 presidential campaign. George H. W. Bush, in contrast, had dismissed the theory as "voodoo economics," a view he necessarily recanted when he became Reagan's running mate. But tax policy proved a continuing stumbling block for the elder Bush. As the 1988 presidential nominee, he promised never to raise taxes. Breaking this promise contributed to his defeat four years later and made an indelible impression on his son. George W. Bush would not repeat his father's political mistake, and his tax cuts stamped him as the Gipper's heir. This phenomenon was examined in "Reagan's Son," an incisive cover story by Bill Keller in *The New York Times Magazine* on January 26, 2003, seven weeks before the invasion of Iraq. Keller, soon to become the executive editor of his newspaper, described a president with Reagan-like priorities in judicial appointments and deployment of American power as well as tax-cutting. Furthermore, wrote Keller, "Reagan DNA" was imprinted in the staffing and training of the George W. Bush administration. Several longtime Reagan aides agreed. One of them, Hoover Institution scholar Martin C. Anderson, who had served as Reagan's domestic policy adviser, said that when he gave tutorials to Bush it felt as if he were briefing a younger version of Reagan. Michael K. Deaver, who had been closer to the Reagans than any other White House aide, also saw Bush's behavior as Reaganesque. "I mean, his father was supposed to be the third term of the Reagan presidency—but then he wasn't," Deaver said. "This guy is."

Why did Reagan have such a magical hold on his followers—and for that matter, on the American people? These questions have been examined in Lou Cannon's books and will, in shorter compass, be reexamined in this one. There are three key points. The first is that conservatives saw Reagan as their champion because he led them out of the political wilderness to national power and, many of them believe, to greatness. This adoration was expressed at a December 1, 1988, Republican dinner by Kemp, who described himself as a "foot-soldier . . . in the Reagan army" and noted that over the years he had introduced Reagan as George Gipp, as a modern-day Sir Thomas More, and as Alexander the Great. Then, with President-elect George H. W. Bush in attendance, Kemp gazed at Reagan and gushed, "with all due respect to Winston Churchill and with all due respect to William Manchester, who wrote *The Last Lion,* Churchill was not the 'last lion' of the twentieth century. He's with us tonight: Ronald Wilson Reagan."[2]

The second reason for Reagan's iconic status is that a significant majority of Americans, including many Democrats and independents, viewed him as a reassuring figure who had steadied the nation in troubled times and, by dealing successfully with the Soviet Union, made the world a safer place. Even though President Reagan's popularity had been nicked by the Iran-contra affair, he finished his two terms with approval ratings ranging from 63 percent (Gallup) to 68 percent (*The New York Times*–CBS), the highest for any president who has left office alive. In a Gallup Poll in 2001, Americans ranked Reagan as the greatest president of all time, slightly ahead of John F. Kennedy, with Abraham Lincoln third. (Even among more skeptical academic historians, Reagan's ratings have slowly advanced. These historians placed Reagan twenty-second when he left office; in four more recent surveys he has ranked anywhere from third to eleventh.)

The third reason Reagan remains popular is that in the eyes of many he benefits in comparison to his successors. The first Bush lost the public's confidence by barely responding to recession—and lost his reelection bid. Clinton's reputation was damaged while he was president by fund-raising and sex scandals, and after he left office by retrospective criticism that he had failed to prepare America for terrorist attacks. Americans across the political spectrum are disillusioned with George W. Bush for a host of reasons, most of all the Iraq War. In their eagerness to discredit him, political liberals who couldn't stand Reagan when he was alive have discovered hitherto unrecognized qualities of greatness in the fortieth president. Disappointed conservatives, meanwhile, have recast Bush as the Anti-Reagan. "Bush is not a conservative," wrote Jeffrey Hart, the conservative academic and author of *The Making of the American Conservative Mind:* National Review *and Its Times*. "He is a right-wing ideologue."[3] In this same essay Hart quoted conservative icon William F. Buckley Jr. as defining true conservatism as "the politics of reality," adding that Bush did not meet this standard. For his part, Bill Buckley cooled first on the Iraq War, and then on the Bush presidency itself. Conservative economist Bruce Bartlett, in *Imposter: How George W. Bush Bankrupted America and Betrayed the Reagan Legacy,* denounces Bush on the book's first page as a "pretend conservative" who, despite cutting taxes, never made any meaningful attempts to rein in federal spending. "He has more in common with liberals, who see no limits to state power as long as it is used to advance what they think is right," Bartlett said of GWB. The phrase coined by Bush defender Fred Barnes—"big-government conservatism"—has been used derisively in *National Review* and other conservative publications.

There are two principal reasons why conservatives have soured on George W. Bush. One is uneasiness about the war. The other is Bush's blithe embrace of deficit spending, necessitated, in part, to finance that war. As the U.S. occupation of Iraq turned into a stalemate, a spirited debate broke out in liberal circles over whether Al Gore would have launched an invasion to oust Saddam Hussein. Gore, who said in the 2000 campaign that his guiding principle as president would be "WWJD" (what would Jesus do?), answered, as many Democrats have, that he would have invaded Afghanistan, but not Iraq. Conservatives began debating a similar question, but their concerns came under the heading of what can be termed "WWRRD?"

"Would Ronald Reagan have invaded Iraq?" Patrick J. Buchanan, Reagan's onetime White House director of communications, asked in a 2004 column days after Reagan's death. "Would he have declared a doctrine of preventive war to keep any rival nation from rising to where it might challenge us? Would he have crusaded for 'world democratic revolution'? Was Reagan the first neoconservative?" Buchanan, who never favored the Iraq War—even when it appeared to be going well and was politically popular with a majority of Americans—argued no. And while it's true that Buchanan is an idiosyncratic conservative and longtime critic of the entire Bush family, he was not alone. Conservative scholars Stefan Halper and Jonathan Clarke, coauthors of *America Alone: The Neo-Conservatives and Global Order,* maintained that it is a "travesty" to even assert, as several prominent Iraq hawks have done, that Reagan would have invaded Iraq.

The purpose of this book is to examine that proposition and the broader questions surrounding it: Did it ever make sense to anoint George W. Bush the rightful inheritor of Reaganism? Once in the Oval Office, did he govern as Reagan governed and lead the nation in the direction Reagan would have led it? Finally, did the forty-third president of the United States ratify the Reagan Revolution—or derail it?

We trust that readers of this book who have followed the authors' works over the years will expect an evenhanded and thorough examination of our subject matter from—in the old sense of the phrase—a fair and balanced point of view. Neither of us is partisan, an outlook made easier by the fact that we are not ideological. We come to our judgments with shoe-leather reporting and analysis based on facts and historical context. Between the two of us, we have covered six of the last seven presidents and interviewed all seven. While reporting this book we drew on Carl's access to Bush aides and former aides, such as Michael Gerson, Karl Rove, Peter Wehner, and Bush media maven Mark McKinnon, formerly a Texas Democrat; and on Lou's longtime relationship with such GOP luminaries as Colin Powell, Michael Deaver, James Baker, Kenneth Duberstein, Edwin Meese, and George Shultz, among others. Carl has twice dined with George W. Bush; Lou had numerous interviews and exchanges with Ronald Reagan. Both of us, particularly Lou, have long known Dick Cheney. We respect these people without identifying with them, or with their Democratic critics. We believe reporters should be beyond politics. We see our role—as contemporary historians and biographers as well as journalists—as one of bearing witness to events and trying to understand them. In the pages that follow, we have tried to describe the essence of these two presidencies, the fortieth and the forty-third, and to compare them in a way that sheds light on what has happened at 1600 Pennsylvania Avenue in the past three decades. We hope that this analysis will be particularly useful at a time when Americans are in the process of choosing their next president.

We realize we are joining a conversation in progress and have no illusion that what we say will be the last word on either Ronald Reagan or George W. Bush. This book is neither an anti-Bush polemic nor an apologia, and it makes no pretense of being a definitive account of how the United States became involved in the war in Iraq, a subject on which there are a wealth of excellent books. Being non-ideological, however, does not mean we are conflict averse. Reporters make judgments every day, and we have tried to confront the difficult questions raised by the George W. Bush presidency. The war in Iraq has revived the traditional American distrust of foreign entanglements, once labeled "isolationism," that persist even in an age of globalism. It has encouraged some conservatives to say aloud what they muttered in the Reagan years: That deficits are a real problem and that many tax cuts are illusory. But the debate over the national direction is taking place during the Bush presidency in a different political context than the one faced by Reagan. Republicans were a minority in the House throughout Reagan's presidency and in the Senate during his last two years in office. Until 2006, Republicans were mostly in control of Congress during the George W. Bush presidency; even now, they are more numerous in the House than at any time in the Reagan years. That fact proved a mixed blessing for Bush during his first six years in office. John Kerry was correct when he asserted that Bush hadn't vetoed any spending bills, but Reagan didn't veto many of them either, and he also, after his ballyhooed tax cuts of 1981, raised taxes several times without suffering much in conservative esteem. Given the Democratic majority in the House, many conservatives excused Reagan as doing the best he could.

Yet for all his second-term travails and the accompanying plunge in his popularity, Bush has unquestionably advanced the Reagan Revolution in significant ways. The Democrats, even while denouncing Bush's tax cuts, have failed to make a serious effort to reverse them. The judiciary, most notably the Supreme Court, has become more conservative. Thus, the assertion made by Bill Keller that "Bush is in a sense the fruition of Reagan" is worth a close examination today, as it was in 2003. So, too, are the implications of Keller's prescient conclusion: "If [Bush] fails, my guess is that it will be a failure not of caution but of overreaching, which means it will be failure on a grand scale."

LOU AND CARL CANNON

1

THREE GENERATIONS

In the midst of the presidential campaign of 2004, Boston genealogist Gary Boyd Roberts established that George W. Bush and John Kerry were distant kinsmen. This revelation was unsurprising to Roberts, who in 1995 had documented that the Bush family was related to *fifteen* previous presidents. But it did raise ancient concerns about birth and privilege. "These people are definitely in the American hereditary upper class," Roberts noted.[1] He might have added that Bush's aristocratic background set him apart from every other modern Republican presidential nominee—except Bush's own father. Kerry was not atypical: Two of the Democratic Party's most beloved twentieth-century presidents, Franklin D. Roosevelt and John F. Kennedy, and several other Democratic nominees were to the manor born. But among modern Republican presidents, the two Bushes are the only ones with aristocratic lineages. Both arguably owed their presidencies to the success of Ronald Reagan.

George W. Bush, mindful of his debt, put Reagan first on his list of political heroes, ahead of Winston Churchill and Theodore Roosevelt. Reagan and George W. Bush shared many traits, including (as columnist George F. Will put it) "a talent for happiness," a supreme (even excessive) self-confidence, and a preference for physical activity. But in his modest upbringing and the near penury of his father, Reagan had more in common with other Republican presidents of the past century. Herbert Hoover was orphaned as a child and knew poverty and hard work in his teenage years; Dwight D. Eisenhower's father opened a clothing store that failed, and then retreated, "financially ruined," to the family farm in Kansas. (The future president was born in Texas at a time when his father was trying to get back on his feet as a railroad hand.) Richard M. Nixon's father struggled to survive as a lemon farmer and made dubious business decisions that often put him on the financial brink. Reagan's father was even less successful; he moved from town to town in Illinois as a dreamy itinerant shoe salesman who tried to make a living for his family between drinking bouts. As a child, Reagan lived in so many Illinois towns and cities that he had no opportunity to develop boyhood friendships except with his only sibling, his older brother Neil. Many years later Nancy Reagan said that the combination of this nomadic existence and his father's alcoholism had created a barrier within Ronald Reagan that not even she could fully penetrate. But Reagan was not crushed by his childhood. He adored and identified with his mother, Nelle, a religious woman with an interest in dramatics that she imparted to Ronald. Like Eisenhower and Nixon before him, Reagan was close to his mother and did the best he could with his father. When Reagan, newly minted as a California governor in 1967, was asked about his parents, he talked for fifteen minutes about his mother and didn't mention his father at all.

Memories of hard times in childhood clung to these future presidents for the rest of their lives. Ronald Reagan, born in Tampico, Illinois, on February 6, 1911, came to politics by way of sports broadcasting in Iowa and a movie career in Hollywood, but he talked more in later life about his experiences in Dixon, Illinois, where he and his brother had attended junior high and high school. "We didn't live on the wrong side of the tracks, but we lived so close to them we could hear the whistle real loud,"[2] Reagan often said. Never prosperous, the Reagans were almost crushed by the Depression, which caused the cement shop where his older brother was working to be shut down, forced his father to close a shoe store he had opened with borrowed money, and sent his mother to work in a dress shop for $14 a week. On the campaign trail Ronald Reagan often told a story about how his father, working for a company as a shoe salesman after his store had closed, opened a special delivery letter on Christmas Eve that he thought might be a bonus. Instead, he found a pink slip informing him that he was fired.

The Bush family couldn't be more of a contrast. George W. Bush, despite his well-documented contempt for elites, is a scion of the select. He was born July 6, 1946, in New Haven, Connecticut, into the bosom of comfort, wealth, privilege, and expectation. "The United States was the most powerful nation in the world, and his own extended family was in a wonderfully favorable position in it" is the way *New Yorker* writer Nicholas Lemann put it. "His father was a war-hero student at Yale, which *his* father, great-grandfather, great-great grandfather, and several uncles and cousins had attended before him."[3] When George H. W. Bush was tapped for membership in the exclusive Yale secret club Skull and Bones, he was the fifth member of the clan to be so honored. (George W. Bush would be the sixth.) And that was only Bush's father's side. Barbara Bush—née Pierce—the wife of one president and mother of another, came from a moneyed and accomplished family of her own. The Bushes were connected by friendship and business to other dynastic American lineages, including the Harrimans and the Rockefellers. "There was," noted Lemann, "almost no place that mattered in business or politics, in the United States or Europe, that was out of the Bush family's range."

If the family's reputation is firmly established in the twenty-first century as one of the most accomplished political dynasties in American history, this was not preordained. It almost didn't happen, and might not have happened except for Ronald Reagan. Three decades ago, an objective chronicling of the Bush fortune could have easily made the case for *downward* mobility.

The patriarch of the modern Bush clan was Prescott Bush, George W. Bush's grandfather. The family was never hard-pressed, but it was Prescott Bush's success as a Wall Street banker with Brown Brothers Harriman in the 1930s and 1940s that ensured his children and grandchildren would begin their own careers in business and politics on solid financial footing. He was known as "Pres" Bush, but the minimalist makeup of that nickname in a family of monikers such as "Pressy," "Poppy," and "Bucky" was an apt elucidation for this tall, imposing, and somewhat detached man. Prescott Bush wore neckties to the family dinner table and encouraged his sons to do the same. "He didn't get down and play with you on the floor," William Bush (Bucky), his youngest son, once explained.[4] Jonathan J. Bush, another of Prescott's son's, put it in more earthy terms in a 1986 interview with *The Washington Post:* "I never heard him fart," he said of his father. Prescott Bush's most famous son, the forty-first president of the United States, liked to tell his own children of the time another man tried to tell their grandfather an off-color joke in the locker room of their club. "Dad walked out on him," George H. W. Bush recalled.[5]

If Prescott Bush was exacting, he was also game and active. An accomplished amateur golfer in his native Ohio, he later became president of the U.S. Golf Association. (His wife, Dorothy, was a fiercely competitive and gifted tennis player.) At Yale, he played varsity golf and football, in addition to baseball, the sport in which his athletic abilities were most celebrated. Prescott Bush was a power-hitting first baseman, and he captained the team. After college, he enlisted in the U.S. Army and was shipped to France, where he saw action as an artillery captain with the American Expeditionary Force serving on the Western Front under Gen. John J. Pershing. After the end of World War I, Prescott Bush went to work in St. Louis before putting down roots on the East Coast. In Connecticut, he became a wealthy banker, and later, as a U.S. senator from that state, he came to be known for his formal manner and his golf swing, which was so picture-perfect that he was regularly invited to accompany presidents on the links.*

George Herbert Walker Bush was Prescott Bush's second son, and in many ways, the one most like his father. He had the height, the natural leadership ability, and the nickname ("Poppy") to prove it. He followed his father into military service, too, enlisting in the Navy on June 12, 1942—his eighteenth birthday—only days after graduating from Phillips Academy in Andover, Massachusetts. One of the youngest American combat pilots in the U.S. Navy, Bush flew fifty-eight combat missions in 1944 in a squadron with horrific casualty rates, and he was awarded the Distinguished Flying Cross and other medals for his contributions. He almost didn't live to see the end of the war. On September 2, in action over

---

*The Eisenhower Library boasts a photograph showing Ike with his hands in the air after incorrectly telling Japanese Prime Minister Nobusuke Kishi that Prescott Bush (also pictured) was a graduate of Harvard. Bush stepped forward and said, "Beg your pardon, it was Yale." Eisenhower exclaimed: "Oh my gosh."

Chichi Jima, his plane was hit by Japanese gunners. He bailed out, as did one of his two remaining crewmen—but that man's parachute never opened, and the other perished in the plane. Bush was rescued at sea by a U.S. submarine. After World War II, Bush enrolled at Yale, where he played first base—Prescott's position—and led his team to the finals of the College World Series in 1947 and 1948. Although he wasn't the hitter Prescott Bush had been, he was an elegant fielder who was also chosen team captain. After college, he left New England for Texas, where he realized some early success in the oil business before forsaking it, as his father had banking, for politics. He served two terms in the U.S. House of Representatives from a district in Houston, but lost two elections in which he attempted to follow his father's career path into the U.S. Senate. Among family friends, it seemed, the only surprising aspect of his life's trajectory was his failure to win a Senate seat. From a young age, Poppy Bush had followed Dorothy and Prescott Bush's wishes so reliably that it seemed to some as if he'd never really been a kid at all.

George W. Bush was another story. Adults in Midland, taking their cue from the Bush clan, called the oldest child of George and Barbara Bush "Georgie" to differentiate him from "Big George," as Poppy was known in Texas. The other kids called him "Bushtail," and he was a handful. If Prescott normally eschewed any word stronger than "jackass," young George knew all the four-letter words by the time he was twelve, a habit he complemented with cigars, swagger, and a constant array of juvenile stunts designed, in the main, to irritate his elders. In contrast to his genteel grandfather, young George developed a lifelong appreciation for flatulence jokes. Some readers expressed distress when Bob Woodward revealed in *State of Denial* that at a 2005 White House senior staff meeting, the president rigged up a kind of high-tech whoopee cushion in a chair for senior political aide Karl Rove. But Bush had been doing these things all his life. "Okay you little wieners, line up," he'd bark to his younger brothers as a Bush relative would cruise up the driveway after arriving at the family compound at Kennebunkport, Maine. Then he'd shoot them with his air rifle, and they'd dutifully flop around as if they'd been mortally wounded. At Sunday morning church services he liked to greet women four times his age, "Hiya, little lady, lookin' sexy!" and Barbara and George Bush would exchange pained looks. "Georgie aggravates the hell out of me at times," Big George wrote to his father-in-law.[6]

Such parental frustrations didn't end with the conclusion of George W.'s childhood. In college he was detained by the Yale police for a prank (stealing a Christmas wreath from a rival fraternity); when he was twenty-six he took his fifteen-year-old brother, Marvin, to a party, and when the two brothers arrived home tipsy, George W. confronted his father insolently; the summer he turned thirty, at a time when his father was director of the Central Intelligence Agency, George W. was arrested for drunk driving; and at the age of forty, an apparently well-lubricated George W. cussed out *Wall Street Journal* reporter Al Hunt at a Mexican restaurant in Dallas because Hunt had possessed the temerity to predict in print that the 1988 Republican nominee would be Jack Kemp. The episode occurred in the presence of Hunt's wife and four-year-old son, and Hunt later recalled thinking, as Bush walked away from his table, "This is a guy who's got problems."[7]

But what kind of problems? Why George W. behaved this way has been a source of speculation among the amateur psychologists in America's political class almost since the day he announced his presidential ambitions. Predictably, the question has engendered the sort of partisan posing that passes for reflection in twenty-first-century America's political climate. Bush's predominantly liberal detractors, citing all of this—his hard-partying college years; his mediocre academic record; his stint in the Army Air Corps Reserves, for which he was barely present in his last couple of years; the family connections that formed the foundation of his dual career in business and politics; and his willing role as the family's media-baiting enforcer when his father ran for the presidency in 1988—said this was the résumé of a callow, spoiled, intellectually incurious bully who suffered from a well-served Oedipus complex. Accordingly, in the faddish parlance of our times, George W.'s critics characterized him as a "dry drunk" who had never really dealt with his alcoholism, let alone his underlying resentments toward his father. He was, his critics maintained, a rebel without a clue.

To his loyalists, however, George W. was a red-blooded American male who had raised a little hell as a young man—but just a little. He had never hurt anyone in the process, and his unilateral decision to give up drinking in adulthood without a serious mishap, let alone an Alcoholics Anonymous–style intervention, was the mark of a dedicated and disciplined family man. Bush's sense of humor, friends said, was one of the most endearing things about him. Democrats who didn't care for his down-home irreverence, they added, were unaccustomed to politicians like Bush who were comfortable in their own skins. His loyalists also insisted, albeit more quietly, that if George W. Bush sometimes came across as inappropriately glib, the unresolved emotion he was exhibiting was neither jealousy nor arrogance. It was grief.

Georgie Bush was six years old when his three-year-old sister, Robin, was diagnosed with childhood leukemia. Barbara and George Bush sought the best medical care in the world for their daughter, which meant Memorial Sloan-Kettering Hospital in New York, where Dr. John Walker, George H. W. Bush's uncle, was a surgeon. Nevertheless, in the 1950s, a diagnosis of leukemia was a death sentence, and the little girl succumbed to the disease seven months later. During that time the other Bush children were sheltered by their parents from the impending tragedy, and her oldest brother, by then a seven-year-old second-grader at Sam Houston Elementary School in Midland, simply had no idea Robin was dying. One October day in 1953, Georgie saw his parents' car pull up in the gravel driveway at school. The boy, who was carrying an old phonograph player to the principal's office when he spotted the car, put his burden down and ran toward his teacher. "My mom, dad, and sister are home," he said breathlessly. "Can I go see them?" He raced toward the family sedan expecting to find Robin in the back seat. But she was already gone.[8]

Barbara Bush had been a dark-haired woman until Robin's illness. In the months she was fighting for her daughter's life her hair turned white, and George W. began mothering his mother. In her autobiography, Barbara Bush offers a single vignette to describe how her oldest son took it upon himself to rescue his mom. One "lovely, breezy day," Mrs. Bush was in her bedroom, mourning, and she overheard her son's brief conversation with a neighbor boy who had come to see if Georgie could come out and play. The boy replied that he wanted to, but he couldn't leave his mother, who needed him. "That started my cure," wrote Barbara Bush, adding that she realized she was asking too much of a little boy.[9] By then Georgie had already started, if not the Bush family's "cure," then it's healing. Barbara and George H. W. Bush had difficulty talking about Robin without crying; well-wishers and family friends had trouble talking about her at all. It was young Georgie who, at a west Texas high school football game, suggested aloud that Robin had a better view of the field from heaven than he did in the stands. And it was Georgie, after learning in school about the rotation of the Earth, who asked his parents if his sister had been buried standing up or sitting down. The sadness that enveloped the Bush household in Midland did not evaporate quickly, but as it did young Georgie Bush forged a bond with his mother that sometimes seemed to exclude other members of the Bush clan. He had learned along the way that he had a knack for making adults laugh, and that wisecracking was an effective way of lightening the emotional load. Bush himself credits his caustic wit to his mom.[10]

These two views of George W. are not mutually exclusive, or even incompatible. In any event, he developed, first as a boy and then as a man, into an unusual archetype: the class clown who possessed a talent for command as well as the expectation that others would turn to him for leadership. It was a duality noticed by his father, who, in that same letter about how maddening his oldest son could be, added: "But then at times I'm so proud of him I could die."

And so this boy who had an impulse to please as well as to exasperate dutifully followed his father and grandfather to Andover and Yale. The family's connections weren't incidental factors in Bush's education. His prep school grades and Scholastic Aptitude Test scores alone were probably insufficient for admission to the Ivy League. George W. appears to have benefited from being a Yale "legacy," the equivalent of affirmative action for the well connected.[11] He is remembered as a garrulous fraternity brother, but in the classroom he was a middling student, posting a high C average,[12] about what Ronald Reagan's grades had been at Eureka, an unpretentious college in downstate Illinois. On the baseball diamond, George W.'s level of talent and dedication took him only as far as being a seldom-used relief pitcher on Yale's junior varsity. After matriculating, with the war raging in Southeast Asia, he also signed up for military service—but in the Texas Air National Guard, flying F-102 fighter interceptors, a billet from which combat posting to Vietnam was unlikely. After college, he earned a master's degree at Harvard Business School and then set out to make his fortune wildcatting in west Texas. He tried but was less successful in the oil fields than his father.

That's about where things stood three decades ago when George H. W. Bush was contemplating running for president against Jimmy Carter—

Reagan was the prohibitive Republican front-runner—and George W. Bush began eyeing a vacant House seat in Midland, Texas. "Dynasty, schmynasty," Jeb Bush would later wisecrack when the Bushes were compared to the Kennedys.[13] But back when the Bushes were plotting the clan's decidedly uphill political campaigns, this skepticism seemed right: The Bush pedigree notwithstanding, the Republican Party in the late 1970s was Ronald Reagan's world and everybody else was just living in it.

This state of affairs was underscored for George H. W. Bush and his eldest son in the summer of 1978 when two faces of the Republican Party—its past and its future—met up in Midland. It was there that the Bushes got their first whiff of the residue of the Reagan army's gunpowder. Although the fate of Reagan, a seasoned speaker and former California governor, and George W. Bush, making his first bid for political office, would be linked in the years to come, George W.'s initial encounter with Reagan on the political battlefield was not a happy one for the younger man. On July 6, 1977, a west Texas congressman named George Mahon had announced his retirement. Mahon had been elected to the U.S. House of Representatives in the second year of the New Deal. He was seventy-seven years old, the longest-serving House member on Capitol Hill. George W. Bush was thirty-one years old, had no experience in government, and had only recently returned to west Texas. But Mahon made the announcement on Bush's birthday, which family members of the ambitious young oilman seemed to see as an omen of sorts.[14] It proved not to be.

Mahon, like all Texas congressmen of his generation, was a Democrat, but southwestern politics had changed profoundly since 1934 when he was first elected. Republican bosses in Texas and Washington, D.C., immediately targeted the seat. Among the west Texas conservatives who thought it was his time was Jim Reese. A stockbroker who had been a local sportscaster and mayor of Odessa, Reese had run for the seat in 1976 and done respectably well, garnering 45 percent of the vote against Mahon. Reese had also been Reagan's point man in west Texas in the 1976 Republican primary, in which Reagan had carried the Lone Star State while nearly wresting the presidential nomination from Gerald R. Ford. By the following year, the elder Bush was himself a presumptive presidential candidate—as was Reagan—and Bush was counting on Texas as his base of support.

Reagan endorsed Jim Reese. Longtime California Reaganite Lyn Nofziger, then running a Reagan-affiliated political action committee called Citizens for the Republic, kicked in money for him. When the Bushes squawked, Reagan called the young congressional candidate's father to smooth things over. The call was vintage Reagan. He told the elder Bush that the Nofziger contribution happened while he, Reagan, was out of the country and would not be repeated. Reagan also said he had nothing against young Bush's candidacy and would be happy to campaign for him—in the general election. But Reagan did not rescind his endorsement of Reese. And if Reagan himself did not go into the district to campaign against George W. Bush, several surrogates associated with the Reagan movement did so. Among them was Oklahoma Republican activist Clarence Warner, who traveled to Texas and promptly raised the far-right canard of the elder Bush's membership in the Trilateral Commission. George W. held a press conference the next day denouncing the attacks on his family. Team Bush also looked for help outside the district (among those contributing to Bush's candidacy were former President Gerald Ford), but Bush's father was peeved and expressed his ire publicly. "I'm not interested in getting into an argument with Reagan," the senior Bush told prominent Washington journalist David S. Broder. "But I am surprised about what he is doing here, in my state. . . . They are making a real effort to defeat George."[15]

The younger Bush managed to best Reese in the primary, but that was not the end of his Reaganite-related troubles. Reese refused to endorse George W. Bush in the general election. More significantly, Reese had shown Bush's Democratic opponent, a wily populist named Kent Hance, the road map for defeating the upstart. Young Bush was portrayed as not authentically Texan, and insufficiently conservative, first by Reese, then by Hance. Reese's campaign sent out a mailer accusing Bush of hiring "Rockefeller-type Republicans such as Karl Rove to help him run his campaign." (In response, Bush minimized Rove's involvement in his campaign in an interview with the local paper, the *Midland Reporter-Telegram,* adding, "I doubt he even supports Rockefeller.") In the general election, Hance echoed this theme of George W. the Effete, telling friends from Lubbock that he doubted young Bush had "ever been in the back of a pool hall in Dimmitt, Texas."[16]

In the primary, George W. Bush had been forced, against his wishes, to buck Reagan. In the runoff, he was cornered into distancing himself from his own father—to the point of asking his father not to campaign with him, and even on occasion pulling out his driver's license to show people he wasn't George Bush Jr.[17] Denying George H. W. Bush in Texas and Reagan anywhere added up to an inauspicious start to George W.'s political career and a predictable outcome: He lost to Hance.

Political junkies who like foreshadowing with their campaign history will appreciate that two years later Bush's father lost to Reagan in the Republican primaries, that Kent Hance's middle name is Ronald, and that while Reagan was president, Hance switched parties and became, literally, a Reagan Republican. Similar things were happening all over the Sunbelt in those days. The Reagan presidential campaigns of 1976 and 1980—never mind George W.'s unsuccessful 1978 congressional bid—signaled the far-reaching changes that were overtaking the Republican Party and, in turn, American electoral politics. It was a taxing journey for the GOP, one that could actually be traced through the travails, and the travels, of a single family: the Bushes.

Prescott Bush, banker, golfer, and family man, was always more interested in government than business, a passion he revealed to the outside world in the spring of 1950 when he announced his candidacy for a vacant Senate seat in a special election in Connecticut. After dispatching a tax protester named Vivian Kellems at the state party convention, Bush began his general election campaign against the Democratic nominee, William Benton, who had been appointed in 1949 by President Harry S. Truman to fill a vacant Senate seat. For most of his life, Prescott Bush had been a "Hoover Republican," a designation signifying an austere approach to domestic government spending and limited interest in having the United States play a decisive role in international affairs. The Great Depression and World War II rendered such a platform untenable, however, and by the 1950s Prescott Bush, notwithstanding his friendship with ranking GOP conservative Bob Taft, was an Eisenhower man. About this time Prescott began describing his own politics as "moderate progressive."[18] His 1950 election-year rhetoric was ardently anti-Communist, fiscally conservative, and moderate-to-liberal on social issues, which generally meant race relations and women's rights. During the campaign, Prescott Bush denounced Truman's proposals for "socialized medicine," warned against the perceived power of "labor bosses" (but not labor unions), and spoke about the corrosive effects on business of "confiscatory taxes." The stalemated Korean War was taking a toll on Truman's popularity even before Chinese troops entered the fight on October 25, 1950, a week before the mid-term election. The Gallup Poll showed Truman's job approval rating dipping below 40 percent that week, revealing a landscape that implied Republican pickups in Connecticut and elsewhere. Indeed, when the election returns rolled in, the Democrats had lost twenty-eight House seats, and six new Republican senators who had ousted Democrats were headed to Washington. Prescott Bush was not one of them.

In the collective memory of the Bush family this loss is attributed to a political attack over a new issue that would come to play a pivotal role in American party politics. In the extensive oral history Prescott Bush and his wife gave to Columbia University in 1966, Bush related how, on the Sunday before the election, thousands of flyers appeared in pews in heavily Catholic towns all over Connecticut instructing parishioners to listen to Drew Pearson's radio broadcast that night at six o'clock. At that hour, Pearson came on the air and intoned that Benton, not Bush, would probably be elected, because it had recently been learned that Bush was involved in the leadership of the American Birth Control League.

Prescott and Dorothy Bush recalled that they had immediately denied the accusation, but the harm had been done. Two days later, Prescott Bush lost to Benton by a total of 1,102 votes out of 862,000 cast. It was a bitter pill, and various Bush family chroniclers have attached great significance to this episode. Peter and Rochelle Schweizer, coauthors of *The Bushes: Portrait of a Dynasty,* wrote that the incident "infuriated [Prescott] Bush and darkened the family's views about the media." It also awakened them to the salience of abortion and family planning issues. Writing the foreword to a 1972 U.N.-produced book called *World Population Crisis,* George H. W. Bush, then ambassador to the United Nations, asserted that Prescott's 1950 campaign provided his initial awareness of birth control as a public policy issue. That lesson, he added, "came with a jolt."

Prescott Bush's loss might have ended the Bush dynasty before it ever began. Two years later, Prescott Bush wanted a rematch against Benton but was denied his party's nomination. Connecticut's second senator, Brien McMahon, died unexpectedly, however, and Bush got his second chance. To win in 1952, Prescott Bush first had to confront the opposition of his old business partner, friend, and Yale classmate W. Averill Harriman. The two men were so close that during the Depression Harriman had used his own family money to help Prescott Bush stave off bankruptcy. He was like family, except that he wasn't—and in the collective memory of Clan Bush—this proved significant.

Like many millions of other Americans (including Ronald Reagan), Harriman had become a liberal Democrat during the New Deal, and in 1952 he sought the Democratic senatorial nomination himself. He didn't get it, but he campaigned in the general election for the man who did, Abraham Ribicoff—despite the fact that Ribicoff was running against his friend Prescott Bush. To political writer Michael Kranish, who wrote a detailed 2001 portrait of the Bush family in the *Boston Globe,* this event—even more than the 1950 defeat over family planning—forged the core of the Bush family political identity, one in which loyalty is valued above all else.

"The Harriman-Bush episode, perhaps more than any other, marks the birth of the Bush family's political soul," Kranish asserted. "No more would there be naive assumptions that all patricians and partners in business would stand together. Over the years, the Bushes would be tagged as elitists. They would often respond that the Democrats were the real elitists, and cite Harriman as a bitter example. Similarly, the Bushes value loyalty above all else, and once again, Harriman helps explain why."[19]

Perhaps so, but these two campaigns also illustrate how, as the United States emerged from the Depression and World War II, there were greater natural forces at work than the Bush family's sensibilities. The tectonic plates in American politics were shifting, to use a California metaphor, and Republicans who didn't change with the times risked being swallowed up. On some level, the Bushes understood this intuitively. After all, their reflexive reaction to the Drew Pearson item was to deny it, even though the allegation was essentially true. (Pearson alleged that Bush was on the board of directors of the Birth Control League. A 1947 national fundraising letter on the stationery of Planned Parenthood Federation of America, its successor organization, lists Prescott Bush as the group's national treasurer.) Family planning was one of the issues that would delineate the old Republican Party from the new version, the GOP in the Age of Reagan. The Republican sea change can be chronicled through the actions of three generations of Bush political candidates.

Generation One: Prescott Bush was an unabashed supporter of family planning.

Generation Two: George and Barbara Bush quietly supported abortion rights, to the point of the occasional monetary contribution to Planned Parenthood. But Bush abandoned that position on the spot when offered the vice presidency in 1980 by Reagan.

Generation Three: George W. Bush and his brother, who came of age politically after *Roe v. Wade,* are simply never on record as backing legalized abortion. Jeb Bush lost his 1994 gubernatorial election in part because he was too hard-right—even for Florida—on social issues. George W. Bush didn't make that mistake, but without saying the words directly, he consistently implied both as a gubernatorial and a presidential candidate that he'd appoint jurists who shared his dim view of *Roe.*

There were myriad other facets to the conservative movement in the Age of Reagan, including fiscal policy, racial politics, cultural differences, and geography. During the three generations of Bushes, the GOP went from being a party dominated by eastern bankers and business leaders, holding its own in the Midwest and on the West Coast but unable to compete in the South, to a Sunbelt-based party whose base voters could be found not in Episcopalian pews, but in evangelical megachurches; not in the stands of the Yale-Harvard football game, but in the infield at NASCAR races. Anti-communism was a core issue for both new and old Republicans wherever they were living, worshiping, or recreating. There was a second issue for the GOP, however, and it became a bright line of demarcation. That issue was taxes. And once again, the evolution on this issue could be traced through three generations of the Bush family.

Generation One: A typical headline in Connecticut newspapers while Prescott Bush was in the Senate would read: "Bush Says Tax Burden May Have to Be Bigger." In that particular article, Bush was quoted in the context of funding national defense, scientific research, and federal support for education, and he said that the Senate must "have the courage to raise the required revenues by approving whatever levels of taxation may be necessary."[20]

Generation Two: George H. W. Bush was a chip off his old man's block—for a while. In the 1980 presidential primaries, he famously referred to the proposed Reagan tax cut, along with the supply-side theory undergirding it, as "voodoo economics." This gibe infuriated party conservatives, and it was to mollify them that Bush coined his famous "Read my lips: No new taxes!" pledge at the 1988 Republican Party convention. For good or ill, Bush reneged on that vow in his 1990 budget deal with the Democrats. It is an article of faith among conservatives that George H. W. Bush broke his word, made bad policy in concert with the Democrats, and paid for it dearly at the polls in his 1992 reelection bid. This view, while widespread, may not be fair or even accurate. Actually, it was independents, many of them followers of Ross Perot, who deserted Bush in droves, not conservatives. These moderate voters did so, in large part, because Bush seemed uninterested in the nation's sluggish economic performance during the last half of his presidency. (The irony here is that by then Bush was a convert to the Reagan laissez-faire school of economic conservatives, and he believed that anything government would do in the way of public works spending would probably make the problem worse.)

Then along came Generation Three: George W. and Jeb Bush. If they were as Catholic as the pope on abortion, on taxes they were more Reagan than Reagan. When George W. ran for office in 2000 the federal budget was in surplus for the first time since 1969. Given the huge national debt, and the enormous annual payments the federal government paid to service that debt—not to mention the structural inequities looming for Social Security and Medicare—this surplus was an illusion. Even so, Bush's response was to propose a huge tax cut designed to put back in Americans' pockets (or, depending on your politics, take from the U.S. Treasury) some $1.6 trillion over ten years. Bush explained, in language Reagan surely would have applauded, that the American people would spend the surplus more wisely than Congress. "If we leave money in Washington, D.C., the people are going to spend it on bigger government and more programs," Bush said at a January 15, 2000, debate in Johnston, Iowa. It was a typical remark for him, and it engendered a typical response from the other Republican contenders: The only argument he got from his principle challenger, Arizona Senator John McCain, was over whose proposed tax cut was larger. (By then, Reaganomics had permeated the Democratic Party as well. After initially deriding Bush's proposed tax cuts as unwise and unnecessary—a "risky scheme," he called it—candidate Al Gore offered a $250 billion tax cut of his own, a number he doubled by mid-summer.)

As president-elect, Bush sought to reassure House Majority leader Dick Armey, an ardent supply-sider, that he wouldn't go wobbly on taxes once he became president. "You know, Dick, I'm more like Ronald Reagan than my dad," Bush said. "The difference is my dad was raised in the East, and I was raised in Texas."[21]

While campaigning in 2000, Bush also stressed his tax-cutting days in Austin, and it is this reference—his Texas connection—that provides a third way of tracing the metamorphosis of the Republican Party in the second half of the twentieth century: geography.

In 1924, Prescott Bush moved his family to Connecticut, where his children were reared in the elite environment alluded to by genealogist Gary Roberts. Prescott Bush's only experience before running for Senate was serving as the moderator for the Town Meeting in Greenwich for seventeen years. When Prescott Bush took his place in the Senate, he joined the New England and eastern-seaboard GOP congressional delegation that was then, as now, more liberal than the Republican Party as a whole. The difference is that, back then, liberals constituted the very face of the national Republican Party—and had real power in the Senate.

The Senate's senior Republican, George D. Aiken of Vermont (nationally famous for suggesting that the United States should declare victory in Vietnam and withdraw its troops), helped secure funding for rural electrification and food stamps. With the New England delegation taking the lead, 82 percent of Senate Republicans—a higher percentage than among Democrats—voted for the Civil Rights Act of 1964. Prescott Bush wasn't one of them, but that was only because he'd left the Senate in 1962. Among Prescott's allies in the Senate was a New Englander from the other side of the aisle, John F. Kennedy, with whom he worked closely during the first two years of the Kennedy presidency. "There was a certain kind of bond," Senator Edward M. Kennedy said. "Prescott Bush was committed to civil rights. He cosponsored the Peace Corps. They both came to the Senate together. My brother thought Prescott Bush was a very principled person."[22]

This was the legacy Prescott Bush's second son left behind when he moved himself and his family to Texas. At times it showed. At other times, it was the Texan in him that stood out. Early in life, George H. W. Bush displayed a willingness to go beyond New England for new worlds to conquer—literally. (At his 1942 prep school commencement ceremony, the speaker lined up by Phillips Academy was Secretary of War Henry Stimson, who told the graduates the war would be a long one, that the military services would need officers, but they should go to college before donning the uniform. "George, did the Secretary say anything to change your mind?" Prescott asked his son afterward. "No, sir," the young man replied. "I'm going in."[23]) And yet, George H. W. Bush's preppy persona, later parodied to hilarious effect by Dana Carvey, underscored the point that no amount of pork rind–eating could change Bush's mannerisms— or his outlook on life. He may have started his career as an equipment clerk in Odessa, but he soon launched an oil exploration firm on money lent him by his family and his family's Wall Street connections.

If making money in the Texas oil fields was tough, however, the sledding in Texas politics was even tougher. George H. W. Bush lost his Senate bid in 1964, suffering from being on the ballot with Barry Goldwater while liberal Democrat Ralph Yarborough was benefiting from the presence of a true Texan—Lyndon B. Johnson—at the top of the Democratic ticket. In 1966 and 1968, Bush ran successfully in a wealthy Houston congressional district that he had helped to create when he was the Republican chairman for Harris County. But in another statewide bid in 1970, he lost again. He had figured that Texans wouldn't support Yarborough a second time and was more prescient than he knew: Yarborough lost to the more conservative Lloyd Bentsen in the Democratic primary. Once again Bush found himself being portrayed as the effete (and liberal) carpetbagger from the East. Bentsen and Bush were not dissimilar in political outlook or life experience. Like Bush, Bentsen had won the Distinguished Flying Cross in World War II (while Bush was in the Pacific, Bentsen was over Italy, ultimately flying thirty-five missions in a B-24 bomber). What set them apart was that the Bentsen family had deep roots in the Rio Grande Valley—and Lloyd had attended law school at the University of Texas.

The real rap against George H. W. Bush, then and always, was that he was an inauthentic Texan. This was in part a calculated attempt to depict him as a carpetbagger, such as when Ralph Yarborough chanted at campaign rallies, "Elect a Senator from Texas, and not the Connecticut investment bankers." It was also a good-natured ribbing mixed with Texas chauvinism. Texan Jim Wright, the Democratic House speaker, kidded Bush at a Gridiron Dinner as the "only Texan I know who eats lobster with his chili." Molly Ivins, the iconic Texas newspaper columnist, nee-dled Bush by writing that he would never be fully accepted in his adopted state because "real Texans do not use the word summer as a verb . . . and do not wear blue slacks with little green whales all over them." Finally, some of the anti-Bush jabs had a touch of class enmity, evidenced by the two most famous insults leveled at him by Texas liberals: Ann Richards's quip at the 1988 Democratic National Convention that Bush was born "with a silver foot in his mouth," and Jim Hightower's insult at the same convocation that Bush "was born on third base and thought he hit a triple."*

As he made the transition from New Englander to Texan, George H. W. Bush was getting this kind of treatment from both directions. Back among his old friends in the East, there would always be concern that he had gone native. As late as 1988, after then–Vice President Bush finished third in the Iowa caucuses at the beginning of his run to succeed Reagan, several of his old Skull and Bones mates groused that Bush's mistake wasn't, as conventional wisdom held, that he was deemed insufficiently conservative by the Republican activists who went to the caucuses. Bush's problem, they believed, was that in his effort to appeal to the Reaganite base, he was striking an unconvincing pose as a southern conservative. "It was not the real George Bush we were getting," complained William J. Connelly Jr., one of Bush's friends from his Yale days. "He was coming off as preposterously conservative."[24]

To win the GOP senatorial primary in 1964, George H. W. Bush had come out against then-pending civil rights legislation "on constitutional grounds." During the general election, he criticized the Nuclear Test Ban Treaty negotiated by President Kennedy, said the United States should withdraw from the United Nations if "Red" China were admitted, char-acterized Medicare as "socialized medicine," and expressed support for expanding the war in Vietnam, even to the point of considering the use of nuclear weapons if "militarily prudent."

The Goldwater campaign was a lost cause for Bush—and Goldwa-ter—but not for Reagan. The nationally broadcast speech he gave in the

---

*Richards's line poked fun at both Bush's background and his propensity for the occa-sional malapropism. Hightower's was aimed at the habit of Bush, even more pronounced in his son, to present himself as a self-made man.

dying campaign's last week made Reagan a household name among conservatives. The day after Goldwater's landslide defeat, Ronald Reagan for President Committees arose spontaneously in cities across the country. Four years later, Reagan mounted a belated favorite-son candidacy from California for the Republican presidential nomination, losing out to Richard Nixon, but surprising even himself by doing better than expected. Meanwhile, George H. W. Bush was in the House of Representatives when the Civil Rights Act of 1968, with its controversial open-housing provision, put every southern member of Congress to the test. It has been reported that Bush incurred the anger of his constituents by voting aye on this bill, which is true. Less remembered is that on the key procedural vote that day, April 10, 1968, Bush sided *against* the liberals, who won a 229–195 vote to beat back a gambit to send the open-housing provisions of the bill back to committee. George H. W. Bush was a man literally caught between two worlds, and his rhetoric and voting record showed it.

This was the lay of the land in Bush World when George W. arrived at Yale in 1964. Yale was just sheltered enough, and Bush was just old enough to be a class or two ahead of the kind of campus unrest that Reagan, as California governor, would call the "mess at Berkeley." The mess would come to New Haven, too, but Bush managed to have a pretty good time in college. He became "commissioner" of an intramural stickball league he helped launch, was elected president of the Yale chapter of the Delta Kappa Epsilon fraternity, and followed his father and grandfather (and John Kerry) into Skull and Bones. Bush roommate Collister (Terry) Johnson recalled their college years as "the last of the happy days." Clay Johnson, another friend, who followed George W. Bush to the White House, used similar language—"the last of the beer days"—to refer to that time.[25] This is reminiscent of Ronald Reagan's nostalgia for a world that never was. In his 1965 autobiography, *Where's the Rest of Me?,* Reagan described his boyhood as "a rare Huck Finn idyll" in which he explored the mysteries of fields and meadows while enjoying pickup games of football with other boys. This is tame stuff compared to the passage where, as an eleven-year-old boy, he comes upon his father Jack "drunk, dead to the world," in front of their house and drags him in from the snow. Ronald was not ruined by this experience, but he also couldn't wait to leave home. He became the first member of his family to go to college, where, typically, he earned his room and board.

George W. Bush's Yale idyll also had a blemish. It certainly wasn't because of anything his father did, although his father figured in the episode, and it wasn't the Vietnam War—not exactly. Yale was where Bush first confronted liberal elitism, and where he discovered, to his surprise, that it was aimed at him and his family. This attitude, and his reaction to it, helped define George W. Bush. In Bush's memory it was epitomized by a single remark, in the form of a gratuitous insult from Yale chaplain Rev. William Sloane Coffin. The exchange occurred during Bush's freshman year and shortly after George H. W. Bush's loss to Ralph Yarborough. Coffin was a Skull and Bones man himself, but he was becoming a leader in the pacifist movement and using his sinecure at Yale to drum up activism against the Vietnam War. Bush introduced himself to Coffin. "I know your father," Coffin replied. "Frankly, he was beaten by a better man."*

Fully thirty years later, in an interview with *Texas Monthly,* George W. Bush still smarted when recalling this episode, an apparent signpost at the beginning of his own ideological journey. "What angered me was the way such people at Yale felt so intellectually superior and so righteous," Bush told Texas writer Skip Hollandsworth in 1994. "They thought they had all the answers. They thought they could create a government that could solve all our problems for us." He added that his reaction was a desire to "get away from the snobs."

As he began his presidential run in 2000, Bush amplified on this theme. "I don't remember any protests at Yale, any big stuff," he told *The Washington Post*'s Hanna Rosin. "I had fun at Yale. I got a lot of great friends out of Yale. And I didn't pay attention. I guess there were some people who paid attention, some of whom you've obviously been talking to. But I didn't want to be friends with these people who *felt* superior." The way he

---

*As Barbara Bush noted in her autobiography, this was an appalling thing to say to a college freshman. For his part, after George W. Bush became governor of Texas, Coffin wrote him a letter saying he didn't remember the conversation, adding that he had difficulty imagining saying such a thing. But he did not directly challenge Bush's recollection and asked him "to forgive what you cannot condone." In a handwritten reply, according to letters made public by Bush's office in 1998, Bush said he was confident that his recollection was correct. "But," he added, "I also know time passes, and I bear no ill will."

accomplished this—the way he exacted his revenge against the William Sloane Coffins—was to relocate himself, body and mind, back to Texas.

The only one of his siblings not actually born in Texas, George W. Bush was the one his brothers and sister considered the most Texan, and the only one to put down roots there. "The formative years of his childhood (from age 2 to the eighth grade) and of his business career (from 1975 to 1987) were spent in Midland, the oil capital of West Texas," author David Maraniss wrote, "and no amount of schooling in New Haven and Cambridge or political dealing in Washington would make him an easterner." Texas suited Bush even better than he seemed to know. *"Don't Mess with Texas"* was the anti-littering slogan coined by the state's highway commission back in the mid-1980s, but it described George W.'s sentiments as well. "People say, 'What's the difference between you and your dad?'" Bush said to Maraniss in 1989. "Well, he went to Greenwich Country Day and I went to San Jacinto Junior High. I think it goes back that far. I tend to speak my mind, which is a West Texas trait. Coming to Washington, where everything is innuendo and suggestion, that's just not me."

If George and Barbara Bush's eldest son was a rowdy kid early on, whether at Andover or at public school in Midland, by the time he showed up for graduate school at Harvard in cowboy boots, a tin of tobacco in his back jeans pocket, wearing his Air National Guard flight jacket, and not hiding his west Texas twang, well, that was something more. The metamorphosis of the Bush clan from East Coast establishment Republicans to Sunbelt conservatives was completed in just three generations. It was as though the Prodigal Son had come home—just to show the old country what he'd become. "His father was perceived to be more of an Easterner, more moderate Republican, and this president is a Texas Republican" was how moderate Maine Democratic congressman Tom Allen explained it in 2001. "He prefers his ranch in Texas, and it's a different climate—and it's a different political climate."[26]

It was a western ranch that got George W. Bush back to Texas in the first place. Before going to business school at Harvard, Bush had applied to the University of Texas law school and been rejected.[27] He didn't take it too hard. After leaving Harvard, he was driving through Texas on his way to a ranch in Arizona when he stopped off at his old stomping grounds in Midland. "All of a sudden it dawned on me that this is entrepreneurial heaven," he explained later. "This is one of the few places in the country where you can go without portfolio and train yourself and become competitive."

Bush was talking about the oil sector of the economy, not the entertainment industry, but the parallel to how Reagan was drawn to Hollywood a generation earlier is palpable. "The barriers to entry were very low," Bush said. "I can't tell you how obvious it was."[28]

Reagan had experienced a similar epiphany on a trip out west of his own. "Dutch" Reagan was then a broadcaster for WHO, the 50,000-watt NBC radio station in Des Moines. He recreated the games of the Chicago White Sox, who trained in the off-season in Pasadena, California, and the Chicago Cubs, whose spring training facility was then on Catalina Island. On his first day in Southern California in 1937, Reagan took a screen test that a friend had helped arrange. He passed, was offered $200 a week— enormous wages during the Depression—just days after returning to Iowa, and cabled back to his newfound agent: "SIGN BEFORE THEY CHANGE THEIR MINDS—DUTCH REAGAN."

Reagan became a movie actor, and a Californian, that quickly. George W. Bush's transformation to full-fledged Texan took a bit longer, but was just as thorough. When Bush went into the oil business in west Texas, his youngest brother, Marvin, took to calling him "J.R.," after J.R. Ewing, the mythical oil baron of the hit television show *Dallas*. George W. married a Texas native, a school librarian then living in Austin who had grown up in Midland. Laura Welch had attended college at Southern Methodist University, taught elementary school in Houston, and received her master's degree at the University of Texas at Austin. With Laura at his side, Bush began running for Congress. In his 1978 campaign, he sought the counsel of prominent Texans when making up his mind. His father took him to see Robert Strauss, the Texas éminence grise in Washington, who cautioned about the dangers of challenging Hance, whom Strauss described as "smart as a whip and mean as a snake." But the younger Bush was so bent on running that he ignored the advice he had solicited. (Strauss was not omniscient, however. In the same meeting, he encouraged the senior Bush to run for president in 1980, adding, "Reagan sure as hell won't be the nominee.")[29]

"He's a personable young man from back East who apparently has been misleading the people of west Texas about his background," Bush's Republican opponent Jim Reese had declared in a 1978 television interview. A more accurate way of saying it would have been that Bush's makeover was not yet complete. But George W. Bush knew enough to blunt the issue of his East Coast heritage—and he charmed audiences in the process—by saying that his only regret in life was that he hadn't been born in Texas. In response to Reese's and Hance's insinuations that there was something wrong with not being a Texas native, Bush would quip that he would have preferred to have been born in Midland, but he needed to be close to his mother, "and she happened to be in New Haven, Connecticut."

After George W. became president, even Molly Ivins, no fan of the man she dubbed "Shrub," or of his politics, concurred grudgingly that he was one of them. "Yes, dammit!" she replied when asked directly if George W. Bush was an authentic Texan."[30] "For all the time Big George spent here, he remained a classic, refined, New England–type WASP person. But George W. clearly identifies with Texas and its mores."* Part of Texas's code is knowing when you are whipped—and why it happened. George W. passed this test, too. "Kent Hance gave me a lesson on country-boy politics," he told *Time* magazine in the summer of 2000. "He was a master at it, funny and belittling. I vowed never to get out-countried again." And he wasn't. Nor did he ever get crosswise with Reagan or Reaganism again—at least until he resided in the White House.

Reagan's own political journey was prodigious: He voted for FDR four times and supported Truman in 1948. As late as 1950, the year Prescott Bush's Senate ambitions were derailed, Reagan campaigned for Democrats, including Helen Gahagan Douglas, who was smeared and defeated by Richard Nixon in her bid to become a U.S. senator from California. Reagan had traveled further than the entire Bush family—he moved from Iowa to California and (in 1962) changed parties. From Prescott's day onward, the Bushes had always been Republican. Reagan himself lived a generation-long process that political scientists would come to see as a great sorting of the two political parties along ideological lines. The final ingredient was what *The Economist* would later characterize as the "sunny optimism" and "sunbelt capitalism" of the Reagan-era GOP. But

---

*Ivins, never at a loss for a good line, quipped that not only was Bush a true Texan, he was "so goddamn dumb about it, he's always coming back to Texas for the month of August."

there was more at work than Reagan's famous optimism.[31] Mother Teresa once said that the first obligation of a Christian is to smile. Reagan behaved as though the first obligation of a politician who loves America is to trust Americans. This came through in his campaigns. You might still win a bar bet in any Capitol Hill watering hole by asking how many negative ads Reagan ran against George H. W. Bush in their 1980 campaign. The correct answer is zero. This approach didn't come naturally to Bush's eldest son, but he evidently paid attention.

In George W. Bush's 1978 congressional race, a local radio host had asked him if he was "involved" or knew anybody who was involved in "one-world government or the Trilateral Commission." This strange question emanated from the fringes of American politics and was a dig at Bush's father, a member of that respected organization of internationalists. Instead of confidently speaking up for his dad—a decorated fighter pilot in World War II—young Bush bristled at the question and assured his listeners, "I won't be persuaded, even by my father." Afterward, George W. ignored the interviewer's proffered handshake, muttering "You asshole," as he walked out the station door.[32]

In his 1994 race against incumbent Texas governor Ann Richards, George W. Bush was the sunny-side-up candidate. When she called him derogatory names, Bush called her "governor." How much of that had to do with Reagan's example is unknowable, but this much is certain: The 1978 west Texas congressional race was the last time Bush put himself before the voters without an exaggerated Texas swagger, the last time he ran without the blessing of the Reaganites, the last time he ran with a divided Republican Party, and the last time he ran with a chip on his shoulder. Not coincidentally, it would be the last election he lost, or even that his party lost with him at the head of the ticket, until the 2006 mid-term elections dominated by concern over the war in Iraq.

In early 1979, George W. Bush had flown to Washington for his father's announcement at the National Press Club that he was running for president. In contrast to his younger brothers, George W.'s role in his father's subsequent presidential campaign would be minimal. Yet he was clearly taking Reagan's measure. He could not help but be impressed by what he saw in 1980 when Reagan got off to a slow start and then polished off George H. W. Bush as the primary season unfolded—and he said so, both publicly and privately.

Later, when he was running for president, George W. told Walter Isaacson of *Time* magazine, "Dynasty means something inherited. We inherited a good name, but you don't inherit a vote. You have to win a vote."[33] Reagan, not Bush's father, had "won the vote" in 1980. It was Reagan's time, he reassured his dad afterward. There might never have been a "Bush time," but somehow George W. Bush seemed to sense that 1980 wasn't the end of it. Before the Reagan team had even focused on it, he was encouraging his father to be receptive to a vice presidential invitation.[34] George W. took to calling Reagan "the Western man," almost as a way of telling himself that a successful Republican must attract voters in the West and the South to be a successful national candidate. At a luncheon speech in Midland, George W. lauded Reagan's "easy-going" style, while simultaneously (and somewhat incongruously) expressing admiration for how decisively Reagan had fired his top aides on the eve of the New Hampshire primary when he was dissatisfied with the campaign's direction. It was "brilliant . . . and there was no hesitancy in it," Bush said. "Reagan is a man of decisive action."[35]

This perception had been borne out at the 1980 Republican convention in Detroit. An attempt to forge a "dream ticket" by offering Gerald Ford the vice presidential nomination broke down. Five minutes after Ford left Reagan's hotel suite, Reagan was on the phone decisively offering the job to George H. W. Bush. Prepped by his eldest son, Bush just as decisively accepted it. This was the pivotal act in forging the Bush dynasty, although few concentrated on that at the time. To many Republicans, the collapse of the putative Reagan-Ford ticket had made the selection of Reagan's running mate anti-climactic. One Republican, namely, the other half of the aborted Dream Team, knew better.

"Some people told us that a ticket with he and I on it would have been unbeatable," Gerald Ford recalled twenty-four summers later.[36] "That's probably right, but it was unbeatable the way it was. *Any* ticket with Reagan on it was pretty unbeatable."

For George W. Bush, the lessons were clear. However difficult it had been for his father to be accepted in his adopted home state, George W.'s own home, and his natural political base, was Texas. The other lesson was that, for now anyway, Texas was the heart of Reagan Country, not Bush Country. Moreover, as big as Texas was, Reaganism was even bigger.

2

WHAT REAGAN WROUGHT

As his presidency recedes into the mists of history, Ronald Wilson Reagan has become an elusive icon. On the Right, Reagan's cheerleaders celebrate him as the undisputed victor in the Cold War, forgetting that they once questioned the wisdom of his summitry with Soviet leader Mikhail Gorbachev and opposed the treaties that pared U.S. and Soviet nuclear arsenals. On the Left, critics who once assailed Reagan's defense buildup as provocative and deplored his straight talk about the Soviet Union now laud his diplomacy, usually to draw a contrast with the perceived intransigence of President George W. Bush. Selective amnesia also prevails in evaluations of Reagan's domestic policies. Conservatives applaud the salutary effect of Reagan's first-year tax cuts but mostly ignore the several tax increases that followed. Liberals take note of Reagan's negotiating prowess and supposed willingness to compromise; during his presidency they pictured him as stubborn and unyielding on issues ranging from the economy to the environment.

Academic historians, few of them sympathetic to conservatives, also are uncertain. When Reagan left office, they judged him mediocre or worse. Over time, in response to an emergent legacy, academics have

grudgingly granted him a higher position in the rankings while still resisting his admittance to the top tier. A few have done more. Political scientist James MacGregor Burns, noted for his excellent books on Franklin
D. Roosevelt, believes Reagan will be remembered as a "great or near-
great" president.[1] Some journalists also have conducted a reexamination.
Howell Raines, a White House correspondent for *The New York Times* in
the early years of the Reagan presidency, wrote in *The Washington Post:*
"My generation of White House correspondents was accused of covering
up Ronald Reagan's supposed stupidity and his reliance on fictional 'facts'
derived from Errol Flynn movies and the John Birch Society. In 1981,
Clark Clifford, the Democratic 'wise man,' entertained Georgetown dinner parties with the killer line that Reagan was an amiable dunce. Twenty
years later we know that Clark Clifford was charged in a banking scandal and the dunce ended the Cold War."[2] Two years later, Raines said in
an interview, "I think what we need as a nation is another leader on Reagan's scale."[3]

By and large, Reagan has been less elusive to ordinary Americans than
to academics or journalists. He was a commanding figure on the political
scene for nearly a quarter century, beginning with the rousing nationally
televised speech he gave on behalf of Republican presidential candidate
Barry Goldwater on October 27, 1964, and extending through the second
term of the Reagan presidency, which ended January 20, 1989. The high
poll ratings Reagan enjoyed as he left office gave rise to a national impulse
to name things—buildings, highways, even airports—after him while he
was still alive. The public's comfort level with Reagan has continued
through the presidencies of his three successors. In 1999, late in the Bill
Clinton presidency, a majority of adult Americans ranked Reagan the best
of presidents. Fifty-four percent of those polled said he would be remembered as "outstanding" or "above average," compared to 12 percent who
said he would be remembered as "poor." In 2007, when voters were asked
in a poll which past president "would you like our next president to be
most like," Reagan was the first choice, followed by John F. Kennedy.[4]

Reagan connected with ordinary people because they believed that he
was one of them. Raised as a Democrat by a religious mother and an alcoholic father in the heartland of America, educated in a struggling, small
college that had been founded by the Disciples of Christ, self-schooled as
a sports announcer in a time and place where sports mattered, trained on

the job in the grind of moviemaking when Hollywood was the dream capital of the world, immersed in the hothouse culture of Southern California when everything seemed possible, called up as an Army reservist and sent to an entertainment unit that made training films and propagandized for the war effort, plunged into a tangle of waivers and union negotiations and congressional investigations in the salad days of the Cold War, self-schooled again as an inspirational speaker for an innovative corporation as he traveled America by train because he feared to fly, converted to the conservative cause in middle age: Reagan followed a unique path to the presidency. He was at once an American everyman who distilled the national experience and a lone outsider who lacked ties to the elite institutions that typically produce American political leaders.

Although Reagan's life was as unlike that of his political idol Franklin Roosevelt as the lives of two American white males could be, his inspirational qualities emulated the president who gave hope and jobs to millions of Americans (including Reagan's father and brother) during the Great Depression. Reagan, no less than FDR, could be polarizing and full of hot air. But Americans recognized in the populist outsider Reagan as they had in the patrician insider Roosevelt an unquenchable optimism and a defining sense of national purpose. Both men believed in the ideals of American democracy and in the capacity of the American people to overcome any obstacle. Because they seemed embodiments as well as apostles of the American dream, they were able to reassure their countrymen when they were most in need of reassurance. Reagan at his best was a shining mirror of a leader, reflecting back to Americans their most precious values and aspirations. He knew this but was not puffed up about it. On the eve of his election in 1980, a radio reporter asked Reagan what it was that Americans saw in him. He hesitated a moment, then responded, "Would you laugh if I told you that I think, maybe, they see themselves and that I'm one of them? I've never been able to detach myself or think that I, somehow, am apart from them."

Reagan's belief that he was inseparable from the American people gave him an advantage in politics. He was less dependent on polls than other politicians, not because he was more principled but because he needed polls less than they did. Pollster Richard Wirthlin, who recognized that Reagan was a natural, quoted French leader François Mitterrand, in a wordplay on the description of Reagan as "Great Communicator," as saying that Reagan was "in communion" with the American people.[5] Early in his campaign for governor of California, Reagan recognized from the responses of audiences long before the issue showed up in the polls that voters were upset by the campus disturbances at the Berkeley campus of the University of California. A decade later, when he sought the Republican presidential nomination against an incumbent of his own party, he detected similar voter concern over the U.S. "giveaway" of the Panama Canal. These were populist issues, and Reagan's opponents considered his exploitation of them demagogic. But Reagan's ability to serve as his own focus group proved equally helpful when the cause was high-minded. As president, Reagan had no doubt that a majority of Americans approved of his dualistic approach to the Soviet Union: blunt statements about the immorality of the Communist system (too blunt for most of the experts) coupled with a consistent appeal to Soviet leaders for negotiation. So we have Reagan, meeting with reporters early in his presidency, paraphrasing Lenin on the duty of Communists to engage in criminal activity if it serves their cause, while privately, over the objections of his first secretary of state, Alexander M. Haig, writing to Leonid Brezhnev with an appeal for a "meaningful and constructive dialogue which will assist us in fulfilling our joint obligation to find lasting peace."

Reagan's self-assurance that he was doing the right thing, another echo of FDR, and also doing what the American people wanted him to do was an essential characteristic of his presidency. For the most part, it served him and the country well, but there were times when Reagan's remarkable political ear fell short of perfect pitch or when he underrated the risks of a course of action he was determined to pursue. In 1986, seeing what he thought was a strategic opening and an opportunity to free Americans held hostage in Lebanon, Reagan allowed himself to be euchred into a secret sale of arms to Iran, later conflated into what became known as the Iran-contra affair. When the scandal inevitably became public, Reagan floundered and lied—partly because he was misinformed by aides—about its dimensions. (Cynics might say that this, too, was an FDR echo. When he was vice president–elect, Harry Truman said his only problem with Roosevelt was that "he lies.")[6] Reagan depended on the trust of the American people to do his best work, and he was at sea for months until Nancy Reagan and her allies persuaded him to make changes in his White House staff and apologize to the American people.

The apology was circumspect—"my heart and my best intentions still tell me that [my earlier denial of arms sales] was true, but the facts and the evidence tell me it is not"—but sufficient. Landon Parvin, the speechwriter who wrote these words, concluded that what Reagan really wanted to say was, "I didn't do it, and I'll never do it again."[7] But it worked. Most of the American people forgave a president they admired, and Reagan was freed in the last two years of his presidency to pursue the critical task of closing the deal with the Soviets on the arms-control agreements that his policies had made possible.

Douglas Brinkley has said that every president in the twentieth century before Reagan lived in the shadow of FDR and that every president since then has lived in the shadow of Reagan.[8] They are long and interlocking shadows. Both FDR and Reagan came to the presidency with solid records as governor, of New York and California respectively, but without much respect from the national press or most of the political community. Early in 1932, Walter Lippmann dismissed FDR as "a pleasant man, without any important qualifications for the office, who would like to be president." *National Review,* which had ardently backed Reagan in his near-miss attempt to wrest the Republican presidential nomination from Gerald Ford in 1976, reluctantly decided four years later that he had become a "middle-aged anachronism." Reagan was opposed, initially, by a half dozen other Republicans, most of whom questioned his age and qualifications. Ordinary Americans were little troubled by such calculations. They turned to the confident FDR and the optimistic Reagan because they promised hope in a time of despair at a time when their well-meant but hapless predecessors seemed overwhelmed by events beyond their control.

After defeating President Herbert Hoover in the 1932 election, FDR had faced the harder challenge of the Great Depression, part of a worldwide economic crisis. Like a life-threatening illness that starts out as a cold, the Depression had crept slowly upon the nation. Even after the stock market crash of 1929, which foreshadowed the collapse to come, many economists believed that the country was passing through a normal recession. Unemployment rose slowly during the two years after the crash, prompting expectations that the nation would resume its prosperous ways, as it had after the recession of 1920–1922. But by 1932, unemployment shot up to 24 percent, nearly a quarter of the workforce, and it became starkly obvious that this was no ordinary downturn. National income in 1933 fell to less than half of what it had been in 1929 and did not reach the 1929 level until 1941, when America was girding for war. Crops rotted in the fields because they fetched less at market than it cost to grow them, and fearsome droughts turned family farms to dust while factories closed, fertility rates plummeted, and banks failed. Half a million homeowners (many of them family farmers) defaulted on their mortgages, and the stock market lost 75 percent of its value.

Under the constitutional standard of the time, FDR did not take office until March 4, 1933, when he made his famous speech proclaiming "that the only thing we have to fear is fear itself—nameless, unreasoning, unjustified terror." On March 5 the new president declared a national bank holiday and called Congress into session. During these three months, FDR put forward legislation to reduce farm surpluses, put young men to work in conservation camps, regulate the securities market, and underwrite home mortgages. He created the Tennessee Valley Authority, a multipurpose public corporation that generated electricity for poor farmers and built dams to control floods and combat soil erosion. These Hundred Days and the other innovative policies of FDR's first term—most notably, Social Security—reshaped American politics with results that are felt to this day.

Reagan, then a twenty-two-year-old college student with a flair for dramatics, was captivated by Roosevelt's inaugural speech. Years later, Eureka College classmates would recall him using a broomstick microphone, on which he customarily did imaginary sports broadcasts, to give a passable imitation of FDR, who became a lifelong hero. Reagan voted for FDR every time he ran for president and venerated his memory long after Reagan's own politics had changed from Democratic to Republican.* He was inspired by FDR's "fireside chats," as Roosevelt called his radio reports to the American people. (The first of these was on March 12, 1933, a week into the Hundred Days.) These became the model for Reagan's own radio speeches, which helped to keep him in the public eye after he

---

*In his diary entry for January 28, 1982, President Reagan wrote: "The press is dying to paint me as now trying to undo the New Deal. I remind them I voted for FDR 4 times. I'm trying to undo the 'Great Society.' It was LBJ's war on poverty that led to our present mess."

left the California governorship, and which evolved into the radio speeches he gave on Saturdays as president. His White House successors have paid him the tribute of continuing the tradition.

The impression of FDR's radio speeches was keenly stamped on Reagan's successful campaign for the presidency in 1980. Reagan had been using FDR's words for his own purposes throughout his political career; in his nationally televised address for Goldwater in 1964 he had proclaimed that Americans had a "rendezvous with destiny." In 1980, paraphrasing a 1934 fireside chat that FDR had used two years after his election to expand the Democratic majority in Congress, Reagan framed his case against President Jimmy Carter in these words: "Are you better off than you were four years ago? Is it easier for you to go and buy things in the stores than it was four years ago? Is there more or less unemployment in the country than there was four years ago? Is America as respected in the world as it was? Do you feel that our security is as safe, that we're as strong as we were four years ago?"

Americans felt neither safe nor strong nor well-off in 1980. Fifty-two Americans had been held hostage by the revolutionary government of Iran since November 4, 1979. President Carter had tried to rescue them with diplomacy and then with military force—an unsuccessful operation on April 24, 1980, that cost the lives of eight of the would-be rescuers. Beginning on Christmas Day 1979 the Soviet Union had launched a bloody invasion of Afghanistan, in which it had installed a puppet government. According to one respected estimate, the Soviets were spending 85 percent more than the United States for military purposes, much of it to enhance a dangerous and bloated arsenal of nuclear-tipped missiles aimed at the United States and Europe. Americans were not sanguine about Soviet adventurism, but their biggest concerns were closer to home. U.S. unemployment had jumped to 7.8 percent in May 1979, the highest rate since the Truman presidency, and averaged 7 percent for the year. Inflation was supposed to march in the opposite direction, according to an established theory of the economy known as the Phillips Curve, but instead had soared to a high of 18 percent, averaging 12.5 percent for the year. The prime rate, the basis of lending, had reached 20 percent in April; it dropped during the summer but was back up to 17 percent by election day. For the first time since the Depression millions of Americans felt they were in danger of losing their homes, their livelihoods, and their futures.

In a less stable country this crisis of confidence might have provided a context for disorder; in the United States it was the stuff of political realignment. Reagan understood this; he paid little attention to the nuts and bolts of politics but was always a party man no matter which party he belonged to. In the final days of Reagan's 1966 campaign for governor of California, a poll showed other Republican statewide candidates losing. Reagan campaigned for the entire ticket with the plea, "Don't send me to Sacramento alone." He carried four of the five trailing Republicans to victory. In 1980, Reagan sought a party victory as much as a personal one and tried, as FDR had done against Hoover, to pin the "failed leadership" of President Carter on the Democratic Party. Pressing the analogy a bit too far, Reagan even announced he was running against the "Carter Depression." When Reagan's economic advisers, notably Alan Greenspan, said this was an overstatement, Reagan amended it: "If he [Carter] wants a definition I'll give him one. A recession is when your neighbor loses his job. A depression is when you lose yours. And recovery is when Jimmy Carter loses his."

In the 1980 election Carter received 41 percent of the vote, the lowest for any incumbent president seeking reelection since Hoover's 39.7 percent. Reagan won in an electoral landslide. The Republican Party picked up thirty-three seats in the House and took control of the Senate by winning thirteen seats. These were the GOP's biggest gains since states began electing senators by popular vote early in the twentieth century. Reagan moved swiftly to consolidate his victory by holding out an olive branch of cooperation to Congress and the Washington establishment, institutions that Carter had alternately shunned or alienated. Reagan received an inaugural-day boost when the Iranian regime—apparently recognizing that it would not get a better deal from the new administration—released the hostages on January 20, 1981, after 444 days in captivity. The news came soon after Reagan finished his Inaugural Address on the restored west front of the Capitol. The speech stirred the crowd on an unseasonably warm Washington winter day. "Let us renew our determination, our courage, and our strength," Reagan said. "And let us renew our faith and hope. We have every right to dream heroic dreams." (Among those Reagan inspired was Michael Gerson, then a high school senior at Westminster Christian Academy in St. Louis. By 1981, Gerson was a Reaganite, and he would go on to become George W. Bush's top speechwriter. After leaving the White House he paid homage to his roots as a Reagan convert by writing a book entitled *Heroic Conservatism*.)

Reagan would soon have a chance to demonstrate his own heroism. When historians examine the many might-have-beens of the Franklin Roosevelt and Ronald Reagan presidencies, they sometimes observe that both might have been aborted by assassination, the fate of four presidents in the history of our republic. In fact, FDR's presidency would not even have begun if the deranged man who had fired at him in an open car in Miami had demonstrated better aim. This happened on February 15, 1933, little more than two weeks before the presidential inauguration. The bullet intended for FDR struck Chicago Mayor Anton J. Cermak, who later died from his wounds. On March 30, 1981, when Reagan had been president for seventy days, the would-be assassin's aim was more accurate, and he used bullets designed to fly apart inside the body. Leaving the Washington Hilton Hotel after a speech, Reagan was hit by one of these bullets, part of a barrage that struck down and severely wounded White House Press Secretary James Brady and also injured a police officer and a Secret Service agent. Reagan was in pain but at first did not realize he had been shot; he thought his ribs had been broken when a Secret Service agent threw him into the presidential limousine. In fact, a bullet had come within an inch of his aorta, lodged near the heart, and caused internal damage. Doctors later said Reagan probably would not have survived had not a quick-witted Secret Service agent diverted the motorcade from its intended route back to the White House to George Washington Hospital.

In these extreme moments both FDR and Reagan demonstrated uncanny self-confidence. Roosevelt cradled Cermak's head on his lap and reassured him. Later in the evening, FDR displayed a calm that an associate described as "magnificent." As for Reagan, he was bleeding internally and struggling to breathe as the motorcade arrived at the hospital. By now he realized he had been shot and was in danger, but the old actor summoned the will for a premier performance. In a brave act, Reagan buttoned his suit coat and strode into the emergency room—then collapsed once he was out of public sight. It was the old actor's premier performance. Displaying his vaunted humor even as he struggled to breathe, Reagan said to the doctors who were about to operate on him, "Please tell me you're Republicans."

Reagan, at age seventy, overnight became a national hero. He had shown vigor and charm, and his approval ratings soared. "When he displayed that same wit and grace in the hours after his own life was threatened, he elevated those appealing qualities to the level of legend," wrote David Broder.[9] With the nation cheering for his recovery, Reagan and his adroit advisers took advantage of the moment and made the case for his economic programs. Less than a month after he was shot, Reagan gave another stellar performance on behalf of his Economic Recovery Plan in a speech to a joint session of Congress. That speech expressed a sense of urgency but was laced with his trademark humor. He read a letter from a Maryland second-grader, which said: "I hope you get well quick or you might have to make a speech in your pajamas."

FDR had pushed an array of policy proposals into law during his first Hundred Days by force of personality and a political strategy that capitalized on congressional fears of a widening depression. Reagan also had a strong personality and a competent political team. Though he lacked FDR's advantage of a majority in the House of Representatives, he was nevertheless favored by timing and circumstances. The inaugural-day freeing of the hostages in Iran enabled Reagan to focus on economic policy without an immediate foreign distraction, and the wave of public sympathy after the assassination attempt gave him leverage with Congress. Reagan's agenda was based on the three main promises of his campaign: reducing income-tax rates, accelerating military spending, and balancing the budget. (Reagan had given different versions of the third promise, at times saying he would balance the budget and at others pledging to move in this direction by slashing domestic spending.) Reagan's political opponents, Republicans as much as Democrats, had questioned the compatibility of these promises. George H. W. Bush, running against Reagan in the Republican primaries, had ridiculed Reagan's belief that reduced tax rates would promote sufficient economic growth to reduce the budget deficit. Independent candidate John Anderson said Reagan could accomplish all three of his promises only "by mirrors." Reagan did not take such ridicule personally—he had, after all, put Bush on the ticket—but he never acknowledged that accelerated military spending coupled with a major reduction of income-tax rates might be incompatible with a balanced budget.

Reagan's defense promise was the most easily accomplished of these goals, and probably the one of greatest consequence, since the bump-up in

U.S. military spending helped bring the Soviets to the arms-control bargaining table. It was made easier by the fact that the much-maligned
Jimmy Carter had responded to the Soviet invasion of Afghanistan and
intelligence reports of a surge in Soviet missile development by boosting
the military budget in 1980—at a time when Reagan was scoring political
points with his contention that the United States was losing the arms race.
("Only the Soviets are racing," Reagan said.) Reagan's defense secretary,
Caspar Weinberger, shrewdly took the last Carter baseline as his starting
point and sought an 8 percent increase in military spending. Congress
gave the administration everything it asked for and more. In later years,
Congress became critical of Weinberger and trimmed some of his requests, but the horse was by then well clear of the barn and out of sight
down the road. Military spending during the Reagan years was roughly
$3 trillion, $800 million more than it would have been had he maintained
the pace of military spending he inherited.

Despite a forty-five-vote Democratic majority in the House, Reagan
also succeeded within five months in winning congressional approval of
most of his proposed income-tax cuts and a budget he believed would reduce the deficit. He did this by cultivating the support of conservative and
moderate Democrats in the South and West, many of them from Texas,
who represented districts that Reagan had carried in the election. Reagan
incorporated some of their lesser recommendations into the budget bill,
which enabled him to say it was bipartisan. At the suggestion of his chief
of staff, James Baker, Reagan even promised that he would not campaign
against any Democratic member of Congress who voted for both his tax
and budget bills. Republican leaders in Texas grumbled at this, knowing
that some of the Democratic-held districts were ripe for the taking. Baker
told Reagan that these districts would go Republican soon enough anyway, as most of them did.

The budget bill passed the House in June by a seventeen-vote margin
but made no dent on the deficit. This was partly because the inflation-
stressed economy soon plunged into recession, throwing millions of
Americans out of work and reducing government revenues. It was also
partly because Reagan and his team didn't realize that Republican members of Congress would be reluctant to cut spending that benefited their
districts, an attitude that foreshadowed their performance during the
George W. Bush years. The 1981 budget bill was promoted as a triumph
of frugality, but in reality it was a Christmas tree measure loaded with

dubious spending projects for supporters. In addition, some of the concessions made to assure passage of the measure reinstated questionable government handouts to favored industries. To win the votes of four
Louisiana Democrats, for instance, the Reagan administration revived a
costly sugar subsidy that had been phased out in the Carter years. After it
was added to the budget bill, a reporter asked one of these Democrats,
John B. Breaux, if his vote could be bought. "No," Breaux memorably
replied, "it can be rented."[10]

But even without these shenanigans and with a milder recession, Reagan would not have accomplished his avowed aim of reducing the deficit,
let alone balancing the budget. He never once in eight years submitted a
budget proposing the revenues necessary to pay for the programs he
thought necessary. Neither Reagan nor his too-clever-by-half budget director David Stockman were willing to tackle the spending built into the
budget in the form of programs ("entitlements") that automatically increased each year. As a result, the budget cuts they made occurred on the
margins in the realm of programs known as "discretionary spending"
that had relatively little impact on budget growth. Reagan made one un-
typical ham-handed effort to rein in Social Security when he signed off,
perhaps unwittingly, on a Stockman initiative that would have made
huge cuts in the monthly checks of recipients taking early retirement.
Congress unanimously repudiated it. Reagan managed to turn this setback into lemonade by appointing a commission headed by Greenspan
that produced a compromise plan that averted a Social Security crisis and
pushed structural reforms into the future. (George W. Bush's abortive attempt to create private accounts aside, Reagan's successors have ignored
the issue.) But after obtaining this compromise, Reagan was ever after
cautious about advocating anything that smacked of restraining Social
Security or any of the other entitlement programs with automatic increases. These programs had been woven into the fabric of American society since FDR's presidency. "Americans are conservative," said
columnist George F. Will. "What they want to conserve is the New
Deal."[11] Will calculated that the middle six budgets of the Reagan administration produced deficits totaling $1.1 trillion and that Reagan had pro-
posed all but about 7 percent of this total, with Congress adding the rest.
Overall, the accumulated operating deficits for the eight Reagan years
amounted to more than $1.5 trillion.

Viewed in isolation, these staggering deficits (higher in proportion to the size of the economy than the George W. Bush deficits) seem a black mark. But history did not end when Reagan left office, and the dividends produced by the accumulated debt were substantial. The United States, along with most other nations, has always run deficits during wartime, and the Cold War was an expensive war, although usually not a shooting one in terms of direct U.S.-Soviet military conflict. (Millions of people nonetheless died in a hundred wars and insurgencies during the Cold War years.) If one believes, as the historical evidence suggests, that the military buildup of the Reagan era hastened the demise of the Soviet empire, then that extra $800 billion of defense spending, roughly half the accumulated deficit, was a negligible price to pay. No price tag can be put on reducing the threat of a nuclear war that could have destroyed civilization. Whether such a war would have occurred is a matter of conjecture. What is not conjectural is that the buildup of the Reagan years was followed by a substantial reduction in U.S. military spending after the Soviet Union collapsed. The disappearance of wartime deficits, albeit temporarily, was a principal reason that a Democratic president and a Republican Congress, neither giving credit to the other, were able to balance the budget in the mid-1990s.

Long before the deferred benefits of the deficits became evident, "Reaganomics" had carried the day on tax and monetary policy. Reagan, while no scholar, was a disciple of the iconoclastic economist Milton Friedman, who served on his economic advisory board. He believed in Friedman's dictum that inflation was the result of excessive money creation—"too much money chasing too few goods," as Reagan often said—and he was resolved to end the "Carter inflation" that had outlived the Carter administration, reaching more than 10 percent during Reagan's first year in office. As a result, Reagan backed Federal Reserve Chairman Paul Volcker, appointed by Carter, in his persistent effort to wring inflation out of the economy by raising interest rates. The immediate result was the 1982 recession. Reagan's approval ratings sank, the Democrats made modest mid-term gains, and Republicans, including Senate leader Howard Baker, joined the political chorus calling for Volcker's scalp. Reagan, unfazed, defiantly proclaimed, "Stay the course." The recession gave way to six years of unprecedented economic growth and, of even more importance, to a long-term reduction of inflation, which in the quarter century since 1982 has reached an annual rate of 5 percent only once. Reagan also sent a vital signal on wage restraint early in his presidency when he fired 13,000 air traffic controllers who had walked off their jobs on August 3, 1981. The decision was not easy for Reagan—the union of the air traffic controllers had been one of the few to endorse his presidential candidacy—but he never again faced a walkout of federal workers, and his action sent an anti-inflationary message that resonates to this day.

The other crucial pillar of Reaganomics was tax relief, which began well but progressed unevenly. Congress in 1981 approved most of the income-tax reductions proposed by Reagan, but as government revenues plummeted during the recession, the administration could not resist a clamor for tax increases. Disguised as tax reform, a 1982 bill restored about a third of the reductions made the year before, and other bills in subsequent years also nudged taxes higher. Even the genuine tax reform passed by Congress in 1986 had a downside: It eliminated or reduced a number of long-accepted tax deductions, which had the impact of raising taxes for those who had claimed them. But for all these ups and downs, Reagan succeeded in his essential goal of reducing the tax burdens for most Americans (which, in turn, meant the largest savings for the wealthy, who pay the most taxes). The marginal tax rate—the rate at which the last dollar of income is taxed—was 70 percent when Reagan came to office. When he left, it was 28 percent, and some 2,000 pages had been removed from the tax code.

Lower tax rates and low inflation are enduring legacies of Reaganomics. They have been accompanied by growing trade imbalances and increased national debt, which ballooned again with the budget deficits of the George W. Bush presidency. Economists differ on the potential impact of this debt on the U.S. standard of living when and if creditor nations, especially China, reduce their investment in the United States. This seemed a remote prospect in the 1980s, and even if Reagan had considered the possibility of it occurring, there is little doubt he would have been willing to run the risks associated with higher long-term national debt. Reagan believed in "globalism" before the term had entered the vernacular. He had been a free-trader throughout his adult life and had called for a "North American Accord" in announcing his presidential candidacy in 1979. (It led to the "framework agreement" with Mexico that was in turn an ancestor of the North American Free Trade Agreement signed into law by President Clinton.) Reagan understood with a clarity equaled by few American leaders that the military buildup he favored required sturdy U.S. economic growth. In Reagan's view the conflict between the West and the Soviet Union was a contest of ideas and economies as much as a competition in military prowess. British Prime Minister Margaret Thatcher, his premier ally abroad, shared this view. Both of them believed that socialism was a bankrupt ideology. Reagan additionally suspected that the strains of empire were putting intolerable and recurrent burdens on the Soviet Union. His insights prompted a prophetic speech to British members of Parliament at the Palace of Westminster on June 8, 1982, in which Reagan foresaw the Soviet demise. Against the backdrop of unrest in Poland, where the then-outlawed Solidarity union was organizing strikes and protests, Reagan said that the Soviet Union, "the home of Marxism-Leninism," was gripped by a "great revolutionary crisis." He predicted "repeated explosions against repression" in Eastern Europe and said a "global campaign for freedom" ultimately would prevail. "It is the Soviet Union that runs against the tide of human history by denying human freedom and human dignity to its citizens," Reagan said. "It also is in deep economic difficulty." After spelling out the dimensions of this failure, Reagan paraphrased a famous line of Karl Marx: "What I am describing now is a policy and a hope for the long term—the march of freedom and democracy which will leave Marxism-Leninism on the ash heap of history as it has left other totalitarian ideologies which stifle the freedom and muzzle the self expressions of citizens."

Despite his optimism about the eventual outcome of the struggle, Reagan was not sanguine. He worried that as cracks appeared in the façade of empire the Soviets would become more aggressive in dealing with Eastern Europe, as had happened before in Poland, Hungary, and Czechoslovakia. And Reagan believed, at times almost obsessively, that as the Soviet Union became more embattled, the risk of a nuclear confrontation between the superpowers would increase. The perceived danger of nuclear war led him to embrace the fantastic vision of a defensive shield that would repel incoming nuclear missiles. After Reagan announced the formation of the Strategic Defense Initiative (SDI) on March 23, 1983, Soviet leaders denounced it as a ploy by which the United States intended to dominate and militarize space. Democrats in Congress were also skeptical. They dubbed the program "Star Wars," after the popular film, and the name stuck. Most of SDI's advocates (although not Reagan himself) accepted the nomenclature, recognizing, as Reagan administration Assistant Secretary of Defense Richard Perle put it, that in the movie, "the good guys won."

U.S.-Soviet relations, severely strained since the invasion of Afghanistan, turned frigid during the early years of the Reagan presidency as the Soviet Union struggled through a succession of geriatric leaders. Washington was not blameless for the increased tensions, although Reagan from the beginning of his presidency called upon the Soviets to negotiate a peaceful end to the Cold War. But Secretary of State Haig set a confrontational tone, epitomized by a gesture in which he denied Soviet Ambassador Anatoly Dobrynin, dean of the diplomatic corps in Washington, his long-standing special basement access to the White House. (Haig said in his memoirs that this rebuff was instigated without his knowledge by underlings, but he did not conceal his pleasure at the discomfiture the gesture produced in the Soviet embassy.) More than a year later, on March 8, 1983, Reagan sent a sterner message to Moscow in a speech to the National Association of Evangelicals in which he called the Soviet Union an "evil empire" and "the focus of evil in the modern world." The speech, the work of Reagan and a conservative speechwriter, was not cleared by the State Department and greatly vexed George P. Shultz, who had succeeded Haig as secretary of state. The speech came at a time when the Soviets were escalating the level of violence in Afghanistan and increasing pressure on the United States by backing proxy military forces in Angola, Cambodia, and Nicaragua. It also came against the backdrop of a concerted Soviet effort to decouple the United States from its allies by preventing promised U.S. deployment of intermediate-range nuclear missiles in Europe, beginning in West Germany, as a counterweight to Soviet deployment of such missiles in Eastern Europe. (More than 2 million Europeans organized by the nuclear-freeze movement would march in protest to the U.S. deployment.) Then, on September 1, 1983, a Korean civilian airliner with 269 people aboard, including 61 Americans, strayed into Soviet airspace and was shot down by a Soviet fighter plane. It is now known that this happened on orders from Moscow, but at the time the Soviets refused to accept responsibility and lied that the airliner was a spy plane. Reagan called the downing of the defenseless airliner a "crime against humanity." But in the administration's internal discussions he sided with Shultz, dismissing the view of Weinberger and others who wanted to break off most contacts with Moscow. The U.S. military buildup was progressing, and Reagan meant to use it as leverage when he could find a Soviet leader willing to sit down with him.

But the Cold War turned colder before progress could be made. Early in November 1983, and largely unknown to the general public, there was a scare that showed just how thin the line could be between cold and hot war. The United States and its allies in the North Atlantic Treaty Organization (NATO), in a routine annual exercise called Able Archer, were testing the communications and command procedures to be used in event of a nuclear war. But elements of the Soviet secret service (KGB) erroneously concluded that U.S forces had been placed on high alert. NATO learned of this from the KGB chief in London, secretly a British agent, and Reagan was informed that the Soviet high command was concerned that the United States might launch a preemptive strike. The information made Reagan more determined than ever to meet face to face with a Soviet leader. Three days after Able Archer ended, the first U.S. intermediate-range missiles arrived in Europe, and the parliaments of Italy, West Germany, and Norway (the latter by a single vote) voted to deploy them. The Soviets promptly walked out of arms talks that were being held in Geneva at which they had hoped to prevent these deployments. By then, the Soviet press was rabidly comparing Reagan to Hitler, and Yuri Andropov, the Soviet leader who had succeeded Brezhnev, was accusing Reagan of risking war. On January 1, 1984, *Time* chose Reagan and Andropov as their "men of the year"; the magazine's cover showed the two leaders standing grimly with their backs to one another. Reagan was unfazed. In a January 16, 1984, speech drafted by Jack Matlock of the National Security Council (NSC) staff, the president called for negotiations to settle international disputes and reduce stockpiles of nuclear armaments. "My dream is to see the day when nuclear weapons will be banished from the face of the earth," Reagan said. This significant speech was dismissed by Reagan's domestic critics, and also by the Soviets, as election-year propaganda. Matlock believes that Ambassador Dobrynin may have compounded Soviet suspicions because he did not understand English as well as he thought he did and misreported U.S. policy to his superiors in Moscow.[12]

Andropov died of kidney failure on February 9, 1984, after sixteen months in power and was succeeded by Konstantin Chernenko, a member of the Soviet old guard who had long been a lieutenant to Brezhnev. Chernenko was seventy-one years old and in poor health; he died only thirteen months later. Reagan had at this point outlasted three Soviet leaders, two of whom were younger than him. He had sent messages to all of them calling for face-to-face meetings, without success. Indeed, said Reagan, he had been willing from the outset of his presidency to sit down with Soviet leaders, but "they keep dying on me."[13] It was an odd locution that caused much merriment in the White House press corps. "Those Communists will stop at nothing; I'll show that Reagan—I'll just die" went one of the many parodies. But Reagan had a point. It is unlikely that a meaningful negotiation between a U.S. president and a Soviet leader could have occurred in the 1980s until the Soviets had a healthy, younger leader in place. That occurred on March 11, 1985, when Mikhail Gorbachev, fifty-four and vigorous, was chosen by the Soviet Politburo to replace Chernenko.

Gorbachev, whose grandfathers had suffered under Joseph Stalin, had more to recommend him than youth and good health. Although a dedicated Communist, he was a moral man who was anxious to reform his country and who recognized that the enormous level of Soviet military spending was an impediment to this goal. Reagan sensed that Gorbachev was a different kind of Soviet leader—in this judgment he had the useful counsel of Prime Minister Thatcher, who had met Gorbachev in London before his ascension to the Soviet leadership. Thatcher had been impressed by him. In a briefing at Camp David on December 22, 1984, she told Reagan that Gorbachev was "an unusual Russian in that he was much less constrained, more charming, open to discussion and debate, and did not stick to prepared notes."[14] (Characteristically, she added that she often said to herself, "the more charming the adversary, the more dangerous.")[15] Reagan was intrigued. On the day Gorbachev assumed power, Reagan dashed off a letter asking him for a meeting that "could yield results of benefit to both our countries and to the international community as a whole."[16]

U.S.-Soviet relations improved in 1985, pushed along by Shultz and his Soviet counterpart, Soviet Foreign Minister Eduard Sheverdnadze. Reagan and Gorbachev met in Geneva in November, initiating a series of summits that would occur in consecutive years in Reykjavik, Washington, and Moscow. No American president since FDR had enjoyed the commanding public support with which Reagan began these negotiations. Running on the theme of "It's Morning Again in America," he had in 1984 won a huge reelection victory, carrying forty-nine states. Gorbachev recognized the importance of such a landslide victory. Pavel Palazchenko, his interpreter and personal aide, remembered that Gorbachev was standing with a group of his subordinates in Geneva when one of them launched into harsh criticisms of Reagan and his policies. Gorbachev cut him off, saying, "This is the president of the United States, elected by the American people."[17]

The most remarkable aspect of these summits in the recollections of those who attended them—and to some extent in the memoirs of the leaders as well—was their unvarnished candor. Reagan and Gorbachev spoke frankly, argued, made up, socialized together with their wives, reconvened, argued some more, and consistently advanced the policy proposals in which they believed. U.S. diplomat Rozanne Ridgway said the sharpness of the exchanges "would have scared a lot of people" who were not prepared for it: "These, I found, were two men who believed everything they said."[18] In this way, these summits invite comparison with the earlier wartime meetings among FDR, Stalin, and Churchill when the Red Army was the decisive force in Europe. Forty years later the leaders meeting at Geneva bore the burdens of post–World War II history and Europe's division into rival blocs with the eastern half under Soviet domination. Reagan was preoccupied with this history and saw an opportunity to change it. Before Gorbachev came to power Reagan and his diplomats had developed a four-part agenda that would change little in substance throughout the balance of the Cold War. It called for reducing nuclear weapons, respecting human rights, opening up the Soviet Union to information from outside, and pursuing disengagement from armed conflicts in third countries. At every summit Reagan gave Gorbachev lists of Soviet dissidents whom he wanted released or allowed to emigrate. (He had been pushing for such action since 1983, when, at Shultz's urging, he had promised Ambassador Dobrynin that he would make no public statements if the Soviets released members of two Pentecostal Christian families who had taken refuge in the U.S. embassy. The Soviets allowed the Pentecostals to emigrate.) Gorbachev had his own concerns, the most pressing of which was to find a way out of the Afghanistan war that Brezhnev had begun and his successors had continued. But even Afghanistan was overshadowed by the debate over what to do about the ever-growing nuclear arsenals of both sides. Both leaders wanted to reduce these arsenals, but Reagan also was intent on gaining Soviet acceptance of SDI, even to the point of proposing to share the technology (an idea that scared the U.S. national security community out of its socks). Gorbachev would have none of it. He was determined to stop "space weapons," as he called them, and asserted that the only reason a nation would build a defensive shield would be to enable it to make a surprise attack.

Today, the world is awash in worries about nuclear proliferation. Will Iran develop a nuclear weapon? Will North Korea keep its promise to abandon its nuclear weapons program? And what if a nuclear weapon somehow finds its way into the hands of a gang of stateless terrorists? These are troublesome questions, but they pale in comparison to the situation facing Reagan and Gorbachev. In 1985, when the two leaders sat down in Geneva, the Soviet Union and the United States between them possessed more than 67,000 nuclear weapons, roughly two-thirds of them in Soviet stockpiles. Of these, just fewer than 12,000 weapons on the U.S. side and nearly 10,000 on the Soviet side were classified as "strategic," meaning that they could be delivered onto the other nation's territory. The premise of nuclear deterrence—a policy more than three decades old when Reagan became president—was that the prospect of these strategic weapons being used was so horrifying that neither side would ever dare use them. For this reason, the policy was known as Mutual Assured Destruction, or MAD. To ensure that neither side would be tempted to launch a first strike that would knock out the other side's nuclear weapons, military doctrine in both the Soviet Union and the United States called for one side to launch at the first sign the other had done so. Reagan believed this was an immoral policy and "truly mad." ("A nuclear war can never be won and must never be fought," Reagan had said many times, most poignantly in a speech to the Japanese parliament on November 11, 1983.) But the premise of deterrence, the moral issue aside, might have had practical validity if the danger of nuclear war had been limited to a deliberate attack. That was not what Reagan feared. Though he allowed for the theoretical possibility that a future Soviet leader (certainly not Gorbachev), either under pressure or deranged, might order such an attack, Reagan focused on the possibility that miscalculation or accident could lead to nuclear war. Indeed, he considered such an outcome probable if the two sides continued to aim strategic missiles at each other under a hair-trigger system in which a response to a perceived attack was nearly automatic.

The operative word in the preceding sentence, it turns out, is "nearly." Although Reagan and probably Gorbachev were unaware of it when they sat down at Geneva, the Unthinkable had almost occurred. On September 26, 1983, less than four weeks after the Soviet downing of the Korean airliner and at a time when Andropov seems genuinely to have feared a preemptive strike, Lt. Col. Stanislav Petrov was in his commander's chair in a secret bunker where the Soviets monitored its early warning satellites over the United States. One of the satellites sent a computer signal indicating that nuclear missiles had been launched and were heading toward the Soviet Union. Petrov informed the general staff and had less than five minutes to decide upon a response. He had been told many times that any U.S. nuclear attack would be massive, in an attempt to overwhelm Soviet defenses in a single stroke, but the electronic signal said that only five missiles were on the way. Petrov also knew the Soviet satellite warning system had been rushed into service—it was "raw," as he later put it—and possibly unreliable. "I had a funny feeling in my gut," he said. "I didn't want to make a mistake."[19] And he didn't. On his own initiative, Petrov decided that there were no U.S. missiles on the way and that no Soviet response was needed. He so informed the general staff. But it had been a near-run thing, almost the nightmare that Reagan believed was the likely outcome of a continual reliance on deterrence to forestall nuclear war. The world did not know this story until February 10, 1999, when it was related in chilling detail by David Hoffman of *The Washington Post*.

Reagan had been thinking about nuclear war since the United States had ended World War II in 1945 by dropping atomic bombs on Hiroshima and Nagasaki. Although he did not wear it on his sleeve, Reagan was a religious man, and he took Armageddon, the biblical story of the end of the world, seriously if not quite literally. He was also, since the 1940s, an avid science-fiction fan—a reading habit that persisted through his presidency—and he was familiar with a recurrent theme of the genre:

An invasion from another world prompts earthlings to put aside their quarrels and unite against an alien invader. Reagan liked this idea so much he tried it out on Gorbachev in Geneva, saying that he was certain the United States and the Soviet Union would cooperate if Earth were threatened by an invasion from outer space. Gorbachev had no idea what he was talking about and changed the subject, which in turn persuaded Reagan that he had scored a point.

But Reagan's fears were based on more than fantasy. The inherent immorality of Mutual Assured Destruction—deliberately annihilating the civilian population of another country in revenge—troubled him. He remembered the warnings of President Dwight Eisenhower, who as a general had opposed the atomic bombing of Japan; in 1953, Eisenhower had delivered his famous "atoms for peace" speech at the United Nations in which he rejected the prospect of "the annihilation of the irreplaceable heritage of mankind" in favor of a quest for peace. (Reagan voted for Eisenhower in 1952, the first time he cast a ballot for a Republican presidential candidate.) After Reagan was narrowly bested for the Republican presidential nomination by President Gerald Ford in 1976, he strode onto the stage of the auditorium in Kansas City and warned that nuclear war was the greatest danger facing the nation and the world. In part because of the late hour, the speech was not covered well in the media, and most of what little attention it did receive focused on its political aspects, not Reagan's warning. Three years later, when Reagan was preparing himself for the next presidential campaign, he toured the headquarters of the North American Aerospace Defense Command (NORAD) at Cheyenne Mountain in Colorado and was told there was nothing that could be done about an incoming Soviet missile except to track it. Reagan was shaken. "We have spent all that money and have all that equipment, and there is nothing we can do to prevent a nuclear missile from hitting us," he said to adviser Martin Anderson as the two of them flew back to Los Angeles.[20]

By the time Reagan reached the first of his summits with Gorbachev, he was focused on two interlocking goals. The first was to eliminate nuclear weapons. The second, since Reagan knew that the first might elude full achievement, was to provide a defensive shield that would protect the civilian population of the United States and the population of any other nation willing to take advantage of what he envisioned as a shared technology. It was a moral but unachievable objective; scientists did not believe that a workable defensive shield was possible, particularly against a barrage of incoming Soviet missiles. But the SDI concept nonetheless introduced a new element into U.S.-Soviet arms discussions, for it promised scientific competition in a variety of technologies in which the Soviet Union would have difficulty matching the United States. Gorbachev knew this, and he was also aware that SDI would require additional military spending at a time when he needed to reduce the Soviet military budget. Gorbachev set out to kill the project in its infancy, but Reagan refused to budge, and the stubbornness of the two leaders made SDI a sticking point in the Reagan-Gorbachev negotiations. The talks nonetheless continued. Both leaders were convinced that it was crucial to reduce nuclear arsenals. In Reagan's case, his utopian attachment to SDI was trumped by a practical impulse. He believed that his background negotiating contracts in Hollywood on behalf of the Screen Actors Guild had prepared him to deal with Gorbachev. When he was asked what he had learned from his experiences negotiating with movie producers, Reagan replied: "That the purpose of a negotiation is to get an agreement."[21]

Reagan's negotiating experience was not limited to Hollywood, however. In his second term as governor of California he had negotiated face-to-face with Democratic legislative leaders to produce a notable welfare reform bill and other measures. The key to a successful agreement, Reagan recognized, was that it be beneficial to both sides. In the protracted Reagan-Gorbachev negotiations, Reagan and his team perceived that the steep reductions in nuclear arms and military forces proposed by the United States would help Gorbachev because they would free up resources for his domestic reforms. (Useful books by Jack Matlock, George Shultz, and Don Oberdorfer trace the path of these negotiations.) Gorbachev eventually came to this view—soon enough to produce the significant arms control treaties that marked the twilight of the Cold War, but too late to rescue his country. Matlock suggested in *Reagan and Gorbachev* that Gorbachev might have saved the Soviet Union had he come to this realization sooner than he did.

It took two years before the two sides agreed to reduce intermediate-range missiles. The breakthrough followed an October 1986 summit in Reykjavik, Iceland, which ended in acrimony when Reagan rejected Gorbachev's demand that SDI be confined to the laboratory. Although Reykjavik initially was perceived in both countries as a failure, Reagan and Gorbachev in their frank discussions had laid the groundwork for an agreement. The diplomats and technical staff transformed this into the Intermediate Nuclear Forces (INF) Treaty, which was signed at the Washington summit of 1987. Ultimately, Reagan obtained every point on his four-part agenda, including Soviet withdrawal from Afghanistan, which Gorbachev announced on February 8, 1988. Within a year, all Soviet troops had left Afghanistan.

Reagan had been expecting a Soviet withdrawal since Geneva. When Gorbachev first discussed Afghanistan at that meeting, he said he had learned of the invasion in a radio broadcast, which Reagan interpreted as Gorbachev's way of saying he had "no responsibility and less enthusiasm" for the war. This was an example of Reagan's observant qualities. He was a good listener who paid attention to body language, which in many situations more than compensated for any deficiencies in formal knowledge. Reagan tended to be impressionistic and intuitive rather than analytical. He made sense of the world through anecdotes, often funny and on point but sometimes neither. He had the capacity to unnerve aides and acquaintances by retelling a joke or story he had related to them dozens of times as if it were brand new. To his staff, which found him alternately focused and detached, he was at once an inspiration and puzzlement. On balance, he dealt boldly and effectively with Gorbachev, often eluding the confines of his briefing papers and saying whatever was on his mind. This wasn't always a successful strategy. At the Washington summit, he told a shopworn anti-Soviet joke that offended Gorbachev and embarrassed Shultz. At the Moscow summit the following year, however, Reagan struck all the right notes with Gorbachev and received a rock star's welcome from excited Muscovites. The highlight was a premier performance at Moscow State University, where, beneath a gigantic white bust of Lenin, Reagan extolled the values of a free society and the "riot of experimentation that is the free market." The students applauded his speech mightily; on the way out of the lecture hall one of the female students said to her companion, "You can see why he is called the Great Communicator."[22] Later, Reagan and Gorbachev strolled together through Red Square, where the president was asked if he still believed the Soviet Union was an evil empire. "I was speaking of another time, another era," Reagan replied.

Although the Cold War did not end formally until George H. W. Bush was in the White House, it was effectively over after the Moscow summit.

Partisans on both sides soon began making extravagant claims about who "won" the war, as if it had been a football game, usually without saying that a protracted conflict between nuclear superpowers that ended peaceably was an enormous victory for mankind. Even short of a nuclear exchange, the Cold War could have ended bloodily if Gorbachev had been willing to shoot East Germans and Hungarians, as his predecessors did, to preserve the boundaries of the Soviet empire. He was not willing to do so, for which he deserves much credit that conservatives in the United States often withhold. Liberals, at least until George W. Bush launched the Iraq War, have been even less willing to credit Reagan. Without evidence, they suggest that what happened was inevitable and occurred mostly because of the internal situation in the Soviet Union. But it was Reagan, in defiance of the liberal orthodoxy of his day, who most accurately assessed the weakness of the Soviet system and exploited it by expanding an arms race in which the Soviets could not keep up. The Cold War, in the words of Condoleezza Rice, was "frozen in time"[23] when Reagan became president, and Reagan, more than anyone else, unfroze it. He ran risks to do so, and his insights and actions were disputed every step of the way until they bore fruit. The words of the British historian C. V. Wedgwood apply: "History is written backward but lived forward. Those who know the end of the story can never know what it was like at the time."[24]

After the Cold War ended, diplomats from both sides, George Shultz and Jack Matlock among them, gathered together at Princeton to discuss what had happened. The diplomats agreed that the Cold War had not ended automatically, and they all gave credit to Reagan and Gorbachev, none more eloquently than Alexander Besstmertnykh, the former deputy Soviet foreign minister:

> Those two men [Reagan and Gorbachev] were very idealistic. They each had their own ideals, which they had tried to follow all through their lives. Their ideals were not similar, but the dedication to those ideals was similar. They both believed in something. They were not just men who could trim their sails and go any way the wind blows. . . . this is what they immediately sensed in each other, and why they made good partners.
>
> Reagan handled negotiations very, very well. He might not have known all the details. He used little cards when he would come to

details. He didn't like the formal part of negotiations. . . . He would try to rush through this formal part, and then he would throw away the cards and then he would start talking the direct way. I was across the table at all the summits and followed this president for all those years, and I personally admired the man very much. He was a good politician. He was a good diplomat. He was very dedicated. And if it were not for Reagan, I don't think we would have been able to reach the agreements in arms control that we reached later, because of his idealism, because he thought that we should really do away with nuclear weapons. Gorbachev believed in that. Reagan believed in that. The experts didn't believe, but the leaders did.[25]

What Reagan most believed in was the power of freedom. This led him to engage the surrogates of the Soviet empire—or those whom he believed were surrogates—in little wars around the globe. Some of these wars turned out better than others, and all of them will be examined in a subsequent chapter. Suffice it here to say that Reagan was confident from beginning to end that freedom would prevail in the long twilight struggle with communism. "Democracy triumphed in the cold war." Reagan wrote, "because it was a battle of values—between one system that gave preeminence to the state and another preeminence to the individual and freedom."[26] Reagan's ally Margaret Thatcher stood with him in this "battle of values" and keenly assessed Reagan's role in it. Writing about his achievements in his final month in office, she said that Reagan had "achieved the most difficult of all political tasks: changing attitudes and perceptions about what is possible. From the strong fortress of his convictions, he set out to enlarge freedom the world over at a time when freedom was in retreat—and he succeeded."[27]

Reagan's contribution in safely ending the Cold War is the transcendent aspect of his legacy. Part of that legacy, it should be noted, is that Reagan not only signed the INF Treaty but also carried it forward to Senate ratification against the vigorous opposition of conservatives, including William F. Buckley. Reagan could not have done this, or indeed done much of anything, without first restoring national confidence, which in turn was followed by a long period of robust economic growth. "National confidence" resists quantifiable measurement but is an important barometer. In the early weeks of FDR's presidency, his success in helping his fellow Americans conquer "fear itself" overshadowed the New Deal's specific legislative measures. This was similarly the case with Reagan. "What I'd really like to do is go down in history as the president who made Americans believe in themselves again." Reagan said six months into his presidency. This was the pre-condition to everything he achieved.

Reagan's magic continued to work its spell beyond his presidency. George H. W. Bush was elected president in 1988, when Reagan was near the peak of public approval. As political scientist John Kenneth White has noted, Bush was then seen by voters as a stand-in for Reagan, who was constitutionally ineligible for a third term. Reagan also had an impact on the opposition. The political success of the Reagan coalition tugged the Democratic Party rightward, creating an opening for the centrist Clinton. When President Clinton was perceived as having overreached, Republicans in 1994 won control of the House for the first time in forty years under Newt Gingrich's banner of the Contract with America, mostly cribbed from Reagan's various State of the Union addresses. By the time the Democrats regained control of the House in 2006 and won the Senate after a campaign waged in repudiation of George W. Bush and the Iraq War, Reagan had become the default position of the Republican Party. Senator John McCain said on *Meet the Press* after the election: "I am a conservative Republican in the school of Ronald Reagan—who, by the way, brought our party back after a defeat in 1976 and gave us hope and optimism."[28] By then, Reagan had passed into the realm of iconic leader for politicians of both major parties. In 2004, upon the news of Reagan's death, Democratic presidential nominee John Kerry pronounced Reagan one of American history's "great optimists." In a speech to graduating high school seniors, Kerry, who had been a relentless critic of Reagan, added, "Free men and women everywhere will forever remember and honor President Reagan's role in ending the Cold War. . . . Perhaps President Reagan's greatest monument isn't any building or any structure that bears his name, but it is the absence of the Berlin Wall."

A year earlier, as the war began in Iraq, progressive writer Harold Meyerson expressed liberals' newfound nostalgia for Reagan even more succinctly by beginning a cover story of the *American Prospect* with the simple declaration: "I miss Ronald Reagan."[29]

Transformational presidents continue to be transforming after they have left the scene. Michael Barone has observed that there were more New Deal Democrats in the Senate during Eisenhower's term than at any time during FDR's lifetime, and during the presidency of George W. Bush there were more avowed Reagan Republicans in Congress and the state legislatures than at any time during the Reagan presidency, even after the Republican electoral setbacks of 2006. The Reagan label helped to obscure the differences that emerged within the conservative coalition once the Soviet Union no longer provided a unifying front of anti-communism. After Reagan left the scene, Republican candidates resembled the wannabes in the Michael Jordan television commercials, who plaintively say, "I want to be like Mike." This is easy to say but hard to do. The basketball superstar was in a class by himself, and so was Ronald Reagan. Other Republicans emulated Reagan, but they could not replicate him.

The politician who staked the most plausible claim to be "another Reagan" was, for a time, George W. Bush. He rallied and unified the country in the wake of the September 11, 2001, terrorist attacks, and his approval ratings briefly exceeded even Reagan's highest levels. While the unity and the poll ratings proved short-lived, Bush modeled many of his policies on the premises of what conservatives call the "Reagan Revolution." This was cheered by conservatives (and deplored by liberals), most conspicuously in *The New York Times Magazine* article, "Reagan's Son," cited in the introduction to this book. Bush believed as firmly as Reagan in the value of tax reductions as a means of promoting economic growth, and his judicial appointments were arguably more conservative than Reagan's. But the persistent comparison to Reagan was ultimately disadvantageous to Bush, for it set the bar at a higher level than he, or for that matter most presidents, could clear. Reagan was a conservative, to be sure, and he advanced many conservative principles. But he was also, as the situation required, a pragmatist, a negotiator, a diplomat, and a statesman. Much like his political idol Franklin Roosevelt, Reagan eluded pigeonholes and was unconfined by ideology. He realized his goal of making Americans believe in themselves, and he left the world safer than he found it. These are large achievements.

3

THE THREE PRESIDENCIES
OF GEORGE W. BUSH

Just after 3 P.M. on November 3, 2004, a tired but triumphant-looking George W. Bush addressed handpicked supporters at the Ronald Reagan Building and International Trade Center a few blocks southeast of the White House. In contrast to the aftermath of the 2000 presidential election, this time there was no litigation, no recount, no Supreme Court decision to help determine the winner, no fluky reliance on the Electoral College after failing to win the popular vote. In 2004, without a taint to his victory, the president evinced few doubts about his ability to follow through on the policy goals he had staked out so clearly on the campaign trail.

Bush had run energetically for reelection, especially across the highly contested states of the Midwest, stressing the same themes everywhere he went: holding firm in Iraq, pressing ahead in the worldwide war against Islamic terrorism, demanding Congress make "permanent" his first-term tax cuts and accede to significant changes in Social Security designed to make that program more remunerative for taxpayers and solvent far into the future. He touted the success of his signature domestic policy achievement, the No Child Left Behind Act, and promised to keep nominating federal judges "who know the difference between personal opinion and the strict interpretation of the law."[1] American voters knew where Bush stood, all right, and returned him to the White House. The results were no landslide, but Bush's 118,601-vote win in Ohio had given him the Buckeye State's twenty electoral votes—and, with them, reelection. In the national popular vote, Bush's margin of victory was just over 3 million.

"America has spoken, and I'm humbled by the trust and the confidence of my fellow citizens," Bush told his supporters. "With that trust comes a duty to serve all Americans, and I will do my best to fulfill that duty every day as your president."

Although he strove for a public tone of graciousness and humility, inside the White House the predominant emotion on the part of Bush and his aides was euphoria. Running against a united Democratic Party, without any spoiler third-party candidate on the ballot, Bush had won a clear majority, drawing far more votes in the process than any presidential candidate in U.S. history. Second-term elections usually bring a decline in voter participation. That was not the case in 2004. In the 2000 election, 105 million Americans cast ballots for president. Four years later, 122 million Americans went to the polls—meaning that 61 percent of eligible citizens participated in the presidential election. John Kerry garnered 8 million more votes than Al Gore had done four years earlier. But the George W. Bush of 2004 attracted 11.6 million more votes than the George W. Bush of 2000. He did so during a year of mixed economic news and in the midst of a stalemated Iraq War that fully half of the voting public had come to consider a misstep. For those reasons, Bush's gratitude toward his campaign organization—at the Reagan Building victory speech he called top political adviser Karl Rove "the architect" of his reelection—was fitting. Still, it was Bush's name on the ballot, and in that halcyon week in November his forward momentum seemed undeniable, and not just to those who labored inside the cloistered gates of the White House compound.

Republicans had retained control in both houses of Congress. In the Senate, they had added to their power, picking up four more Senate seats, for a more comfortable 55–45 working majority. The stock market, reassured by continuity, rose 350 points in three days. By the end of election week, the U.S. Department of Labor had posted the October employment numbers, and 337,000 new jobs had been added to the economy—

twice as many as had been expected. "It was," Bush campaign aide Mark McKinnon recalled later, "a good time to be us."[2]

This elation would not last. Although hardly anyone predicted it, least of all the demoralized Democrats, the last few weeks of 2004 constituted the zenith of the Bush presidency. In his second term, conditions would unravel inexorably, as Bush's standing would fall victim to hurricane and hubris, to evidence of corruption in his political party, and to questions of competence in his White House. But mostly, the Bush administration's reputation and momentum would erode because of events halfway across the world in the unforgiving sands of the Iraqi desert and on the bloody streets of Baghdad.

Presidencies, like marriages and life itself, go through iterations. One famous example, related firsthand by Franklin Roosevelt, was how after Pearl Harbor, FDR transfigured himself from "old Doctor New Deal" to "Doctor Win-the-War."[3] Ronald Reagan's presidency was divided, at least in the minds of contemporary commentators, between the years before Iran-contra and after Iran-contra. Many of those who worked inside the Reagan White House or who covered it for the press refer to three distinct chapters of the Reagan presidency delineated by who occupied the job of White House chief of staff. The first, and most successful, years were when James A. Baker was chief of staff—Reagan's entire first term. The troubled middle years came after Baker and Treasury Secretary Donald Regan persuaded Reagan to let them switch jobs. The final act came after the team of Howard Baker and Kenneth Duberstein was brought aboard for damage control, and Reagan's wagon train regained its course.

Bill Clinton's tenure in the White House also had three distinct incarnations: The first consisted of his rocky initial two years in office. This period was marked by the successful passage of Clinton's budget bill, which tweaked the Reagan-era tax formulas for those in the top tax brackets, and enactment of the Reagan-envisioned North American Free Trade Agreement (NAFTA). But Clinton's first two years also featured a high-profile failure to get Congress to take up his sweeping health care proposal, his waffling on no-win issues such as gays in the military, and his catastrophic refusal to thwart genocide in Rwanda. Elected in a three-way race in 1992 with only 43 percent of the vote, Clinton during his first two years in office was also bedeviled by persistently middling poll numbers, which made few members of either party on Capitol Hill fear displeasure from the White House.

Counterintuitively, the successful second act of Bill Clinton's presidency was heralded by the Republican takeover of Congress in the 1994 mid-term elections, an upheaval that was partly a reaction by voters against the reign of the Clintons. After initially demoralizing the president, Newt Gingrich's ascendance to Speaker of the House galvanized Clinton and those inside his White House and led to the successful middle years of his presidency. This period brought balanced budgets, welfare reform legislation, military and diplomatic successes in Kosovo and Bosnia—and reelection.

The final phase of Clinton's presidency, abridged by scandal and impeachment, constituted a kind of holding action in which neither Clinton nor his Republican nemeses on Capitol Hill could move much beyond trench warfare to address policy issues. These years also resulted, paradoxically, in the highest job approval ratings of Clinton's presidency. True, the American public was affronted by Clinton's fundraising schemes, which famously featured the renting out of the Lincoln Bedroom to wealthy Democratic donors, and even more so by an exploitive sexual liaison between the president and an intern in the Oval Office itself. But a sizable majority of voters was more sorely vexed by what they considered the Republicans' excessive—and, in many instances, hypocritical—overreaction to the president's transgressions.

In Austin, George W. Bush was paying attention. When it was his turn to run for president, Bush positioned himself as someone who would simultaneously avoid tawdriness and float above partisan pettiness. In Bush's vow to restore dignity to the office of the presidency, Republican voters heard, quite correctly, that Bush was promising never to indulge himself at the White House with a woman half his age, or to give Americans cause to doubt his fealty to Laura Bush. Also, and in contrast to Al Gore's much-parodied circumlocution about the administration's fundraising excesses ("There is no controlling legal authority that says this was in violation of law," Gore claimed repeatedly), Bush vowed that in his administration he would "ask not only what is legal but what is right, not what the lawyers allow but what the public deserves."*

---

*At this October 26, 2000, campaign rally in Pittsburgh, Bush was introduced by Colin Powell. The same day, at a press conference in Washington, D.C., Ralph Nader publicly blew off Democratic entreaties to withdraw from the race, saying that it didn't matter to him if his presence on the ballot helped Bush defeat Gore, because both political parties were mired in "decay."

Bush additionally promised to elevate the tenor of the nation's political discourse, and carefully cast his famous promise to be "a uniter, not a divider" in bipartisan terms. In his first speech after clinching the GOP nomination, Bush decried "the arms race of anger" in American politics, adding pointedly that both major political parties were to blame.[4] Bush amplified this point the following night in an interview with Jim Lehrer of PBS, and again while accepting the nomination at the Republican National Convention in Philadelphia that summer. "I don't have enemies to fight," Bush proclaimed in that speech. "And I have no stake in the bitter arguments of the last few years. I want to change the tone of Washington to one of civility and respect." Bush wasn't specific how he intended to attain that goal, but the Bush biography peddled by him and his campaign staff included obligatory references to Bob Bullock, the powerful Texas Democrat who served as lieutenant governor when Bush was in Austin. With Bullock, Bush had found common purpose on legislation and style—to the point that Bullock endorsed Bush when he ran for reelection as governor. Bush himself would also invoke the name of a west Texan named James E. (Pete) Laney, the longtime speaker of the Texas House of Representatives, as an example of how he could forge a close working relationship with Democrats of goodwill. The record in Austin confirmed that this picture of Bush the Bipartisan was accurate enough. Bush also sought to convey the image of a candidate who was so at ease with himself that the possibility of losing wasn't a particularly catastrophic thought. In an early 1999 interview with a New Hampshire television reporter, Bush, who was then fifty-one years old, volunteered that he didn't wake up when he was fifteen thinking "I really want to be president"—nor had he done so at twenty-one, thirty-one, or forty-one. He was thinking of it now, he conceded, but not in a desperate way. "If I were to decide to run for president and it not work out, it's okay," Bush said. "I got a pretty good life right here."[5]

The veiled swipe at Bill Clinton notwithstanding, implicit in Bush's pitch that he could play well with others was the notion that if elected, he would eschew the ad-hominem attacks routinely used against Clinton—and *by* the Clintonites (including the first lady)—against their adversaries. But Bush had always been highly competitive, with an occasional mean streak, and the rough tactics used by his campaign in the 2000 South Carolina primary against John McCain sorely tested Bush's commitment to the high road. It was a test that the McCainiacs thought Bush and his top political aide Karl Rove failed miserably. ("I want the presidency in the best way," an embittered McCain said after he lost South Carolina to Bush. "Not the worst way.") Likewise, the extremely close general election against Gore, with the acrimonious Florida recount and attendant litigation that ultimately resolved the question, made it imperative for Bush to begin his presidency on an inclusive note. Bush—and, for that matter, Gore—met this challenge in their gracious public statements on the night the 2000 election was finally decided. And the day he took the oath of office, Bush made another conciliatory gesture. "I thank President Clinton for his service to our nation," he said at the beginning of his Inaugural Address. "And I thank Vice President Gore for a contest conducted with spirit and ended with grace."

So began Act I of the man who would be Reagan.

In his first eight months in office Bush kept his half of the bargain he had forged with the American people. Like Clinton, he was forced to troll for votes for his tax increase almost exclusively in the ranks of his own party. This was a testament to how polarized Congress had become along ideological lines since the Reagan era rather than a sign that there was any lack of persuasiveness on the part of Clinton or Bush. If anything, Bush's rhetoric on the budget was less partisan than Clinton's, and Bush actively reached across party lines in search of support for the No Child Left Behind Act, just as Clinton had done on NAFTA. Bush found willing partners among two influential liberals, Massachusetts Senator Edward M. Kennedy and California Congressman George Miller. At his inaugural Bush had stressed the importance of education in language that revealed just how much the expectations of the federal government had changed in twenty years, even among conservative voters. While running for president in 1980, Ronald Reagan had expressed skepticism about the utility of the U.S. Department of Education, a historic backwater that had been upgraded to cabinet status by Jimmy Carter in fulfillment of his campaign promise to the teachers' unions. "President Carter's new bureaucratic boondoggle," Reagan called it. As president, Reagan made no serious attempt to dismantle the Department of Education. The federal portion of K–12 spending increased during his presidency, and it has steadily increased even more under the next three presidents. (Reagan never, however, changed his dim view of the Department of Education.

In his 1984 State of the Union address he said: "Excellence does not begin in Washington. A 600-percent increase in federal spending on education between 1960 and 1980 was accompanied by a steady decline in Scholastic Aptitude Test scores. Excellence must begin in our homes and neighborhood schools, where it's the responsibility of every parent and teacher and the right of every child.")

In 1996, Republican presidential nominee Bob Dole talked this way during his campaign, too, and for his troubles succeeded in doing little more than reinforcing his image as a curmudgeon. This was most decidedly not George W. Bush's approach to education. As he began running for president, Bush would tell educators' groups that he loved teachers so much he had married one, and upon becoming president he appointed Houston's African-American school superintendent as his secretary of education. Meanwhile, Bush reassured anyone on Capitol Hill who would listen that if public school districts needed more money, he would help deliver it, provided those districts used the money for reforms to tangibly improve their record of educating the nation's hardest-to-reach kids.

"Together, we will reclaim America's schools, before ignorance and apathy claim more young lives," Bush vowed in his Inaugural Address. Bush never alluded directly to Reagan in this speech (the only president he mentioned other than Clinton was his predecessor's namesake, Thomas Jefferson), but in prose penned by Michael Gerson and his team of speechwriters that was obviously inspired by Reagan's farewell presidential address of 1988, Bush offered up his version of American Exceptionalism. "We have a place, all of us, in a long story ... the American story—a story of flawed and fallible people, united across the generations by grand and enduring ideals," Bush said. "The grandest of these ideals is an unfolding American promise that everyone belongs, that everyone deserves a chance, that no insignificant person was ever born."

Such language was an agreeable surprise to many Democrats. "George W. Bush's first week as president of the United States began with a speech that, taken as a whole and judged purely as a piece of writing, was shockingly good," wrote *The New Yorker* magazine's Hendrik Hertzberg, a liberal who had helped draft Jimmy Carter's 1977 Inaugural Address. "It was by far the best inaugural address in forty years," Hertzberg added. "Indeed, it was better than all but a tiny handful of all the inaugurals of all the presidents since the Republic was founded." Regarding education policy, what helped Bush govern more than inspired rhetoric was his pragmatic decision to quickly jettison the conservatives' will-o'-the-wisp of vouchers for private school tuition. With that chit in their pockets, Miller and Kennedy were able to shepherd Bush's sweeping education reform bill through Congress. It may have been an illusion—and it was certainly premature—but on that day the outlines of George W. Bush's tenure as president seemed sketched out. Bush had promised in 2000 to "fix" Social Security and put Medicare on "firm financial ground," but his emphasis was primarily on two issues: getting the GOP in the game on national education policy and cutting taxes. Candidate Bush proposed eliminating the estate tax; lessening the income-tax burden for every American, including lowering the bottom rate from 15 percent to 10 percent; doubling the child tax credit; increasing the amount of credits parents could claim for putting away money for college; reducing the so-called marriage penalty; and capping the top income-tax rate, which was then 39.6 percent, at 33 percent. If such a program would result in deficit spending, which seemed obvious, Bush didn't register much concern. For him the sin was that, for the first time since Richard Nixon was president, the U.S. Treasury was taking in more in tax receipts than it was dispersing. "Today, our high taxes fund a surplus," Bush said simply, in words that could have been uttered by Reagan. "The surplus is not the government's money. The surplus is the people's money."[6]

For post-Reagan Republicans, the political logic of Bush's position was unassailable, which even Al Gore eventually came to realize. In 1999, the Republican-controlled Congress had passed a tax cut that would have put an estimated $792 billion back into the pockets of Americans over the ensuing ten years. The legislation also would have negated President Clinton's hard-fought 1993 budget bill, but some Republicans believed that Clinton, weakened by the Lewinsky scandal, would sign it anyway. Instead, Clinton vetoed the GOP tax bill with a flourish, taunting Republican presidential candidates—Bush included—by dismissing the Republican bill as a pre-election ploy designed to help Republicans run on a platform of tax cutting. Go ahead, Clinton told them, but just be sure to tell the American people about the high-flying economic conditions in the country that led to the surplus. Undeterred, Bush seized the initiative by proposing a tax cut even larger than the one Clinton had vetoed. Gore, noting that the federal government's books were in the black for the first time in a generation, repeatedly derided Bush's proposal as a "risky scheme." But by the summer of 2000, with the federal budget in surplus for the third straight year, Gore began to hedge his bet. Still denouncing Bush's plans, Gore proposed a $500 billion tax cut of his own, meaning that even before the election, Bush—acting as a Reagan acolyte—had framed the national agenda on taxes.

By the time Bush assumed office, the economic picture in the country had been altered. Bush didn't waver in his desire to cut taxes, but his underlying rationale for the tax cut changed twice. Initially, Bush asserted as a kind of moral proposition that Americans should not have to pay more than one-third of their income in federal taxes. As the surplus increased in the last year of Clinton's presidency, Bush employed his anti-Washington-spending language. By the time Bush was inaugurated, it was clear that a looming economic slowdown he had inherited would doom the surplus. Not to worry; Bush shifted gears yet again. The new justification for tax cuts was that they would stimulate the economy and tamp down the effects of any coming recession. In the first week of Bush's presidency, Federal Reserve Board chairman Alan Greenspan testified that Bush's proposed tax cuts—he was now asking for a $1.6 trillion cut over ten years—would not harm the already cooling economy and might do some good. That gave Republicans cover, but the precise reasons cited by the president were not the deciding factor. Bush got his tax cut because by 2001 tax cutting was post-Reagan Republican catechism—and, as had been the case for Clinton eight years earlier, the new president had just enough of his own crowd in Congress to pass his budget bill on a virtual party-line vote.

In the end, Bush wrangled out of Congress tax cuts estimated at $1.3 trillion to $1.4 trillion over ten years. The measure was signed by Bush in the East Room on June 7, 2001. It exempted millions of Americans from paying any taxes, and created a new (and lower) 10 percent bracket for the working poor, while lowering the top three brackets: By 2006, the top tax rate was to decline from 39.6 percent to 35 percent; the 36 percent rate to 33 percent, and the 28 percent rate to 25 percent. "A year ago, tax relief was said to be a political impossibility. Six months ago, it was supposed to be a political liability. Today, it becomes reality," Bush said as he signed it into law. Amid Bush's elation, some dissenting voices warned of trip wires buried in the legislation. One was that if the economy were to slow further, the effects on the federal deficit could be explosive. Another was that some portions of the measure, such as phasing out inheritance taxes, took effect gradually, and that there would be political pressure to expedite them, adding to future deficits. But such fears were trumped by the tangible truth of the government's returning excess money to wage earners—and it wasn't a symbolic idea. Even as Bush spoke at the bill-signing ceremony, $300 and $600 rebate checks were being mailed to American taxpayers. This idea originated with Representative Bernie Sanders of Vermont, which some White House aides found ironic, Sanders being the only socialist in Congress. But droll irony is Vermont's stock in trade, and as it regarded Bush, it cut two ways. In Bush's first year as president, the Vermont congressional delegation would cause no minor amount of heartburn inside the White House. In late May, Senator James Jeffords, the state's junior senator, abruptly switched parties. It wasn't the loss of a vote in the Senate that hurt: Jeffords was so liberal a Republican that he had not only voted against Bush's tax cuts but had voted against *Reagan's* tax cuts twenty years earlier when he was in the House. Under Bush's reign, the Senate had been divided fifty-fifty, and with Vice President Dick Cheney seated in his constitutionally prescribed role as Senate tie-breaker, the Republican Party had effective control of the Senate. Jeffords's defection changed all that. Overnight, South Dakota Democrat Tom Daschle replaced Mississippi Republican Trent Lott as Senate majority leader. Even worse, from the standpoint of Bush and the conservatives, the Senate Judiciary Committee fell under the chairmanship of Jeffords's fellow Vermonter Patrick Leahy, a fiery liberal who became the de facto gatekeeper for Bush's nominees to the federal bench.

Nonetheless, as his first summer in office wound to a close, Bush was seeing forward movement. Jeffords had kept his word and did not attempt to re-open the tax bill. By September, the House and Senate had passed their versions of No Child Left Behind, and the differences were being ironed out in a joint conference committee. Eager to sign an education bill before momentum could build against it, Bush embarked on a trip to Florida for some made-for-television schoolhouse events designed to maintain public support for the legislation. The next morning in Washington, Laura Bush was scheduled to testify before Senator

Kennedy's Senate Education Committee about the results of the summit she'd hosted at Georgetown University that summer on early childhood cognitive development. Kennedy had actually attended those July sessions, and he had personally invited the first lady to Capitol Hill.[7]

And so on that evening, September 10, 2001, George W. Bush's tax cut was law, his education package was on its way to becoming law, and nothing too threatening was evident on the horizon. Bush seemed content to let the recession he'd inherited run its course, was unconcerned about the rising budget deficit, and was pushing no particular foreign policy agenda. His job approval ratings were respectable—but hardly formidable—and had dipped to 51 percent, the lowest of his presidency up to that point. Perhaps that slump would have been temporary, but George W. Bush seemed destined to preside over an inoffensive, relatively unambitious one-term presidency. Fred I. Greenstein, the influential Princeton political scientist who helped form the framework through which his profession views presidents, opined that Bush wasn't "up to speed" on the specifics of his own policies and had demonstrated a "minimalist" approach to presidential communications, a crucial part of the job of any modern president.[8] Preeminent *Washington Post* political writer David Broder, picking up on this theme, adjudged that the American people lacked a "clear definition" of their new president.

Yet, Bush wasn't at war with anyone, and he was on pretty good personal terms with those from other branches of government and the institutions designed to keep a watch on him. On the humid Florida morning of September 11, 2001, Bush went for a brisk, four-and-a-half mile early morning run on a golf course on Longboat Key with White House correspondent Richard Keil of Bloomberg News, a member of the traveling press "pool," before heading to Emma T. Booker Elementary School in Sarasota to read *The Pet Goat* to a class of schoolchildren. At the Pentagon, Secretary of Defense Donald Rumsfeld ate a routine breakfast with members of Congress. Across the Potomac River, Laura Bush headed by car to Capitol Hill. Two blocks from the White House, at the St. Regis Hotel, Democratic Party professionals and personalities Bob Shrum, Stanley Greenberg, and James Carville were regaling journalists attending a *Christian Science Monitor* "Sperling Breakfast" with poll data and sound bites purporting to show that Bush already looked like a one-term president. Greenberg, a pollster, brandished a recent survey he'd done in which 45 percent of respondents agreed with the postulate that Bush was "in over his head" as president.

"He's not formidable, politically," Greenberg told the reporters.

"Is he vulnerable?" host Godfrey Sperling asked Shrum. "Is he a pushover?"

The Democrats thought so, but invoked Reagan as a caveat—and as a way of undermining Bush.

"In 1982, Ronald Reagan looked like he was in terrible shape after the congressional elections," Shrum replied. "But then he won in '84. I think there are two fundamental differences. One: He ain't Ronald Reagan in terms of his capacity to move the country. . . . And number two, Reagan came in at a time when people believed the country was not only weak overseas, but that there was a real economic crisis."

Carville chipped in, quoting himself: "My line is: We're busted at home and distrusted around the world." Later Carville added, "The myth is that this is a strong president; he is not." To win the elections of 2002 and 2004, the Republicans would have to run "on their successful foreign policy," Carville said sarcastically. About that time, cell phones began ringing around the table—the first being Shrum's own. The call came from his office. Because he'd left precise instructions not to be disturbed except in an emergency, Shrum answered the call with trepidation. He was so shocked by what he heard that he repeated it to the room: "A plane has just crashed into the World Trade Center."

"What kind of plane?" Shrum asked audibly, and again, repeated the answer: "A 737."

Almost simultaneously, Greenberg's assistant phoned to tell him a second plane had hit. Reporters were getting similar messages from their desks. Carville's thoughts went to his wife, Mary Matalin, who worked in the Bush White House and who would, at the urging of Secret Service agents, soon be sprinting in her stocking feet to a safe location. Perhaps for that reason, or perhaps because he has peerless political instincts, Carville realized, sooner than anyone else in the room, that a seismic event had just occurred. "Disregard everything we just said!" Carville barked to the journalists starting to scramble out of the room. "This changes everything!"[9]

In her limousine, the first lady learned about two planes striking the World Trade Center before arriving on Capitol Hill. Other than those in her own entourage, Ted Kennedy was the first government official Laura Bush saw as her husband's presidency was transitioning—in an instant—from the languid backdrop of its first act. In the months ahead, Kennedy would emerge as a strident opponent of the Bush administration's foreign policy. But that morning the Massachusetts senator who had seen so much tragedy in his own life met Mrs. Bush's limousine and personally escorted the first lady up to his office.

Phase two of George W. Bush's presidency had begun.

By Bush's second term in office, each side of the great divide that constitutes the modern American electorate had settled on its mythology surrounding his reaction to 9/11. To Bush's supporters—and they were legion—he was the second coming not just of Ronald Reagan, but also of Abraham Lincoln. Meanwhile, the president's many detractors formed the belief that Bush was over his head and utterly lost without his White House wordsmiths. To these critics, the true measure of the man was the deer-in-the-headlights expressions on his face while sitting in that Florida classroom reading to students for a full five minutes after he was informed by White House chief of staff Andrew Card what had happened to the World Trade Center. ("A second plane hit the second tower," Card told the president. "America is under attack.") This scene was milked, with actual television footage, to devastating effect in Michael Moore's anti-Bush and antiwar film *Fahrenheit 9/11.* The president would explain later that he didn't leave the classroom immediately because he didn't want to startle the children. Perhaps he was contemplating the harrowing implications of what was occurring on American soil. If so, five minutes doesn't seem too long to do that, considering the stakes. Certainly this was the verdict of the American people: In the hours, days, and months following the attacks of September 11, Bush was seen by most Americans, even those who had little use for him, as the unflinching commander-in-chief who had rallied a stricken nation with his empathy and his steely resolve. "The attacks . . . transformed Bush's presidency, giving him an extraordinary opportunity to achieve greatness," liberal historian Sean Wilentz wrote later. "Some of the early signs were encouraging. Bush's simple, unflinching eloquence and his quick toppling of the Taliban government in Afghanistan rallied the nation."[10]

Boarding Air Force One in Florida, the president had the presence of mind to instruct White House press secretary Ari Fleischer to write down what he saw and heard that day. According to Fleischer's notes, in a phone call to Vice President Cheney from Air Force One, Bush said, "We're at war, Dick. We're going to find out who did this and kick their ass."[11] Bush himself told CBS News that he'd made a similar comment to Rumsfeld.[12] In this reaction, Bush epitomized the mood of the country he was leading. "Everybody's so angry," said Tom Daschle. "They just want to [attack] somebody." A woman in New York emerging from the wreckage of the World Trade Center told a CNN camera crew, "Whatever we have to do to eradicate the world of this vermin, I hope we do. I hope Bush will do it."[13] A year later, in his interview with CBS, Bush recalled going to Ground Zero and hearing amid the chants of "USA! USA!" an undercurrent of rage—and desire for revenge. "There was a lot of blood lust," Bush noted. "People were pointing their big old hands at me saying, 'Don't you ever forget this, Mr. President. Don't let us down.'"

Bush's conversion to wartime president, although profound, was not seamless. Speaking at the school in Sarasota, Bush vowed to hunt down and to find "those folks" who committed the acts of terrorism, a jarringly informal colloquialism. Then, partly because of a false alarm relayed from the Federal Aviation Administration (FAA) to the Secret Service about a possible threat to Air Force One itself, and partly because Bush and Card acquiesced to the warnings of their protective detail and the vice president, Bush and his traveling party did not head immediately back to Washington. The president's plane instead left Florida for Barksdale Air Force Base in Louisiana. There, the president taped a message to the American people. "Freedom itself was attacked this morning by a faceless coward." Bush began. It was an awkward opening, given that the American people couldn't see Bush, either, and he was heading away from the flames. From Barksdale, the president's plane next flew even further from Washington, to Offutt Air Force Base in Nebraska with its elaborate command and control facilities and ability to house up to fifty people in the president's party. At 3:15 P.M., Bush convened a meeting of his top national security aides via a secure video conference. "We're at war," Bush said bluntly.[14] Afterward, according to the testimony accumulated by the 9/11 Commission Report, Bush himself insisted that he return to Washington. As Marine One, the presidential helicopter, ferried

Bush from Andrews Air Force Base to the White House, the still-smoldering Pentagon was visible from the chopper. Once inside the White House, Bush gave an Oval Office speech in flat tones and abstract language. The president, though seeking to reassure the nation, looked shaken. (His aides knew it, too. They dubbed it the "Oval Awful" speech.)[15]

The following day, Bush was more sure-footed. At an emergency White House cabinet meeting, flanked by Cheney and Secretary of State Colin Powell, he turned to the pool cameras and delivered remarks that employed the repetitious cadences that Americans of a previous generation had associated with Franklin Roosevelt.* "The American people need to know that we're facing a different enemy than we have ever faced," Bush said. "This is an enemy who preys on innocent and unsuspecting people then runs for cover. But it won't be able to run for cover forever. This is an enemy that tries to hide. But it won't be able to hide forever. This is an enemy that thinks its harbors are safe. But they won't be safe forever." Bush also said that the United States would rally the world to its cause and that it would be patient, but steadfast and focused. He said victory would take time, adding, "But make no mistake about it: We will win."

On Thursday, two mornings after the attack, White House pool reporters were ushered into the Oval Office because Bush had something further he wanted to make clear. "Understand," he said, "this is now the focus of my administration." The next day Friday, September 14, Bush delivered an address at the Washington National Cathedral that managed a tone both spiritual and martial. "This conflict was begun on the timing and terms of others," he said. "It will end in a way and at an hour of our choosing. Our purpose as a nation is firm, yet our wounds as a people are recent and unhealed and lead us to pray." The cadence and the language in his speech sounded Lincoln-esque, a deliberate gesture by Bush's gifted stable of speechwriters to evoke the greatest of American wartime presidents. That afternoon in New York, however, it was Bush Unplugged—and the effect was galvanizing. At Ground Zero, walking

---

*FDR's most famous use of the rhetorical device of repeating phrases came, fittingly, in his "Day of Infamy" speech to a joint session of Congress on December 8, 1941, the day after Pearl Harbor.

through the immense wreckage of the World Trade Center, Bush scrambled atop a pile of rubble and began talking. When someone from the crowd yelled, "We can't hear you," Bush, his arm around a grizzled firefighter, grabbed a bullhorn and replied, "I can hear you! The rest of the world hears you. And the people who knocked these buildings down will hear all of us soon."

He had found his voice. It would usher him through the second phase of his presidency, carrying him for the next three years through triumph and peril, and on to reelection.

The Great Communicator had proven—and FDR had shown before him—that presidential articulation is no small thing. FDR wasn't sure where he wanted to lead Depression-ridden America in 1933, but he knew he had to revive the hopes of its citizenry—hence "the only thing we have to fear is fear itself" of his stirring first inaugural. Ronald Reagan believed that his greatest service as president had been to restore the self-confidence of Americans during a time of stagnation and self-doubt. In the midst of the only recession of his presidency, he preached "Stay the Course" until he was blue in the face. Late in 2001, Kathleen Hall Jamieson, professor of communications at the University of Pennsylvania, observed that public discourse isn't an extraneous role for a president, or even an exclusively modern one. "Rhetoric *is* leadership," she said. Presciently, given what would happen in Iraq, she added this thought: "Leadership for Lincoln was not simply in trusting Grant."[16]

The Taliban turned out to be a wholly owned subsidiary of al Qaeda, not merely Osama bin Laden's protectors, and Bush's second incarnation was not a month old before the United States began the military campaign in Afghanistan designed to eradicate both organizations. In a nationally televised address announcing the invasion, Bush deployed Churchillian rhetoric. "We will not waver," the president said. "We will not tire, we will not falter, and we will not fail." This slogan would make its way onto T-shirts and websites, was repeated respectfully at the U.S. service academies, and was quoted in the conservative press. With those words, Bush began his second presidency.

In the next two years, Bush would oversee the dislodging of the Taliban from power in Kabul and the scattering of bin Laden's forces to the badlands between Afghanistan and Pakistan. He would successfully rouse his nation to the cause of invading Iraq, maintain job approval ratings far higher than Reagan's, help his party recapture the Senate in 2002, and himself win reelection—with the Republicans again holding Congress. A month after the 2004 election, Bush would be selected *Time* magazine's Person of the Year for the second time in the decade. (Reagan was also twice designated Person of the Year, in 1980 and 1983, although the second time, when he shared the honor with Soviet Premier Andropov, the recognition was a two-edged sword as the magazine emphasized the supposed nuclear brinkmanship of both leaders.)

The zenith of Bush's time at the helm came in May 2003. U.S. troops had swept away Saddam's armies, and although the dictator was still in hiding, his massive statue had been torn down in Baghdad and defiled, Iraqi-style, by being struck with the soles of citizens' shoes. On May 1, Bush demonstrated his familiarity with the cockpit of an airplane by copiloting a Navy jet onto the deck of the USS *Lincoln.* Looking jaunty and ruggedly handsome in his green flight suit, the commander-in-chief was greeted with roars of approval from the hundreds of sailors who crowded toward him. In his speech aboard the ship Bush warned that the transition in Iraq "from dictatorship to democracy will take time," and that while al Qaeda had been wounded, "it was not destroyed," but the triumphal posture of the president was undeniable. In the second term, Democrats would ceaselessly remind Republicans that Bush spoke that day under a "Mission Accomplished" banner; they would also recall the president's dubious assertion aboard the aircraft carrier that "major combat operations in Iraq have ended." At the time, however, the Democrats' complaint was that Bush was hogging the credit for the military success and that his victory lap aboard a Navy ship of war gave his political party an unfair edge.

In May 2003 the American public couldn't have cared less. According to two Gallup Polls done at that time, some 70 percent of Americans approved of the job Bush was doing as president. Another survey taken that month, this one by the Pew Research Center, asked respondents to furnish one or two words that they believed best described George W. Bush. Of the twenty-five responses that garnered 5 percent or more, only two, "arrogant" and "idiot," were unambiguously negative. Two others, "aggressive" and "cowboy," could be read that way. The other twenty-one answers had positive connotations, most of them quite approving.

The responses, in order, along with the percentages they received, were as follows:

Honest (29)
Good (21)
Arrogant (20)
Leader/Leadership (16)
Great (13)
Confident (12)
Courageous (12)
Aggressive (11)
Christian (11)
Determined (11)
Integrity (11)
Patriotic (10)
Cowboy (9)
Competent (8)
Decisive (8)
Idiot (8)
President (8)
Strong (8)
Adequate (7)
Excellent (7)
Fair (7)
Dedicated (6)
Honorable (5)
Okay (5)
Powerful (5)

"The president's personal image is very strong," the Pew Report stated. So was his record of achievement at this point in his tenure. In the second chapter of his presidency, Bush's accomplishments, for better or worse, were also undeniable. He created a Department of Homeland Security designed to protect Americans from further terrorist attacks. He shepherded through Congress the unfortunately named USA Patriot Act, a measure designed to break down the bureaucratic barriers that made it harder for the FBI to stop the 9/11 attacks. He proposed and signed a vast expansion of Medicare, which for the first time included a prescription drug benefit for seniors. The recession, and the accompanying job losses of his first year in office, gradually gave way to a robust economy featuring employment gains, low inflation, rises in productivity, and continued increases—begun in the Clinton administration—in the rate of home ownership. Bush also began compiling an impressive record on the most sensitive racial questions facing the country—and did so despite the implacable, often demagogic enmity expressed by prominent black Democrats. ("We've got a president that's prepared to take us back to the days of Jim Crow segregation and dominance," NAACP president Kweisi Mfume said of Bush. The Republicans' "idea of equal rights is the American flag and Confederate swastika flying side by side," added NAACP chairman Julian Bond.)[17]

Yet, it was a matter of record that the concept of school reform was introduced by Bush to address the consistent achievement gaps by Latino and African-American students. His famous phrase, "the soft bigotry of low expectations," was a challenge to the complacency of liberal educators and conservative policy-makers. California congressman George Miller, in fact, had gone to Austin and met with President-elect Bush just a week after the Supreme Court affirmed Bush's election and did so explicitly because of Bush's vow to "disaggregate the data" on minority student reading—meaning he'd dismantle the sleight-of-hand used by the education establishment to mask the fact that black and Latino children were not reading at the same levels as white students.

Even before they came to Washington, it took little prompting for Bush or those in his inner circle to disparage former California Governor Pete Wilson for alienating Latinos with his support for referendums aimed at illegal immigrants—including one that would have prevented the children of illegals from attending public school. Wilson's proposals had garnered him a second term but made him a villain to many Mexican-American voters. In a less political but more evocative vein, Bush was a white man who spoke unabashedly of aspiring, as a boy, "to be Willie Mays" when he grew up.

Bush went beyond symbolism. Under America's "first black president" (African-American author Toni Morrison's dubious but enduring description of Bill Clinton), the administration had done nothing to stop genocide in Rwanda and had discouraged the United Nations from acting on its own. By contrast, Clinton's successor requested—and got—nearly twice as much money in federal aid to sub-Saharan Africa as the United States had been spending; in 2003, Bush vowed to spend $15 billion combating HIV/AIDS in Africa. White House officials characterized this figure as a threefold boost. It was something less than that, but it was a huge increase. In 1998, Clinton had made a trip to Africa, the first such trip by an American president in twenty years, where he was received by fawning African political leaders, adoring crowds, and adulatory news coverage both in the United States and abroad. Five years later, during the first summer of the Iraq War, George W. Bush made a similar trip—with dissimilar results. Nelson Mandela promptly announced that he wouldn't be seen with Bush, crowds in the post-9/11 world were not allowed to mingle much because of security concerns, and the press coverage was discernibly begrudging. Julian Bond dismissed it as a "photo-op." Both presidents made the pilgrimage to the onetime slave ship debarkation port at Goree Island, Senegal. Bush was the more eloquent of the two, but wire stories concentrated on complaints of Senegalese citizens quarantined miles away from Bush in a hot soccer stadium, apparently because of the Senegalese government's overcautious approach to protecting the president.

Reagan was often criticized by African-American leaders for his insensitivity to racial symbols, from his 1976 campaign trail references to the "Chicago welfare queen"—a woman with many aliases who drove a Cadillac—to his 1980 speech in support of "states' rights"—the battle cry of southern segregationists—in Philadelphia, Mississippi, the site of the infamous triple murder of civil rights workers. As president, Reagan appointed one black man to his cabinet, put him in a second-tier position (Housing and Urban Development), and then failed to recognize him, addressing him as "Mr. Mayor" at a reception. George W. Bush was more attuned to the damage such slights can cause, and he did more than try to avoid offense; he was proactive on questions of race.

Clinton vowed to appoint a cabinet that "looks like America," and in his first term, 47 percent of his appointments were women or people of color. Bush promised no such thing, but wound up with the exact same percentage of women and minorities.[18] These weren't token jobs: Although he did not make a big deal of it, Bush's secretary of state and his national security adviser were African American. Bush also accomplished what neither Clinton nor Bush's father could do, which was to round up the votes necessary to pass Georgia Democratic congressman John Lewis's long-standing proposal to create a National Museum of African-American History and Culture. Bush persuaded Congress to set aside land and $250 million toward its construction, half its estimated cost. He didn't stop there. He and Laura were among the first to write checks to the Smithsonian for the museum; later, Bush would donate $5 million for the museum in unused campaign funds.

If officials in the opposition party were slow to give Bush credit for such acts, that wasn't a universal reaction among progressive activists and commentators. Liberal journalist Eleanor Clift lauded Bush's racial sensitivity in her column.[19] Irish singer and songwriter and veteran African-relief activist Bob Geldof said the Bush administration was "the most radical—in a positive sense—in its approach to Africa since Kennedy." Another Irish-born musician, international rock-star Bono, bonded with Bush over the issue of aid to Africa. Actress Ashley Judd told herself happily, after Bush's 2003 State of the Union address: "They get it, they really get it."[20]

Ultimately, Democratic Party reluctance to give Bush credit for anything came across as poor sportsmanship, or worse. "Few Democrats have faced up to the reality that Bush and his fellow Republicans know how to manage the government," wrote *USA Today* political columnist Walter Shapiro in December 2002, after the Bush-led victories in the mid-term elections.[21] The same month, a book called *The Leadership Genius of George W. Bush* began showing up in bookstores, and conservative editorial writer John Podhoretz churned out *Bush Country: How Dubya Became a Great President while Driving Liberals Insane.* This was a bit much, but the sentiment wasn't confined to conservatives. "This is the best-run White House since Eisenhower," asserted Stephen Hess of the Brookings Institution. In an updated edition of *Organizing the Presidency,* Hess and his coauthor James Pfiffner wrote that the nation's first MBA president had imposed his own vision of how to run an executive office "by making structural changes reflecting his priorities, goals and general approach to governing."[22]

The precise nature of that approach fascinated presidency scholars, many of whom, prior to 9/11, had been all-too-willing to dismiss Bush as an inconsequential lightweight. But the obvious successes of the second phase of his presidency generated an impulse to reconsider. One explanation, encouraged by those around Bush, was that this president was more disciplined than his predecessor—and had surrounded himself with better, more experienced aides. "Organizationally, many of us would give him high points for putting together a highly professional team," Fred Greenstein told a National Public Radio audience on November 12, 2003.

In the words of conservative writer David Frum, Bush was the "un-Clinton." This characterization wasn't entirely sympathetic. "The Bush team lived clean . . . upright and hygienic," Frum wrote in his 2003 book *The Right Man: The Surprising Presidency of George W. Bush*. Frum said Bush had a cabinet that was "able, solid, and reliable," but contained no "really high-powered brains." In another passage, Frum wrote dryly, "If the country wanted an un-Clinton administration, they had hired the right man. Was Clinton famously unpunctual? Bush was always on time. Were the Clintons morally slack? Bush opened every cabinet meeting with a prayer." Frum, a Canadian-born Yale- and Harvard-educated intellectual, was also less than thrilled with the anti-academic impulses of some of the president's closest aides. "Conspicuous intelligence seemed actively unwelcome in the Bush White House," he wrote.[23] Frum was complimentary of Karl Rove, a voracious reader, but scornful of another high-ranking White House aide, Karen Hughes, who, he said, "rarely read books and distrusted people who did."[24]

But if Bush is the "un-Clinton" in Frum's telling, he is also, less obviously, the un-Reagan. George W. Bush consciously selected as advisers the kind of people who could easily submerge their own ambitions for the boss—and the team. Bush's chief of staff, Andrew Card, told Frum how, in the Reagan White House, aides would quickly be pegged as belonging in the orbit of either James Baker or Edwin Meese. Card insisted that this did not ever happen in George W. Bush's White House. "You are not Karl's people or Karen's people," Card told his subordinates. "You are all the president's people." To Frum, the lesson was simple: "There must be no bickering."

At the time Frum's book came out, there was little reason to question the inference implicit in such an anecdote: In mid-2003, with his poll numbers high, his domestic policies enacted, the Taliban decimated, and the war in Iraq proceeding apace, Bush's style of leadership seemed to be working. So did the relationship between Bush and Cheney, a vice president with no independent presidential ambitions of his own. At Princeton and the University of London, academic conferences were convened with the purpose of providing an early assessment of George W. Bush's presidency. What the attendees at these sessions did, really, was to *reassess* a man who'd formerly been given short shrift by academics and other intellectual elites.

Fred Greenstein was the grand eminence at the Princeton conference, and Princeton itself had a pivotal role in the presidential scholarship. That role goes back to the beginning of the twentieth century, when a talented young scholar from Michigan, named Edward S. Corwin, came east in search of employment. Corwin obtained an audience with the president of Princeton, Virginia-born intellectual Woodrow Wilson. The two men hit it off, and Wilson became a mentor to Corwin, whom he hired as a professor. In 1908, Corwin assisted Wilson on updating Wilson's history of the United States, *Division and Reunion,* and when Wilson left Princeton to serve as governor of New Jersey and then president of the United States, Corwin became an academic star in his own right. In 1918, while Wilson served as a wartime commander-in-chief, Corwin assumed Wilson's old chair, the McCormick Professorship of Jurisprudence. In 1924, the college inaugurated a Department of Politics, naming Corwin as its first dean. Nicknamed "The General" by his students, Corwin helped create a new academic discipline: presidential scholarship. Until then, biographers and historians tended to write about a specific president or a specific age. But new ways of looking at government were emerging, and one of them was from the inside: After a five-year stint in Franklin Delano Roosevelt's administration, Corwin returned to Princeton in 1940, a confirmed believer in what one of his devotees, historian Arthur M. Schlesinger Jr., would later call "the imperial presidency." In no area was this concept more significant than war-making. Approvingly citing Lincoln, Corwin asserted an implicit constitutional war-making power in an office that included the title "commander-in-chief," and he described the Constitution as "an invitation to struggle for the privilege of directing American foreign policy." He published a book, *The President: Office and Powers,* centering on this contention, hoping his influence would spread beyond Princeton's walls. And it did.

Corwin's view of executive power was so entrenched among Democratic academics that Schlesinger later wrote of being "astonished" when Corwin insisted that Truman needed congressional approval to wage war in Korea.[25] This debate has never really been settled, in either the Democratic Party or academia, and Bush's invasion of Iraq rekindled it at Princeton in late April 2003. The same discussion arose three weeks later across the Atlantic Ocean at the University of London.[26]

In London, Bush critic Richard M. Pious of Barnard College insisted that the post-9/11 Bush White House had asserted claims of "prerogative power" broader than any other administration's. This contention might have surprised Corwin, whose change of heart about the necessary limits on presidential authority was caused by his horror at a truly gross violation of civil liberties: the 1942 decision by his former boss FDR to incarcerate more than 110,000 Japanese Americans and resident aliens of Japanese descent living on the West Coast. But if the scholarship in the first three-quarters of the twentieth century was devoted to defining and chronicling the ever-broadening scope of presidential prerogatives, in the past twenty-five years the trend in political science has been to devise models that measure exactly how effectively a president uses all this executive power. That's where Fred Greenstein comes in. More than two decades ago, Greenstein mined the documents in the Eisenhower administration archives and found a trove of evidence showing Dwight Eisenhower to be a sharper, more engaged, and politically astute operator as president than was known at the time. Greenstein's book on Ike, *The Hidden-Hand Presidency: Eisenhower as Leader,* made Greenstein's reputation and profoundly altered presidency scholarship. In contemplating why Eisenhower had been underestimated, and in trying to establish common yardsticks by which presidents' effectiveness can be gauged outside of ideology or party affiliation, Greenstein formulated a list of six "touchstones" by which to judge presidents. His criteria, which have been widely (if not universally) accepted, are: an ability to communicate publicly; organizational efficiency within the White House; "external" political skills, including how a president sells his agenda to Congress; the scope of a president's vision; his brain power, which used to be called "book-smarts," but which Greenstein defines as "cognitive" ability; and finally, "emotional intelligence"—that indefinable trait that Oliver Wendell Holmes Jr. once called (alluding to FDR) "temperament."*

Some of these traits are purely subjective, and even those that are not are difficult to measure. But in 2003, even among a cohort of liberal academics, George W. Bush received such good mid-term grades that one participant at the Princeton conference, Thomas Mann of the Brookings Institution, remonstrated aloud, at the opening session, that Bush's presidency may have exposed the very limits of political science. "Don't we run the risk of being dazzled so much by what he's accomplished that we don't judge it?" Mann yelled in frustration, adding that at some level the real question about Bush's policies wasn't how effective he'd been at implementing them, but whether they were "good or bad."

One question about Bush had always been his intellectual firepower. But once his focus shifted to war, he seemed helped by the presence of seasoned foreign-policy advisers such as Cheney, Rumsfeld, Rice, and Powell—or so thought the academics. "It's like adding memory to your computer," said Greenstein, who summed up his 2003 early assessment of Bush this way: "Whatever the future has in store for George W. Bush, he has proved to have a highly distinctive, and often impressively effective, political style."

Not all of Greenstein's fellow academics agreed with him, although they were careful not to quarrel too overtly with their eminent host. Allen Schick of the University of Maryland portrayed Bush as a scheming and effective anti-government ideologue. Professor Schick said Bush was a student of recent political history who knew better than to reprise Reagan's broad rhetorical war on government, or to repeat his father's mistake of talking tough on the budget and then signing a big tax increase. Bush's strategy, Schick maintained, was to avoid incendiary language while orchestrating tax cuts that starved social programs. Clinton administration refugees Ivo H. Daalder and James M. Lindsay of the Brookings

---

*Among presidency scholars, the concept of "emotional intelligence" is often attributed to Greenstein. The phrase was actually coined by Harvard-trained psychologist Daniel Goleman, a professor at Rutgers University's graduate school and author of the 1995 best-seller *Emotional Intelligence*. In Greenstein's own 2000 book, *The Presidential Difference: Leadership Style from FDR to Clinton,* Greenstein amplifies on his criteria, while giving Goleman his proper due.

Institution sounded a similar theme in the area of international affairs. "Bush is leading a revolution in American foreign policy," they wrote, not necessarily as a compliment. "An America that acts as it sees fit may be able to remake the world—for the better, but an America unbound also may be seen by others as arrogant rather than principled."*

Yet even after comparing Bush to Gary Cooper in *High Noon* and suggesting that Bush was overconfident and underinformed, Daalder and Lindsay gave Bush high marks for effectiveness. Echoing Tom Mann's concerns about political science's way of measuring a president's performance, they lauded Bush's management skills while questioning his policies. "Even before September 11, he demonstrated that he understood how to be an effective president to an extent that surprised even his most ardent supporters; he was decisive, resolute, and in command of his advisers," they wrote in the paper submitted to the conference. "This is not to say that history will necessarily judge all his choices as wise." Greenstein responded by implying that he had voted Democratic in every election since 1952 and had been evaluating presidents for almost as long, and that he was "a little old" to suddenly change the criteria because an unprepossessing Texas governor had come into the White House and aced the exams.

But this was only 2003, midway through the second phase of Bush's presidency—too early, in other words, to be assigning final grades—a point accentuated at the London conference by the one American presidential scholar who might have been said to outrank Fred Greenstein. He was Harvard-trained political scientist Richard E. Neustadt, who had worked in the administrations of Roosevelt, Truman, Kennedy, and Johnson, who had known Edward Corwin personally—and was influenced by him—and whose seminal book, *Presidential Power,* was still being used four decades after it was published. In his keynote address at the University of London, Neustadt spoke about presidents and war-making, and while he didn't contest Bush's constitutional authority to commit U.S. troops to Iraq, he most certainly questioned the wisdom of the decision. Asserting that Americans "hate" long wars and that they also hate to lose, Neustadt predicted that the people of this country would come to

*Daalder and Lindsay turned their critique into a book, *America Unbound: The Bush Revolution in Foreign Policy,* published in 2003 by the Brookings Institution Press.

rue the invasion of Iraq and that Bush himself would regret his decision to frame the struggle against terrorism as war in the first place.

If Bush's "second presidency" was a smashing success by previously accepted standards, it would become plain that the seeds of future failure were planted within it—and the problem wasn't only Iraq.

In 2000, Bush had stood for election as a "compassionate conservative," a designation intended to appeal both to the solid majority of his own party, made up of people who identified themselves as staunchly conservative, and to right-leaning and centrist independents, for whom "compassion" was the stronger lure. That Bush managed something slightly less than a statistical tie with Al Gore demonstrated the limits of such an appeal, however, and showed how much the electorate had changed since Reagan had defeated Jimmy Carter by 8.4 million votes, a margin of nearly 10 percent (and 440 electoral votes), in 1980. It took a while for Team Bush to recognize the new landscape. Throughout Bush's first two years in office, Karl Rove hinted publicly at a grand realignment of the country into a GOP-majority nation. Rove's frame of reference was Texas, where he had gone to work as a political operative at a time when Democrats held every single statewide office in the Lone Star State. At the end of Rove's last Texas campaign—George W. Bush's lopsided re-election victory in 1998—every statewide office had been captured by a Republican. This was a phenomenon Rove hoped to replicate on a national scale. To be sure, there were skeptics, including the student who asked Rove, on November 13, 2002, at a University of Utah forum, about the value of having all three branches of government in Republican hands at a time when the nation was so clearly "split fifty-fifty" between Democrats and Republicans.

"It was closely split in 2000," Rove replied. "I am not certain it is so closely split now. Nothing stays in gridlock in American politics. Things move one direction or the other." Rove then cited the evidence that they were moving the Republicans' way: the GOP gains in the House and Senate in the 2002 off-year elections; the large Republican margin when vote totals were aggregated nationally that year; the steady Republican pickups in state legislatures; Bush's strong popularity. "Something is going on out there," Rove said. "I attribute it to the president, to the president's agenda, to quality candidates and quality campaigns, to some tactical advantages in our ground game—our getting out the vote—but I think something else more fundamental is happening there, but we will only know it retrospectively, in two years or four years or six years [when we] look back and say the dam began to break in 2002."[27]

He didn't say so that day, but the "something else more fundamental" Rove alluded to was conservatives' consistent numerical advantage over liberals among the electorate. Rove's goal of realignment was based on factors more sweeping than superior Republican get-out-the vote efforts. In the autumn of 2003, a Gallup Poll showed 41 percent of Americans self-identifying as conservative, 19 percent saying they were liberal—and most of the rest reporting they were moderate. Those numbers had been essentially unchanged for a generation, but changes in the makeup of the political parties convinced Rove, among others, that the GOP was on the verge of a historic breakthrough. The demise of southern Democrats as a de facto third political party, and the gradual sorting of the two major parties along ideological lines, had produced a nation in which the Republican Party was home to most of America's conservatives, and the Democratic Party was all but officially a liberal party. In such an environment, post-Reagan conservatives had come to believe that if the philosophy, candidates, and issues guiding conservatism's political party could get anything resembling an even break from the media, and from elites in Washington, New York, Hollywood, and academia, Americans would be choosing Republican national leaders more often than not. An important point eluded this narrow logic: On a host of domestic policy issues, ranging from environmental regulation to workplace protection and wage regulation, American voters were more in sync with the Democrats' policy prescriptions than with the Republicans'. Furthermore, national elections hinge on the personality, character, confidence, competence, spouse, running mate, and luck of the nominee—not just the candidate's ideology. Republican activists were not incognizant of this reality. It was why they turned to George W. Bush in the first place: They were trying to recreate the magic of the Reagan years.

But the 2000 results were sobering for realignment-minded Republicans, including those working for Bush. One of those most puzzled by the closeness of that election was prominent Bush campaign strategist Matthew Dowd, a former Democrat who, like Mark McKinnon, had been lured away from the Democratic Party because he'd been charmed by Bush. Dowd decided to review the 2000 election to find out what worked and what didn't—and who voted, and why. Dowd's findings would dismay him (and eventually lead to his estrangement from Rove and Bush) and set Bush on a course that clashed with compassionate conservatism. With fewer Republican or Democratic voters breaking party ranks, Dowd focused most closely on self-described "independents" to see how truly independent they were. The answer was, not very. When examining an electorate, political ad-men use the word "persuadables" to describe those whose vote is up for grabs. In Dowd's calculation, the percentage of voters who could really be persuaded to cross party lines had declined from 22 percent of the electorate in 1980 to 7 percent in 2000. Dowd put all this on paper, complete with graphs and trend lines, and took it to Rove, who was planning the 2004 reelection strategy. "So 93 percent . . . or 94 in 2004 . . . was going to be already decided either for us or against us," Dowd explained after the reelection campaign ended. "You obviously had to do fairly well among the 6 or 7 [percent], but you could lose the 6 or 7 percent and win the election, which was fairly revolutionary, because everybody up until that time had said, 'Swing voters, swing voters, swing voters, swing voters, swing voters.'"[28]

Thus, Rove's youthful questioner in Utah turned out to be possibly more attuned to the ways of the modern American electorate than the man Bush had dubbed "Boy Genius." But if Rove wasn't a genius, he was certainly a quick study and an adroit political operator, and the 2004 campaign strategy was adjusted accordingly. Republican Party chief Ken Mehlman would protest that the media's fixation on the "base strategy" was overblown. "The press, unfortunately for them, believes that it's zero-sum, that it's either a base or a swing strategy," he said. "The fact is, we appeal to both."[29] Rove made a similar point, arguing in mid-2007, "The fact of the matter is you don't win the kind of percentages we did, or get a majority of the vote, or increase dramatically the share of the vote . . . by playing to the base," he said. "That's revisionism."[30] This is a fair point. But in the end, much of the passion, energy, and money in the 2004 Bush campaign was directed at getting slightly more Republicans than Democrats to participate in the election. That is what came to pass, and given the results of the 2004 election returns, it was hard to fault, at least tactically.

The problem that would develop in George W. Bush's second term wasn't so much how he campaigned, it was how he governed. Operating under the (mistaken) conventional wisdom that his father had been hurt in his unsuccessful reelection bid by defections from the Republicans' conservative base, Bush and Rove worked overtime to keep the base mollified. Had they heeded the counsel of the Texas pol closest to Bush's father—and the man who had been Ronald Reagan's first chief of staff—they wouldn't have fallen into this trap. "You can't always govern by appealing to the base, sometimes you have to govern by appealing to the center—by reaching a consensus," Jim Baker explained.[31] Rove didn't see it that way. As one prominent Republican political operative told the authors: "Karl's philosophy is you play to your base. Whatever you do, you play to your base. You play to your base when you run, you play to your base when you govern. . . . The reason they didn't fire Rumsfeld was that Karl thought the base wouldn't like it, you'd lose your base, and the only thing you've got is your base. They barely won the 2004 election by orienting everything to the base."

Rove, citing No Child Left Behind, the Medicare prescription drug benefit, and Bush's staunch support in 2007 for a doomed immigration reform bill favored by Senate Democrats (and John McCain), but by few prominent Senate Republicans, protested that the accusation that Bush catered to the base in governance is a misconception. The second-term problems of forging bipartisan consensus is one Rove blames less on the Bush White House and more on Democratic Party intransigence and "an increasing degree of polarization in Washington."[32]

Nonetheless, as the view took hold in the nation, and not only among liberals, that the Bush White House and the Bush campaign operation were one and the same, Bush—and Rove—began to pay a price. The perception developed, for example, that the exigencies of base politics, and not the merits of public policy, pushed Social Security privatization to a higher priority in Bush's White House than, say, tax simplification. Many issues came to be viewed through this prism. The president expressed skepticism about global warming, asked Americans for little in the way of sacrifice after 9/11, came out in vocal opposition to gay marriage, allowed stem cell research only under the narrowest of circumstances, and even launched a war in Iraq because it was popular with the conservative base—or so went the accusation. Some of these allegations were easier to rebut than others. Certainly neither old-line conservatives nor "neo-cons" had anything against sacrifice, or even compulsory public service. As far as the war in Iraq went, the notion that the war was motivated by politics left Bush loyalists scratching their heads. (Grover Norquist, president of Americans for Tax Reform and a leading conservative player, insists that if not for the Iraq invasion, Bush would have equaled Reagan's 58.5 percent reelection margin in 1984. "Clinton jumped six points from 1992 to 1996, and Reagan's margin increased almost ten points," he said in a 2007 interview. "Iraq was the anchor. What other than Iraq?")[33] Nonetheless, those peddling this line included Senator Kennedy, one of the few Democrats who would have had reason to believe otherwise. In 2002, in a joint appearance at Boston Latin School, Kennedy had showered Bush with praise, presenting him with a framed reproduction of an early draft of the Declaration of Independence signed by one of its editors, John Adams. The gift, Kennedy said, was a "small token" of Bush's leadership on education. But only a year and a half later, the Massachusetts senator excoriated Bush over the war in Iraq, asserting that the rationale for the invasion was a "fraud" that was "made up in Texas" for political advantage.[34]

It was not only Democrats who concluded that the "base strategy" had spilled over from politics into policy. Newt Gingrich, analyzing events with the benefit of hindsight following Republican losses in the 2006 midterm elections, characterized the 2004 reelection strategy as "manically dumb." The results, Gingrich said, left Bush precisely lacking in the political capital he thought he'd earned. The only thing Rove and the Bush campaign team had proven in 2004, Gingrich told journalist Jeffrey Goldberg, was "that the anti-Kerry vote was bigger than the anti-Bush vote."[35] Republican Christine Todd Whitman came to a similar conclusion. As a member of Bush's first-term cabinet, she had overseen an area—environmental protection—generally considered a relatively safe harbor away from the wedge issues of the "culture wars."

Whitman was tapped to be administrator of the Environmental Protection Agency (EPA), where it was thought that her brand of GOP liberalism (as governor of New Jersey she had vetoed a ban against partial-birth abortion) wouldn't get the White House too crosswise with conservatives and might burnish Bush's reputation among centrists. It didn't work out that way. Just a month into her job, Whitman voiced support for capping carbon dioxide gases blamed for the greenhouse effect. "There's no question but that global warming is a real phenomenon, that it is occurring," she told a Senate subcommittee. "The science is strong there."[36] A week later, in a confidential memo to Bush, Whitman warned that global warming was an important test of the new president's credibility abroad. Bush had mused aloud during the campaign about the federal government classifying carbon dioxide emissions from U.S. power plants as pollutants—something that would have placed them under the jurisdiction of the EPA—and Whitman may have figured she was on safe ground. Actually, she was way out in front of herself. By Earth Day 2001, Bush had backtracked on power plant regulation, suspended the EPA rules governing cleanup of toxic mining sites, and signaled that the United States would withdraw from the Kyoto Treaty on global warming. The treaty had been negotiated by Al Gore, but the Senate had rejected it by a vote of 95–0. Europeans treated Bush's repudiation of Kyoto as American denial of global warming itself. (This was hardly a stretch, given Bush's tepid remarks on the issue.) Secretary of State Colin Powell was the administration aide best positioned to hear the displeasure from America's allies on this subject. In solicitude for Whitman's predicament, Powell told her she was a "wind dummy," the military term for a manikin thrown out of a moving plane in a landing zone to see how troops can exit an aircraft safely. Phil Clapp, president of the National Environmental Trust, had another description. "No EPA administrator has ever been so consistently and publicly humiliated by the White House," he said.[37] In her letter of resignation, Whitman avoided any criticism of Bush, whom she appears to like personally, or even his White House operation. She wanted only, she told the president, to "return to my home and husband in New Jersey, which I love just as you do your home state of Texas."

Once she was back home, a bucolic, 230-acre farm estate in Oldwick, New Jersey, it began to dawn on Whitman that she'd been ill-used by the Bush administration—and that Republicanism was being ill-served by it. She wrote a book, *It's My Party, Too: The Battle for the Heart of the GOP and the Future of America;* helped revive a moribund centrist group called the Republican Leadership Council; and gave an interview to PBS in which she theorized that considerations over the sensibilities of "the base" were responsible for the friction between the EPA and the White House. Whitman claimed that the antipathy for her agency was so pervasive that even when the EPA was allowed to pursue environmental-friendly policies, White House officials refused to let her publicize it for fear of alienating conservatives. "[Environmental protection] never polled high with the base," she said. "The base basically said they don't care about it, and so it was never high on the list of things that you communicated."[38]

In her book, Whitman told of being taken aside by Rove after she had met with Bush and Cheney during the transition and accepted her post. The president's top political aide told her that she was one of three cabinet officials who could have the most impact on Bush's reelection. She took that to mean that Bush wanted to expand his party's appeal. But if he made such a prediction (Rove has never confirmed her account), Rove was already of two minds. The same month, December 2001, at an appearance before the American Enterprise Institute, Rove asserted that by his reading of the 2000 election data, some 4 million white evangelical or fundamentalist Protestants (out of 19 million total) had stayed home on election day, adding, "I think we may have failed to mobilize them."

Numerous attempts would be made to mobilize them in 2004, and Republicans such as Whitman came to believe that those efforts narrowed Bush's policy options—and thus came with a price that eventually would have to be paid. "Karl Rove focused on 4 million evangelicals who had not gone to the polls in 2000 and he felt they were Bush voters, and they should go out for him, and if he was able to capture those 4 million, that the president would be reelected," Whitman told PBS. "I mean, he's done a brilliant job for what he's supposed to do, which is to ensure that the president has a Republican Congress and was reelected. And he did all those things exceedingly well. My fear is at what cost to governance and what cost to the future of the party, because by hardening the base, by everything being aimed at that base of the evangelicals and the social fundamentalists, there was no effort to reach out to the middle."

Whitman stated one other thing: This was decidedly *not* the example set by the conservative president modern Republicans claimed to be emulating. "I think Ronald Reagan would have been very uncomfortable with much of what he would see today," she said. "One of the things [Reagan] did do was to reach out to dissident Democrats. He was building a base. What I see happening now . . . this idea that instead of building your base once you're in office, you harden that base."

Although George W. Bush didn't govern exactly like Reagan, he didn't always campaign like him either. In 1980, Reagan lost the Iowa caucuses to George H. W. Bush and responded by replacing his own top campaign aides on the eve of the New Hampshire primary. The Reagan campaign aired no negative ads against Bush, and it sanctioned no personal criticism of him. Twenty years later, George W. Bush was soundly defeated in New Hampshire by John McCain, and when the Republican nominating contest shifted to South Carolina, it became a mud bath. Each side ran negative ads against the other, while a subterranean guerrilla campaign, evidently spearheaded out of Bob Jones University, took aim at McCain. The vilest hit was the anonymously done "poll" in which callers would telephone likely Republican voters and ask them whether they'd be more or less likely to vote for McCain knowing he had fathered an illegitimate black child. (What McCain had actually done, along with his wife, Cindy, was adopt a dark-skinned girl from Bangladesh whom they had originally brought to the United States for medical care.) McCain's staff blamed Rove for this kind of thing. Rove's response was that the McCain campaign had aired the first negative ads, and that no one had ever produced evidence that he or anyone in the Bush campaign had sponsored the infamous "poll" about an out-of-wedlock child. He was right, but it was also true that during the South Carolina primary Bush did not disavow the ugly tactics used on his behalf.

Winning at all costs—the accusation leveled by McCain in South Carolina—came to be a hallmark of George W. Bush's administration as well. After Jim Jeffords's defection from the Republican Party, Rove and others in the White House were nettled by media coverage that tended to canonize Jeffords as the second coming of Edmund G. Ross, the Kansas senator who voted courageously against Andrew Johnson's impeachment. Inside the White House, Jeffords was not considered a profile in courage, but a petty hack. It was believed that he had not bolted from the party out of principle, but because he wanted a committee chairmanship. Jeffords asserted that public support for education was the final straw. Pointing out that Bush had secured more federal money for education than any previous president in history, Republican or Democrat, Bush aides surmised that Jeffords actually had thrown his fateful snit over not being invited to a Rose Garden ceremony honoring a Vermonter as Teacher of the Year. But biased news coverage doesn't explain Bush's unwillingness to compromise with the Democrats, specifically with Patrick Leahy, after Jeffords's party-switch. What does explain it is Rove's and Bush's desire to appease the base on judicial appointments, a matter of vastly greater import to conservatives than Christine Whitman's would-be environmental policy.

Bush assumed office with 48 percent of the vote—he polled half a million voters fewer than Al Gore—and the narrowest of Electoral College victories, but upon taking the oath of office had assumed, quite rightly, that there could be only one president at a time, that he was that president, and that he shouldn't govern shyly or apologetically. In this, Bush displayed a grasp of the exigencies of leadership and constitutional democracy, but his necessary boldness led him to the borders of intransigence. A president who took seriously his pledge to unite the country might have sued for peace with Senator Leahy and begun negotiating a formula for nominating federal judges that would have given Democrats some say-so—and, yes, some of their judges. This was apparently never considered by Bush and his aides, who began planning a more fundamental solution to their problem.* That is, they began plotting how to take back the Senate. In the days after 9/11, Bush had given Tom Daschle (and House Democratic Leader Dick Gephardt) big bear hugs when he went to Capitol Hill, and he spoke of them in laudatory terms in public, going so far as to thank them during a September 20, 2001, address to a joint session of Congress for "your friendship, for your leadership, and for your service to our country."

Ridding themselves of Leahy required recapturing the Senate, which meant, in turn, marginalizing Daschle, along with several of the Senate's most vulnerable Democrats, including the recently widowed Jean Carnahan of Missouri and Max Cleland of Georgia, a disabled veteran. In the new Republican narrative, Daschle the 2001 Friend of Bush became Daschle the 2002 Obstructionist to Bush. Ostensibly, the Republican complaint was that Daschle's Democrats had dragged their feet on legislation creating a Department of Homeland Security because they did not want the new agency to be exempt, as the administration proposed, from union rules. Republican-paid ads on behalf of Georgia Republican Saxby Chambliss showed Cleland's picture slowly changing into images of Sad-

---

*In a March 2002 interview with Carl Cannon, Rove termed "naive" any suggestion that Democrats be given a hand in choosing judges. "Do you think they would they do that for us?" he replied pointedly.

dam Hussein and Osama bin Laden. The protest was immediate and loud. White House officials responded that they had nothing to do with such ads, but—once again—Bush did not denounce them. Quite the opposite: While campaigning vigorously for Republican candidates in the 2002 mid-term elections, the president himself asserted on two occasions that Democrats were "more interested in special interests" than in the security of the American people.[39]

This remark generated a furor, as Daschle took to the Senate floor and excoriated the president for his "outrageous" characterization. Whether by design or confusion, Senate Democrats responded as though the president had been discussing Iraq, which he had not, and Bush was so unimpressed by their condemnation that he repeated the phrase, word for word, in the last days of the campaign. Nonetheless, this was a hell of a thing to say about Cleland, a former Army captain who had lost both his legs and an arm in a grenade explosion during the Vietnam War, and whose appointment by President Carter to head the Veterans Administration was hailed as a breakthrough for Americans with disabilities. The willingness to target Cleland was significant for another reason, too: Cleland (and Carnahan) had voted for No Child Left Behind, as did almost all Senate Democrats, and they were among only ten Democrats in that chamber who backed Bush's 2001 tax cuts. They both also voted aye on the 2002 Iraq War resolution. Thus, on the two domestic policies dearest to Bush's heart, and on his most important and controversial foreign policy initiative, they had backed the president. They were not targeted because of Daschle's haggling on the Department of Homeland Security. They were targeted because Bush wanted the Senate, especially the Senate Judiciary Committee, back in Republican hands—and because Rove, Bush, and Republican Senate Leader Bill Frist thought they could be beaten. Two years later, to solidify their gains, the Republicans targeted Daschle himself. He would lose his seat, too, in a campaign in which the Republican National Committee actually sent a letter protesting Daschle's use of video footage of Bush hugging him after 9/11. Politics ain't beanbag, the saying goes, and it was ever thus. But these were not the actions of a "uniter," and the opposition party took note. While plotting their revenge, some of these Democrats would invoke Ronald Reagan's name. President Reagan wasn't much of a hugger, although he did once have a beer with Tip O'Neill in a Boston bar. But in 1981, White

House chief of staff James A. Baker had made, and Reagan honored, a promise not to campaign personally against the "Boll Weevil" Democrats, led by those in the Texas delegation, who voted for Reagan's tax cuts.[40]

Two of those conservative Texas Democrats (their nickname had by then evolved to "Blue Dogs") were still in Congress twenty years later when George W. Bush sent his tax cuts to Congress. One of them, Charlie Stenholm, voted against Bush. The other, Ralph Hall, voted with Bush. No matter. In the unprecedented 2002 gerrymander of Texas's congressional districts, spearheaded, with Rove's approval, by Republican Minority Leader Tom DeLay, both Hall and Stenholm were targeted for extinction along with every other white Democrat in the Texas delegation. Stenholm's hometown of Abilene was put into an adjacent district. Hall's district was carved up so effectively by DeLay's computers that it was no longer winnable for even the most conservative Democrat in Congress, which Hall probably was. Hall switched parties; Stenholm ran as a Democrat and lost. And so it went. But this was not what Bush had promised.

On December 13, 2000, in his first speech to the American people, the president-elect spoke from the House chamber in the Texas legislature, the very setting, Bush said, of the "bipartisan cooperation" that epitomized his governorship. Predictably, Bush mentioned Bob Bullock. He also singled out Texas House speaker Pete Laney, who had made the introduction of Bush that night, as a "friend" whose example in finding "constructive consensus" Bush would take with him to Washington. In 2002, however, it fell to Laney to battle DeLay's mid-term gerrymander, and though DeLay managed to get himself indicted over his fundraising methods associated with the "Tommymander," Laney couldn't prevent the decimation of white Democrats in his state's congressional delegation. Laney lost his majority in Austin and his speakership along with it, and sat helplessly as Republicans celebrated their triumph by stripping Bush's "friend" of legislature committee assignments just for spite. Democrats with Texas backgrounds, such as Paul Begala, complained bitterly that Bush could not be compared with his father, or with Reagan, but with only one previous Republican president: Richard Nixon.[41]

Such criticism was inevitable, because Bush had committed himself to two incompatible goals—ensuring Republican control in Congress and bringing the country together. There were other shortcomings as well.

John F. Kennedy had appointed a prominent Republican, Douglas Dillon, as secretary of the treasury, and Bill Clinton had tapped Republican Senator William Cohen as defense secretary during his second term. In this spirit, Bush took a member of Clinton's cabinet, former California Congressman Norman Y. Mineta, and made him secretary of transportation. Bush's affection for Mineta was genuine, but considering how close the 2000 election was, a lone Democrat was not enough of a gesture to accomplish Bush's avowed goal of bi-partisanship. One member of Mineta's inner circle, Democrat Les Francis (who supported Bush on the war in Iraq), put it this way: "In the Bush White House, Norm was *Home Alone*."[42]

Meanwhile, George Miller and Ted Kennedy began complaining that the administration had shortchanged them on funding for No Child Left Behind. Whether this was actually true is debatable, but given the heat these Democrats were feeling from their own base, including the teachers' union, which hated the new law, such grousing was predictable. What wasn't foreseeable, given the staggering sums the government was spending in Iraq, was that the president and his budget officials would allow discontent to foster over a relatively small amount of money. In 2002 and 2003 combined, some $46 billion in federal money was funneled to the public schools. Miller, asserting that the nation's schools needed $4.2 billion more in fiscal year 2002 and $5.4 billion more in 2003, accused the president of consistently breaking his word on No Child Left Behind. Miller's frustration was mainly with Republican congressional leaders, but he felt that a push from the president could free up the money he was looking for. With war looming, it seemed absurd for Bush to alienate the Democrats who had worked most closely with him, but Bush kept himself at arm's length from the messy budget and legislative battles on Capitol Hill. The upshot was that Bush left the details of governing to a partisan, conservative Republican congressional leadership that passed legislation with narrow majorities while ignoring the minority party.

If Bush seemed publicly impervious to any such protestations that he was the problem, privately he expressed bafflement. At the White House Correspondents' Association dinner in May 2004, Bush asked the president of the association, "What happened with Ted Kennedy?"[43] Bush was referring to Kennedy's description of the war as a "fraud" undertaken for political advantage. On one level Kennedy's criticism made little sense:

Iraq was always a risky proposition, and it had clearly eroded Bush's popularity. On another level, however, Kennedy's frustration was quite real, and more widespread among Democrats than had been generally understood at the time of the invasion. What "happened" to Ted Kennedy had happened to most of the Democrats in Congress; they had begun to feel disenfranchised, including on the most important question of war and peace, and most of them didn't much like the war they had been asked to support. The vote in the Senate on October 11, 2002, was 77–23, but an examination of the partisan breakdown shows how divided the Democrats were. Twenty-nine Democratic senators backed the president, compared to twenty-one who opposed him. The numbers in support were inflated by those with presidential ambitions (Daschle, John Kerry, John Edwards, Hillary Clinton, Joseph Biden, Evan Bayh, and Chris Dodd all voted in support) who had been reluctant to buck a president's war-making authority, but who nonetheless expressed misgivings about the invasion and had publicly called on Bush to give weapons inspectors in Iraq more time. Though the vote the day before in the "people's house" had attracted less attention nationally, it was a better barometer of the mood among Democrats. In the House of Representatives, a clear majority of Democrats opposed the resolution. With then-Democratic Whip Nancy Pelosi leading the way, 127 Democrats* voted against the resolution, with only 81 following Minority Leader Dick Gephardt's example of supporting the president.

The prevailing view among Democrats was that Bush didn't really consult them on the war; rather, he had thrown down the gauntlet and forced them to choose between two bad options. The first choice was defying a popular president on issues of war and peace just a year after the nation had been attacked. The second was invading a sovereign nation most Democrats did not believe presented an impending threat to the United States. They believed Bush had bullied them with his popularity that wasn't legitimately his to use in this way. They had a point. In April and May 1981, in the months following his assassination attempt, Ronald Reagan had attained a Gallup job-approval rating of 67 and 68 percent,

---

*That total of 127 includes Bernie Sanders, who is technically designated as an independent, but who caucuses with the House Democrats.

respectively, a number he hit only one other time, in May 1986. George W. Bush had numbers that high or higher—sometimes much higher—for a solid year after the 9/11 attacks. His approval ratings had started coming back to earth before the Iraq invasion, then spiked back upward as Americans rallied behind their commander-in-chief, as they invariably do at the outset of war.

As 2003 turned into 2004 and the Iraq War began to stall, it was as if Bush hadn't understood what had made him so popular in the first place. In those disconcerting days after 9/11, Americans had been impressed not only by Bush's resolve but also by his willingness to reach out to Democrats, to foreign governments, and to peace-loving Muslims. Bush's actions at that time, observed Joanne B. Ciulla, a professor of leadership studies at the University of Richmond, were a "beautiful example" of building consensus. Ciulla made another observation that would, in the years ahead, seem astute: The rapid rise in the esteem with which Bush was held by his countrymen in the waning weeks of 2001 wasn't his accomplishment alone. Americans rallied behind him for their own purposes as much as Bush's. "This is a classic example of this country making Bush into the leader they need," she said. "We all realized we have to have a great president right now."[44]

In his second term, as his popularity sank, Bush would often remind his inquisitors in the media that historians were still evaluating the tenure in office of the first president named George. This was true, but it is also true that George Washington detested partisanship and would have found a "base strategy" anathema to good government. "I think you could really call Washington the apostle of unity in America. It was at the heart of what he was all about," Philander D. Chase, editor-in-chief, The Papers of George Washington at the University of Virginia, said after 9/11. "He would have been the first person (in the current situation) to organize relief efforts. He would be very proud of the recent national unity, with political parties laying down their differences."[45]

By 2004, with the war in Iraq turning more contentious by the week, Bush waded, albeit reluctantly, into the latest "wedge" issue in American politics—gay marriage. This stance helped Bush with evangelical voters, particularly since Democrat John Kerry's position was so murky, but it also led to speculation that Bush was trying to lead half the nation—the half that considers itself conservative. "How divided is the country?"

pollster and political analyst William Schneider asked a week before the 2004 election. "The (Gallup) poll asked voters whether they felt President Bush is more of a 'uniter' or a 'divider.' The answer: 48 percent call Bush a uniter; 48 percent call him a divider."

That was how Bush stood on the eve of his victory. It proved an ominous omen, especially when Bush served notice within hours of his 2004 reelection that he believed he had been given an unqualified mandate to keep to his chosen course. This was an attitude that mystified a generation of political scientists, the scions of Corwin, Neustadt, and Greenstein. "Look at what happened to George W. Bush," said George W. Edwards III, a professor of political science at Texas A&M and editor of *Presidential Studies Quarterly*. "He did not win a plurality of the vote in his first election. He won 50.7 percent of the vote in his re-election. He seemed to be very relieved, and two days after the election, he declares he has earned political capital and is going to spend it. He announces a bold and aggressive agenda. This is interesting because this is the chief executive with the smallest electoral vote of any newly re-elected president since Woodrow Wilson—and the biggest agenda of any second-term president since FDR. It just doesn't mesh. He grossly overestimated his political capital. Perhaps it was second-term hubris. The bottom line is that he did not have a lot of political capital. His analysis was wrong."[46]

"I think he misread the election returns," concurred another prominent political scientist, Louis L. Gould, author of *The Modern American Presidency*. "A majority of voters said, 'We prefer you to Kerry, but please don't change anything.' But Bush heard a different voice."[47]

The voice Bush heard was his own, uttered daily on the 2004 campaign trail. There, to adoring handpicked audiences, he had promised to keep on being himself. In his second term, however, that would not be enough. No one seemed to know it then, least of all the forty-third president of the United States, but that November 3, 2004, press conference at the Ronald Reagan Building signaled the end of the second part of George W. Bush's presidency. The third part would not be so kind. An increasing number of political scientists came to view Bush as a president who talked like Reagan while governing like Jimmy Carter, and a majority of everyday Americans reached the conclusion, many of them reluctantly, that George W. Bush was no Reagan—indeed, that he wasn't even his own father.

4

SAFE FOR DEMOCRACY

George W. Bush's attempt to establish a beachhead of democracy in Iraq did not spring unbidden and full-blown, like Athena from the brow of Zeus. Although America's leaders have long paid homage to the dictum of George Washington to have "as little political connection as possible" with foreign nations, the nation has been enmeshed in such connections from its founding. President Thomas Jefferson purchased Louisiana and more than a fifth of the modern United States from France in 1803; President James Polk invaded Mexico in 1846 and annexed much of the present-day Southwest; President Andrew Johnson purchased Alaska from Russia in 1867. These are only the highlights. America was a world power long before its leaders proclaimed it as such during the Spanish-American War in 1898. At the time of that war, Woodrow Wilson was a professor of political science at Princeton University, of which he became president in 1902. Fifteen years later, he would take his country into World War I on the side of Britain and France, a conflict in which the United States played a decisive role in defeating an exhausted Germany. Two decades later, after an interregnum of global withdrawal, the aid "short of war" provided by President

Franklin D. Roosevelt to Great Britain helped that island nation to hold out against Nazi Germany—until Pearl Harbor plunged America into World War II and vindicated Winston Churchill's prediction that "the New World would come storming to the rescue of the Old."[1] The United States became, in FDR's words, the "arsenal of democracy" and the pivotal member of the Grand Alliance that crushed Nazi Germany and Imperial Japan. During four subsequent decades of Cold War, punctuated by hot wars in Korea and Vietnam, the United States led the anti-Communist alliance that culminated in the tearing down of the Berlin Wall and the collapse of the Soviet Union. In the early years of the post–Cold War era, through the Gulf War and beyond, America remained the world's dominant military and economic superpower.

Most American presidents have believed that national interests may require military action in the cause of freedom; they have differed widely, however, on the circumstances in which such action is necessary. In his State of the Union address to Congress on January 6, 1941, nine weeks after assuring America's mothers and fathers that their "boys are not going to be sent into any foreign wars," Franklin D. Roosevelt delivered a more ominous message: "I find it unhappily necessary to report that the future and the safety of our country and of our democracy are overwhelmingly involved in events far beyond our borders. No realistic American can expect from a dictator's peace international generosity, or return of true independence, or world disarmament, or freedom of expression, or freedom of religion—or even good business. Such a peace would bring no security for us or for our neighbors. Those who would give up essential liberty to purchase a little temporary safety deserve neither liberty nor safety."

This was the speech to Congress in which FDR articulated what he called the "Four Freedoms"—freedom of expression, freedom of worship, freedom from fear, and freedom from want, *everywhere in the world.* It was that magic phrase, everywhere in the world, repeated after the enunciation of each "freedom," that gave the speech its loft and rhetorical power. And it did indeed resonate in the world, even though the Soviet Union—the U.S. ally that suffered the most and inflicted the decisive blows to Nazi Germany—denied all of the freedoms that FDR so grandly espoused.

FDR's call was answered, in time, by 18 million Americans, among them Joseph P. Kennedy Jr., who would not survive World War II, and his younger brother John, who served heroically in the South Pacific, and who would succeed the supreme allied commander, Dwight D. Eisenhower, in the White House. John F. Kennedy espoused and epitomized the values of a generation that had seen its nation attacked and assumed the necessity of protecting liberty on foreign shores. President Kennedy's 1961 Inaugural Address became the gold standard for interventionist rhetoric among twentieth-century presidents. The United States, JFK told the world, would "bear any burden . . . support any friend, oppose any foe to assure the survival and success of liberty."

The United States bore many burdens in the years ahead, most notably in Vietnam. All were made heavier by the Cold War, in which the United States claimed to advance the cause of liberty by containing the Soviet Union even when this meant supporting authoritarian governments. The U.S. position—essentially that the enemy of my enemy is my friend and hence promotes the cause of democracy—extended to the shadow world of covert activity. The United States both resisted Soviet subversion and aided irregular forces that opposed Marxian regimes. Winning the Cold War, in this view, required unsavory choices. Near the Cold War's dawn, President Harry S. Truman told Congress that in the name of "free peoples" the United States should intervene against Communist insurgents in Greece on behalf of a reactionary government of which he personally disapproved. In the twilight of this war, President Ronald Reagan described the Nicaraguan contras, violent rebels against the Sandinista government, as the "moral equal of the Founding Fathers."* The rhetoric, while overblown, expressed Reagan's consistent view that opposition to pro-Communist regimes promoted universal freedom. President Reagan's most expansive expression of this long-held belief came on June 8, 1982, when he

---

*Reagan used these words in a speech to the annual Conservative Political Action Conference in Washington, D.C., on March 1, 1985, in the context of honoring members of the Afghan anti-Soviet resistance, one of whom was present. Then he said: "I've spoken recently of the freedom fighters of Nicaragua. You know the truth about them. You know who they're fighting and why. They are the moral equal of our Founding Fathers and the brave men and women of the French Resistance. We cannot turn away from them, for the struggle here is not right versus left; it is right versus wrong." Subsequent references to Reagan's policy by supporters and foes alike often used the phrase "moral equivalent" instead of "moral equal."

told British parliamentarians at Westminster Palace, "We must be staunch in our conviction that freedom is not the sole prerogative of a lucky few, but the inalienable and universal right of all human beings." The headline from this speech was Reagan's prediction, in a paraphrase of Karl Marx, that "the march of freedom and democracy will leave Marxism-Leninism on the ash heap of history." And in time, with no small boost from Reagan, it did.

George W. Bush's declarations on the presumed U.S. obligation to advance the cause of democracy abroad are in the mainstream of this rhetorical tradition. Some four months after the terrorist attacks of 9/11, Bush said, in his 2002 State of the Union speech, that "history has called America and our allies to action, and it is both our responsibility and our privilege to fight freedom's fight." This was more than a year before Bush launched the Iraq War. Two months into that war, Bush said, in a speech to the Coast Guard Academy, and in words that could have been used by either JFK or Reagan: "The advance of freedom is more than an interest we pursue. It is a calling we follow. Our country was created in the name and cause of freedom. And if the self-evident truths of our founding are true for us, they are true for all."

In the ensuing three years, the language of these three presidents—Roosevelt, Kennedy, and Reagan—were never far from the minds of Bush and his wordsmiths. The imagery of "axis of evil" in Bush's 2002 State of the Union address was consciously borrowed from FDR's 1942 State of the Union—a speech that employed both the words "axis" and "evil." Speaking to the National Endowment for Democracy in November 2003, Bush quoted directly from Reagan's Westminster address, comparing the democratic world's current struggle with another historic analogy, the Cold War, while predicting a similar result for the ultimate outcome. Bush would use these two examples, Nazism and communism, interchangeably during his second term, gradually (and gingerly) replacing the rhetorically amorphous "War on Terror" with the more politically resonant concept of a war against radical Islamic "fascism." Ultimately, he took to referring to these adversaries of the United States (and the enemies of the fledgling Iraq government) simply as "al Qaeda." In a Labor Day 2006 radio address—a convention begun by FDR and regenerated by Reagan—Bush termed the war with radical Islamic forces "the decisive ideological struggle of the twenty-first century."

Bush and his communications team were not coy about whom they were emulating and would expound on it when asked—at times even when not asked. Michael Gerson, Bush's eloquent chief speechwriter, insisted that Bush's formulation that "freedom is not America's gift to the world, it is the Almighty God's gift to every man and woman in the world" was Bush's own.[2] Perhaps that's true, but it is also clear that the president's speechwriters spent a lot of time studying John Kennedy, and they were particularly inspired by then-Senator Kennedy's 1959 assertion that "the magic power on our side is the desire of every person to be free, of every nation to be independent."

"Kennedy said we would pay *any* price to assure the survival of liberty. That we would bear *any* burden," Gerson deputy John McConnell, another top Bush speechwriter, said when asked about the president's wartime rhetoric. "Not *some* price, not *a little bit* of burden."[3] Standing in the White House driveway, McConnell continued, faithfully recalling Kennedy's words—delivered before he was born—word for word: "Meet any hardship. Support any friend. Oppose any foe. And then Kennedy said: 'This much we promise—and more.'"[4]

Bush began the start of his second term by articulating a vision every bit as encompassing as Kennedy's—and with similar implications. "We are led, by events and common sense," Bush said in his second Inaugural Address, "to one conclusion: The survival of liberty in our land increasingly depends on the success of liberty in other lands. The best hope for peace in our world is the expansion of freedom in all the world."

The handy label applied to such talk, and the military action that it often accompanies, is "Wilsonian," used a bit contradictorily to describe both a failed idealism on behalf of world peace and a promotion of U.S. involvement in the affairs of other nations on behalf of democratic principles. In the first sense of the adjective, Wilsonian policies are seen as utopian. The story line is that Woodrow Wilson, the twenty-eighth president of the United States, conceived of a League of Nations but was too impractical and unbending (or, more convincingly, too ill) to persuade the American people or the U.S. Senate of its necessity. The U.S. rejection of the League set in motion a chain of events in which the weakened League failed to halt Japanese and Italian aggression and then collapsed, hastening World War II. This is the Wilson whom FDR admired but was determined not to emulate as he laid the groundwork for what became the

United Nations. This is the Wilson whom Henry Kissinger had in mind in his book *Diplomacy,* where he divided American leaders of the twentieth century into categories of "realists," led by Theodore Roosevelt, and "idealists," headed by Wilson. (William Bundy, observing that TR was at times idealistic and Wilson realistic, called Kissinger's categorization "at best an over-simplification, at worst a serious distortion.")[5]

It is the second sense of the adjective—the evocation of Wilsonian principles as justification for overseas intervention—that resonates with contemporary Americans. This is the Wilson who sent U.S. troops to Europe in World War I supposedly to "make the world safe for democracy" in "the war to end all wars." (The latter phrase, sometimes attributed to Wilson, was coined by the French leader Georges Clemenceau.) This is the Wilson described by Dean Acheson, who wrote that Americans, "and none more than Woodrow Wilson," believed in the "Grand Fallacy" that the liberal principles that animate democratic legislatures could be applied to foreign affairs.[6] This is the Wilson who in contemporary imagination would have approved of the effort to establish democracy in Vietnam, where the United States ran into the downside of revolutionary self-determination. U.S. involvement in this war, explored by Eisenhower, tentatively begun by Kennedy, enormously expanded by Johnson, and continued by Nixon, was seen as a failure of Wilsonian principles, ironically so because Johnson considered Wilson a "self-righteous prig," while Ho Chi Minh, the North Vietnamese leader, was a Wilson admirer. In 1919 when Wilson arrived in Versailles for the signing of the postwar peace treaty, Ho was so inspired by Wilson's Fourteen Points that he drafted a statement which said that "all subject peoples are filled with hope by the prospect that an era of right and justice is opening to them."[7] (Ho hoped to hand the statement to Wilson but never met him.)

Wilsonian analogies and references have permeated the debate over the Iraq War. Conservative pundit William Safire approvingly linked Bush's action in Iraq to the "Wilsonian" approach of President Nixon, for whom Safire once wrote resonant speeches. Neoconservative historian Francis Fukuyama, who favored the Iraq intervention but later turned against it, called the Bush policy "neo-Wilsonian." Within the Bush administration, according to Fred Barnes, Condoleezza Rice, Bush's national security adviser at the time of the Iraq invasion and afterward his secretary of state, was fascinated with Wilson and the "great missed opportunities" after World War I.[8] Barnes defended Bush's Iraq policy in his book *Rebel-in-Chief* but added: "To a typical conservative, 'Wilsonian' is a slur, not a compliment."[9]

Nor is the word necessarily a compliment when used by Bush's liberal or centrist critics. University of Chicago political scientist John Mearsheimer, an outspoken opponent of the Iraq War, has termed Bush's approach to foreign policy "Wilsonianism with teeth."[10] Stanford history professor David M. Kennedy, who was also skeptical of the Iraq invasion, said that the theory Bush articulated in his second Inaugural Address was "Wilsonism on steroids."[11] To such writers, Bush's policy seems an excess of Wilsonism. New Republic senior editor John Judis has gone further, arguing in his book *The Folly of Empire* that Bush has abandoned the "ideal of collective security" fostered by Wilson on behalf of "a toxic mixture of nationalism and neo-conservatism."[12]

What would Woodrow Wilson have made of all this? Because Wilson made distinctions among wars, he might be taken aback by the wide range of foreign policy adventures to which his name has been applied. At the same time, as a student of history, he might also be pleased at the backhanded tribute conferred by the use of "Wilsonian" to describe any and all efforts to establish global democracy. For Wilson, like him or not, was the first great architect of U.S. internationalism in the twentieth century. In the words of Harvard professor of international relations Joseph S. Nye Jr., Wilson envisioned a "transformation of world politics through the spread of democracy and the creation of new international institutions."[13] Nye found, as have many others, that Wilson's reach exceeded his grasp, and he implicitly blamed Wilson for the fact that the United States distanced itself from Europe in the 1920s.

So Wilson is faulted on one hand for being too starry-eyed in his pursuit of world peace, and on the other for providing too broad a rationale for military interventionist policies. Neither interpretation is fair to Wilson. No president in American history has worked as hard and as long as Wilson to avoid a war into which belligerents were determined to drag the United States. When World War I began, Wilson advocated neutrality in thought and deed and called for "peace without victory" in Europe. He was outraged by the German violation of Belgian neutrality in 1914 and angered by a German submarine's torpedoing of the British liner *Lusitania* off Kinsale Head, Ireland, in 1915. Nearly 1,200 lives, including

100 children, were lost in this incident, 128 of them Americans. In the context of the time—long before unrestricted aerial bombardments of defenseless cities, let alone suicide bombers flying planes into towers—submarine warfare was a formidable terror weapon. And German U-boats were certainly weapons of mass destruction. Wilson sent a stiff note of protest (in fact, three notes) to Germany but resisted the clamor for war. In Britain he was denounced as a coward. During the next two years he made repeated diplomatic efforts to keep the United States out of war, emphasizing his opposition to submarine attacks on unarmed ships while also protesting a British blacklist of American firms that did business with Germany. Wilson used diplomacy for a time to encourage Germany to be more cautious about its submarine targets, justifying the slogan of his 1916 reelection campaign: "He Kept Us Out of War." But within weeks of Wilson's reelection, Germany—strangled by the British naval blockade—resumed unrestricted submarine warfare. Wilson, more peacefully inclined than his countrymen, believed he had been given no choice. On April 2, 1917, Wilson asked Congress for a declaration of war against Germany.

It was in this speech that Wilson said, "The world must be made safe for democracy." They are the best-remembered words he ever uttered, but they are often used out of context. A leading historian of the Vietnam War, for instance, quoting these words, said that Wilson wanted the world to be made safe for democracy "under American auspices."[14] That is neither what Wilson said nor what he meant. Wilson was a master stylist who chose in this instance to use the passive tense. In the words of Wilson biographer John Milton Cooper Jr.: "[Wilson] was very careful with language and tenses. He never used the passive tense carelessly. He did NOT say that the United States should make the world safe for democracy. He meant that the United States should be part of a broader effort involving other nations that would make the world safe for democracy. The distinction is important."[15]

Other passages in the speech suggest that Wilson was a reluctant warrior. In asking for a national draft, he said that the "status of belligerent" had been "thrust" upon the United States. With his voice rising, he began his peroration by saying, "It is a fearful thing to lead this most peaceful people, into the most terrible and disastrous of all wars. . . . But the right is more precarious than peace, and we shall fight for the things which we have always carried nearest our heart." He ended on an almost querulous note. After saying that "America is privileged to spend her blood and her might for the principles that gave her birth and happiness and the peace that she has treasured," Wilson concluded, "God helping her, she can do no other."

All presidents are products of their time and culture and technology, and it can be risky to speculate on what they might have done in another era. We don't know how George Washington would have responded to the Great Depression or what Grover Cleveland would have made of the bombing of Dresden. But based on Woodrow Wilson's track record, we can say with a reasonable degree of certainty where he would have stood on the U.S. interventions examined in this book. We can be fairly sure, for instance, that Wilson would have gone along with the Reagan-ordered U.S. deployment in Lebanon that ended so disastrously. The U.S. Marines were part of a multinational force, an approach dear to Wilson's heart. In 1918, after a bit of foot-dragging, Wilson yielded to the entreaty of the British and dispatched 5,000 U.S. troops into newly Bolshevik Russia as part of a multinational Allied force. (The intervention failed.) And Wilson no doubt would have sent U.S. forces into Grenada, as Reagan did, after receiving urgent requests from the surrounding island nations.

Would Wilson also have ordered an invasion of Panama to remove Manuel Noriega, an undertaking that Reagan declined in the last year of his presidency, but that was later carried out by President George H. W. Bush? Probably. Wilson was less reluctant to use military force in the hemisphere than to become involved in the affairs of Europe. Prodded by U.S. business interests and congressional war hawks, and seized by what one of his best biographers called "an itch to intervene,"[16] Wilson sent U.S. troops into Mexico in 1914 in an intervention that is instructive about the limits of Wilsonism when Wilson was practicing it. Mexico was a mess at the time. It was ruled by the despotic Gen. Victoriano Huerta, who had ascended to power by murdering a democratically elected president. Revolutionaries prowled the countryside and sometimes crossed into U.S. borderlands. Germans, rehearsing tactics for the European war, played an advisory role and in April 1914 were preparing to unload an arms shipment for the Huerta government at Veracruz. While this was happening, the regime arrested two American sailors at nearby Tampico, and Wilson sent an invasion force to rescue them. He expected token

opposition, but government troops resisted and anti-American riots exploded across Mexico. Six thousand troops were needed to secure Veracruz harbor, an action in which seventeen American sailors and five
Marines were killed. Instead of widening the attack, Wilson and his secretary of state, William Jennings Bryan, asked Argentina, Brazil, and
Chile to act as mediators. The U.S. troops stayed in Veracruz during the
mediation while Mexican rivals fought among themselves. Huerta was
forced to resign in July, and U.S. Secretary of War Lindley Garrison
asked Wilson to send the American troops to Mexico City to install a new
government. Wilson refused in a letter to Garrison in which he said that
the United States had "no right at any time to intervene in Mexico to determine the way in which the Mexicans are to settle their own affairs."[17]

So it is clear from the record—and most of all from his learning experience in Mexico—that Wilson would not have launched a preemptive
war against Iraq, no matter how odious the barbarities of its ruler or how
provocative its policies might have seemed. Wilson eschewed preemptive
military action. When he felt it necessary to resort to military force, he relied on first principles—usually defensive ones—as justification. "Freedom of the seas" had been a cardinal U.S. principle since the early days of
the republic, and Wilson realized even before the sinking of the *Lusitania*
(and especially afterward) that German submarine warfare and the
British blacklist in response to it menaced U.S. trade and commerce. He
nonetheless for three years sought a diplomatic solution that would keep
the United States out of war, displaying a caution that infuriated supporters of intervention (even as his eventual decision to go to war alienated
opponents of the war). Nor did Wilson ever authorize a U.S.-led intervention anywhere to replace a dictator with a democracy. In Mexico, he
explicitly repudiated his own secretary of war for advocating such a
course of action. Outside the hemisphere, Wilson was cautious to the
point of hesitancy, especially in the region where Bush has sent thousands
of American troops into harm's way.

Wilson did not lack for opportunities to intervene in this region if he
had wanted to do so. In 1919, when the world was inflamed with the stories of what became the Armenian genocide, Wilson dismissed appeals
for U.S. troops to protect the Armenian populace from atrocities at the
hands of the Turks. "If you want to put out a fire in Utah, you don't send
to Oklahoma for the fire engine," he said in a speech in Salt Lake City. "If

you want to put out a fire in the Balkans, if you want to stamp out the smoldering flames in some part of Europe, you don't send to the United States for troops."[18] The notion that the Iraq War is somehow an expression of Wilsonian ideals does not withstand examination either of what Wilson said or what he did.

The word "Wilsonian" has nonetheless clung to the Bush policy in Iraq, mainly in the other sense, as a synonym for failed idealism. Wilson hoped after World War I to advance his belief in "peace without victory" by bringing a defeated Germany back into the family of nations and by creating the League of Nations to prevent future wars. He was frustrated on both counts. After the appalling casualties of the war, Britain and even more France were determined to extract revenge, which they did at the Treaty of Versailles in terms of reparations that bankrupted Germany, produced revolution and unrest, and paved the way for the rise of Hitler. Wilson meanwhile put his trust in the League, saying that it would "break the heart of the world" if the United States refused to join. But Wilson was unwilling to accept reservations attached to U.S. approval of the Treaty of Versailles by Senator Henry Cabot Lodge and other opponents of the League. In a complicated series of votes culminating on March 19, 1920, the Senate rejected the treaty and U.S. participation in the League. At the time, Wilson was faulted, even by some of his supporters, for his "rigidity." He still is. Nye, echoing the view that Wilson deserves the blame for what happened, has contended that George W. Bush has shown more "emotional intelligence and self-mastery" in dealing with his foreign policy crises than Wilson did in the League fight.[19] But such comments ignore the probable reason for Wilson's behavior. Wilson, his moralistic tendencies aside, was a gifted politician. He maneuvered to win the presidential nomination against a frontrunner, and as president, before his debilitating stroke, often displayed a preference for compromise that alienated extreme partisans. With the wisdom of modern medical insight, a consensus has emerged that it was Wilson's physical condition, rather than his temperament or his moral judgments, that was the decisive factor in his conduct during the League fight. Wilson scholar Arthur Link, neurologist Edwin Weinstein, and latter-day biographer Cooper have all contended that the stroke affected Wilson's judgment in a way that made him literally "incapable of compromise."[20]

So the United States stayed out of the League and retreated into a distanced foreign policy under three Republican presidents. But Wilsonian ideals survived. In his lyrical (and adulatory) dual biography, *Roosevelt and Hopkins,* playwright Robert Sherwood said that Franklin Roosevelt was "haunted by the ghost of Woodrow Wilson."* FDR, assistant secretary of the navy in the Wilson administration, repeatedly saw Wilson at his shoulder. In Sherwood's account, FDR realized after he was elected to a third term in 1940 that he, like Wilson, could stand accused of winning on a pledge of peace and then leading the nation into war. Later, at his meeting with Churchill and Stalin at Yalta (which has done its own share of haunting), FDR was mindful that Wilson had failed to secure the peace after the war was won.

Drawing upon Sherwood, Cooper suggested that all U.S. foreign policy is haunted by Wilson. The United States never came to terms with its participation in World War I or with the desolate postwar outcome in Europe (not to mention Iraq, which the British cobbled together in 1920 from three pieces of the decaying Ottoman Empire). In the aftermath of the war, America experienced labor unrest, race riots, lynchings, and a Red Scare. This was followed by a long hiatus in which a majority of Americans wanted no part of the world. Even Franklin Roosevelt, in a successful bid to win the support of William Randolph Hearst in 1932, repudiated his belief that the United States should join the League of Nations. It took the bombing of Pearl Harbor to destroy the cages of isolationism as, sixty years later, the bombing of the Twin Towers and the Pentagon shattered the new isolationism that had gained currency after the Vietnam War.

The failure of the League of Nations still resonates with American policy-makers. It was on President Truman's mind as he launched the United Nations, and it has been cited ever since whenever the United Nations has proved impotent or unwilling in the face of aggression or genocide. In the run-up to the Iraq War, Defense Secretary Donald Rumsfeld argued that the United Nations would be going down the "path of

---

*Sherwood related that Roosevelt wrote his World War II speeches on a table in the Cabinet Room and would look up from time to time at the portrait of Woodrow Wilson over the mantelpiece. "The tragedy of Wilson was always somewhere within the rim of his consciousness," Sherwood wrote (p. 227).

ridicule" that had "discredited" the League if it refused to back the United States in Iraq. Later, the Bush administration's difficulties in trying to build a stable government in Iraq would be explicitly compared to Wilson's shortcomings. "Bush defined a vision that failed to balance ideals with national capacities; Wilson made the same miscalculation," wrote Joseph Nye. "Both, moreover, failed to manage information flows in their administrations." And while they showed an "admirable" persistence in clinging to their goals, "strength of character is not an adequate substitute for contextual intelligence and organizational competence."[21]

Their problems went beyond "information flows" and organizational shortcomings. Neither Wilson nor Bush had a military background, and both relied on a small circle of advisers—arguably, too small a circle—in making military decisions. American troops in the field paid a price for it. Wilson is faulted even by admirers for massive deficiencies in U.S. mobilization that sent an untrained Army into the field. Although U.S. casualties in World War I pale in comparison to the losses of the British, French, Germans, and Russians, they were hardly trivial: 116,000 dead and more than 200,000 wounded in a year and a half of war. As it became evident that the war had solved nothing, Americans increasingly thought of these casualties as wasted sacrifices.

Woodrow Wilson's dream of a cooperative world order in which nations would unite against an aggressor died in the vengeful Versailles aftermath of World War I. Italy and Japan, allied with the winners, felt cheated out of a share of the spoils of victory and turned, respectively, to fascism and militarism. France was ungovernable. Germany, ruined by the war, suffered through revolution, upheavals, and economic calamity that culminated in the triumph of Hitler. Britain, reeling from 3 million casualties, had lost its taste for war, and the Oxford Union passed a resolution declaring that "this House refuses to fight for King or country." In the United States, World War I was seen in the rearview mirror as a betrayal of first principles. America, at its peril, had ignored George Washington's warning against political connections with foreign nations and Thomas Jefferson's advice to avoid "entangling alliances." In the post-Wilson era, the United States wanted no part of Europe and no longer welcomed its "teeming masses," or for that matter the masses from anywhere else. Congress in 1921 and again in 1924 passed restrictive immigration bills that were signed into law by Republican presidents.

"Rejection of Europe is what America is all about," wrote novelist John Dos Passos. Americans believed that in doing so they were also rejecting war. German writer Erich Maria Remarque's antiwar novel, *All Quiet on the Western Front,* was an American best-seller in 1929. A year later it became an acclaimed movie that was voted best picture of the year.

It was in this context of disillusion, at once patriotic and faintly pacifist, that a twenty-year-old young man attending college in the isolationist Midwest wrote a short story about the war. The young man, although not an accomplished writer, had a narrative gift and a sense of the public mood. His story flashed back to the western front, where one war-weary U.S. soldier sarcastically tells another that they are doing the "noble work" of "making the world safe for democracy." His comrade replies that the war will seem "worth fighting" only when it ends. In a subsequent attack, one of the soldiers is gassed and sent to a military hospital. The story is narrated by the other soldier, who loses track of his buddy after the war and reads about his death in a newspaper. The gassed soldier, now a penniless "tramp," was trying to reach a veterans' hospital for treatment, and when boarding a moving freight train, fell under the wheels. The story was titled "Killed in Action."[22]

The college student graduated and was altered by the world. As the Great Depression stalked the land, he became enthusiastic about Franklin Roosevelt, the new president. Later, at a time when many of his boyhood friends thought that isolationism was the path to peace, the former college student, now an actor, became apprehensive about the rise of Hitler and supportive of FDR's efforts to aid embattled Britain. Many years later, he went into politics, still an internationalist, but no longer a Democrat. By then, Ronald Reagan dismissed the story he had written at Eureka College in 1931 as an expression of youthful pacifism, and he could not even remember why he had written it. All he recalled were the words—Woodrow Wilson's words—that he had put into the mouth of one of his soldiers. The war they fought, said Reagan, had not in fact made the world safe for democracy.

5

NOBLE CAUSES

T he antiwar sentiments that Ronald Reagan had expressed in his short story as a college student were buried in the mists of memory by the time he reached the White House. Over the course of half a century, he had first become a militant internationalist, championing the cause of embattled Britain against Nazi Germany, and then, after Pearl Harbor, part of the Hollywood propaganda machine that emerged during World War II. Reagan, spared from overseas duty because of poor eyesight, served comfortably in the First Motion Picture Unit in Culver City.

The unit was formed through a collaboration between Jack and Harry Warner—Reagan's peacetime employers—and Gen. Henry (Hap) Arnold, who headed the Army Air Corps (later the Army Air Force) and preached the decisiveness of air power in the war against Germany and Japan. The First Motion Picture Unit made films that sought to "increase enlistments, train servicemen, build morale, define the enemy, create unity, and promote air power."[1] Reagan narrated or acted in at least eight such films, beginning with a role in *Rear Gunner* in 1942, made at Arnold's request because the Army Air Corps had a surfeit of pilots and a shortage of gunners.[2] The other movies included *Westward Bataan,* in which Reagan as narrator explained and lauded the island-hopping strategy of General Douglas MacArthur in the South Pacific, and *Target Tokyo,* which celebrated the B-29 bombings of Japan. Reagan's participation in these movies, and his viewing of countless reels of film from American bombings, stayed with him for the rest of his life. While he became an advocate of air power, he never forgot the scenes of the devastation caused by aerial bombardment. When, in August 1982, he watched television pictures of sections of Beirut reduced to rubble by eleven hours of Israeli bombing, President Reagan was reminded of what Allied bombers had done to Germany and Japan.

Reagan reasoned inductively, generalizing about the universal from personal experience. He was a Democrat (not unlike many other Americans) because President Franklin D. Roosevelt and his New Deal had provided government jobs to his father and brother during the Depression. Reagan's appreciation of FDR deepened during World War II, in which he saw himself as part of the war effort. Although he never met FDR, he felt he knew him after narrating the propaganda film *Beyond the Line of Duty* (1942), the only movie to feature the voices of both Roosevelt and Reagan. Reagan would write later that he was at the time a "near-hopeless hemophilic liberal";[3] it would be more precise to say that he was a New Deal Democrat with a hero-worshipping appreciation of the president who had saved Reagan's family in the process of saving the country. The label of liberalism nonetheless clung to Reagan for years after the war. As late as 1952, the Los Angeles County Democratic Central Committee rejected Reagan as a potential congressional candidate on grounds he was "too liberal."[4] That same year, Reagan served on the advisory board of the United World Federalists, a utopian organization.

Forces were at work in Reagan's life, however, that propelled him toward conservatism. Reagan made his best-known film, *Kings Row,* in 1941; it was released in 1942 when he was in the Army. Reagan's strong performance in this film enabled his agent to negotiate a contract that was fabulous for its day: $1 million over a seven-year period. So when Reagan returned to civilian moviemaking after four years in the Army, he was making big money for the first time when the marginal income-tax rate was at a record high and individuals were not allowed to average their income. (Reagan told a friend there should be a "personal depreciation allowance" for actors, similar to the depreciation allowed to oil companies.) Reagan's resentment over his tax bill made him receptive to conservative arguments that high tax rates were the inevitable fruit of costly social programs initiated by the New Deal. His epiphany on this issued coincided with an unhappy period in his life. A bout of pneumonia nearly killed him, and his marriage to Jane Wyman disintegrated—she would walk out on him in 1947, and they would divorce a year later. Hollywood was at the time beset by labor strife and anti-Communist investigations and worried by the looming threat of television. As president of the Screen Actors Guild (and secretly, if briefly, an FBI informant), Reagan was politically active. He became convinced that the Communist Party in Hollywood was a leading wedge of a Moscow-directed worldwide conspiracy. This story has been told from many points of view: Suffice it here to say that Reagan's clashes in Hollywood with avowed or suspected Communists made him a lifelong anti-Communist. As a Democrat, Reagan cheered the anti-communism of President Harry Truman. As he moved rightward during the late 1950s, Reagan denounced the Soviet Union, which he described as the "slave master" of captive people. Until he met Mikhail Gorbachev, Reagan never wavered in the view that the Soviet Union was, to again use the words of his "evil empire" speech, "the focus of evil in the modern world." Gorbachev was different, Reagan explained to fellow conservatives, because he was the first Soviet leader to abandon the goal of world domination.

It is not surprising that Reagan saw the competition between the industrialized democracies and the Soviet Union as a contest between good and evil. This Manichean view derived naturally from his religious upbringing, his dramatic tendency, and his wartime experience as a Hollywood propagandist who had described the struggle between the Allies and Nazi Germany in similar terms. Depicting the Soviets as the embodiment of evil produced snickers among the political elite, which pronounced Reagan's views as "simplistic" or "provocative," but resonated with ordinary Americans. George W. Bush's Manichean view would have similar resonance in the United States after 9/11, even though the military threat did not compare to the ones that had been posed by Germany and Japan in World War II or by the Soviet Union during much of the Cold War. In language his speechwriters borrowed from both Roosevelt and Reagan, Bush in his 2002 State of the Union address described a supposed

"axis of evil" involving Iraq, Iran, and North Korea that defied logic—
the three nations barely speak to one another, let alone constitute an
"axis"—but appealed to the sentiments of Americans who were accustomed to believing that their country held the moral high ground in every
conflict.

Reagan's logic as he evolved into an anti-Communist was not always
impeccable either. He had during World War II faithfully echoed the
FDR party line and lauded the Soviets as gallant allies. After he became
an anti-Communist, Reagan discarded all references to Soviet valor and
to the key role the Soviet Union had played in the wartime alliance
against Nazi Germany, when its military forces and civilian population
had suffered by far the greatest losses at German hands. In a 1951 magazine article shortly after his conversion to the anti-Communist cause,
Reagan wrote that "the real fight with this new [Soviet] totalitarianism
belongs to the forces of liberal democracy, just as did the battle with
Hitler's totalitarianism."[5] What was in fact "new" was not Soviet totalitarianism but Reagan's recognition of it.

Reagan wrote this article, in which he expressed the view that communism was a "hoax" masking "Russian aggression aimed at world conquest," in the context of the Korean War, a conflict that would alter his
opinion of the ways the United States should respond to such aggression.
Korea, freed from Japanese rule by World War II, had been partitioned
at the 38th Parallel into a Communist north and a non-Communist south.
On June 25, 1950, North Korea launched a surprise attack, routing South
Korean forces and marching on to capture Seoul, the South Korean capital. President Truman sent troops into South Korea under United Nations auspices, which he was able to do because the Soviets were
boycotting the Security Council, in which they had a veto power. The
World War II hero Douglas MacArthur commanded the U.N. forces, the
majority of them American. In mid-September MacArthur's forces made
a daring amphibious landing at Inchon, a port west of the South Korean
capitol of Seoul. He then recaptured Seoul in heavy fighting and pursued
the North Korean army beyond the 38th Parallel. As MacArthur's troops
neared the Yalu River separating China from North Korea, Mao Tse-
tung ordered units of the People's Liberation Army, described as volun-
teers, to join the fight. MacArthur's supply lines were overextended, and
he underestimated the strength of the Chinese. In late November, the

Chinese troops came out of hiding, overwhelmed South Korean forces, and flanked the U.S. Eighth Army, which suffered heavy casualties and was forced into the longest retreat in U.S. military history. The Chinese recaptured Seoul before being thrown back by a reconstituted Eighth Army. MacArthur wanted to pursue the retreating Chinese into China if necessary, but Truman instructed MacArthur to use only Korean forces near the Chinese border. When MacArthur disobeyed these instructions, Truman removed him from command.

The firing of MacArthur on April 21, 1951, produced "quite an explosion," as Truman wrote in his diary.[6] Americans overwhelmingly sided with MacArthur—69 percent opposed his dismissal, according to Gallup—and gave him an adoring welcome home. A half million people cheered MacArthur in San Francisco; he flew on to Washington and delivered an emotional address to a joint session of Congress. Truman's approval ratings never exceeded 33 percent after the MacArthur firing; he was down to 22 percent in February 1952 when he announced he would not seek reelection. Meanwhile, Dwight Eisenhower, the revered commander of Allied forces in Europe during World War II and the Republican nominee for president that year, promised he would go to Korea if elected. He was, and he did, but the war dragged on until July 1953. When it ended, the two Koreas were again divided at the 38th Parallel. Four million people, half of them civilians, had died in the war, and Korea's industry and much of its housing were in ruins. U.S. military deaths during the war were more than 54,000, including 33,686 combat deaths, and 103,248 wounded. The combat death toll alone in three years was ten times the comparable figure of U.S. losses during the first four years of the Iraq War.

Reagan believed that Truman's reputation was irreparably damaged by the MacArthur firing and the inconclusive outcome of the Korean War. "In my view, the only thing that kept Harry Truman from real greatness was his decision not to completely back General Douglas MacArthur and win the Korean War,"[7] Reagan wrote in his memoirs. He claimed that MacArthur had made a "prophetic remark": "If we don't win this war in Korea, we'll have to fight another war—this time in Vietnam." Reagan gave no source for this unlikely quotation. Whether or not MacArthur ever said these words, there is no doubt that Reagan viewed Vietnam through the lenses of Korea and found it inexcusable to sacrifice American lives merely to maintain the status quo. Korea became a template for evaluating such sacrifice, although Reagan as president would extol the U.S. soldiers still stationed there as manning the barricades on the "front lines of freedom." Ironically, Korea would also become a template of sorts for the George W. Bush administration, which explored the long-term U.S. deployment as a potential model for maintaining a similar military role in Iraq.

By the time the United States became involved in Vietnam, Reagan had completed his political transition from liberal to conservative. He had also undergone a personal transition, marrying Nancy Davis, who became his valuable partner for the rest of his life. Reagan's film career was now near its end, but he made a successful transition to television as host (and occasionally an actor) on the popular *General Electric Theater.* Off screen, he became an inspirational speaker. In 1960, while still a Democrat, Reagan supported Richard Nixon for president. In 1962, the year President John F. Kennedy increased the number of U.S. advisers in Vietnam from 700 to 12,000, Reagan changed his registration to Republican. Two years later, with JFK assassinated and Lyndon B. Johnson in the White House, Reagan joined the crusade of Senator Barry Goldwater of Arizona to transform the Republican Party into a conservative institution.

Goldwater was unflinching in his view of the Soviet Union. In his 1964 political manifesto, *The Conscience of a Conservative,* he warned that the United States was "in clear and imminent danger of being overwhelmed by alien forces. We are confronted by a world revolutionary movement that possesses not only the will to dominate absolutely every square mile on the globe but increasingly the capacity to do so."[8] (Reagan echoed this warning in the nationally televised speech he gave for Goldwater a week before the election.) Goldwater's solution was to put the Soviet Union on notice: "to make sure the enemy knows he cannot and will not win any war that he might be tempted to start."[9] The Arizona senator believed such candor would help keep the peace. But Goldwater's bristly demeanor and his undisciplined remarks, including a careless quip about wanting to lob a grenade into the men's room of the Kremlin, abetted the Democratic strategy of depicting him as an unstable warmonger. The Democratic campaign was epitomized by a television commercial known as Daisy Girl, which began with a little girl standing in a meadow picking petals off a daisy and counting them. When the count reached "nine," a man's voice began counting down a missile launch. When his countdown reached "zero," there was the sound of an explosion. As the telltale picture of a mushroom cloud filled the screen, President Johnson's voice could be heard saying, "These are the stakes. To make a world in which all of God's children can live, or to go into the dark. We must either love each other, or we must die."* The commercial, although used only once, became the touchstone of a campaign in which the Democrats portrayed Johnson as a man of peace.

Truth, famously described as the first casualty of war, is also an early victim of political campaigns. Johnson was not truthful about his intentions in Vietnam, but the demonization of Goldwater and the laxness of the media in prodding LBJ to explain his own post-election plans enabled the president to avoid a serious debate about the war. Historian Frederik Logevall has documented in his important book *Choosing War* that Johnson planned to escalate the U.S. military presence in Vietnam once the election was over. Logevall found little difference in the views of Johnson and Goldwater about the war,[10] although it seems likely that Goldwater, with his Air Force background, would have relied more on aerial attack and less on a ground war. In his acceptance speech at the tumultuous Republican National Convention in San Francisco, Goldwater attempted to prompt a debate on Vietnam, but his comments were overshadowed by his defense of "extremism" and other issues. Still, Goldwater tried. "Don't try to sweep this under the rug," he said at the convention. "We are at war in Vietnam. And yet the president who is commander in chief of our forces refuses to say—refuses to say, mind you—whether the objective there is victory, and his secretary of defense continues to mislead and misinform the American people."

As U.S. troops poured into Vietnam late in 1965, conservatives told a bitter joke: "They said if I voted for Goldwater we'd be at war within a year, and I did, and we are."** Conservatives believed, with reason, that

---

*These lines—"We must love each other or die"—were cribbed from a famous poem written by W.H. Auden, "1 September 1939," without Auden's permission. Auden was so furious at this unauthorized use that he removed the poem from his canon.

**In his column of May 9, 1965, at a time when U.S. warplanes were conducting a sustained bombing of Vietnam, Art Buchwald expressed a close variant of this gallows humor. Buchwald wrote that it was "frightening" to imagine what it would be like if Goldwater were president. "For one thing, we would probably be bombing North Viet-Nam now if Goldwater were in office," he wrote. "The people who voted for Johnson would scream at their Republican friends, 'I told you if Goldwater became president he'd get us into war.'"

President Johnson had deceived them, but they were restrained by a belief that it was imperative to resist communism in Southeast Asia. As a result, conservatives largely swallowed their distrust of LBJ and supported
the war, in the process accepting a military strategy that many of them
disliked. With Korea in mind, MacArthur had often warned that it
would be folly for the United States to become bogged down in a land
war in Asia. When President Kennedy, a hundred days into office, was
pondering intervention in Laos, MacArthur told him (according to
Arthur J. Schlesinger Jr.) that "anyone wanting to commit American
ground forces to the mainland of Asia should have his head examined."[11]

This was not a unique opinion. Prescott Bush also believed relatively
early on that Vietnam was a misguided venture. Speaking for a 1966 oral
history, four years after he left the Senate, Bush said that if he'd still been
in Congress he would have opposed the buildup started by President
Kennedy and escalated by President Johnson.[12] The fissures regarding
Vietnam were complicated, however, and transcended party, ideology,
even family lines. The same year, his son George H. W. Bush ran successfully for a House district in Houston vowing to support the war. "I will
back the President no matter what weapons we use in Southeast Asia,"
George H. W. Bush said, adding his antipathy for "faint-hearted Americans" who questioned America's role in Vietnam.[13] He kept that promise
as a congressman even through the tough year of 1968, the year his oldest
son eschewed active military service in Southeast Asia by enlisting in the
Texas Air National Guard.

Democrats had their own differences. The preference on the Left, asserted softly at first and then more loudly after the Tet offensive of February 1968, was to withdraw U.S. troops and leave the South Vietnamese to
fend for themselves. Liberal opponents of the war disputed the view (expressed by Johnson and Goldwater alike) that the loss of South Vietnam
would send a signal of weakness and lead to other Communist victories
in Asia. On the Right, the clear preference was for victory, which at the
outset of the U.S. intervention seemed within reach. After Johnson had
ordered bombing raids and the first heavy deployment of U.S. troops in
October 1965, Reagan had given a sanguine and somewhat jingoistic assessment: "We should declare war on Vietnam. We could pave the whole
country and put parking stripes on it and still be home by Christmas."[14]
By the time of Tet, more than two years later, Reagan and other conserva-

tives held a more realistic view. Although they still talked of victory, they meant by this the preservation of a non-Communist South Vietnam. Bombing or attacking North Vietnam was advocated as a means of saving South Vietnam, not with the goal of occupying the north. So it could be said, although it rarely was, that conservatives were committed to the limited war in Vietnam that they had renounced in Korea.

The political problem for conservatives was that their talk of "winning," however defined, inevitably raised the prospect of a nuclear conflict. MacArthur had favored dropping nuclear bombs on China and Manchuria after China had sent troops across the Yalu, and both Truman and Eisenhower had considered using nuclear weapons in the Korean War (although in a much more limited way than MacArthur had in mind). Popular opinion in 1952 was evenly divided, with half the American people saying they favored using nuclear weapons, if necessary, to end the war in Korea. By the time of the Vietnam deployments, however, only a quarter of Americans favored a nuclear option. In the interval between Korea and Vietnam, a significant event had taken place that had frightened Americans and made them more aware of the probable consequences of nuclear war: the Cuban missile crisis. It was this event, more than any other, that explains why the Daisy Girl commercial had been so effective. And it explains why, in 1965, when Johnson sent 200,000 U.S. troops into Vietnam, conservatives mostly backed him, despite their resentment over LBJ's misrepresentations in the 1964 election campaign.

Reagan was one of these conservatives. His belief that Vietnam was on the front lines of a worldwide struggle between freedom and communism trumped his reservations about Johnson, whose domestic policies he often criticized. The principal U.S. involvement in the war, if dated from the Johnson military buildup, roughly corresponded to Reagan's political career in California. President Johnson approved Gen. William Westmoreland's request for forty-four additional combat battalions in July 1965, when Reagan was meeting with his political strategists to discuss the 1966 campaign. By November 1966, when Reagan was elected governor of California, more than 400,000 U.S. troops (of an eventual 540,000) had been deployed in Vietnam. Reagan was governor for eight years. His second term ended in January 1975, a few months before the evacuations from the U.S. embassy rooftop in Saigon that marked the final victory of the Communist forces. During these eight years Reagan often commented about the war, but it was not an obsession for him. The cabinet minutes of the Reagan governorship suggest that he was usually focused, as he should have been, on the panoply of issues that confronted him as governor rather than on U.S. foreign policy. But by the mid-1960s the Vietnam War had become the central issue of American politics, as the Iraq War would be four decades later, and Reagan did not shrink from the controversy. In a CBS "Town Meeting of the World" on May 16, 1967, Reagan appeared with Senator Robert F. Kennedy on an internationally televised forum to answer questions from young people around the world. The questioners were hostile to U.S. policy in Vietnam, and Reagan, well prepared, gave a good account of himself. Kennedy, who was privately critical of the war, did not. He was reluctant to endorse the intense anti-Americanism expressed by the foreign students and was on the defensive during most of the program. Reagan was measured in his answers, even to a Soviet student. In response to a skeptical question about U.S. motives in the war, Reagan said "our goal" was preserving the right of the South Vietnamese people to self-determination instead of "a government or a system forced upon them."

Reagan ran abortively for the Republican presidential nomination in 1968, entering the race when Richard Nixon was on the verge of locking it up. But he made a strong showing in the South and West that foreshadowed his appeal in future elections. The Democratic coalition that, aside from the Eisenhower interregnum, had governed America for fifty-five years was unraveling in the face of urban disorders and increasing domestic protests against the war, paving the way for the presidential candidacy of George C. Wallace. Reagan tried to appeal to Wallace voters without embracing Wallace's racism. This was easier to do on foreign policy than in domestic issues, and Reagan began to emphasize his criticisms of Johnson's strategy in Vietnam. "The president," Reagan told the *Chicago Tribune,* "should say to the American people: We are at war. We can win and we must win."[15]

The prevailing sentiment in America after Tet was less for winning than for withdrawal. On February 27, 1968, in the wake of the Tet offensive, Walter Cronkite, "the most trusted man in America," delivered a gloomy assessment of the war. President Johnson told his aides that if he had lost Cronkite he had lost the country, as indeed he had. In March, Senator Eugene McCarthy of Minnesota, running as an antiwar candidate, nearly defeated Johnson in the New Hampshire Democratic primary. Robert Kennedy entered the race, and Johnson announced on March 31 that he would not seek reelection. Kennedy conducted a passionate eighty-five-day campaign and might have become the Democratic nominee, but he was assassinated on June 5, just hours after he had won the California primary.

Johnson still controlled the party machinery, and the Democrats nominated his vice president, Hubert Humphrey, at a Chicago convention marked by police violence against antiwar demonstrators. Nixon, the Republican nominee, straddled the war issue. He gave so few details about what he intended to do in Vietnam that Democrats mocked what they called Nixon's "secret plan" to end the war. But Humphrey's own straddling alienated both supporters and opponents of the war, and the Democrats after Chicago were damaged beyond repair. Reagan, campaigning for Nixon in the fall, continued to call for victory in Vietnam. "Wouldn't it be nice," he said at a Houston speech, "if the government, when it asks our sons to put on a uniform to fight and, perhaps, die for freedom and their country, would assure them that it would make them its No. 1 priority and put the full resources of this nation at their disposal to win as quickly as possible?"[16] After Nixon won, Reagan supported his war policy through its twists and turns while always sounding a bit more hawkish than the president. Summarizing his position in a 1979 letter to a conservative columnist, Reagan said: "I supported the mining of Haiphong Harbor and the bombing of Hanoi enthusiastically and was, indeed considered a hawk because I have continued to say that the only immorality of the Vietnam War was that our government asked young men to die in a war that the government had no intention of winning."[17] As time went by, Reagan focused less on what he considered the justified reasons for U.S. intervention in Vietnam and more on this "only immorality." Personal encounters were always paramount for Reagan, and he was moved to tears when he and Nancy met with returning U.S. prisoners of war in 1973 and heard their stories of hardship and torture. On May 4, 1974, at a dedication in the Angeles National Forest to California's war dead, Reagan recalled his meetings with the returning prisoners. "There are those who say that Vietnam was a war without heroes because the conflict became a controversy that divided our people for so long," Reagan said. "I do not accept that. They were all heroes, especially those we were honoring today."

By the time Reagan gave this speech, American troops had been with-drawn from Vietnam, and the North Vietnamese army, in violation of the Paris accords to which its government had agreed, was moving toward victory. Nixon resigned in August because of the Watergate scandal, and the war ended in April 1975 on President Gerald Ford's watch. By this time Reagan was poised to oppose Ford for the 1976 Republican presi-dential nomination. The Vietnam War was an emotional subtext of his challenge. "Let us tell those who fought in that war that we will never again ask young men to fight and possibly die in a war our government is afraid to win," Reagan said repeatedly. It was an inevitable applause line—and one that would have historical resonance. When George W. Bush ran for president, he would declare in his campaign autobiography, *A Charge to Keep:* "We must not go into a conflict unless we go in commit-ted to win."[18]

Reagan returned to this theme in 1980, running against an incumbent president at a time when Americans were frustrated over the inability of their government to rescue the hostages in Iran. Speaking to the Veterans of Foreign Wars on August 18, Reagan once more said that Americans should not be sent to die in wars that their government was unwilling to win. Veterans gave him a standing ovation and cheered again at a line that Reagan had written by hand into a prepared text of his remarks. Speaking of the sacrifices American troops had made in Vietnam, Reagan told the assembled veterans: "It is time we recognized that ours, in truth, was a noble cause."

The phrase had honorable antecedents. George Washington had first used the words "noble cause" in an otherwise routine order to his troops in 1776.[19] Harry Truman had used it, too, but in a different context: "the noble cause of peace."[20] The more common phrase was "just cause." As expressed in a stanza of our national anthem ("then conquer we must, when our cause it is just"), it has a bit of an imperial ring. Reagan, who had a good ear, liked the sound of "noble" and its connotation of altruism. He meant the words literally. While he felt strongly that Lyndon Johnson had bungled the conduct of the Vietnam War, Reagan believed the U.S. intentions had been to preserve democratic government and halt the ex-pansion of communism.

But at the time he addressed the VFW, "noble cause" was widely con-sidered to be a political blunder on Reagan's part. The polls showed a negative reaction to the remark, and Reagan's strategists believed it was a mistake to bring up a war that had caused so much divisiveness in America. The strategists wanted Reagan to let the past be and focus on the easier message of President Jimmy Carter's "failed leadership." They may have been right in terms of the politics of the moment,* but Reagan was on to something. His remarks about the war, well remembered by voters because Reagan had been making them for so many years, tapped into the disillusionment of Americans with their government after an accumulation of grievances: Vietnam, Watergate, domestic riots, gas lines, and the humiliation of the hostage crisis. Reagan, optimistic and resolute, was the candidate of the disillusioned. He hoped to restore the nation's military prowess and the faith of its citizens in themselves and their country. This could not be done, Reagan realized, without facing the legacy of Vietnam. There was simply no ducking the war. One could defend it, as Reagan did, or consider it a failed undertaking, as Carter and Bill Clinton did, but the war could not be dodged.

For a generation after Reagan, the Vietnam War would prove a crucible, personally and politically, for politicians with national aspirations. Clinton's 1969 letter expressing his "loathing" of the military was unearthed on the eve of the 1992 New Hampshire primary, nearly upending his candidacy. Al Gore responded to criticism of his namesake father—a Tennessee Democrat who voted to end the war and lost his U.S. Senate seat in part because of it—by enlisting in the Army. This did not inoculate him from criticism that he'd gone to Vietnam as an information specialist, not an infantryman, and had spent most of his tour stateside. John Kerry was a combat veteran of Vietnam, where he was wounded and decorated. Even so, some veterans viewed him with suspicion for his antiwar activities after he returned. This suspicion crested in the Swift Boat

---

*Reagan was supposed to make safe speeches in August to dependable constituencies and then focus on undecided voters after the formal campaign opening on Labor Day. But he was undisciplined at this stage of his candidacy: Reagan caused a flurry of controversies with unscripted comments about civil rights, creationism, and Taiwan in addition to the flap over "noble cause." Reagan capped off this disastrous stretch on Labor Day by inaccurately accusing President Carter of opening his campaign in the city that gave birth to the Ku Klux Klan. Wirthlin's polls found "noble cause" to be the most damaging of these episodes. It differed from the others in that it was a deliberate statement rather than a stray remark.

Veterans for Truth, who demonized Kerry in the 2004 presidential campaign. Democrats suffered the most from the war, and understandably so,
since Lyndon Johnson was principally responsible for U.S. involvement,
and other Democrats (Gene McCarthy, Robert Kennedy, George McGov-
ern) became its most fervent critics. But Republicans were not immune.
George H. W. Bush's running mate, Dan Quayle, and later Bush's son,
George W., were dogged by suspicions they had parlayed family connections into safe billets in the National Guard at a time that few of these
units were sent into combat.

Reagan, whose military service had not taken him beyond the boundaries of California, was alone among presidential aspirants in being politically unscathed by Vietnam, unless one counts John McCain, who spent
five and a half years in North Vietnamese prison camps. Despite the fact
that he had no combat experience, Reagan was a hero to McCain and his
fellow POWs long before he ever ran for president. Deep into his time as
a prisoner in Hanoi, McCain began hearing from more recently detained
American servicemen about the pro-veteran sympathies of a recently installed governor in Sacramento. "When I was in prison, all we had was a
cell and a loudspeaker. And, of course, I heard all the antiwar statements
by prominent Americans," McCain recalled later. "But we never heard
about this new governor of California until newer guys started getting
captured. And they began to tell us about this guy Reagan and his wife—
and their commitment to the POWs."[21]

McCain biographer Robert Timberg has credited Reagan with changing the way Americans looked at its Vietnam veterans to the point that
this altered perspective made possible McCain's political career. McCain,
who went into politics by running for Congress in 1982, said he was inspired to do so by Reagan. After the Vietnam War was over, California,
with its numerous Navy bases and Pacific ports, hosted many parties for
the returning POWs, and Ronald and Nancy Reagan attended some of
them. The governor (as did John Wayne) came to McCain's party, held in
San Francisco, and McCain came to know Reagan. "He asked me to speak
at his last National Prayer Day Breakfast as governor of the state of California, which was in 1974," McCain recalled. "He literally was responsible
for my career change. I wanted him to be president, and I wanted to be a
foot soldier in what became widely known as the Reagan Revolution.
. . . That really was one of the major motives of me wanting to serve in
Congress."[22]

In 1980, McCain preferred Reagan to fellow Navy flier George H. W. Bush, a World War II hero. He wasn't the only one. In the ensuing Republican primaries Reagan routed Bush. The furor caused by "noble cause" also gave Reagan an added boost from veterans groups in the fall campaign against President Carter. Once in office, Reagan and his secretary of defense, Caspar Weinberger, easily persuaded Congress to increase military outlays, as Carter, without receiving much credit for it, had begun to do a year earlier. But Reagan realized that he did not have (nor did he seek) a free hand in waging war. The Vietnam War cast a long shadow. Military men who had been junior officers in Vietnam were now in positions of command, especially in the Army. The lesson they had learned from Vietnam was that it was impossible to wage a long war, however well conceived the military effort, without popular support. Reagan and Weinberger recognized this, too. Indeed, Reagan's oft-repeated view that troops should not be sent into battle except in a war the United States intended to win imposed its own set of limitations. It required, for starters, an assessment of whether a war was winnable and at what cost. Such assessments usually passed through the Joint Chiefs of Staff, notable during the Reagan years for cautious recommendations about involving the United States in what the military called "small wars."

Reagan was also cautious about such involvements, more so than his first secretary of state, Al Haig, had anticipated. Haig, who lacked prior experience with Reagan, took his anti-Communist rhetoric at face value and was mindful of Reagan's campaign declaration that there would be "no more betrayal" of friends of the United States in a Reagan presidency. But Reagan was a balancer. As we have seen, his desire to defeat the Soviet empire was balanced by a sensible worry about accidental nuclear war. In Central America, balancing meant not only resisting Soviet and Cuban subversion but also recognizing the widespread resentment against the United States that existed because of past displays of military power, economic influence, and political manipulation. Reagan called the United States "the colossus of the North." He used this phrase a dozen times publicly as president, beginning with a March 3, 1981, interview with Walter Cronkite in which he promised that sending military advisers to El Salvador would not take the nation down the path of Vietnam. In that interview, Reagan said that our "southern friends . . . have memories of the great colossus of the north." The "colossus" phrase popped up again in Reagan's memoirs and in various conversations with aides. William P. Clark, a trusted Reagan troubleshooter, heard it on April 18, 1983, as Clark departed on a secret mission to obtain Venezuelan assistance in combating Cuban penetration in nearby Suriname. The United States, Reagan told him, must not behave like the colossus of the north. While the administration's deeds did not always match Reagan's words, his awareness of historic anti-American attitudes in the region introduced a note of restraint when there were proposals on the table for use of U.S. military power.

Reagan's caution was evident from the salad days of his presidency. Ten days before he took office, leftist guerrillas launched what they called a final offensive in El Salvador, where they sought to replace a democratically elected government with a pro-Communist regime. They were cheered on and to some degree supplied by the Sandinista regime in neighboring Nicaragua. The Sandinistas had seized power in 1979 after the overthrow of strongman Anastasio Somoza. Under the banner of human rights, the Carter administration had encouraged a democratic resistance in Nicaragua, contributing to Somoza's downfall. But the Sandinistas were Marxists with as little regard as Somoza for human rights. In his final days in office, Carter was embarrassed by the Sandinista-supported leftist offensive in El Salvador. He suspended U.S. aid to Nicaragua and sent $10 million in arms and equipment and nineteen military technicians to El Salvador. When Reagan took office, Haig sought to make the El Salvador situation a test case of resistance to hemisphere subversion. Reagan, to Haig's surprise, didn't want to discuss it. Haig then tried to make the case publicly, talking on television about "going to the source," by which he meant Cuba, and denouncing "Cuban adventurism."[23] This brought a rebuke from White House Chief of Staff James Baker, who, with Reagan's approval, called Haig and urged him to limit his television appearances.[24] Baker, a Texan, was a political realist. Reagan needed Democratic votes to pass his economic programs, and Baker was cultivating Democrats from districts in Texas that Reagan had carried against Carter in the election. Central America was a divisive subject in these districts, and Baker wanted no distraction from his effort to forge a bipartisan coalition on behalf of the Reagan economic plan. Whenever Central America came up during the early months of the Reagan presidency, Baker changed the subject.

Haig continued to press. He wanted to lay down "markers" that would send a clear signal to the Soviet Union and Cuba about the risks of continued subversion. He had a basis for his concern, for the Soviets had stepped up military aid to Cuba, which in turn transshipped weapons to Nicaragua and the rebels in El Salvador. (In 1981, Soviet deliveries to Cuba tripled from the previous year to 66,000 tons, the most since the Cuban missile crisis.) Haig directed preparation of a State Department "white paper" to document the flow of weapons to the El Salvadoran rebels from Cuba and Nicaragua. Reagan, at Baker's behest, delayed it for three weeks. When the paper was issued, members of Congress expressed alarm that it presaged military involvement, confirming Baker's view that Central America was a no-win situation. Frustrated, Haig became blustery in private meetings, never an effective tactic in dealing with Reagan. At one meeting, according to Reagan's closest aide, Michael Deaver, Haig responded to a comment that Cuba was the source of Central American subversion by saying, in words reminiscent of Reagan's 1965 comment about Vietnam, "Give me the word, and I'll make that island a fucking parking lot." This frightened Deaver, the White House aide closest to Reagan. "Good God, I cannot believe that I'm in the room with the president of the United States and the secretary of state's talking about bombing Cuba," Deaver remarked to William Clark, then Haig's deputy, at the end of the meeting. Clark said Haig was saying it for effect. "Well it certainly had a good effect on me," Deaver said. "It scared the shit out of me."[25] Reagan also found Haig's approach counter-productive. In his memoirs Reagan said he had been told that Haig had "shocked" members of Congress "by giving them the impression that if it were up to him, he'd deal with some of our problems in Central America with a bombing run or an invasion."[26]

Such war talk also alarmed Defense Secretary Weinberger, who worried that Congress might become skittish about the ongoing defense buildup. So Weinberger and the White House staff, often at odds, on this occasion made common cause in resisting any suggestion of U.S. military involvement in Central America. The combined weight of their opinions was crucial in the middle months of 1981, when Reagan was recuperating from the bullet wounds of the assassination attempt and focused on pushing his income-tax plan and budget through Congress. Meanwhile, William Casey, Reagan's nominee for director of central intelligence, was awaiting a Senate committee's inquiry into his financial dealings as a private citizen. On December 1, 1981, Casey received backhanded clearance from the committee, which said it had found no evidence that he had done anything wrong. This was sufficient for Casey, who that same day sought Reagan's signature on a presidential finding to funnel covert U.S. aid to rebels, known as contras, who had begun to conduct an armed resistance against the Sandinista government.

Before his clearance, Casey had been busy behind the scenes. On November 16 he had joined Thomas O. Enders, assistant secretary of state for Latin America, in making the case for the contras to Reagan at a meeting of the National Security Council. Enders was a celebrated but contentious foreign service officer—one of the "best and the brightest" who in the 1960s had favored civil rights at home and the Vietnam War abroad. Enders described the contras (an abbreviation of the Spanish word for counter-revolutionaries) as a small part of a large program aimed at preserving democracy in El Salvador and resisting Communist intervention in Central America. The contras, he said, would provide an alternative to the "empty box" of Cuban interdiction and to U.S. military intervention in the region. Their mission would be to put pressure on the Sandinista government and prod it to hold new elections.

On December 1, Reagan convened a National Security Council Planning Group to discuss the proposal. This time Casey made the presentation, asking for $19 million to train a 500-man rebel force in Argentina. His audience was unenthusiastic. Haig, the only one in the room with substantial military experience, was skeptical because he recognized that "in order for covert aid to be effective in this situation, it would have to be of a scope that by its very nature could not remain covert."[27] But he wanted something done and had been unable to prod Reagan to do anything else. Weinberger meanwhile was aware that at least one general advocated the use of special forces in Nicaragua; the secretary of defense deplored the idea and believed that covert action was preferable to any use of U.S. troops. Baker, Deaver, and White House counselor Edwin Meese went along with the plan because it *was* covert and therefore less likely (or so they believed) to become a public issue that would divert attention from the Reagan economic program. Vice President George H. W. Bush, without saying much, agreed. Reagan signed a presidential finding the same day authorizing covert aid to the contras.

It is doubtful if anyone at this meeting, Casey included, anticipated that the contras would become the touchstone of administration policy in Central America. Reagan certainly did not. Although the decision to aid the contras was disclosed by *The Washington Post* on January 14, 1982, Reagan rarely mentioned them for more than a year, in part because he was reluctant to talk publicly about a covert operation. Reagan's opponents in Congress were not similarly reluctant, and on May 3, 1983, they voted (for the first of three times) to cut off U.S. assistance to the contras. The following day, Reagan, who had foregone his midday rest and was tired, talked about the contras in a question-and-answer session with selected reporters in which he confused the issue by describing Salvadoran leftists as "the freedom fighters in El Salvador." Subsequently, Reagan began calling the contras "freedom fighters," explaining that he was expropriating a favorite phrase of Soviet propagandists. Later (in words written by his speechwriters), Reagan extravagantly called the contras the "moral equal of the founding fathers." But conservatives wanted more than analogies. They called upon Reagan to rally support for the contras in a nationally televised address. The White House staff under James Baker resisted, and Reagan was in no rush to do it. He didn't give the televised speech until May 9, 1984. By then, the contras had been introduced to the American people by their opponents, primarily liberals in Congress and also by the Sandinistas, who had the wit to hire U.S. lawyers and public relations experts. As communicators, the opponents lacked Reagan's candlepower, but by mid-1984 the administration's Central American policy had been compromised by the mining of Nicaraguan harbors, a stunt that even Richard Nixon—presumably an expert because of the mining of Haiphong Harbor—called "Mickey Mouse."[28] (The mines in the Nicaraguan harbors, while a violation of international law, were designed to scare away ships, not destroy them.) The mining cost Reagan the support of prominent Republicans, most notably Barry Goldwater, who had hitherto supported him; the Senate, by an 84–12 vote, passed a "sense of the Senate" resolution condemning it.

Bad as the relations were between the White House and Congress, they were even worse within the administration, where the contras had become a litmus test. Contra supporters called themselves "conservatives" and labeled their opponents "prags," for "pragmatists." The pragmatists regarded the conservatives as "crazies." A favorite villain of the pragmatists was Constantine Menges, the CIA national intelligence officer for Central American affairs whom Casey shipped to the National Security Council staff. Menges, known as "constant menace" to the pragmatists, was able, but obsessive on the subject of Soviet-sponsored subversion within the hemisphere. He was not alone. Conservatives were well represented on the NSC staff and among the White House speechwriters, while pragmatists dominated the upper reaches of the White House staff and the State Department. But the divisions weren't tidy. Some NSC staff members—and some CIA officials, for that matter—came to believe that the claims made for the contras were highly overblown. At the same time, some diplomats recognized the utility of the contras.

Why did the contras become such an emotional touchstone? Certainly it was not because of their military prowess. The contras at their creation were a tiny force; most of the soldiers were peasants without a military background led by officers who had served in the National Guard during the Somoza years. At its zenith in the mid-1980s, this somewhat rag-tag guerrilla army numbered at most 7,500. Colin Powell had it right when, as deputy national security adviser, he told a reporter that the contras were a highland fighting force that might exert pressure on the Sandinistas but lacked the capability of marching upon Managua.* To conservatives, however, the contras embodied the strategy of rolling back communism, a strategy they had repeatedly advocated during the Cold War as an alternative to the prevailing doctrine of containment. Menges had been making this argument since 1968, when he wrote an essay for the California think tank, the RAND Corporation, calling for what he termed the "bizarre alternative" of competing with the Soviets in launching "national liberation movements" in the Third World. In the Reagan years the contras became the embodiment of this alternative. Such arguments had little resonance at the time, when public attitudes had turned against the Vietnam War. But they received a fresh hearing in reaction to what conservatives deemed the appeasement of the Carter years. From the conservative perspective, the Soviets and their surrogates were in the early 1980s everywhere extending their reach, and nowhere more so than

---

*The reporter was Lou Cannon. Powell gave him a dispassionate analysis of the capabilities and liabilities of the contras, much as if he were addressing a well-meant student who knew little (as certainly was the case) about the military situation on the ground.

in Central America. Fidel Castro thumbed his nose at the United States. The United States had ceded control of the Panama Canal to Panama. The Salvadoran government was clinging to power, while the Mexican government made excuses for the Sandinistas. If the United States was unwilling to take direct military action, it could at least sponsor indigenous movements to resist communism. In this context, conservatives romanticized the contras as American-style revolutionaries.

Liberals held a mirror image. They had liked the sound of human rights in the Carter years, although its most tangible by-product in Central America had been the triumph of the Sandinistas. To liberals, the contras stirred memories of the bad old days of the CIA when the agency worked behind the scenes to destabilize legitimate regimes. The worst suspicions of the liberals were confirmed later in the Reagan presidency by the antics of Oliver North, a Marine officer and veteran of Vietnam attached to the NSC staff who funneled some of the proceeds from Iran arms sales to the contras. North did for the liberals what they could not have done for themselves by providing Congress with an acceptable rationale for ending aid to the contras.

North's actions were symptomatic of the Reagan administration's unsuccessful struggles to fashion a coherent policy in Central America. Coherence was doomed from the start by the unremitting battles between the conservatives and the pragmatists—and by Reagan's inability to deal with the rivalrous factions and personalities in his government. As the child of an alcoholic, Reagan recoiled from disharmony; he found something to like in all of the options presented by his quarrelsome aides but withdrew from the resolution of their arguments. To the frustration of Secretary of State George Shultz, who favored an aggressive diplomatic effort in the region, Reagan let his subordinates fight it out. This led to considerable confusion on Capitol Hill and in the region about what exactly was the "Reagan policy," since it was interpreted in different ways by the various players in the Central America melodrama. Jeane Kirkpatrick, the Reagan ambassador to the United Nations and one of these players, said it well: "Ronald Reagan was the somewhat remote sort of king who was really absent from these debates. He wasn't absent in NSPG [National Security Planning Group] meetings when he directed discussion or made decisions. He did that. But he was absent from all this [conflict among subordinates.] Just absent. Just not there."[29] The absence of the lead actor was hard on the supporting cast. Kirkpatrick, controversial in her own right, was chewed up by the power struggles, bungled initiatives, and conflicting visions that marked the administration's Central America policy. So were six national security advisers, two secretaries of state, and various ambassadors and envoys. Consensus eluded all of them. During one brief period in 1984, when the National Bipartisan Commission on Central America, known popularly as the Kissinger Commission, issued a report on the situation, it appeared that a consensus might be obtainable. The commission pleased liberals by proposing a substantial program of economic aid contingent on human rights and free elections, and it pleased conservatives by rejecting a power-sharing formula in El Salvador and by recognizing that it was in the national interest to resist the spread of communism in the region. Reagan lauded the report, but neither he nor his surrogates followed up, and nothing came of it. The revelation of the mining of the Nicaraguan harbors ended a brief truce between Congress and the administration, where infighting soon began anew, and the disclosure in November 1986 that funds from the Iran arms sales were being diverted to the contras provided fresh ammunition for Reagan's congressional critics. Although the contra share of the arms-sales loot was small, Congress eventually (in February 1988) rejected Reagan's budget request for continued U.S. aid to the contras.

The Iran-contra affair was a severe political setback for Reagan, mostly because the public was outraged at the secret dealings with Iran. White House pollster Richard Wirthlin, whose surveys went beyond raw approval numbers to explore nuances of opinion, found that a majority of Americans were opposed to the contras but had no strong feelings about them because they didn't know who they were. In fact, many Americans were also confused by the term "freedom fighters" and, even after Reagan's nationally televised speech, couldn't distinguish the contras from the Sandinistas.[30] This distanced and uninformed public view contrasted with the interest level in Washington, where the fate of the Sandinistas and the contras preoccupied both the media and the political community. Wirthlin did not find this surprising. As a general rule, he believed, Americans (with regional exceptions) had limited interest in what happened south of the border and even less interest in what occurred south of Mexico's border. They became involved in foreign policy only when the lives of Americans were at stake, as they had been in Korea and Vietnam.

Reagan at no time considered committing U.S troops to Central America beyond a few advisers. When he was asked at a news conference on February 18, 1982, under what conditions he might send troops to El Salvador, Reagan smiled and said, "Well maybe if they dropped a bomb on the White House, I might get mad."

Because there were no U.S. troops in Nicaragua, Reagan had time and running room in Central America. Time, particularly, was on his side. As the Soviet Union declined in the 1980s, so did its military aid to Cuba, reducing the latter's mischief-making capacity in the hemisphere. The Sandinistas meanwhile overplayed their hand: Their oppressive tactics ignited two small revolts to their rule within the country in addition to the contras, and two brief incursions by Nicaraguan troops into Honduras in 1986 raised regional alarms. In September of that year Costa Rican President Oscar Arias gave an eloquent speech at the United Nations in which he accused the leaders of Nicaragua of betraying a revolution that had been aimed at restoring democracy. Coming from the highly respected Arias, an opponent of the contras (and subsequent winner of the Nobel Peace Prize in 1987), these words carried weight. Shultz and U.S. special envoy Phil Habib tried to capitalize on them by launching an intensive diplomatic effort aimed at getting the Sandinistas to agree to new elections. This diplomatic initiative failed, in large part because the Reagan administration found it difficult to speak with a single voice. Conservatives feared that Shultz was selling out the contras. Reagan favored negotiation, but, as Shultz understatedly noted, "did not impose the discipline needed to allow the negotiating track to proceed in an unambiguous way."[31]

Eventually, however, momentum for democratic change in Nicaragua proved irresistible. It was an article of faith among conservatives that no Marxist state had ever allowed itself to be voted out of power, but that was just what the Sandinistas did. As with the Soviet Union, the policies that produced the regime's demise began under Reagan and ended during the presidency of George H. W. Bush. On February 25, 1990, Violetta Chamorro defeated Daniel Ortega and became president of Nicaragua.* The contras, by then disbanded, had helped determine the outcome. No

---

*At this writing Ortega is president again after having won a free election in which a former contra was his running mate.

one recognized this better than Shultz, who at a key moment during his diplomatic offensive of 1987 joined Habib in toasting the contras for the vital role they had played "in getting Ortega to the negotiating table."[32] In so doing, they accomplished the role set out for them when Reagan approved the covert aid that made the contras possible. The contras were certainly not the moral equal of the Founding Fathers, to use Reagan's most extravagant phrase in describing them. But in helping to erase the Marxist beachhead in Nicaragua, they qualified for Reagan's definition of a noble cause.

6

THE SHORT WARS
OF RONALD REAGAN

Nobility of purpose was also proclaimed by U.S. leaders engaged in military intervention to preserve democracy in Lebanon. In a tape-recorded message to the troops deployed there, the president of the United States once said, "You have served a noble cause in the best tradition of American servicemen."[1] The president who said this was not, however, Ronald Reagan, but Dwight D. Eisenhower. He was, on October 18, 1958, thanking the 9,000 U.S. Marines and soldiers who by landing on the beaches near Beirut had helped Lebanon's embattled government fend off an insurrection backed by Egypt and Syria.

A quarter century later, President Reagan would invoke Eisenhower's name as he paid tribute to the Marines that he twice sent into Lebanon. But Reagan had done almost everything differently than Eisenhower: The Marines dispatched by Reagan to Lebanon were a small and vulnerable force, many without ammunition in their weapons, who were plunged into an ill-guarded position in which adversaries held the high ground during the midst of a war. Eisenhower's intervention—an almost trivial deployment for the man who been supreme commander of Allied forces on D-Day—secured some of Lebanon's finest beaches and propped up a tottering central government. (Ike had rejected landing on the docks of Beirut with an even larger force, explaining later, "If the Lebanese army were unable to subdue the rebels when we had secured their capital and protected their government, I felt, we were backing up a government with so little popular support that we probably should not be there.")[2] The U.S. intervention was so successful that it was cited as a prime example of Eisenhower's decisiveness by his speechwriter and resident in-house critic, Emmet John Hughes.[3] Without taking casualties, Eisenhower sent a message that bolstered wavering U.S. allies throughout the world. In contrast, Reagan's second deployment was so catastrophic and resulted in such heavy casualties that it forever after influenced him against military intervention. It, too, sent a message, but an unintended one, still resonant, of the limits of American power.

Lebanon, roughly contiguous to ancient Phoenicia, is a narrow strip of mostly mountainous land 135 miles long but only 20 to 55 miles wide. With an area of slightly less than 4,000 square miles, it is one of the world's smallest sovereign states. It boasted a cosmopolitan capital, a lively culture, and the renowned American University, but it had for decades been a cockpit for violence. Modern Lebanon was a French mandate, a colony by any other name, from the end of World War I to 1945, when the French withdrew. It became independent in 1946, functioning under an unwritten agreement known as the National Pact that was intended to distribute power equally among the country's various minorities. Under this arrangement, the president of Lebanon was a Maronite Christian, the prime minister was a Sunni Muslim, and the speaker of the National Assembly a Shiite Muslim. On its face this compromise seemed favorable to the Muslims; in practice it gave a slight advantage to the Christians.* Nonetheless, this power sharing worked

---

*Though the proportion of Christians in the country steadily declined in the ensuing years because of the higher Muslim birthrate, at the time of independence Christians made up roughly half the population. Parliamentary seats at independence were distributed on the basis of a 1932 census by the French mandate, which gave the Christians a 6–5 advantage over the Muslims. This has been a consistent sore point for Muslims in Lebanon, where population estimates are of dubious accuracy. A government estimate in 1956 put the population at 1.4 million, with Christians at 54 percent and Muslims (including Druze) at 44

reasonably well for a time, and Lebanon became a functioning democracy and a principal commercial and banking center in the Middle East.

Lebanon's stability was soon threatened, however, by an influx of several hundred thousand Arab refugees from Palestine, who resettled in southern Lebanon, many in camps, in the wake of the 1948–1949 Arab-Israeli war that followed the creation of the state of Israel. Pan-Arab sentiments surged in the region in the wake of the Suez crisis of 1956; in 1958, Syria and Egypt formed the United Arab Republic (UAR) and encouraged insurrection in Lebanon. Jordan's King Hussein proposed a Jordan-Arab alliance to counter the UAR; this was forestalled by a military coup, probably organized in Egypt, in which the young Faisal II, the Hashemite king whom the British had installed as ruler of Iraq, was executed by the coup plotters along with the entire royal household. The UAR called for a revolt against Hussein, as well; it was this crisis that prompted Lebanese President Camille Chamoun to ask Eisenhower for the U.S. troops that helped preserve his government.

Despite the temporary success of the U.S. intervention, Lebanon remained beset by the militancy of the Palestinian refugees. In 1970, the Palestinian Liberation Organization (PLO) was driven out of Jordan with heavy casualties and established its headquarters in Lebanon. The PLO launched raids into northern Israel, which prompted retaliation from the Christian-led Lebanese government. By 1975, the fighting had degenerated into full-scale civil war. In 1976, as the Christians began to lose the war, Syria sent 20,000 troops into Lebanon to forestall an Israeli invasion. Over the next five years, cease-fires alternated with periodic outbreaks of fighting. Much of Lebanon was in ruins. The country was divided into warring factions of Christians, Sunnis, Shia, and Druze (an esoteric offshoot of Shia Muslims), each with its own militia. It was in this unsettled context that the Reagan administration would become involved in Lebanon.

---

percent. Muslims disputed these figures. There was no census during the civil wars of the 1970s and early 1980s. A U.S. State Department estimate in 1983 put the population at 2.6 million but included Lebanese abroad and excluded 400,000 Palestinian refugees. A 1986 CIA estimate showed a Muslim majority. According to the CIA breakdown of confessional groups, only 24 percent of the population was Christian, two-thirds of these Maronites and the remainder Greek Orthodox and Catholics.

In Central America, despite the persistent lack of discipline, Reagan and the other shapers of U.S. policy agreed on the need to resist Communist subversion, if at all possible without the use of U.S. troops. The conflicts within the administration about what to do in the region were almost entirely about means, not ends. In the Middle East, however, and especially in Lebanon, the ends themselves were in question, and Reagan's advisers were rarely on the same page. Furthermore, because Reagan tended to split the difference when trusted subordinates were at odds, his secretaries of state and defense were encouraged to continue their battles with each other rather than seek a compromise. Reagan's penchant for taking parts of one proposal and bits of another had its virtues in some circumstances; it would yield catastrophic results in Lebanon, which at the time Reagan became president was in turmoil after six years of civil war. While a weak central government struggled to exert its authority, militias representing various Muslim and Christian sects vied with each other and with the PLO for control of Beirut. In southern Lebanon, entrenched PLO forces regularly fired rocket and mortar rounds into northern Israel.

President Reagan came into office believing in the identity of U.S. and Israeli interests, a view that reflected his deep-rooted sympathy for the Jewish people and the prevailing sentiment in the Hollywood community. Reagan had cheered the creation of a Jewish state in 1948, and his opinion of Israel had changed little during his long metamorphosis from New Deal Democrat into conservative Republican. Early in his presidency, however, Reagan's pro-Israeli views were tested, first by an Israeli air strike that destroyed a French-made nuclear reactor in Iraq, and then by an Israeli air raid on Beirut that had a declared objective of wiping out the PLO's headquarters. Reagan issued a statement condemning the destruction of the nuclear reactor (on June 7, 1981) and briefly delayed a shipment of F-16 fighter planes to Israel. This was pro forma. Privately, Reagan accepted Israel's explanation that it needed to destroy Saddam Hussein's capacity to manufacture nuclear weapons. But on July 17, 1981, Reagan was appalled by the televised pictures of the bombing of Beirut, in which more than 300 civilians were killed and another 800 injured. In the wake of this attack Reagan indefinitely postponed sale of the F-16s and instructed special envoy Philip Habib to arrange a ceasefire between Israel and the PLO, which Habib accomplished with help from Saudi

Arabia. The Saudis wanted something in return, namely the purchase from the United States of sophisticated Airborne Warning and Control System (AWACS) aircraft. The Israeli lobby in Washington was on the brink of defeating the AWACS sale in the Senate when James Baker urged Reagan to make it a test of his prestige, then sky-high with Republicans in Congress. Reagan held a news conference in which he said, in an implicit warning to Israeli Prime Minister Menachem Begin: "It is not the business of other nations to make U.S. foreign policy." Reagan then met privately with forty-three Republican senators and asked them to be loyal to him instead of the pro-Israel lobby. When Senator Slade Gorton, a Republican from Washington state, protested that the lobby did not control his vote, Reagan replied, "That may be so, senator, but the world will perceive that they do."[4] The Senate (on October 28) approved the sale by a four-vote margin.

Lebanon did not reappear on Reagan's mental radar screen until the following June, as he was just beginning his first presidential trip to Europe. On June 2, 1982, Shlomo Argov, the Israeli ambassador to Great Britain, was shot and wounded in an assassination attempt by the Fatah Revolutionary Council, headed by Abu Nidal, a Palestinian terrorist who rejected any negotiation with Israel and who had broken with PLO leader Yasir Arafat. (Nidal himself would be murdered in August 1982 in an assassination believed to be ordered by Saddam Hussein.) Israel responded to the attempt on Argov's life by blowing up an ammunition depot in Beirut. The PLO then bombed towns in Galilee, prompting Israel to send its army, the Israeli Defense Forces (IDF), into Lebanon. Although Israel had warned the Reagan administration that it might send troops into Lebanon to root out the PLO, the timing of the invasion upset Reagan. "Boy, that guy makes it hard for you to be his friend,"[5] Reagan said of Begin.

It was even harder to be a friend of Israeli Defense Minister Ariel Sharon, whose swift advances in Lebanon went beyond the instructions of the Begin cabinet. Israeli forces swept up the coast toward Beirut while Israeli planes were destroying Syrian planes in the air as well as surface-to-air missiles in the Bekaa Valley. The Israeli Defense Forces were soon in sight of Beirut, to which they laid siege. In response to a message from Reagan on June 10, Begin agreed to a ceasefire, but it lasted only two days. During the next two months, Lebanon became a living hell. Late in

July, Israeli warplanes bombed Beirut for seven consecutive days. These two months were also marked by tumult within the Reagan administration as Secretary of State Haig was forced out and replaced by George Shultz. Haig's days in the Reagan cabinet were numbered before the invasion; Reagan had tired of his squabbles with the White House staff and concluded that the secretary of state "didn't even want me to be involved in setting foreign policy—he regarded it as his turf."[6] But the Israeli invasion probably hastened Haig's departure. National Security Adviser William P. Clark and Defense Secretary Caspar Weinberger believed that Begin and Sharon had been deceptive about Israel's intentions in Lebanon and that Haig had been taken in by them. Whether or not that was true, Haig at best seemed clueless about Israeli intentions. During Reagan's European trip early in the invasion, Haig told the traveling press corps that the Israelis would stop at the Litani River, but Israeli troops barely paused there. Subsequently, he said the Israelis would halt far short of Beirut. These inaccurate predictions contributed to the president's loss of confidence in his secretary of state.

On Monday, June 14, two days after returning from Europe, Reagan called Haig into his office and rebuked him for sending instructions on his own to Habib, who was shuttling among Middle East capitals in an effort to stop the fighting in Lebanon. Haig responded that unless Reagan was willing to make changes to "restore unity and coherence to his foreign policy" he should get another secretary of state.[7] Reagan was eager to make a change, but he wanted the onus on Haig. The process of ousting him took twelve days, during which Reagan indirectly rebuked his secretary of state again by rejecting his conciliatory proposal (and endorsing Clark's hard-line plan) for dealing with European firms that were helping the Soviet Union construct a gas pipeline to Europe. On June 24, in a final meeting with Reagan at the White House, Haig presented a "bill of particulars" describing what he saw as interference in his conduct of foreign affairs. He brought with him a letter of resignation that he held in his hand but never gave the president. No matter. Reagan's staff had informed him that Haig was coming in to resign, and that was good enough for him. Haig's bill of particulars accused Clark of interference and called upon Reagan to reduce Clark's authority, which the president had no intention of doing. Besides, Reagan had already decided on a replacement. On June 25, he had Clark track down Shultz in London, where Reagan offered him the job over the phone. Shultz accepted. Reagan went to the White House briefing room and issued a statement accepting Haig's resignation and announcing the Shultz appointment.[8] "This has been a heavy load," Reagan confided to his diary.[9]

Shultz seemed an inspired choice. He was as principled as Haig but more broad-gauged and more experienced in dealing with the whims of presidents and the contending passions of their White House entourages. He had held three positions, two of cabinet rank, in the Nixon administration, and he had mastered the art of deferring to presidential prerogatives without giving ground on matters of substance. "It's the president's agenda," he often said, even when he was trying to change it. Shultz also had the benefit, as Haig never did, of having allies on the White House staff, in Baker and especially Deaver, who smoothed Shultz's path with Nancy Reagan. But Shultz's appointment did not bring the harmony Reagan sought. At the time Reagan asked him to become secretary of state, Shultz was president of Bechtel, a global construction firm at which Weinberger had worked as special counsel. Shultz and Weinberger had also both served in the Nixon administration. Whether at Bechtel or in the White House, they had differed on many issues, often quarreling. Shultz, an economist versed in labor relations, had preferred to settle legal claims against Bechtel. Weinberger, a lawyer with an extensive political background, believed that huge settlements encouraged other lawsuits, "some of which would be virtually legal blackmail."[10] When Shultz was director and Weinberger deputy director of the Office of Management and Budget in the Nixon administration, they had clashed so often that Frank Carlucci, the next in line at the agency, once said to them in exasperation, "For God's sake, can't you guys talk sensibly to each other?"[11] The answer was no. Reagan was unaware of the Shultz-Weinberger history and wrongly assumed he had put cabinet wrangling behind him by removing Haig. Instead, the discord grew worse. It was this sort of destructive rivalry that Andrew Card would have in mind two decades later when he warned presidential aides that in the Bush White House there were to be no factions, that everyone was a George W. Bush loyalist—period. Reagan, who took loyalty for granted and treated his subordinates as grown-ups, issued no such instruction. Nevertheless, he soon became disheartened by the frequent (and often petty) quarrels between Shultz and Weinberger;

but he was not about to have a third secretary of state, and he valued Weinberger too much to send him packing.[12]

As Shultz learned the ropes at the State Department, the war continued unabated in Lebanon. The carnage caused by Israeli bombings of Beirut was regularly highlighted on the nightly news, causing reactions within the Reagan administration that cut across the usual conservative-pragmatist divisions. The speechwriters were appalled; one of them, Landon Parvin, refused to write remarks for Reagan when Begin visited the White House for a chilly visit in June. On August 12, after Israeli planes had bombed Beirut for eleven consecutive hours, Deaver told Reagan he couldn't continue to be part of "the killing of children" and intended to resign.[13] Shultz and Clark had been sending similar signals to Reagan, albeit more diplomatically. Reagan, also disgusted at the bombings, took the unusual step of calling Begin. "Menachem, this is a holocaust," he told him.[14] In a voice that the aide who monitored the conversation said was "dripping with sarcasm," Begin replied: "Mr. President, I think I know what a holocaust is."[15] But Reagan persisted. Begin called back twenty minutes later to say he had given the order to stop the bombings. After he hung up the phone, Reagan said to Deaver, "I didn't know I had that kind of power."[16]

All went well in Lebanon for a time after this phone call. On August 14, Syria offered to withdraw its troops and the PLO fighters from Beirut. The following day, the Israeli cabinet accepted Habib's plan for a multinational force to oversee the PLO expulsion. French paratroopers and Italian troops arrived in Lebanon. On August 25, two days after the election of Christian Phalangist leader (and secret CIA "asset") Bashir Gemayel as president of Lebanon, 800 U.S. Marines joined the French and Italian military contingents. The Marines were interposed between 30,000 Israeli troops and 15,000 Syrian and PLO fighters, a situation that caused the Joint Chiefs misgivings. But there was no violence. The PLO fighters were evacuated, and the Syrians left West Beirut. On September 1, Reagan interrupted his summer vacation in California to make a televised speech, largely crafted by Shultz, in which he said that the war in Lebanon, "tragic as it was," had provided a new opportunity for Middle East peace. Reagan proposed to give Palestine autonomy "in association with Jordan" while requiring Israel to forfeit most of the territory it had acquired in the 1967 Arab-Israeli War. King Hussein of Jordan hailed the speech as the "most courageous stand taken by an administration since 1956."

Reagan's speech had referred to the Lebanon war in the past tense, a point not lost on Weinberger and General John Vessey, chairman of the Joint Chiefs. They pressed for swift withdrawal of the Marines, contending they had accomplished their mission of overseeing the PLO evacuation. Now it was the turn of Shultz and Habib to have misgivings. But Reagan agreed with Weinberger and his military advisers, and on September 10 the Marines were loaded onto the ships that had brought them to Lebanon. Italian and French forces were also withdrawn. On September 14, a massive bomb rocked the office of the Phalangist Party in East Beirut, killing President-elect Gemayel. The following day, Israeli forces violated the agreement under which the PLO had been evacuated and entered West Beirut, claiming that this would prevent revenge killings of Palestinian civilians by Gemayel's militia. Instead, the militia entered Palestinian refugee camps at Sabra and Shatilla over the next two days and slaughtered more than 700 people, including at least three dozen women and children.

Reagan, horrified, spent the weekend of September 18–19 closeted in the family quarters of the White House, watching on television the gruesome reports of the Sabra-Shatilla killings and reading his briefing papers. Yasir Arafat was furious; Habib had promised him that Israeli forces would not reenter Beirut. Shultz, Habib, and the National Security Council staff contended that the Sabra-Shatilla killings were made possible by the withdrawal of the multinational force. (The entrance to the camps had been guarded by the Italian military contingent.) Robert C. (Bud) McFarlane, at the time Clark's deputy, joined Shultz in advocating a new multinational force. In its most expansive form, this force would have consisted of three U.S. and two French divisions that supposedly could have forced withdrawal of both the Israelis and the Syrians from Lebanon. Weinberger opposed deploying any U.S. forces. So did General Vessey, who told Reagan that Lebanon was the "wrong place" for U.S. troops to be engaged.[17] When it became evident to Weinberger and the chiefs that Reagan was leaning toward sending in the Marines, they asked that the State Department first obtain an agreement that foreign forces would be withdrawn from Lebanon. Shultz thought this put the cart before the horse, since it was unlikely the Syrians or Israelis would pull back without a credible threat of U.S. military power.

Two decades later, President George W. Bush would be accused of paying insufficient attention to adverse views in reaching a single-minded decision to invade Iraq. When it came to redeploying the Marines in Lebanon, Reagan suffered from a surfeit of conflicting advice. His decision drew from all the proposals of his advisers and satisfied none of them. With Sabra-Shatilla as the tipping point, he agreed to send the Marines back into Lebanon, which pleased Shultz and McFarlane, but he rejected out of hand their proposal to deploy a major military force. Instead, he sent into Beirut the 24th Marine Amphibious Unit, some 1,200 strong and with only five tanks and six howitzers. They would become part of a new multinational force that included French and Italian troops and a few British observers. The chiefs were unhappy with even this limited deployment. "I don't think anybody had any expectation we could turn it around [in Lebanon],"[18] said Vessey, a hardened warrior who had received a battlefield commission at Anzio in World War II and won the Distinguished Service Cross in Vietnam. The Marines were assigned to the Beirut International Airport along the sea at the southern end of the city. Their commander also wanted to occupy the hills east of the airport but was not allowed to do so for diplomatic reasons. If the Marines held this high ground, convoys resupplying Israeli troops would have to pass through U.S. lines, making it appear as if the Marines and the Israelis were working together.

Reagan announced the new deployment in a televised speech on September 20, referring to the "heartrending" killings in the refugee camps and calling for "restoration of a strong and central government" in Lebanon and the removal of all foreign forces. He said the multinational force would stay in Lebanon for a "limited period of time," which Vessey understood to be sixty days—about as long as the Eisenhower-sent troops had spent there in 1958—and this was the figure used by Vessey in communiqués to European commanders who were providing men and material for the deployment. "We figured that once we got over our feeling of guilt and a little bit of law and order was established, the Marines would be withdrawn," Vessey said.[19]

And so began more than a year of living dangerously in Lebanon. The first signs were positive. Bashir Gemayel's older brother Amin was unanimously elected president of Lebanon by a parliament usually divided along religious lines. Public opinion within Israel turned against the Begin government in disgust over Sabra-Shatilla and increasing concern about Israeli casualties in Lebanon. Sharon resigned in February 1983 after an Israeli commission found him "personally responsible" for the killings in the refugee camps. A deceptive quiet descended upon Lebanon as the Soviet Union resupplied Syria with weapons and equipment, including surface-to-air missiles to replace the ones that had been destroyed by the Israelis.

The quiet ended on April 18, 1983, when a delivery van loaded with explosives detonated on the grounds of the U.S. embassy on Beirut's waterfront. The explosion killed sixty-three people, including seventeen Americans, one of them Robert C. Ames, the chief CIA analyst of Middle Eastern affairs. His death left a void in intelligence gathering at a time when it was particularly needed. When the bodies of the Americans were returned to Andrews Air Force Base, Reagan gave an emotional speech in which he said the United States would fail the murdered Americans by withdrawing. In the wake of the attack, Shultz renewed his diplomacy, obtaining an accord between Israel and Lebanon, known as the May 17 agreement, to withdraw foreign troops from the country. The CIA and Weinberger thought the agreement was a non-starter because Syria, which objected to the strengthening of a Christian government in Lebanon, had not been consulted. "It was nothing, not even an agreement," Weinberger said scornfully. "It gave the Syrians a veto power, and they exercised it."[20]

Weinberger continued to press for withdrawal of the Marines, but Reagan, convinced by Shultz and his own rhetoric that peace and stability were just around the corner, paid little attention to the unraveling of the precarious consensus in Lebanon. President Amin Gemayel, a weaker leader than his slain brother, was distrusted by the various Muslim factions in parliament. The Muslims who had welcomed back the Marines after the Sabra-Shatilla massacres now saw them as a prop for the Gemayel government. The Syrians were also active, arming and backing groups opposed to the government. One of these groups, the Druze, proclaimed a National Liberation Front and battled the Gemayel militia and the Lebanese Army, which was supported by the U.S. government and bolstered by Marine patrols. Inexorably, as would happen in even greater measure with the U.S. forces sent to Iraq by George W. Bush, the Americans were gradually caught up in a civil war in a foreign land where few U.S. troops knew the terrain, the language, or the history of the country they were sent to pacify. In June, the Druze shelled the Beirut airport, temporarily closing it and wounding three Marines. The Israelis mean-while had bowed to public opinion at home and decided to evacuate the Chouf Mountains east of Beirut to south of the Awali River. This de-prived the Marines of the high ground and made them the principal tar-gets of the Druze and various Shiite militia groups. Bud McFarlane, who had replaced Habib in Lebanon, urged that U.S. Marines be allowed to accompany the Lebanese Army and occupy the positions that had been held by the departing Israeli forces. He sent an urgent message to Clark at the White House, which became known as "the-sky-is-falling cable," saying that the Lebanese Army was in danger of being overrun. At the recommendation of Clark and against the advice of Weinberger, Reagan authorized artillery bombardment and air strikes in support of the Lebanese Army. Once again, Reagan gave something to everyone. In a concession to Weinberger and the chiefs, the presidential order said that nothing in the authorization "shall be construed as changing the mission for the U.S. multinational force."

And what was this mission? It was hazily defined in the deployment order as establishing a "presence" for the purpose of assisting the Lebanese armed forces "to carry out their responsibilities in the Beirut area." This was so vague that Weinberger said it amounted to no mission at all. The mission statement instructed the Marines, who were to use their weapons only in self-defense, to "occupy and secure" positions along a designated line from south of the Beirut International Airport to the presidential palace. What they were to do in these positions wasn't clear, and Shultz, McFarlane, Clark, Weinberger, Vessey, and the military com-manders on the ground had varying interpretations of the mission state-ment. After receiving the presidential order allowing shelling of the Druze positions to help the Lebanese Army, Col. Timothy Geraghty, bat-talion commander of the 24th Marine Amphibious Unit at the Beirut air-port, delayed using it because he feared it would transform the Marines from peacekeepers into full-scale participants in the war. A week later, however, McFarlane and commanders of the 8th Lebanese Brigade per-suaded Geraghty that the Lebanese forces were in danger of being driven out of the market town of Souk al Garb with devastating consequences for the Lebanese Army. Geraghty then gave the order to bomb Druze-held positions on the ridgeline above the town.

Geraghty's fears were soon realized. U.S. Marines on patrol became targets, producing a modification in the rules of engagement to allow the Marines to actively engage the snipers who were shooting at them. Reagan and his advisers should have realized at this point that the Marines were being steadily drawn into the war. Instead, they became preoccupied by reports in *The Washington Post* and on NBC News that the administration had changed the rules of engagement.[21] Since these reports were based on classified information, CIA director William Casey, White House counselor Ed Meese, and Clark saw an opportunity to expose "leakers," whom they assumed to be Baker and Deaver or those who worked for them. Baker and Deaver in turn became accusative of their accusers. At Clark's urging, Attorney General William French Smith was brought into the fray, and he and Meese persuaded Reagan to sign an order authorizing polygraph tests for cabinet officials. Baker and Shultz convinced Reagan to rescind this order. (Shultz famously said that if he were asked to take a polygraph test he would do it only once, meaning that he would then resign.) No "leakers" were ever identified. The episode had a comic-opera aspect, and it distracted Reagan at a time when Marines were being picked off one by one by sniper fire. Congress refocused attention on Lebanon by trying to invoke the 1973 War Powers Resolution, which would have required the president to remove U.S. forces within ninety days. Reagan opposed it and was rescued in the Democratic-controlled House by Speaker Thomas P. (Tip) O'Neill, who had doubts about the new deployment but did not want to undermine the Marines in the field. After winning close votes in both houses of Congress that allowed deployment of the multinational force for another eighteen months, Reagan linked Lebanon to the global struggle against communism. In a radio speech from Camp David on October 8, he said, "Can the United States or the free world stand by and see the Middle East incorporated into the Soviet bloc?" Eight days later, after a sixth Marine was killed by sniper fire, Reagan was asked by a reporter why he was allowing Marines to die in Lebanon. "Because I think it is vitally important to the security of the United States and the Western world that we do everything we can to further the peace process in the Middle East," the president replied.[22]

The Marines were now sitting ducks in Lebanon, pinned down at Beirut International Airport with the Israelis gone and Muslim militia occupying the surrounding high ground. Snipers were not the principal menace. U.S. intelligence agencies had viewed terrorism as a clear and present danger in Lebanon as early as 1982 and especially after the destruction of the U.S. embassy in April. Between May and October these agencies received more than a hundred warnings of prospective car-bomb attacks. But no one in the Reagan administration connected the dots between the destruction of the embassy and the vulnerability of the Marines at the airport. No one talked of the worst-case scenario of this precarious deployment.

The worst case arrived at 6:22 A.M. on Sunday, October 23, 1983, when a grinning young man with a bushy mustache drove a yellow stake-bed Mercedes truck through the parking lot of the four-story headquarters building where members of the 1st Battalion, 8th Marine Regiment, were sleeping. In the words of the official report: "The truck drove over the barbed and concertina wire obstacle, passed between two Marine guard posts without being engaged by fire, entered an open gate, passed around one sewer pipe barrier and between two others, flattened the Sergeant of the Guard's sandbagged booth at the building's entrance, penetrated the lobby of the building and detonated while the majority of the occupants slept. The force of the explosion ripped the building from its foundation. The building then imploded upon itself. Almost all the occupants were crushed or trapped inside the wreckage."[23]

Of the 350 servicemen in the building, most of them Marines, 346 were casualties. The death toll, including those who were extricated from the wreckage and later died, was 241, the worst loss of U.S. troops in any single incident since the battle of Iwo Jima in World War II. Many survivors were permanently injured. FBI experts determined that the bomb had exploded with the force of 12,000 pounds of TNT, producing what was then the largest non-nuclear explosion on record. The bombing had been part of a coordinated attack aimed at driving the multinational force from Lebanon. Soon after it occurred, another bomb exploded in West Beirut, two miles from the Marine headquarters. It brought down a nine-story building, killing fifty-eight French paratroopers.

Reagan was asleep in the master suite of the Eisenhower Cottage at the Augusta National Golf Club, where he was spending the weekend, when the attacks took place. He was awakened at 2:27 A.M. by McFarlane, now his national security adviser,* who told him there had been a "terrible attack" on the Marines. Years later, Reagan would remember the calamity as the "saddest day of my presidency, perhaps the saddest day of my life."[24] In retrospect, he mostly blamed himself, saying, "Part of it was my idea—a good part of it."[25] McFarlane, a Korean War combat veteran who had made the case that the Marines should remain in Lebanon and had visited the Marines in Beirut, was inconsolable. Shultz, a Marine combat veteran of World War II, who had been the most outspoken advocate of the deployment, was also shaken. At one meeting of the National Security Council after the Beirut bombing, he said, "If I ever say send in the Marines again, somebody shoot me."[26]

Despite their anguish, however, Reagan and Shultz—and to a lesser degree McFarlane—opposed withdrawal of the Marines after the catastrophe at the Beirut airport. Reagan's sorrow soon turned to anger. He denounced the suicide bombing as a "despicable act" that demonstrated the "bestial nature" of those who would drive the United States out of the region. "We must be more determined than ever that they cannot take over that vital and strategic part of the earth," he said.[27] This was pure Shultz, who repeatedly referred to Lebanon as if it were synonymous with the entire Middle East. Testifying to Congress the day after the suicide bombing, Shultz said: "To ask why Lebanon is important is to ask why the Middle East is important—because the answer is the same." In a nationally televised address from the Oval Office three days later, Reagan asserted that the region was of "strategic importance" and claimed that the Marines had been targeted because they had been successful in doing

---

*Reagan had more national security advisers than any other president. McFarlane was third of six, following Richard Allen and Clark and preceding John Poindexter, Frank Carlucci, and Colin Powell. McFarlane inherited the post after conservatives, including Clark, persuaded Reagan to block a plan that would have made James Baker national security adviser with Mike Deaver becoming White House chief of staff. Clark was forced out of the national security job after a running battle with Shultz, who had the crucial support of First Lady Nancy Reagan. But Reagan always found a place for Clark, on whom he had relied since the early days of his governorship. In this case, Clark became a convenient replacement for Interior Secretary James G. Watt, who was forced to resign after making statements offensive to handicapped persons and minority groups.

what they had been sent to do: "to help bring peace to Lebanon and stability to the Middle East." Reagan had come full circle from Vietnam, using military forces for diplomatic purposes in a war in which there was no talk of victory. But unlike Vietnam, the war in Lebanon had never been supported by the president's generals or by his secretary of defense.

Reagan's attention—and that of his generals—was soon diverted from Lebanon to the small island nation of Grenada, where the United States would wage a short and winnable small war. Grenada (examined later in this chapter) gave Reagan political running room, but it did not solve the problem of Lebanon, where the surviving Marines remained with an uncertain mission and in too few numbers to affect the outcome. Reagan's congressional critics pressed the point. On the *Today* show, Senator Ernest Hollings, a South Carolina Democrat, said of the Marines: "They do not have a mission. If they were put there to fight, there are too few. If they were put there to die, they are too many." The phrasing was demagogic—neither Reagan nor anyone in his administration had intended for the Marines "to die"—but the observation was accurate. The Marines, even after they were reinforced to make up for their losses, were unable to play an active role in Lebanon. To protect them from another suicide bomber, they were dispersed in underground bunkers and had virtually no contact with anyone in Beirut.

The next move was up to Weinberger and Vessey, both of whom second-guessed themselves over the bombing. Weinberger told Colin Powell, his military deputy (who also opposed the second deployment), that he wished he had been "more persuasive with the president."[28] Vessey told David C. Martin and John Walcott, authors of the definitive book on terrorism during the Reagan years: "None of us marched in and told the president that the United States is going to face disaster if the Marines didn't withdraw."[29] In the wake of the bombing, Weinberger and Vessey were determined to extricate the surviving Marines, but first they had to deal with Reagan's public promise to retaliate against the instigators of the suicide bombing. The options were limited. Weinberger had criticized the Israelis for retaliations that killed civilians and opposed any similar U.S. action. Reagan, remembering the Israeli bombings of Beirut, agreed. He wanted a strictly military target. The chiefs, after much debate, reluctantly settled upon the Sheik Abdullah barracks in Baalbeck, the headquarters of the Iranian Revolutionary Guards and their Shiite allies in Lebanon. This fit the criteria of avoiding civilian casualties and striking at the suspected perpetrators of the suicide bombing, for which the CIA blamed Iran and Syria. In the opinion of Schulz and Don Rumsfeld, who had replaced McFarlane as the negotiator in Lebanon, an air strike would also serve as a warning to Syria, which had been firing on U.S. reconnaissance planes. Vessey raised a caution flag, warning that U.S. planes could be lost to the Syrian anti-aircraft batteries that ringed Baalbeck. When the raid was carried out on December 4 from the carriers *Independence* and *Kennedy,* the Syrians shot down two A-6 bombers, killing one U.S. pilot and capturing another who was later released. At the loss of two gun emplacements and a radar shed, the Syrians had scored a propaganda coup.

With this embarrassing retaliation out of the way, Weinberger turned his full attention to withdrawing the Marines. He had to contend with Reagan's reluctance to pull out under pressure and with Shultz's determination to maintain a U.S. military presence to support the fragile Lebanese government. Weinberger's relationship with the president went back a long way—he had been finance director in the Reagan governorship—and he knew that appearances mattered to Reagan. With this in mind, Weinberger began talking about "redeployment" instead of "withdrawal." It was a distinction without a difference; Weinberger proposed to redeploy the Marines on ships that would then sail away from Lebanon, never to return.

Weinberger's first weapon in his campaign to extricate the Marines was a Defense Department inquiry into the October 23 bombing. He handpicked Admiral Robert Long, who had a reputation for integrity and candor, to head the commission of inquiry. Long proved equal to his reputation, producing a thorough report that was in Weinberger's view too critical of the Marine commanders on the ground, Col. Timothy Geraghty and Lt. Col. Howard Gerlach, who had suffered a broken neck and lost the use of his legs in the bombing. The Long Commission faulted the officers for security breaches; Weinberger thought they had done their best with an impossible job. But the report also did what Weinberger had most hoped, which was to question the premises of the deployment. In what amounted to a slap at Reagan and Shultz, the Long report found that "as progress toward a diplomatic solution slowed," the administration had relied on military options without paying attention to changing political conditions in Lebanon or the threat of terrorism. "It was contemplated from the outset that [the Marines] would operate in a relatively benign environment," the report said.[30]

The report was delivered to Reagan on Friday, December 23. On December 24, McFarlane held an interdepartmental meeting at the White House in which he floated a proposal (by Dennis Ross, a Pentagon official) to move the Marines to a safer place, such as Christian East Beirut, while the United States tried to prod concessions from Syrian President Hafez Assad in return for withdrawal. The participants agreed to bring back recommendations from their departments at a follow-up meeting. It never took place. When Weinberger heard about McFarlane's meeting from Assistant Defense Secretary Richard Armitage, he canceled participation of the Defense Department in the entire exercise. He wanted the Marines out, not moved around in Lebanon.

Weinberger acquired allies during the holiday season. Democrats were already calling for a pullout, and Republican members of Congress, home for a long recess, were also hearing withdrawal sentiments from their constituents. So, too, was White House Chief of Staff James Baker, who was thinking ahead to the 1984 presidential campaign and knew that Lebanon would be an issue unless the Marines were withdrawn.* On November 30, 1983, *The Washington Post* reported that Baker had joined Weinberger in urging withdrawal from Lebanon. Baker also conferred with Senate Majority Leader Howard Baker of Tennessee, who had never been enthusiastic about the Lebanon intervention and saw its continuance as a threat to Republican control of the Senate. James Baker kept Reagan aware of the restiveness in Republican congressional ranks and quietly kept up the pressure inside the White House. McFarlane recalled that Baker questioned him: "Gently but persistently, Jim began to say,

---

*Reagan had high approval ratings before and after the suicide bombing in Beirut, but the published public opinion polls didn't tell the full story. White House pollster Richard Wirthlin was in the field when the bombing occurred, and his survey found a precipitous decline in Reagan's approval rating the day afterward. The ratings rebounded after the Grenada invasion two days later. "Most of the polls that came in after Grenada found it impossible to disentangle the two events," Wirthlin said. "Because of when we were polling we were able to isolate them." The poll findings reinforced Baker's view that Lebanon was a potential campaign liability.

'Bud, what is the light at the end of the tunnel here?' And I had to tell him, 'There really isn't any.'"[31]

Shultz and the president were the remaining holdouts. On January 25, 1984, two days after Congress returned from its recess, Shultz testified before the Senate Foreign Relations Committee and decried the "pullout fever" in Washington, saying it would be devastating to "cut and run." This phrasing was echoed by Reagan in his radio speech from Camp David on February 4, when he said there was "no reason to turn our backs and cut and run. If we do, we'll be sending one signal to terrorists everywhere. They can gain by waging war against innocent people."

But events on the ground in Lebanon discredited the Shultz-Reagan assertions even as they spoke. The United States had placed its reliance on the weak reeds of the Lebanese Army and the Gemayel government, both of which were fast disintegrating. On February 2, the Lebanese Army shot and killed a Shiite militiaman in retaliation for the sniper deaths of two soldiers. Enraged Shiite fighters took to the streets and overran two army posts. The army responded with shellfire. On February 4, Nabih Berri, leader of the leading Shiite militia group, urged Muslims to resign from the government and Muslim members of the army to lay down their arms. On February 5, the Gemayel government collapsed, and on February 6, Shiite and Druze militiamen took control of Beirut while the Lebanese Army stayed in its barracks.

Reagan left Washington on February 6 for a sentimental journey to his alma mater, Eureka College in Illinois. He then flew on to Las Vegas for two speeches and then to California for a vacation at his Santa Barbara–area ranch. Shultz departed for a long-planned trip to South America and Central America. Weinberger seized the moment. On Tuesday, February 7, while Reagan was speaking in Las Vegas and Shultz was flying to Grenada, Weinberger made the case for getting the Marines out of Lebanon to a National Security Planning Group meeting. It was presided over by a hitherto invisible ally, Vice President George H. W. Bush, who met beforehand with James Baker, his former campaign manager and future secretary of state. Baker and Bush were of one mind on Lebanon—and in agreement with Weinberger. Bush has always been close-mouthed about the key role he played in the decision to quit Lebanon, but we have a sense of it from a caustic comment by Shultz, who wrote in his memoirs that the vice president was "panicked" to get out of Lebanon.[32] This is unfair: Bush, like Shultz and Weinberger a combat veteran of World War II, was consistently reluctant to gamble with the lives of U.S. troops, as he demonstrated when he became president. He was also a "realist," a word that would be used pejoratively by neoconservatives a generation later against critics of the Iraq War. Realism in 1984 meant getting out of Lebanon. This was recognized by everyone at the NSPG meeting on February 7 except for Undersecretary of State Lawrence Eagleburger, who was sitting in for Shultz. His was the only voice to oppose withdrawal of the Marines.

Later, McFarlane would say that the decision to withdraw from Lebanon was made at this NSPG meeting even though it was phrased as a recommendation to Reagan. Bush conveyed the sentiments of the group to the president, who was by then on a secure phone in a Las Vegas airport hangar. At Weinberger's suggestion, Bush described the withdrawal as redeployment and said the United States would continue to support the fallen government of Lebanon by naval gunfire and air support. Reagan laconically agreed. The White House statement distributed to reporters traveling with the president emphasized the gunfire and the air support and described the withdrawal backhandedly as a request to Weinberger to submit "a plan for redeployment of the Marines from Beirut Airport to their ships offshore." Bush and McFarlane informed a travel-weary Shultz of the decision when he reached Grenada that night. To Rumsfeld fell the harder task, at midnight Lebanon time, of breaking the bad news to Gemayel in the basement of his bombed-out presidential palace.

The Marines began their pullout to awaiting ships on February 25 and completed it by month's end. They had lost 264 men in the 18-month deployment, most of them in the October 23 attack. (The French, who lost 77 men, stayed until March, and departed, flags flying, in a display of military brio.) As the Americans pulled out, the battleship *New Jersey* fired 288 shells from its 16-inch guns toward Syrian positions in the Lebanese hillsides. Without forward observers this deadly barrage was inevitably inaccurate, and it killed an undetermined number of Shiite civilians without inflicting any military damage. The U.S. defense attaché in Beirut called it "senseless shelling." This unnecessary barrage would come back to haunt the Reagan administration in June 1985 when TWA Flight 847 was hijacked and a U.S. Navy diver murdered. The hijackers shouted "Marines" and "New Jersey" as they boarded the plane.

The idea of sending the battleship *New Jersey* to Lebanese waters had arisen with the National Security Council staff, but Weinberger had ordered it there, and much of the blame for this shelling rests on him, ironically so because he was normally sensitive about avoiding civilian casualties. But Weinberger was frustrated by his inability to persuade the president that the Marines were in danger, and, mindful of Reagan's desire not to "cut and run," he wanted to provide an alternative to total defeat. The *New Jersey* barrage was the naval gunfire that he had promised at the NSPG meeting and that had been incorporated into the statement given the press after Reagan signed off on withdrawal. Reagan was not bloodthirsty either, but he wanted a show of force against Syria and didn't understand how inaccurate a 2,000-pound shell could be at a distance of twenty miles in the absence of forward observers. It was one more part of the puzzle that eluded him. Lebanon was Reagan's great failure, far costlier in terms of casualties and consequences than the Iran-contra affair. It was, to be sure, a failure of good intentions, born of misunderstanding about Lebanon's importance to the United States. McFarlane, who had supported a larger deployment than Reagan was willing to authorize, said it best. "Ronald Reagan called Lebanon vital to United States national security interests, which, in any context, it is not," McFarlane said. "If Lebanon disappeared, it wouldn't affect the United States' security interests very much."[33]

Terrorism by Muslim militants against the United States was in its infancy in the Reagan years. From the perspective of a nation hardened by the September 11, 2001, terrorist attacks in New York City and Washington, some of the reactions to the suicide bombing at the Beirut airport seem naive. Reagan, for instance, called the perpetrators of the crime "cowards," hardly the right description of a suicide bomber (and the precise misnomer George W. Bush would repeat after 9/11), and complained that they had unfairly targeted innocent civilians. (He put the Marines in the category of the innocents since they were in Lebanon to keep the peace.) Two decades later, President George W. Bush and Vice President Dick Cheney would assert that the Lebanon attack had ushered in an era of terrorism that extended in a straight line from 9/11 through the bombing of the World Trade Center and the killing of U.S. soldiers in Mogadishu in 1993, the killings at Khobar Towers in 1996, the attack on U.S. embassies in Kenya and Tanzania in 1998, and the attack on the USS *Cole* in 2000. The common thread of these assaults, Cheney told a pro-Israeli conference in 2006, was the belief of terrorists that "we would not hit back hard enough." Bush made this point more compactly as early as September 7, 2003, saying in a televised address to the nation: "In the past, the terrorists have cited the examples of Beirut and Somalia, claiming that if you inflict harm on Americans, we will run from a challenge." The implication was that Reagan's withdrawal from Lebanon had emboldened terrorists. Bush and Cheney implicitly contrasted the earlier withdrawals with their determination to remain in Iraq.

The Bush-Cheney timeline of terrorism begs the important question of whether staying in Iraq (or going to Iraq) was an effective way to meet the challenge they described. That aside, many analysts have found in Lebanon a template for examining the U.S. entanglement in Iraq. National identity is an issue in both cases. In Iraq, this identity is historically recent; Britain created Iraq out of three pieces of the former Ottoman Empire after World War I. Lebanon has an ancient lineage but has long been dominated by Syria, which considers it a province; Syria does not even show Lebanon as independent on its maps. Shiite Muslims and their militias play a crucial role in Lebanon, where they are a minority that has been historically underrepresented in the government; in Iraq, where they are a majority, they were cruelly repressed by Saddam Hussein. In both countries the principal loyalties of the people are tribal or religious (confessional groups, in the language of Lebanon). The central government in Lebanon was and remains weak. It was weaker still in Iraq after Saddam was deposed. The army in Lebanon reflected the impotence of the government. This foreshadowed what would happen in Iraq two decades later when U.S. policy-makers attempted to reinstate the Iraqi military as a stabilizing national influence, failing to comprehend that the ineptness of the armed forces inevitably reflected the ineffectual nature of the central government in Baghdad. In times of crisis soldiers were more receptive to appeals from confessional groups than to the orders given by their officers. More than any other factor, the collapse of the Lebanese Army in the face of pressure from the Shiite and Druze militias doomed the U.S. intervention in Lebanon.

If an analogy is defined as a comparison in which essential similarities outweigh essential differences, the link between Reagan's deployment in Lebanon and George W. Bush's invasion of Iraq fails the test. On scale alone, it is not comparable: Lebanon is the size of Connecticut with a population of 3.5 million people, and Iraq is the size of California with a population of more than 26 million. Lebanon, for all its fratricidal factionalism, was and remains a parliamentary democracy, albeit a shaky one, and unlike Iraq, had not been brutalized by decades of murderous dictatorship. The U.S. interventions had opposite purposes. Reagan sent the lightly armed Marines into Lebanon neither to fight nor to occupy but to prevent killings of civilians and to promote diplomatic efforts to restore peace. The peacekeeping aspect of the ill-defined Lebanese mission was so exaggerated that the Marine sentries did not have ammunition in their weapons when the suicide bomber drove his bomb-laden truck into their headquarters.* U.S. actions in Lebanon caused no civilian casualties until the *New Jersey* bombardment, which occurred as the Marines withdrew; at this writing, upwards of 80,000 civilians have died in the war in Iraq. And, unlike the Iraq War, the Lebanon intervention had no discernible impact on U.S. politics. With the Marines withdrawn and the U.S. economy booming, Reagan was reelected in 1984 in one of the huge landslides of presidential elections. In 2006, in an election driven primarily by anger over the Iraq War, Democrats regained both houses of Congress.

While Lebanon caused Reagan no political damage, it affected him in other ways. Although not poll-driven, Reagan was attuned and connected to the American people—intuitively and through letters and phone calls with ordinary citizens—and he shared their reluctance to risk U.S. troops abroad. He had rejected the notion of using U.S. forces in El Salvador or Nicaragua and had also turned down the proposal from Shultz and Mc-Farlane to send a larger military contingent into Lebanon. Reagan did not even fully comprehend that he was sending the Marines into harm's way. Despite the warnings of Weinberger and Vessey, he (along with Shultz, the NSC, and the CIA) underestimated the vulnerability of the small Marine force at the Beirut airport. Reagan ever after retained a sense of sorrowfulness about what had happened there, as his phrase, "the saddest day of my life," suggests. Lebanon left a mark on Reagan that would make him even more disinclined to risk U.S. troops in foreign adventures.

---

*Because the Marines were under instruction not to provoke anyone, they often did not have live ammunition in their weapons. As shocking as this sounds from a military standpoint, it probably was not a determining factor in the destruction of the Marine headquarters. The Long Commission concluded that the force of the explosion was so great it would have collapsed the building even if the truck had blown up in the parking lot.

On its face this statement would appear to be contradicted by the invasion of Grenada, which occurred in the penumbra of the bombing of the Marines in Beirut. But planning for the Grenada invasion had been under way before the Beirut bombing in response to urgent developments on that island nation. Grenada, a former British colony in the eastern Caribbean with a population at the time of 83,000, had been a U.S. concern since 1979. That year the New Jewel Movement took power in a nearly bloodless coup while the prime minister was out of the country. Espousing a mix of Marxism and nationalism, the movement's leader and new prime minister, Maurice Bishop, promised to address economic inequities and hold new elections. Instead, he established "revolutionary democracy," violating human rights and imprisoning critics of the regime. Bishop established close ties with the Soviet Union and Cuba, which sent laborers to Grenada to work on construction projects, including a new airport on the southwestern corner of the island with a 10,000-foot runway. On a visit to Barbados in April 1982, Reagan became aware that Grenada's neighbors, most of which lacked armies, were fearful of its military intentions. From then on, he paid attention to Grenada. In the March 23, 1983, nationally televised speech in which he unveiled the Strategic Defense Initiative, Reagan displayed aerial photos of the runway, then under construction, and said it was financed by the Soviet Union. "Grenada doesn't even have an air force," Reagan said. "Who is this intended for?" Reagan answered his own question two weeks later as part of an appeal to Congress for aid to the contras. He said the runway could be used by Libya and other U.S. foes to send arms and supplies to the Sandinistas, emphasizing the strategic importance—accurate in this case—of the Caribbean to U.S. interests. But as Reagan invariably did with perceived threats in the hemisphere, he tried diplomacy before exploring other options. Bishop was invited to Washington in May 1983 to confer with Clark and a State Department official. Nothing came of the meeting; Bishop blandly insisted that the new airport lacked military significance and was part of a plan to expand tourism.

Back in Grenada after his Washington meeting, Bishop was plunged into a power struggle with an extreme radical faction of his movement. Deputy Prime Minister Bernard Coard, the head of this faction, resigned from the government on October 12. The next day, Coard placed Bishop under house arrest and installed himself as prime minister. On October 19, a crowd of thousands marched to Bishop's residence and freed him.

Soldiers loyal to Coard then surrounded Bishop and seven others, marched them into a fort, bound their hands, and shot them to death with automatic weapons. Radio Free Grenada, run by Coard's wife, Phyllis, announced the deaths and the formation of a military revolutionary council, which proclaimed a shoot-on-sight curfew.

Shultz, asleep in the Eisenhower cottage of the Augusta golf club, was awakened at 2:45 A.M. Saturday, October 22, by a call from McFarlane, who said there had been critical developments in Grenada. McFarlane then telephoned Reagan, and the three of them gathered in the solarium of the cottage to discuss what had happened. Bishop's murder had alarmed the half-dozen island nations that were loosely banded together in the Organization of Eastern Caribbean States (OECS). Eugenia Charles, head of this group and prime minister of Dominica, was particularly concerned; a year earlier, she had survived a Grenadian-sponsored coup. Led by Charles, the OECS requested U.S. aid to restore order and democratic government in Grenada.

Even if the OECS had not sought help, the United States had reason to intervene. There were some 800 American medical students in Grenada. Reagan and his advisers, mindful of the Americans who had been held for 444 days in Iran, feared they might become hostages, all the more so after a Pan-Am charter sent to evacuate them was refused permission to land and a cruise ship sent to bring them out was denied permission to dock. Reagan authorized planning for a U.S. invasion, described as a rescue attempt. For the first time in his presidency, Reagan's advisers—Shultz, Weinberger, and McFarlane as well as the CIA and the White House—agreed on a general course of action despite differences on timing and details. The case for sending U.S. forces into Grenada was so strong that it met even Weinberger's restrictive tests for waging war.* It was good for Reagan that this was so, because the

---

*Speaking to the National Press Club on November 28, 1984, Weinberger listed six tests for committing U.S. combat troops overseas. He said troops should be used only in the national interest, in winnable engagements with defined objectives, and with sufficient force to accomplish the goals. Furthermore, troops should be used only when there was "reasonable assurance" of popular and congressional support, and as a last resort. Colin Powell generally agreed but believed Weinberger made his tests so restrictive that they would almost never permit a U.S. military engagement. Powell used a looser version of the Weinberger tests when he became chairman of the Joint Chiefs; this became known as the "Powell Doctrine."

weekend and the Monday after it were among the most harrowing days of his presidency.

He was awakened at 5:15 A.M. Saturday by Shultz and McFarlane with the news about Grenada. Shortly after 9 A.M., Reagan spoke by telephone to a National Security Planning Group that Vice President Bush had convened in the White House. Bush suggested that the United States ask Venezuela to participate in the invasion so that the operation wouldn't look like the action of a large English-speaking power against a small one. Reagan said there was no time to bring in Venezuela, a comment that everyone in the group interpreted as a sign that he strongly backed an immediate invasion. At 2:15 P.M. Saturday, while Reagan and Shultz were golfing, a bearded man wearing a flannel shirt and jeans crashed his pickup through the club gate and waved a .38-caliber pistol at the people in the pro shop, among them White House assistant David Fisher. The gunman demanded to talk to Reagan. Fisher calmly said he would find him and walked over to the 16th hole, where Reagan, at the insistence of the Secret Service, had taken refuge in his armored limousine. Reagan tried without success to talk on the phone with the gunman, who insisted on seeing him in person. Two hours later, the Secret Service talked the gunman, an unemployed pipefitter, into surrendering. Reagan, annoyed that he had been unable to finish the golf game, had dinner and went to bed, only to be awakened by McFarlane's call at 2:27 A.M. with the terrible news from Beirut. On the plane ride back to Washington after a few hours' sleep, Reagan worked on the speech he would give at the White House south portico. Then he presided for an hour and forty-three minutes at an NSPG meeting in the White House situation room with, as an aide put it, "pain and hurt" showing on his face.[34] After a break, the meeting resumed at 4 P.M. and lasted for three hours, with the discussion beginning with Lebanon and concluding with Grenada. At one point Reagan tried to read a supportive letter from a father whose son was a Marine in Lebanon. He was overcome with emotion and could not get through it.

By Monday, familiar cracks were showing in the façade of unity hitherto displayed by Reagan's advisers. Shultz sought to push ahead with the invasion, while Weinberger insisted that more information was needed about Grenada's defenses. In his memoirs Shultz called this "the counsel of no action at all."[35] That was not the way Weinberger and Vessey saw it;

they knew Reagan favored an invasion, and they wanted to be sure that U.S. forces were sufficient in case any surprises awaited them on the beaches of Grenada. It was an understandable concern, especially in the aftermath of Beirut. "Be sure we have enough strength," Weinberger told Vessey.[36] The commander of the Joint Chiefs had already decided that more troops might be needed; he added the 82nd Airborne Division to the invasion force. At 6:55 P.M. on Monday, with military plans completed, Reagan signed a formal order authorizing the invasion. He was briefing congressional leaders on his decision at the White House shortly after 8 P.M. when he was interrupted by a call from British Prime Minister Margaret Thatcher. Shultz had already informed Reagan that Thatcher opposed the invasion, but she now proceeded to make her views known in customarily blunt terms. Her argument was that the invasion would be seen as "intervention by a Western country in the internal affairs of a small independent nation, however unattractive its regime."[37] Reagan never liked a disagreement with Thatcher, and he was surprised by her stand, as he had received an urgent request for intervention from Governor General Sir Paul Scoon, head of state of Grenada, which was still a member of the British Commonwealth. (The request was kept secret until after the invasion because of concern for Scoon's life.) But Reagan did not want to argue with a foreign ally whom he also considered a trusted friend. He told Thatcher her request came too late because "we are already at zero."[38] After this call Reagan finished briefing congressional leaders and went upstairs to the residence with his advisers in tow. McFarlane told the president that the situation room had been upgraded with many capabilities and suggested that he might want to watch the action from there. Reagan asked Vessey what he was going to do. "I'm going to go home and go to bed," Vessey said. "The situation is now in the hands of the combat commanders, and they know what to do."[39] Reagan thanked Vessey for the "good advice" and also went to bed.[40]

At 5:36 A.M. Monday, 400 Marines from the helicopter carrier *Guam* landed at Pearls Airport on the western shore of Grenada. Thirty-six minutes later U.S. Army rangers parachuted onto the uncompleted runway that the Cubans were building at the southeastern tip of the 133-square-mile island. They encountered heavier than expected anti-aircraft fire and resistance on the ground from the Cubans, described as laborers but organized into military units and armed with AK-47s. But it was an uneven match, and the outnumbered Cubans surrendered after two days of fighting. Leaders of the radical faction that had murdered Bishop were captured, and an immense cache of arms, enough to provision a force of 10,000 men, was discovered along with armored vehicles and patrol boats. The United States attacking force numbered 5,000; its casualties were 19 dead and 115 wounded. Of the 800 Cuban defenders, 59 were killed and 25 wounded. The rest surrendered and were returned to Cuba. Forty-five Grenadians died in the fighting, and 337 were wounded. "We blew them away," exulted Vice Admiral Joseph Metcalf III, commander of the U.S. task force in Grenada. Taking note of Metcalf's statement, Richard Harwood of *The Washington Post* said Grenada had been made safe for tourism. "For the American military forces it had been, as soldiers use the term, a lovely little war," Harwood wrote.[41]

Reagan wasn't gloating, however. He was still in shock from the Beirut catastrophe and regretted the U.S. casualties, light as they were. The success of the Grenada operation produced one of the most overtly religious entries in the Reagan diaries: "Success seems to shine on us, & I thank the Lord for it. He has really held us in the hollow of His hand."[42] Reagan had reason to be thankful. The Grenada operation had in one stroke taken the edge off the Beirut tragedy, rescued Americans who could have become hostages, and removed a leftist thorn in the side of the United States in the Caribbean. Democrats could not believe Reagan's good luck and hinted darkly, as Tip O'Neill put it, that Grenada was "all about Lebanon" even though the actions were not related.[43] But not everything had gone as well in Grenada as it seemed. After-action reports revealed, as Weinberger had suspected, that the U.S. invaders lacked adequate information about Grenada's defenses. Four SEALs (Navy commandos) had drowned on a reconnaissance mission intended to produce better intelligence. Other U.S. casualties appeared to have been victims of friendly fire. "Relations between the services were marred by poor communications, fractured command and control, interservice parochialism, and micromanagement from Washington," wrote Colin Powell, who called the invasion "a sloppy success."[44] As Grenada demonstrated, risks attend even the most lopsided of small wars.

Politically, however, Grenada was a rousing and unmitigated success. Rescued medical students kissed the tarmac when they arrived in Charleston, South Carolina, providing a television clip that would be shown repeatedly in Republican campaign commercials. Reagan on October 27, 1983, gave a nationally televised speech that linked Lebanon and Grenada and the Soviet downing of the Korean airliner KAL 007 in a single narrative of patriotism and anti-communism. "The events in Lebanon and Grenada, though oceans apart, are closely related," he said. "Not only has Moscow assisted and encouraged the violence in both countries, but it provides direct support through a network of surrogates and terrorists." Reagan asserted that U.S. security was threatened in "far-away places" and said it was "up to all of us to be aware of the strategic importance of such places and to be able to identify them." This statement might plausibly have served as an indictment of U.S. policy in Lebanon, but it did not play that way. By adeptly wrapping the disaster of Beirut in the cloak of the victory in Grenada, Reagan had quieted the doubts of Americans about his foreign policies and bought the time he needed to extricate the Marines from Lebanon. A Gallup Poll in November 1983, slightly less than a month after Reagan's speech, provides a useful snapshot of public opinion. Americans favored the intervention in Grenada by more than a 2–1 margin and were evenly divided on the question of whether sending the Marines into Lebanon had been a mistake. By a 72–17 percent margin, however, they favored withdrawing the Marines from Lebanon. The withdrawal three months later enabled Reagan to seek reelection as the apostle of peace and prosperity, always the preferred theme for incumbent presidents who are able to use it. Reagan's updated version of this theme was the upbeat slogan "Morning in America." To be sure, the revived economy was a big part of the "morning." But it also helped that U.S. troops were no longer in combat in any part of the globe.

Reagan did not deploy ground troops again during the nearly five years of his presidency that remained after the last Marine left Lebanon, and, with one exception, he was also unwilling to use U.S. air power in retaliation for terrorist attacks. On June 19, 1985, Salvadoran guerrillas attacked a sidewalk café in San Salvador that was frequented by off-duty U.S. servicemen. The death toll was 13, including 4 Marines. The same day, a bomb went off in the airport in Frankfurt, West Germany, killing 3 and wounding 42. (Sikh terrorists downed an Air India Boeing 747 three days later, killing all 329 aboard.) Reagan attended the funeral for the Marines killed in El Salvador and promised that their killers "will not evade justice on earth." But when two of Reagan's political advisers (Patrick J. Buchanan and Ed Rollins) urged him to retaliate for these killings, the president turned to Bud McFarlane and asked if there were any guerrilla staging areas in San Salvador that could be bombed. Not without large-scale killing of civilians, McFarlane replied. Reagan decided on the spot against retaliation.[45]

The exception to this cautious approach was Libya, led by the volatile strongman Moammar Gadhafi. Libya had been a troublemaker from the U.S. perspective throughout the Reagan years. In August 1981, two U.S. Navy F-14 fighters flying off the Libyan coast were attacked by Soviet-made Libyan jets. The F-14s returned fire and downed the attackers. In March 1986, U.S. naval forces maneuvered in the Gulf of Sidra, a deep bay near the Libyan coastline that the United States (and most other nations) considered international waters. Libya, which claimed the gulf as its own, attacked U.S. aircraft with shore-based missiles. U.S. forces shelled the missile sites and sank a patrol boat. Such incidents were little more than annoyances, but U.S. intelligence agencies took a darker view of Gadhafi's capacity for terrorism. On April 5, 1986, a bomb exploded at a popular disco in West Berlin, killing two U.S. soldiers and injuring more than 150 people, about a third of them Americans. After the bombing, U.S. intelligence sources intercepted a Libyan communication from East Berlin saying that the operation had been carried out successfully.

Reagan, awakened at his California ranch with news of the bombing by National Security Adviser John Poindexter, quickly decided that the evidence of Libyan involvement required a retaliatory strike. Poindexter so informed Shultz, who was all for it. In short order, the Pentagon and the Joint Chiefs were on board. Two days later, with Reagan back at the White House, representatives of all these agencies plus Director of Central Intelligence William Casey met with the president at the White House to discuss a potential list of targets. They settled on three: a Gadhafi military compound near his residence, a terrorist training camp, and the Tripoli Air Base. But when Reagan asked Margaret Thatcher for permission to allow American F-111 bombers to fly from British bases, she was hesitant. Thatcher was concerned, among other things, with the safety of 5,000 British nationals in Libya who might be harmed or held hostage. She consulted with her foreign secretary, Geoffrey Howe, exchanged notes with Reagan, and reluctantly assented to the U.S. request. (France and Italy, in contrast, refused to allow overflights of their territory, adding to the distance and the risk taken by the American pilots.) On April 14, U.S. planes dropped more than 300 bombs on the Libyan targets, hitting the Gadhafi barracks. Gadhafi, sleeping in a tent outside the compound, escaped injury during the forty-minute raid, but a fifteen-month-old girl whom Gadhafi claimed was his adopted daughter was killed, and two of his sons were wounded. Reports of casualties varied widely, from a dozen to more than a hundred. Two U.S. aviators were lost. The raid produced a torrent of denunciation in Europe and in Muslim countries, but it accomplished its purpose of instructing Gadhafi that he could not engage in terrorism with impunity. Reagan, writing in his diary when results of the raid were still sketchy, called it a "success."[46] Thatcher retrospectively agreed. As she wrote in her memoirs, "There was a marked decline in Libyan-sponsored terrorism in succeeding years."[47]

After Libya, Reagan never again sent U.S. military forces into battle. Nor was he explicitly asked to do so, although Kenneth Duberstein, Reagan's fourth and final White House chief of staff, has said that unnamed ultra-conservatives wanted to use military force in Nicaragua after Congress cut off aid to the contras. "Those sonsofbitches won't be happy until we have 25,000 troops in Managua, and I'm not going to do it,"[48] Duberstein quoted Reagan as saying. Duberstein is a reliable witness, and these words are consistent with Reagan's sentiments opposing use of U.S. troops in Central America—a view that, as we have seen, predated Lebanon. In an interview after he left office Reagan reiterated the point, saying, "Now some of the people far to the right, they'd have marched in the troops."[49] But there was no stomach in Congress or the country, even among conservatives, for sending U.S. forces to Nicaragua. Reagan's remark to Duberstein reflected his generalized concern, not a rebuttal to a specific proposal for invading Nicaragua.

Panama was different. There was sentiment, as Reagan recognized, for using force to depose Panama's corrupt strongman, Gen. Manuel Antonio Noriega. Reagan resisted it. He detested Noriega, but he detested war more, and he saw the opportunity to oust the brutal Panamanian leader without bloodshed. In the last year of his presidency, Reagan sought a negotiated outcome in Panama against the opposition of Vice President Bush, Attorney General Meese, director of Central Intelligence William Webster (who had succeeded Casey), Treasury Secretary James

Baker, and the Joint Chiefs of Staff. The president's only allies were Shultz and Colin Powell, now the national security adviser.

The United States did not have clean hands when it came to Noriega. He had been on the CIA payroll for a number of years, and Casey may have used him as an emissary to Cuba during the invasion of Grenada. Moreover, the Drug Enforcement Agency within the U.S. Justice Department had collaborated with Noriega on drug interdiction, going so far as to give him a citation commending him for his help. By 1988, however, Noriega had become a serious embarrassment to his U.S. allies. On February 4, in a move that Shultz complained was done without adequate consultation with the White House and the State Department, the Justice Department indicted Noriega for drug trafficking and racketeering. Later that month, the Senate Foreign Relations Committee held dramatic hearings in which Noriega was accused of multiple murders by Jose Blandon, a former adviser. Emboldened Panamanians launched a general strike, and Eric Arturo Delvalle, the Panamanian president, fired Noriega as head of the Panama Defense Forces. Noriega responded by convening the National Assembly and replacing Delvalle with a crony. The Reagan administration continued to recognize Delvalle and at his request impounded U.S. funds that would have flowed to the government from the operation of the Panama Canal. With Panama bankrupt and unable to meet its payrolls, Reagan and Shultz believed that the time was ripe for a deal. Noriega was told that if he yielded power and took refuge in a friendly country, the United States would not extradite him. Spain consented to be the friendly country. Noriega considered the offer but rejected it. Reagan then offered to quash the U.S. indictment if Noriega would leave Panama. Michael Kozak, a respected State Department lawyer, was sent to Panama. He met frequently with Noriega and his lawyers during the next three months in an effort to persuade them to accept the offer or some variation of it.

Back home, however, Reagan was swimming upstream against a gathering movement, which he and Nancy Reagan had much encouraged, for a "zero tolerance" policy toward drugs. Vice President Bush, going with the current, feared that Reagan was also undermining his budding presidential campaign. Bush, who had clinched the Republican presidential nomination in March, had taken a hard line against drug dealers, and his campaign operatives were depicting Michael Dukakis, the anticipated

Democratic nominee, as soft on crime. Dukakis had seized the initiative on Noriega. How was it possible, Dukakis asked on the campaign trail in California on May 20, to tell Americans to "say no to drugs when we've got an administration in Washington that can't say no to Noriega?" On May 21, in a meeting at the White House, Bush denounced the offer to Reagan's face.

By the standards of previous presidents, Reagan was uncommonly generous to his vice president.* He recognized that Bush had a campaign to win, and he offered to tell the world that Bush opposed any deal with Noriega. This green light permitted Bush to make his case against giving amnesty to Noriega in the pages of *The Washington Post,* among other papers. That was not enough for Bush, who on this issue showed Reagan little of the loyalty that Reagan was displaying to him. Bush had more allies in the inner circle than Reagan did. At the contentious May 21 meeting, even Attorney General Edwin Meese, who had been with Reagan throughout his political career and had supported the offer to Noriega, switched sides and opposed the deal. Meese told Reagan that if he quashed the indictment he would be acting against the wishes of the law enforcement community. "You've just lowered my respect for people in the law enforcement field," Reagan replied. "How is it better to leave him [Noriega] in charge?"[50]

The meeting continued in this vein, with only Shultz speaking up for Reagan. On the other side, in addition to Bush and Meese, were the "two Bakers"—James, now treasury secretary, and Howard, the White House chief of staff. Howard Baker and his deputy, Kenneth Duberstein, reflected the concern on Capitol Hill, where the Senate had by an 86–10 vote opposed any amnesty for Noriega. Duberstein told Reagan he had been unable to recruit a single congressional ally because of "the hysteria in the country now on drugs."[51] Reagan replied that it was Congress and the press that were whipping up this hysteria, adding, "There is no alternative

---

*Reagan made it known in little ways around the White House that he wanted Bush as his successor even though he wasn't going to endorse him in the primaries, and this view was reflected in his diary. After Howard Baker, then about to leave the Senate, came by the White House on November 27, 1984, Reagan wrote in his diary: "He checked me out as to whether I'd be neutral in '88. I must say this will be a tough one for me. I've always believed the party should choose the nominee but when the time comes I'm afraid my heart will be with George B. if he makes the run" (*Reagan Diaries,* p. 281).

to this deal except troops."[52] Later in the meeting Reagan reiterated this point when James Baker suggested he should reserve the right to intervene if Noriega plunged Panama into further crisis. Reagan said, "What you guys are settling for is that we have to go in there with considerable loss of life, and how does that look to the rest of Latin America?"[53] This was Reagan's position, and he would not budge from it. Exasperated by the criticisms, Reagan told his rebellious inner circle: "I'm not giving in. This deal is better than going in and counting our dead. I just think you are as wrong as hell on this."[54]

Nothing came of Reagan's prescience. Noriega, well aware of the dissension within the Reagan administration and overconfident of his ability to dodge crises of his own making, turned down the deal. In December 1989, President George H. W. Bush authorized a U.S. invasion of Panama. This short war, which the invaders called Operation Just Cause, ousted and arrested Noriega at the cost of 24 U.S. military dead and 325 wounded. Panamanian military casualties were numbered at 50; civilian casualties were variously estimated from 500 to 4,000. Thousands more were homeless. The heavily populated El Chorillo neighborhood in downtown Panama City was destroyed.

Was this an avoidable short war? Shultz believes Noriega might have accepted a deal had the Reagan administration acted swiftly and spoken with a single voice. Reagan thought so, too, despite the perfunctory endorsement he gave to the Bush invasion in his ghostwritten memoirs, which omit discussion of the May 22, 1988, meeting and much else. Reagan's true feelings were conveyed in an interview a year after this meeting when he was asked why he hadn't ousted Noriega by force. "We would have lost every friend we've got in Latin America if we had sent in the troops," Reagan said.[55] (Indeed, when Bush did send in troops, the Organization of American States passed a resolution deploring the invasion and calling for withdrawal of U.S. forces from Panama.) In this interview, as so many times in the past, Reagan recalled that the Latin image of the United States was of "the big colossus of the north sending in the Marines."[56] Reagan did not lightly send in the Marines or any other U.S. forces. He never forgot what had happened in Lebanon, where the Marines had been sent not to fight but to keep the peace. As president of the United States, he was a reluctant warrior who much preferred negotiation to counting the dead.

7

THE LONG WARS
OF GEORGE W. BUSH

George W. Bush responded to al Qaeda's aggression and, later, to the threat he perceived in Iraq by chasing the ghosts of his predecessors in the Oval Office. In the process he pursued his own ghost as well.

As a first-time presidential candidate, Bush believed that Bill Clinton had set a dangerous precedent in abandoning Somalia, but his antipathy for this operation went beyond the view that it had emboldened terrorist groups. Bush also made it clear that he was skeptical of the practicality, or even the achievability, of the nebulous doctrine known as "nation-building." By mid-2007, as the breakdown in Iraq united congressional Democrats against him and induced deep concern in his own party, Bush tried to reassure worried Republicans by invoking Korea as an example of a long-term U.S. military deployment that succeeded, and Vietnam as an example of a war effort the United States abandoned too early. Both were tortured analogies for a number of reasons, and they were also at odds with Bush's previously stated views. This was particularly true of Korea.

In 1999 and 2000 as he ran for president, Bush expressed skepticism that American troops should ever be used as "peacekeepers," or that they should be placed as long-term buffers between two armed factions with ancient enmities. In his first major foreign policy address of his campaign, delivered at the Citadel on September 23, 1999, Bush extolled a view of the efficacy of military power that was striking in its realism and sense of limitations:

> The problem comes with open-ended deployments and unclear military missions. In these cases we will ask, "What is our goal, can it be met, and when do we leave?" As I've said before, I will work hard to find political solutions that allow an orderly and timely withdrawal from places like Kosovo and Bosnia. We will encourage our allies to take a broader role. We will not be hasty. But we will not be permanent peacekeepers, dividing warring parties. This is not our strength or our calling.

Two months later, speaking at the Ronald Reagan Presidential Library in Simi Valley to an audience that included Nancy Reagan and George Shultz, Bush declared that Americans were living in "the nation President Reagan restored, and the world he helped to save." Bush stated that national defense must be a president's primary focus and, indeed, is the first duty spelled out for a president in the Constitution. Once again, Bush set about defining the national interest, and he delivered a cautionary warning about what America can rationally expect to achieve on the international stage. "In the defense of our nation, a president must be a clear-eyed realist," he declared. In the next sentence Bush also outlined what he saw as the boundaries to international negotiations. "There are limits to the smiles and scowls of diplomacy," Bush said. "Armies and missiles are not stopped by stiff notes of condemnation. They are held in check by strength and purpose and the promise of swift punishment."

In speeches and in *A Charge to Keep,* his hurriedly assembled autobiography ghostwritten by Karen Hughes, Bush's campaign pronouncements about when, where, and how he believed it was appropriate to use American military power emphasized the constraints of time. Bush demonstrated an understanding that military operations of short duration were far more palatable to a free people than open-ended conflicts of uncertain outcomes. His guiding principle for going in seemed to be how fast you could get out. It was a lesson he would forget as president, but it was the right instinct. When asked, as he often was in the ensuing interviews and debates, about what kind of military operations he favored, brevity was one constant. The other was having a clear, easily explained, and clearly delineated military objective, an echo of one of the six tests articulated by Caspar Weinberger in the Reagan years and in modified form by Colin Powell under Bush's father. George W. Bush was on record as supporting Clinton's incursion into Kosovo, one undertaken by NATO planes from the skies, which lasted two weeks, and which was done both for humanitarian considerations (Serbs were engaged in "ethnic cleansing" of Albanian Muslims) and geopolitical strategic reasons: The Clinton administration feared a wider Balkans war if the Kosovars were forced out of Kosovo. Purely humanitarian uses of troops, such as in Haiti, did not interest him. Nation building? Forget about it.

Bush's worldview was on display in his second debate with Al Gore on October 11, 2000, when moderator Jim Lehrer asked both candidates to comment about previous U.S. military incursions. Bush indicated support for Reagan's short wars, including Lebanon, and his father's short war in Panama, even quipping, "Some of them I've got a conflict-of-interest on, if you know what I mean."

"Somalia?" Lehrer asked.

"Started off as a humanitarian mission and it changed into a nation-building mission, and that's where the mission went wrong," Bush replied.

"The mission was changed and, as a result, our nation paid a price," Bush continued. "And so I don't think our troops ought to be used for what's called nation-building. I think our troops ought to be used to fight and win war. I think our troops ought to be used to help overthrow the dictator when it's in our best interests. But in this case, it was a nation-building exercise—and same with Haiti—I wouldn't have supported, either."

Bush was so wed to this position he wouldn't even second-guess Gore on the Clinton administration's failure to send troops to Rwanda to prevent the grisly genocide of Tutsis at the hands of frenzied Hutu nationalists. Gore asserted disingenuously during the 2000 presidential campaign that the administration had sent troops to assist in the "humanitarian relief measures" in the slaughter's aftermath. This was a meaningless assertion: By the time the first U.S. peacekeeper was on the ground in Rwanda, a

Tutsi rebel army had liberated the country and 800,000 people had been slain, most of them hacked to death with machetes. The Clinton administration had refused to send troops and had discouraged the United Nations from acting on its own, thereby contributing to a human rights catastrophe that remains the biggest blight on his presidency—and Clinton's own great regret.[1] Gore's defensiveness, in other words, was understandable; Bush's defense of his rivals' mistake came across as cavalier and unbending.

"I think the administration did the right thing in that case—I do," Bush told the American people in that debate. "It was a horrible situation, no one liked to see it on our TV screens, but . . . we can't be all things to all people in the world, Jim."

A week later, in the 2000 campaign's third and final presidential debate, which took place in St. Louis on October 17, Bush returned to this theme. "It . . . must be in our vital interests whether we ever send troops," he said. "The mission must be clear. Soldiers must understand why we're going. The force must be strong enough so that the mission can be accomplished. And the exit strategy needs to be well-defined."

On the surface, Bush's stated reticence about American power seemed at odds with his swaggering persona. The man who vowed to run a "humble" foreign policy was also the macho fellow who disdained what he saw as Bill Clinton's timidity in foreign policy and his preoccupation with trivia on domestic issues, ranging from midnight basketball programs in a crime bill to support for school uniforms in a federal education appropriation. Midway through Bush's seventh year in office, Karl Rove was still declaiming that in this sense, Bush was Reagan's true heir, skipping over Bush 41 and scoffing at Clintonism. "It's not about school uniforms," Rove said of the presidency, "it's about defeating communism."[2] Inside the White House, Bush would derisively employ a baseball term, "small-ball," to describe the kind of game he was not interested in playing: Bush was a power hitter, more interested in swinging for the fences in hopes of launching three-run homers than in sacrifice bunts or stolen bases calculated to bring in one run at a time.

The image Bush and his top aides sought to convey was of a leader both muscular *and* prudent; a man of action, yes, but not heedless action, not endless action, and not action for action's sake. He was, in Rove's portrait, sort of a cross between Ronald Reagan and management guru Peter F. Drucker. "He has a great sense of history and its forces," Rove said of

Bush in a November 2002 speech at his old school, the University of Utah. "He is the first president to be an MBA, a Harvard MBA. I had read Peter Drucker, but I had never seen Peter Drucker in action until I saw George W. Bush as governor of Texas."

Later, in the same talk, Rove took issue with those (including conservative icon William F. Buckley Jr.) who maintain that the duties of the presidency are too varied and demanding for anyone to succeed in the job. "I disagree," Rove said. "There was a sign on Ronald Reagan's desk when he was president, and it said simply, 'It can be done.'"*

This duality represented the yin and yang of Bush and his team from the outset, and both sides of Bush's brain—the one that stressed the need for clear exit strategies and the one that tended to think nothing was impossible—looked to Reagan for validation. Less than nine months after taking the oath of office, however, while the rubble of the Pentagon and the World Trade Center still smoldered, Bush would put aside all his caution concerning the efficacy of American military power. The new Bush would precipitously embrace a diametrically different view, one that seemed to him like Reaganism, but proved to be something else. Spreading democracy to every corner of the globe—by force, if necessary—became his mission, "the calling of our time," Bush said.** The prose he used to rally the nation to this vision, whether his own words or those penned by a White House speechwriting team led by Michael Gerson, was often beautiful. It was also ominous.

The violence directed against the United States, its interests, its citizens, and everyone residing under its umbrella was indeed, as Bush said in his famous September 14, 2001, National Cathedral speech, "begun on the timing and terms of others." But that conflict did not start suddenly on 9/11. It unfolded gradually, over the better part of a decade and during the tenures of three U.S. presidencies, in a process that began long before any commander-in-chief—or the American people—fully fathomed the nature of the forces arrayed against them.

---

*The sign on Reagan's desk actually said: "There's no limit to what a man can do or where he can go if he doesn't mind who gets the credit."

**The president used this phrase repeatedly from 9/11 onward through mid-2007. The first time was September 14, 2001, in his address at the National Cathedral in Washington, D.C.

The first act of aggression occurred on December 29, 1992—after Bill Clinton's defeat of George H. W. Bush, but before Clinton's inauguration—in a bomb detonated at the Gold Mohur Hotel in Aden, the capital of Yemen. Two Austrian tourists were killed, but the attack was botched. The real targets, 100 U.S. servicemen who had been billeted in the hotel en route to Somalia, had already departed. The incident attracted little notice in the world news media, and it did not register in political circles within the United States. Ronald Reagan was living in retirement in California. His successor, the first President Bush, was preparing, as he told the White House press corps, for his next career, "in the grandfather business." President-elect Clinton, busy trying to assemble a cabinet that "looks like America," was running into a snag in his determination to name the first female attorney general. (His third choice, Janet Reno, would serve a controversial eight years in the job.) George W. Bush, who had not yet entered politics, was involved in organized baseball as the public face of the Texas Rangers' front office.

At CIA headquarters in Langley, a veteran Arab expert named Frank Anderson began putting together the clues of the Hotel Mohur attack, evidence that would lead him to a name few Americans had ever heard of: Osama bin Laden.[3] The CIA knew this name because bin Laden was part of a shadowy network of radical Muslim Arabs who had migrated east to wage holy war on the Russians after the 1979 Soviet invasion of Afghanistan. In a Cold War machination that looks questionable in hindsight, the CIA began funneling money through the Saudis and Pakistani intelligence service to these *mujahadeen.* It seems to have dawned on no high-ranking U.S. policy-maker that this policy, begun during the Carter administration and continued under Reagan, contained seeds of peril for the United States. (When he claimed that the Afghan "freedom fighters," along with the Nicaraguan contras, were the moral equal of America's Founders, Reagan was inadvertently including bin Laden in this characterization.) Two books about this dubious venture provide no evidence that the CIA directly gave money to bin Laden,* but he didn't need

---

*The books, riveting in their detail, are *Charlie Wilson's War: The Extraordinary Story of the Largest Covert Operation in History,* by George Crile, and *Ghost Wars: The Secret History of the CIA, Afghanistan, and Bin Laden, from the Soviet Invasion to September 10, 2001,* by Steve Coll.

American dollars. Bin Laden had his own fortune, which he brought with him to the Afghan front. Eventually, the ten-year conflict in Afghanistan, often called the Soviet Union's Vietnam, provided bin Laden with something worth much more than U.S. currency. It gave him the confidence that he and his fellow jihadists could defeat a great Western power.

At the time of the Hotel Mohur bombing, bin Laden was operating out of the Sudan; from there, he had dispatched al Qaeda fighters to battle U.S. troops in Somalia. On February 26, 1993, barely two months after the Yemen Hotel bombing, the United States itself was targeted, the attack coming in the form of a truck bomb at the World Trade Center in New York. Six Americans were killed and several hundred injured. At the federal trial of Omar Abdel Rahman, the "blind sheik," and his codefendants, evidence emerged that those in the dock weren't acting on their own. They had received logistical help from a terrorist network called al Qaeda, Arabic for "the base." It was a name that would soon be known worldwide. One of the al Qaeda men, Ramzi Yousef, the Sunni Arab who had planted the truck bomb at the World Trade Center in 1993, later told U.S. authorities that he had hoped to kill 250,000 people. Yousef was arrested in Pakistan in 1995 after Philippine police in Manila learned of his plot to hijack airlines and either blow them up or crash them into occupied European monuments.[4]

As the 9/11 Commission would later conclude, these events signaled a new challenge from terrorists, "whose rage and malice had no limit." Yet, the ability of the American people and their elected officials to comprehend the depth of this strategy was severely limited. What followed between the first and second attacks on the World Trade Center was a drumbeat of ever-escalating attacks. In October 1993, al Qaeda–trained gunmen shot down two U.S. Blackhawk helicopters in Somalia; they killed eighteen American soldiers, wounded seventy-three, and dragged the corpse of a slain serviceman through the streets of Mogadishu. In November 1995, five Americans training Saudi soldiers were murdered by a car bomb in Riyadh. The suspects apprehended by Saudi authorities reportedly said they'd been inspired by bin Laden; whether they were also trained by his organization is unknown. The Saudis executed them forthwith.[5] Seven months later, in the same country, nineteen American servicemen were killed and hundreds wounded in the Khobar Towers bombing, an event that generated a permanent rift between President Clinton and FBI director Louis Freeh, who felt thwarted by White House officials in his attempts to prove Iranian complicity. U.S. anti-terrorism officials subsequently came to believe that logistical support for that attack was provided by bin Laden's organization as well. Such a collaboration heralded a menacing new mutation in the pathology of the Middle East. It showed that Sunni and Shiite extremists were willing to work together—provided the United States was the target—and to do so irrespective of whether the terrorist partners were states, stateless terrorist organizations, or both working together. No one in Washington seems to have contemplated the implications of such partnerships, a failure of imagination that would have lethal consequences in the administration of George W. Bush in Lebanon and, even more so, in Iraq.[6]

In the summer of 1996, bin Laden praised the two bombings on Saudi soil during an interview with a British journalist, asserting that they "signaled the beginning of war between Muslims and the United States."[7] In August, bin Laden issued a rambling 11,500-word *fatwa,* or religious edict, that he dubbed the "Declaration of War against the Americans Occupying the Land of the Two Holy Places." Bin Laden, who lacks formal religious training and has no official standing in any Arab nation, had no legal basis to make such a decree. Nor did it read as the product of a rational mind, which hardly made it less foreboding. Bin Laden also released a threatening poem he had written, addressed to the U.S. secretary of defense, William Perry, which he signed "From the Peaks of the Hindu Kush, Afghanistan."

> *O William, tomorrow you will be informed*
> *As to which young man will face your swaggering brother*
> *A youngster enters the midst of battle smiling, and*
> *Retreats with his spearhead stained with blood* [8]

Bin Laden turned up his rhetorical pressure in February 1998, when, with Egyptian Islamicist Ayman El-Zawahiri and other radicals, he announced the formation of "the International Islamic Front for Jihad against the Jews and Crusaders." In this second fatwa, the militants asserted that it was the duty of all good Muslims to "kill the Americans and their allies, civilian and military," anywhere they came across them in the world. "Strikes will continue from everywhere, and Islamic groups will appear one after the other to fight American interests," the communication said.[9] Two months later, in May 1998, bin Laden elaborated on his violent worldview in an interview from his mountaintop hideaway in southern Afghanistan with intrepid ABC reporter John Miller. "We do not differentiate between those dressed in military uniforms and civilians," bin Laden said. "They are all targets in this fatwa."[10]

Bin Laden claimed his top priority was to persuade the government in Washington to remove U.S. military bases in Saudi Arabia. "Every day the Americans delay their departure, they will receive a new corpse," bin Laden told Miller. When the American journalist noted that the U.S. troops were there at the request of the Saudi royal family, bin Laden gave a response tinged with a bloody prophesy: "It does not make a difference if the (Saudi) government wants you to stay or leave," he said. "You will leave when the youth send you [away] in wooden boxes and coffins. And you will carry in them the bodies of American troops and civilians. This is when you will leave."[11] In saying this bin Laden was expressing conventional regional wisdom that the United States lacked the stomach for taking casualties. Five years earlier, in the summer of 1983, Syrian Foreign Minister Halim Abdul Khaddam had predicted to his Lebanese counterpart, Elie Salam, that U.S. forces would not stick it out in Lebanon. "The Americans are very, very far away," Khaddam reportedly said. "A few Marines will be killed, and they will leave."[12] Sadly, it turned out to be more than a few: 241 U.S. servicemen, most of them Marines, died in the October 1983 blast that occurred when a suicide bomber drove his explosives-laden truck into the Marine bunker in Beirut. By the following February, U.S. forces were gone from Lebanon.

In the late 1990s, American intelligence operatives in the field who were alarmed by bin Laden's increasing bloodlust began devising ways to kill or apprehend him. These efforts ran aground in the lethargic politics of Washington during that period. In May 1998, a strategy by field-level CIA operatives in Afghanistan to capture bin Laden was scuttled somewhere in the nexus of meetings and briefings among CIA Director George Tenet, Clinton National Security Adviser Samuel Berger, and an interagency Counterterrorism Security Group that seemed to talk every action plan into oblivion. In early June, the same thing happened to a pitch by Richard A. Clarke, the top anti-terrorism adviser in Clinton's

National Security Council, who proposed using Tomahawk cruise missiles to take out bin Laden.

Later that summer, bin Laden began delivering on his threats.

On August 7, 1998, two explosives-laden trucks driven by al Qaeda suicide bombers drove into the U.S. embassies in Kenya and Tanzania within five minutes of each other. Twelve Americans and 201 Africans were killed in the Nairobi attack. Eleven more people were killed in Dar es Salaam, none of them Americans, and thousands injured. By the time of the 1998 bombings in East Africa, CIA analyst Frank Anderson was long since retired, but there was no mystery about who was responsible for this handiwork.[13] In response, President Clinton labeled bin Laden "Public Enemy Number One" and authorized the launching of cruise missiles at sites in Sudan and Afghanistan. The Khartoum target was a pharmaceutical factory partly financed by bin Laden. The goal in Afghanistan was bolder: bin Laden himself. Tenet possessed intelligence showing that "the Sheik," as his followers called him, was holed up in a terrorist camp near the town of Khost. Inexplicably, the Clinton administration was in no rush. The missiles weren't fired at bin Laden's camp until August 20. The action had been delayed by numerous deliberations and considerations, including sending the vice chairman of the Joint Chiefs of Staff to alert Pakistanis to the mission, ostensibly so they'd know the missiles fired into Afghanistan weren't coming from India. This overabundance of caution came with a cost. Bin Laden was not killed that day. Later, the 9/11 Commission was told that he evacuated his Khost hideout hours before the missile strikes, possibly having been tipped off by Pakistani intelligence officials.

Bin Laden was not coy about his responsibility for the East Africa attacks. He had declared war on the United States and wanted to show he was prosecuting that war. In a December 22, 1998, interview, bin Laden said it was permissible to kill other Muslims in order to carry the fight to America, and that he had issued a "crystal clear" fatwa to this effect. He was also proving himself increasingly lethal. Still, Americans could not be shaken from a false sense of security. Clinton has been accused of dithering, but he wasn't alone. Congress and the media were consumed with a presidential sex scandal that was heading toward a distracting impeachment proceeding. The partisanship infecting Washington was taking its toll—on Americans' safety. Even terrorism was filtered through a political prism. Several prominent Republicans dismissed the missile attacks on Khartoum and Khost as attempts by Clinton to change the conversation.* Some of them mentioned the 1997 movie *Wag the Dog,* in which a president facing a sex scandal launches a needless attack on a smaller nation. This story line was prominent in the media as well. At Defense Secretary William Cohen's Pentagon briefing on the missile strikes, he was asked how he would respond to those who say "this bears a striking resemblance to *Wag the Dog.*" ("The only motivation driving this action today was our absolute obligation to protect the American people from terrorist activities," Cohen replied evenly. "That is the sole motivation.") The Clinton critics' circular logic, if one can call it logic, reached its nadir in an assertion by then–Republican House Leader Dick Armey. "The suspicion some people have about the president's motives in this attack is itself a powerful argument for impeachment," Armey said in a prepared statement.[14] So impeachment proceedings against Clinton chugged along, and the administration did next to nothing, even as bin Laden melted back into the mountains to plan his next attack.

That assault came in the October 12, 2000, bombing of a U.S. Navy ship of war, the USS *Cole,* anchored in the Yemen port city of Aden. The terrorists approached from the sea in a small boat loaded with explosives and manned by suicide bombers, who rammed the ship, blowing a hole in its hull. Seventeen American sailors were killed and forty were wounded; the *Cole* was nearly sunk. Once again, military intervention was contemplated—this time, a U.S. invasion of Afghanistan. Once again action was not taken. Long afterward, testifying on March 23, 2004, before the 9/11 Commission, Cohen conceded that the Clinton administration "can be faulted" for not responding. At the time, he testified, he didn't think an invasion would enjoy broad support in the United States or abroad. "I just don't think it was feasible," Cohen said.** In the ensuing years, Bill Clinton has displayed a hair-trigger sensitivity on this issue, which

---

*One of those Republicans was *not* George W. Bush. Asked his view of the U.S. air strikes, then-Governor Bush replied: "I think you give the commander-in-chief the benefit of the doubt. This is a foreign policy matter. I'm confident he's working on the best intelligence available, and I hope it's successful."

**One commission member, former Democratic Senator Bob Kerrey of Nebraska, disagreed. "We had a round in our chamber and we didn't use it," he told Cohen. "I'll just say for the record: Better to have tried and failed than to have not tried at all."

reemerged in his wife's 2008 presidential campaign. More than once he has flashed in anger when asked about his inaction against bin Laden. In July 2007, when asked gently about this matter by journalist Elizabeth Drew at the Aspen Ideas Festival, Clinton snapped at her for even asking the question. He noted irritably that he had endured *Wag the Dog* criticism when "I tried to get him" in 1998. Clinton followed this point with the incongruous claim that he couldn't go after bin Laden after the bombing of the *Cole* because the CIA and FBI hadn't "jointly certified" that al Qaeda was responsible, "even though we all knew it." Clinton ended by saying that he and his national security team had been "obsessed" with bin Laden, whereas his successor's national security team was focused on Saddam.

The available record shows that both presidents were more preoccupied with Saddam Hussein than with Osama bin Laden. In fact, to justify the attack on the pharmaceutical plant, Clinton administration officials had told ABC News correspondent John McWethy that one reason the plant was on its radar was that phone calls from the plant to an Iraqi official had been intercepted. ABC identified the official as the man "who runs that country's chemical weapons program." Thus, Osama bin Laden's financial interest in the plant was not the only reason it had been targeted.[15]

In the seven years since the Persian Gulf War had ended, the United States and Iraq had remained in a low-level conflict that existed out of sight of most Americans. This conflict was a kind of twilight zone somewhere between a blockade and a shooting war. Trade sanctions remained in place, but a U.N.-approved oil-for-food loophole meant billions of dollars were flowing into Saddam's coffers. Meanwhile, his propagandists claimed, perhaps speciously, that millions of Iraqi children were malnourished. Saddam's air force routinely made incursions into the Kurdish areas of northern Iraq, and in the Shia south U.S. pilots trying to maintain the integrity of the no-fly zone were regularly fired upon by Iraqi gunners. Clinton administration officials became convinced that Saddam had reconstituted his chemical, biological, and nuclear weapons programs.

They weren't the only ones. In January 1998, Clinton received a letter from a group of prominent and conservative Republican foreign policy hawks called the Project for a New American Century. They argued that "containment" was no longer a prudent option when it came to Iraq. "Our ability to ensure that Saddam Hussein is not producing weapons of mass destruction . . . has substantially diminished," said the authors of the letter. "Given the magnitude of the threat, the current policy, which depends for its success upon the steadfastness of our coalition partners and upon the cooperation of Saddam Hussein, is dangerously inadequate. The only acceptable strategy is one that eliminates the possibility that Iraq will be able to use or threaten to use weapons of mass destruction. In the near term, this means a willingness to undertake military action as diplomacy is clearly failing. In the long term, it means removing Saddam Hussein and his regime from power. That now needs to become the aim of American foreign policy."

It soon was just that, codified into U.S. law in the form of the "Iraq Liberation Act," signed by Clinton on October 31, 1998. Regime change in Iraq was now official American policy, and with that policy came large appropriations of money for Iraqi opposition groups wanting to replace the existing government with a democracy. "The United States favors an Iraq that offers its people freedom at home," Clinton said in words that George W. Bush would echo many times. "I categorically reject arguments that this is unattainable due to Iraq's history or its ethnic or sectarian make-up," Clinton added. "Iraqis deserve and desire freedom like everyone else."

Saddam Hussein's response was to boot U.N. weapons inspectors from Iraq. Two weeks later, Clinton made an explicit call for "a new government" in Baghdad and spoke openly of arming Iraqis opposed to Saddam Hussein. In mid-November, Saddam allowed weapons inspectors to return, but those inspectors, led by Australian diplomat Richard Butler, faced so many obstacles that Butler and his team concluded that Saddam had reconstituted his banned biological weapons program, particularly with regard to weaponized anthrax and other germs. In mid-December Butler pulled his team out of Iraq in anticipation of a joint U.S.-British missile attack dubbed Operation Desert Fox.* Saddam Hussein had "abused his last chance," Clinton told the American people in a televised address that took place against the backdrop of impeachment proceed-

---

*Iraqi Foreign Minister Mohammed Said Al-Sahaf had another name for it: "Operation Villains in the Arabian Desert."

ings. "Saddam must not be allowed to threaten his neighbors or the world with nuclear arms, poison gas or biological weapons," Clinton said. In this speech, Clinton hinted at a more profound U.S.-British goal as well, saying that the best way to end the threat posed by Saddam and his regime "once and for all is with a new Iraqi government—a government ready to live in peace with its neighbors, a government that respects the rights of its people."

Operation Desert Fox was planned and directed primarily by U.S. Marine Corps Gen. Anthony Zinni, and its objectives were straightforward: identifying 100 forbidden weapons sites on Butler's list—and obliterating them with airpower. Much later, in the aftermath of the stalled war in Iraq, and with Hillary Clinton emerging as the Democratic Party's frontrunner for the 2008 presidential nomination, some former Clinton administration officials would claim that Operation Desert Fox had apparently destroyed Iraq's weapons programs. This is implausible. The 100 targets were chosen from a much larger list compiled by Butler, who said as he left Iraq that his team could not account for some 32,000 chemical munitions, 4,000 tons of chemical precursors, and 550 mustard gas–filled bombs—in a nation geographically the size of California. U.S. intelligence agencies also believed Iraq remained in possession of a dozen Scud missiles and that it was busily producing propellants for those missiles that would make them operational far beyond the range allowed by U.N. resolutions. For his part, Cohen used a more modest term—"degrade"—in explaining how he hoped to affect Saddam's capabilities. With too many potential targets to hit them all, U.S. military planners chose to maximize the impact of the air war with the element of surprise, concentrating on sites believed to house Iraq's missile research and development and production program.

On December 16, the first night of Operation Desert Fox, the United States fired 250 Tomahawk missiles at the Iraq targets; those strikes were supplemented by forty sorties launched from the aircraft carrier USS *Enterprise*. Zinni's premium on surprise paid off: The U.S. military later reported that it hit half of the 100 targets that first night. By the end of the 71-hour air war, the United States and Great Britain—but mostly the United States— had flown 650 air strike sorties (including cruise missiles) into 97 of the targets, with a success rate estimated at 75 to 85 percent, setting Iraq's banned weapons programs back by an estimated one to two years. Killing only a few

Iraqi civilians, and losing nary an American life, "Operation Desert Fox was a highly successful operation," Cohen said succinctly.[16]

Others weren't so sure.

"As executed, Desert Fox was a face-saving punitive strike imbued with the *hope* that the regime would collapse," wrote Air War College professor Mark J. Conversino. "The U.S. and U.K. employed brute force to destroy elements of Saddam's power, without seeking a change in his behavior," he added, "and, therefore, seemed to pursue no concrete political objectives."[17] Prominent defense analyst Anthony H. Cordesman said the true test of the operation's success was "what it did or did not do to reshape Iraqi behavior" and its impact on America's position in the Middle East and the world.[18] Another yardstick, invoked by Clinton administration officials, was the notion that air strikes had weakened Saddam Hussein's hold on power. Secretary of State Madeleine Albright, speaking on January 5, 1999, on *The NewsHour with Jim Lehrer,* spoke of "Saddam's increasing isolation and desperation," while Zinni claimed Saddam was displaying a "degree of desperation that we hadn't seen before."

These statements proved to be wishful thinking. If anything, the strikes rallied Iraqis around their government and solidified Saddam's grip on his nation. The cessation of the bombing was greeted with banner headlines in government newspapers proclaiming victory. On January 3, the government media announced that Saddam would pay a bounty of $14,000 to any Iraqi army unit that shot down a coalition airplane patrolling the no-fly zones—more for the capture of a live pilot. In a bellicose address on January 6, he exhorted his nation to rally behind the government while ridiculing the notion that the British or Americans should have any influence on who rules Iraq. "Revolt against those who are proud of America's friendship, those who are directed by Cohen, the Jew," he exhorted with his customary crudeness.

A week later, in his annual "Mother of All Battles" speech, Saddam was equally defiant. Meanwhile, Iraqi air defenses stepped up their harassment of coalition air patrols, and the Iraqi government stepped up its propaganda efforts, seeking to drive a wedge in international public opinion. Moscow needed little prompting: Russian President Boris Yeltsin greeted news of the bombing with expressions of "dismay and deep alarm."[19] Western powers that had backed the United States in the first Gulf War started peeling away. France, Russia, and China called for a review of sanctions. The French let it be known that they would no longer allow their planes to be used to patrol the no-fly zones. Saudi Arabia and Turkey began backpedaling, too. The difference of opinion among the nations on the U.N Security Council presaged a rift that would haunt the United States and its next president during a much more ambitious military operation, launched in 2003, called Operation Iraqi Freedom.

So it was that as he came into office, George W. Bush inherited a mess in Iraq, one that neither his father nor his immediate predecessor had resolved in twelve years of trying. In his first eight months on the job, Bush revealed himself as a commander-in-chief inclined to avoid Carter's perceived pacifism, Reagan's small wars, his father's quick but inconclusive large war, and Clinton's lengthy and ineffectual low-grade conflict. But to paraphrase Leon Trotsky, while Bush may not have been interested in war, war was interested in him. Bush absorbed this lesson on 9/11, and his conversion was rapid and complete. Campaigning for reelection in 2004, Bush put it plainly to an audience in Lancaster, Pennsylvania: "September 11 changed me." Earlier, Bush had told Bob Woodward and Dan Balz of *The Washington Post* that the first thought he had after Andy Card whispered in his ear that a second plane had hit the World Trade Center and that America was under attack was: "They had declared war on us, and I made up my mind at that moment that we were going to war."[20]

Inside the George W. Bush administration, the identity of the "they" in the president's formulation was open to interpretation. The day after the attacks, Tenet came to Bush with yet another CIA plan to go after bin Laden. This time, there was no question. Bush responded to his intelligence chief: "Whatever it takes."[21] Bush had a pretty good idea of what it might take to kill or capture bin Laden. He told Woodward and Balz that the "antiseptic notion of launching a cruise missile into some guy's, you know, tent, really is a joke." (Privately, Bush was more graphic, telling the Senate delegations from New York and Virginia in the Oval Office, "I'm not going to fire a two-million-dollar missile at a ten-dollar empty tent and hit a camel in the butt.* It's going to be decisive.")[22]

---

*One of the U.S. senators present in the Oval Office was Hillary Rodham Clinton. If she considered Bush's comment a subtle criticism of her husband, she kept it to herself.

At the same time, the civilian leadership of the Pentagon began identifying military objectives beyond al Qaeda, namely Iraq. This alarmed the brass. While the smell of smoke still lingered in the Pentagon hallways, Marine Lt. Gen. Greg Newbold was startled by a comment from Undersecretary of Defense Douglas Feith. "Why are you working on Afghanistan?" Feith asked pointedly. "You ought to be working on Iraq."[23] At Camp David that weekend, Tenet presented the president with a "Worldwide Attack Matrix" that envisioned going after al Qaeda in some eighty countries, and Secretary of Defense Donald Rumsfeld and his top deputy, Paul Wolfowitz, brought briefing papers identifying Iraq as a potential target.[24] Bush waved aside the talk of Iraq, telling his war council that he wanted to concentrate on bin Laden—for the time being.

For Tenet's plan, Bush signed a Memorandum of Notification giving the CIA legal authority to interdict and, if necessary, use lethal force against bin Laden. Reagan had signed the original version of the anti-terrorism memorandum on May 12, 1986, and it had been updated five times by Clinton. The version signed by GWB was the most sweeping. Among other things, it explicitly allowed CIA agents the run of Afghanistan, bin Laden's base of operations when planning the attack against the United States. It was there that the first of Bush's long wars would begin. The second one was already taking shape in Wolfowitz's briefcase.

U.S. planning in Afghanistan was complicated by the assassination of Ahmad Shah Massoud, military leader of the Northern Alliance, the only viable anti-Taliban force still operating in Afghanistan. Massoud, known as the "Lion of the Panjshir," was murdered two days before 9/11, apparently on bin Laden's orders, and his absence left a vacuum of power, as it was intended to do. Another aggravating factor was that the Pentagon, which had long-standing plans on the shelf for attacking Iraq, had nothing in writing about how to deal with the mountainous, landlocked, primitive, and sparsely populated Afghanistan. The Taliban had no army to speak of—its gunmen raced around the countryside in Toyota pickup trucks— and little in the way of targets worthy of an aerial bombing campaign. Yet, as it became evident that Taliban leader Mullah Omar had neither the ability nor the inclination to expel bin Laden and his confederates from his country, it became necessary to find something to hit. The president, who had emphasized the necessity for speed with regard to military operations, was still preaching it now, prodding his staff to move quickly. And so, on September 26, 2001, fifteen days after the terrorist attacks, the CIA's most experienced Afghan hand was in-country, doling out money to the Northern Alliance and promising that the Americans would strike hard at the Taliban. "You're going to be impressed," the CIA man told the remnants of the Northern Alliance's leadership.[25] "You have never seen anything like what we're going to deliver onto the enemy."*

In those halcyon days, America's enemies were the world's enemies. Jordan's King Abdullah began rounding up suspected terrorists in Amman, and Russian President Vladimir Putin offered help attacking Afghanistan—as did the Saudis and the emirs of Qatar. General Pervez Musharraf, leader of Pakistan, agreed to pull the plug on the Taliban, which had been supported by ISI, Pakistan's notorious intelligence service. These world leaders were in sync with the sentiments of their people. At Buckingham Palace, the regimental band of the Coldstream Guards played the "Star Spangled Banner," the French newspaper *Le Monde* proclaimed the Kennedyesque sentiment "Nous Sommes Tous Américains" ("We Are All Americans Now"), and in Kosovo, 10,000 ethnic Albanians—mostly Muslims—attended a candlelight vigil in honor of the Americans killed on 9/11. Similar sentiments reigned in the United States, and Bush was one beneficiary. His job approval rating soared from 51 percent at the time of the attacks to nearly 90 percent in less than a month, as Americans demonstrated their historic tendency to find solidarity by rallying around their president.

Hurried along by their commander-in-chief, the U.S. military began its war in Afghanistan just twenty-six days after America had been hit. That night, October 7, 2001, U.S. warplanes began a punishing barrage of aerial bombardments and missile attacks against the Taliban and allied al Qaeda units. In this war, although it took a few weeks to shake out, the United States essentially used air power as artillery—bombing Taliban infantry units surrounding the northern Afghan city of Mazar-e Sharif as well as units aligned in a flat plain thirty-five miles from the main Northern Alliance army. This battery was supplemented by ground attacks

---

*This riveting detail of the CIA's early forays into Afghanistan comes from *Bush at War,* the first book in Bob Woodward's trilogy on the long wars of the forty-third president.

from U.S. Special Forces and CIA teams and several anti-Taliban tribal militias, some of whom rode on horseback. The Americans encouraged—with U.S. dollars as incentives—previously pro-Taliban warlords to switch sides in the fight. Although Bush's top aides suffered through nervous days in mid-October (and three weeks into the campaign, R.W. Apple of *The New York Times* wondered in print if Afghanistan was "another Vietnam"), the Taliban collapsed in the face of this onslaught. Kabul fell to the Northern Alliance on November 13. By Thanksgiving, the Taliban and al Qaeda had been driven into the forbidding caves and mountains of Tora Bora along the Pakistani frontier. Neither Mullah Omar nor Osama bin Laden had been captured, it was true, but an adroit and educated Afghan, Hamid Karzai, assumed the helm in Kabul. America's first front in the nation's "war on terror," as the president called it, was a smashing success.

At the White House, Bush and his aides liked to think that Ronald Reagan would have approved of the way the president prosecuted this phase of the war on terror—and of George W. Bush generally. George Shultz, removed to the scholarly life at the Hoover Institution, had sought to reassure the conservatives' old guard during the 2000 campaign that "this young man" would grow into the mantle of the next Reagan. Once in office, the comparison arose often, sometimes at Bush's instigation. In June 2001—before the war—when Bush had gone to Slovenia for a summit meeting, he had created a stir by saying, after meeting Putin face-to-face for the first time, that he had "looked the man in the eye" and thereby "was able to get a sense of his soul." By way of damage control, Bush gave an interview to *Wall Street Journal* columnist Peggy Noonan, a prominent former Reagan speechwriter. "With all due modesty, I think Ronald Reagan would have been proud of how I conducted myself," Bush told Noonan. "I went to Europe a humble leader of a great country, and stood my ground."[26]

The following year, in the context of both the war on terror and Bush's decision to call for Palestinian statehood—with the ground rule that the new nation-state would be a democracy—Bush speechwriter David Frum also thought Bush had done Reagan proud. "Bush had found what all the great American presidents have believed," Frum later wrote. "War had made him, as it had made Roosevelt and Reagan, a crusader after all."[27]

Bush's efforts at modeling himself after the fortieth president were based on his belief that Reagan had embodied a resonant national optimism. At the Republican convention in Philadelphia in 2000, Bush had concluded his acceptance speech with a vignette about a landscape that hung in his Austin office by renowned west Texas artist Tom Lea. Bush explained that the painting captured his own feelings about "our great land, a land I love," and quoted Lea's own description of the picture. He and his wife, Sarah, Lea explained, lived on the east side of the mountain. "It's the sunrise side, not the sunset side. It is the side to see the day that is coming, not to see the day that has gone." This was nothing if not Reaganesque—and Bush knew it. Lea died nine days after Bush was inaugurated, but Bush brought the painting with him to Washington, hung it in the Oval Office, and was still speaking about it as he launched his second term as president.

In a 2005 interview with Brian Lamb of C-SPAN, Bush virtually grafted Reagan onto the Tom Lea story while asserting that he'd been able to "plant the flag of freedom" as an ideal around the world, and not just a geopolitical strategy designed to benefit Americans. Democracy, Bush asserted, was more than a political movement. It was "an overarching concept," he said, "and is universal." Asked by Lamb if he could remember when this idea became the "backbone" of his governing philosophy, Bush gave this reply: "You know, I think if I had to have a mentor, a public figure that reminded me on a regular basis about the power of freedom and liberty, it would have been Ronald Reagan. He was a stalwart when it came to proclaiming as clearly as possible the need for people to be free."[28]

Reagan surely would have lauded the deliverance of Afghanistan; it was a far-off place where both he and George W. Bush had committed American power to the cause of liberation. Yet, as 2001 drew to a close and Afghanis threw off their Taliban-required clothes, with music wafting through the streets of Kabul for the first time in ten years, trouble loomed on Bush's beloved "sunrise side of the mountain." The days that were coming were not destined to be sunny ones. Although few people in the White House openly used this term, what the United States had signed itself up for in Afghanistan was indeed nation-building—and that job was far from complete. Even more forebodingly, the attention of Bush and his team had already shifted to another, much larger challenge.

Success, or the illusion of success, had come quickly in Afghanistan, too quickly as it turned out. George Tenet had understood, correctly, that because the Taliban and al Qaeda were so entwined, going after al Qaeda in Afghanistan translated into regime change in Kabul. This is precisely what the United States accomplished, thus setting a precedent that proved impossible for Team Bush to resist attempting to replicate. If Bill Clinton had reacted too feebly to Osama bin Laden's previous attacks because he was preoccupied with Saddam Hussein, Bush repeated this mistake, with a fateful wrinkle. His approach was to conflate the threats of al Qaeda and the threat of Saddam, a response that would prove the most controversial judgment of his presidency, dividing the country and the world—and Bush's cabinet.

In hindsight it's striking how quickly after 9/11 the battle lines over Iraq were drawn within Bush's councils of war. Rumsfeld and Wolfowitz raised the possibility of attacking Iraq in the first twenty-four hours—before decisions about Afghanistan had even been made. Dick Cheney quickly fell in line. As secretary of defense during the Gulf War in 1991, Cheney had been the point man in the effort to mollify conservatives who thought President George H. W. Bush should have finished the job and toppled Saddam. (On a PBS *Frontline* program fifteen months after the Gulf War, after noting that the coalition forces could have captured Baghdad, Cheney said, "I don't know how we would have let go of that tar baby once we had grabbed hold of it. . . . How many additional lives is Saddam Hussein worth? And the answer I would give is not very damn many.") Retrospectively, said a friend who had known him for many years, Cheney wondered if the critics had a point, although he never second-guessed the decision in public. This time, however, Cheney would be unwilling to settle for halfway measures.

Meanwhile, Secretary of State Colin Powell and his deputy, Richard Armitage, were appalled by talk of waging war on Iraq.[29] Initially, at least, Bush kept his eye on the ball. Bin Laden first, he kept reminding them. We can talk about Iraq later. But according to one eyewitness account, on September 20, 2001, Bush personally broached the possibility of military action against Iraq with British Prime Minister Tony Blair at a White House dinner. Sir Christopher Meyer, British ambassador to the United States at the time, recalled that Blair urged Bush to go slow, concentrating on al Qaeda and the Taliban first. "I agree with you, Tony," Meyer quoted Bush as saying. "We must deal with this first. But when we have dealt with Afghanistan, we must come back to Iraq."[30] One fascinating facet of this exchange is that Blair's inclination to put the Taliban first was nearly identical to Bush's reaction to his own staff. Soon enough, however, both leaders would jump aboard the neoconservatives' Iraq bandwagon.

Bush's own public comments reveal that one of his first reactions after 9/11—it was also Blair's—was to imagine the horror of what might happen to Tel Aviv or New York (or Washington, Los Angles, London, Paris, or Moscow) if Osama bin Laden and his ilk were able to get hold of a nuclear weapon. This fear, although not Bush's solution to it, was authentically Reaganesque. As far back as the 1976 Republican National Convention in Kansas City, Reagan had publicly underscored his long concern about the danger of nuclear war. Called to the stage unexpectedly by the winning GOP candidate, President Gerald Ford, Reagan didn't fawn over the nominee, as so many losing candidates do. Instead, Reagan's impromptu speech at once foreshadowed his 1980 presidential campaign and the attempt he would one day make in concert with Soviet leader Mikhail Gorbachev to reduce the threat of mutual nuclear annihilation. (Reagan, speaking without a text or even notecards, told the delegates of writing a letter for a time capsule that was to be opened in Los Angeles in a hundred years. "And suddenly it dawned on me, those who would read this letter a hundred years from now will know whether those missiles were fired," Reagan said. "They will know whether we met our challenge. Whether they have the freedoms that we have known up until now will depend on what we do here. Will they look back with appreciation and say, 'Thank God for those people in 1976 who headed off that loss of freedom, who kept us now one hundred years later free, who kept our world from nuclear destruction'?")

Since Reagan left office, however, neither war nor negotiation had diminished Saddam Hussein's cravings for the types of weapons Reagan feared would threaten the human race, and after 9/11 Bush (and Blair) began contemplating the unthinkable: a rogue nuclear device being used against a Western democracy or one of its allies, including Israel. They were not alone.* For several years, a group of conservative, experienced,

---

*On December 15, 2001, two months after 9/11, *National Journal* published a cover story by defense writer Sydney J. Freedberg, called "Beyond Duck and Cover," exploring the damage that a nuclear explosion or a so-called dirty bomb would do to Washington, D.C. The magazine's cover was an aerial photo of the capital with concentric circles superimposed over it, as if in a target.

and well-educated U.S. foreign policy hawks had worried over this possibility as well; most of their attention had centered on Iraq as the likely source of such a catastrophe. These were the signatories to the 1998 letter to Clinton urging him to pursue regime change in Iraq. Their ranks included veterans of several previous Republican administrations, among them Rumsfeld (Nixon and Ford); Wolfowitz, Richard Perle, Richard Armitage, and Elliott Abrams (Reagan); John Bolton and William Bennett (Reagan and Bush 41); and Robert Kagan and Robert Zoellick (Bush 41). Also represented were conservative intellectuals such as William Kristol, Paula Dobriansky, and Jeffrey Bergner, several of whom would later work in the executive branch under the presidency of GWB. Most of this group, with the notable exceptions of Rumsfeld and Armitage, were known as neoconservatives, or "neocons," a word that, as Iraq descended into chaos in 2004, would come to be used as a form of slur. By 2007 the phrase had entered the realm of farce, epitomized by a caller from Ohio to the BBC who asserted that the centrist Democratic Leadership Council was a "neoconservative institution," by which he meant "believing America has a sacred right to hydrocarbons, where it might find them around the globe." Conservative writer Jonah Goldberg, citing the BBC example, opined that "neoconservative" had come to mean "All Bad Things"—and suggested it was time to retire the term. He had a valid point, but in 2001, at a pivotal point in history, the neocons had a pronounced geopolitical vision, which, with the help of others, they were about to impose on the world. The others, to use John Judis's term, were "nationalists," such as Rumsfeld and Cheney, who "had an expansive view of the U.S. national interest"[31] and unbridled faith in the efficacy of U.S. military power. George W. Bush was by this standard a nationalist. In the heady run-up to the Iraq War, it was a distinction without much difference as nationalists and neocons made common cause.

Nonetheless, as originally defined, the neocons, although never numerous, were an important component of modern conservatism. (The word was first used derisively by social critic Michael Harrington to describe liberals he believed were behaving as conservatives; the neocons embraced the term.) Many were Jewish intellectuals and former leftists (Irving Kristol, a founding neocon, had been a Trotskyite) who became disillusioned with the Democratic Party for being insufficiently anti-Communist. Other neocons, such as Jeane Kirkpatrick and Richard

Perle, had supported or worked for senators and presidential candidates like Hubert H. Humphrey or Henry Jackson, the last of the Cold War liberals. When the Democratic Party rejected Humphrey and Jackson, moved left in opposition to the Vietnam War, and nominated George Mc-Govern in 1972, Perle and Kirkpatrick moved right. Ronald Reagan, planning his 1980 presidential campaign, became interested in Kirkpatrick after reading an article in the neocon magazine *Commentary* in which she argued that President Carter's administration had acted unwisely in deposing anti-Communist dictators in Nicaragua and Iran.[32] (Read today, Kirkpatrick's article sounds like a brief for "realism," the pragmatism now so distrusted by the neocons. Indeed, Kirkpatrick was realistic in the ordinary sense of that word: A posthumous memoir published in 2007 quotes her as saying she had "grave reservations" about Bush's invasion of Iraq.)[33] Reagan appointed Kirkpatrick U.N. ambassador and made her a member of his cabinet. Perle wound up in the Pentagon, under Caspar Weinberger. Reagan listened to both of them but often did not follow their counsel: He sided with Britain in the Falklands War while Kirkpatrick leaned to Argentina, and he signed the Intermediate Nuclear Forces (INF) Treaty, about which Perle had reservations. Years later, Jack Matlock would say that "Reagan used the neoconservatives, the neocons use George W. Bush."[34]

Neoconservatism, whatever else can be said about it, has a respectable intellectual pedigree. It derives from a school of political philosophy espoused by Leo Strauss, a cerebral college professor whose family had fled Nazi Germany. At the University of Chicago, a young Paul Wolfowitz became one of Strauss's students. Wolfowitz's father had come to the United States from Poland after World War I; all of the members of his family who had stayed behind had perished in the Holocaust. Strauss was not a particularly partisan man, especially in contemporary terms, and, as Fukuyama has noted, he said little about specific U.S. foreign policies.[35] But Strauss's reading of history, forged by the furnaces of the Holocaust, inevitably led to an abiding respect for the natural rights of man and specific admiration for freedom's great European champion, Winston Churchill, the man who stood up to Hitler. "The tyrant stood at the pinnacle of his power," Strauss wrote. "The contrast between the indomitable and magnanimous statesman and the insane tyrant—this spectacle in its clear simplicity was one of the greatest lessons which men can learn, at any time."[36]

In *Rise of the Vulcans,* a penetrating examination of the lives and influences of the top members of George W. Bush's foreign policy team, author James Mann noted that Strauss, who died in 1973, also provided an intellectual framework for opposing communism, which was, after all, another form of totalitarianism. Mann wrote that "one of the great political milestones" for Straussians was President Reagan's denunciation of the Soviet Union as an evil empire. (Natan Sharansky, then in a Soviet prison, said he and his fellow inmates were "thrilled" when this speech was reported in *Pravda.)* [37] Strauss protégé Alan Bloom was also struck by Reagan's words. In his 1987 book, *The Closing of the American Mind,* Bloom wrote: "What was offensive to contemporary ears in President Reagan's use of the word 'evil' was its cultural arrogance, the presumption that he, and America, know what is good; its closedness to the dignity of other ways of life; its implicit contempt for those who do not share our ways." This is exactly what Straussians liked about Reagan's line; all men may be created equal, but all ideas and governments are not. George W. Bush, trying to make his point about the universal nature of freedom's appeal, would paraphrase this thought in a more politically correct way, stripping the overtly American jingoism from the idea while retaining its essence. Strauss's (and Reagan's) sentiments would be rendered by Bush this way: "The liberty we prize is not America's gift to the world; it is God's gift to humanity." [38]

This view was a long time in the making, and not merely a reaction to 9/11. But what were its implications? For some, it was epitomized in a piece written in June 2001 by neoconservative columnist Charles Krauthammer headlined "The New Unilateralism." September 11, 2001, was a catalyst for both neoconservatives and Bush, who responded to the attacks by chewing on this question: Exactly *where* might al Qaeda acquire a nuclear bomb or devastating biological weapons? Bush and his British ally settled on Iraq as the most likely culprit. Alone among current world leaders, they emphasized, Saddam had already used chemical weapons in a theater of war: What would stop him from doing it again? Moreover, the Iraqi dictator retained what Richard Butler called a clinical "obsession" with obtaining more weapons of mass destruction.

In truth, the list of potential places to obtain such weapons was extensive. Among the other possibilities were Iran, busily building atomic capabilities while its leaders continued to characterize America as "Satan"; North Korea, with proven nuclear capabilities as well as a starving population, meaning it was desperate for cash; the remnants of the Soviet Union, with its extensive nuclear arsenal and economies that had devolved into something resembling organized crime; and Pakistan, which in the 1990s had stolen nuclear secrets, developed a nuclear capability, and tested an atom bomb that was hailed in the Muslim world as "the Islamic bomb." Pakistan had underwritten the Taliban to begin with and, as American intelligence subsequently learned, had received inquiries from al Qaeda about obtaining a crude radiological device, or "dirty" bomb. The exigencies of alliance being what they are, however, in his 2002 State of the Union address Bush and his speechwriters granted a kind of clemency to any nation helping in the war on terror. This left Iran, Iraq, and North Korea holding the bag, although it was apparent in that speech that one nation was first among equals in Bush's "axis of evil." Here is what Bush said:

> The Iraqi regime has plotted to develop anthrax, and nerve gas, and nuclear weapons for over a decade. This is a regime that has already used poison gas to murder thousands of its own citizens—leaving the bodies of mothers huddled over their dead children. This is a regime that agreed to international inspections—then kicked out the inspectors. This is a regime that has something to hide from the civilized world. States like these, and their terrorist allies, constitute an axis of evil, arming to threaten the peace of the world. By seeking weapons of mass destruction, these regimes pose a grave and growing danger. They could provide these arms to terrorists, giving them the means to match their hatred. They could attack our allies or attempt to blackmail the United States. In any of these cases, the price of indifference would be catastrophic.

The threat of WMD, as weapons of mass destruction came to be known, was not the only rationale cited by the president in his campaign to rid the world of Saddam Hussein. Between the 2002 State of the Union address and the March 19, 2003, invasion of Iraq, Bush gave 164 speeches or talks in which he discussed Iraq.[39] In all of them, he mentioned multiple reasons. These included Saddam's sponsorship of terror, Saddam's history of invading his neighbors, Iraq's thwarting of U.N. resolutions, the positive example of having a democratic Arab nation in the region, Bush's hope that peace between Israelis and Palestinians would be easier to obtain if Iraq was a democracy, and Bush's desire to end Iraqis' misery by extending human rights to them. This last reason moved Bush most. It's not every day an American president uses the phrase "rape rooms." Bush did, and he would often choke up while discussing Saddam's savagery. Nonetheless, the first reason and the last reason Bush cited were weapons of mass destruction. The administration took its evidence, such as it was, to Congress, which gave the president a green light, and to the United Nations, which gave him a yellow. Bush sped through it anyway.

By then Bush was not only one of the "Vulcans," but a de facto neocon. On matters of natural rights and human history, the neoconservatives could be quite eloquent. Bush's critics would disparage him for being messianic, suggesting that when it came to his desire to spread freedom to every corner of the globe he had one foot planted in the New Testament and the other on a banana peel. His loyalists, such as Peter Wehner, the administration's in-house intellectual, would counter that Bush's expressions about the universal appeal of freedom were rooted in the Reagan canon and in the past words of all strong U.S. presidents, including John F. Kennedy and Franklin Roosevelt—indeed, in the words of the Declaration of Independence itself. Certainly it was true that Bush's formulation wasn't different in kind from Thomas Jefferson's sentiment that "the God who gave us life gave us liberty at the same time."* And Bush's expressions for the hopes and desires of the Iraqi people did indeed echo those that Reagan had asserted on behalf of the millions of souls living behind the Iron Curtain.

If Bush and his neoconservative speechwriters were solid in their grasp of the historic meaning of American Exceptionalism—in its best sense—as well as the long body of rhetoric on this point by previous U.S. presidents, there was also a great deal they did not know. They did not know enough about Iraq, as it turned out. They did not know enough about war.

---

*"The palpable truth," Jefferson wrote on June 24, 1826, in the last letter he ever penned, was "that the mass of mankind has not been born with saddles on their backs, nor a favored few booted and spurred, ready to ride them legitimately, by the grace of God."

Colin Powell, who did know war, cautioned Bush in August 2002 about the perils of invading Iraq and of trying to build a democratic nation among disparate ethnic factions who'd never experienced anything other than despotism. In a two-and-a-half-hour meeting in the White House residence attended only by Powell, Bush, and Condi Rice, Powell also warned the president of the likely chaos that would ensue if their optimistic plans for Iraq went awry. "I tried to avoid this war," Powell said publicly at the Aspen Ideas Festival on July 5, 2007. "I took (Bush) through the consequences of going into an Arab country and becoming the occupiers."[40] Rice had said little during Powell's presentation, he recalled in a subsequent interview, though afterward she phoned Powell and asked him "to give the same exact briefing" to White House Chief of Staff Andy Card, which he did.[41]

In private, Powell and Armitage, best friends and fellow Vietnam veterans, referred to the "Pottery Barn rule"—if you break it, you own it. (In fact, Pottery Barn has no such rule; Powell had borrowed the inaccurate aphorism from *New York Times* columnist Thomas Friedman, who admitted somewhat sheepishly to *Times* literateur William Safire that he had made it up to illustrate a point.)[42] In any event, Powell was more formal in his presentation to the president, and more evocative as well. "You are going to be the proud owner of 25 million people," he told Bush. "You will own all their hopes, aspirations and problems. You'll own it all."[43]

The secretary of state, who had been arguing this way for months, made two other points in his private session with the president. First, he predicted bluntly that Iraq would come to define the Bush presidency. "It's going to suck the oxygen out of everything" is the way Powell put it. "*This will become the first term.*" Second, in an effort to counter the neoconservatives' flowery rhetoric about the beauty and inviolability of liberty, much of which had already emerged from Bush's lips, Powell reminded the president that Iraqis had never experienced democracy and might not know what to do with it: "So you need to understand that this is not going to be a walk in the woods."[44]

From the beginning, those on the other side of the debate had been telling Bush just the opposite. Only nine days after the attacks of September 11—the same night Bush hosted Tony Blair at the White House—Iraqi exile Ahmed Chalabi spoke at a meeting of the Defense Policy

Board, a part-time panel then chaired by Richard Perle, tasked with providing advice to the secretary of defense. Chalabi, a convicted swindler who had ingratiated himself into the confidences of the neoconservatives, advocated skipping Afghanistan altogether and heading straight for Iraq. With bin Laden still at large, it was a goofy idea, but some of the participants found themselves believing Chalabi's assertion that pacifying Iraq would be the easier mission. Perhaps they wanted to believe it. "He said there'd be no resistance, no guerrilla warfare from the Baathists, and a quick matter of establishing a government," one participant told *New Yorker* correspondent Jane Mayer.[45]

This notion animated the neoconservatives who were advising Bush on foreign policy. As had been the case in the Reagan White House, it wasn't strictly ideology that divided the president's aides; it was something closer to life's experiences and personal temperament. The opposite of a pragmatist is not a conservative, it's a romantic. As he prepared to invade Iraq, Bush had surrounded himself with dreamers telling him what they hoped would happen. He listened to them when he should have listened to his own inner voice. Underwhelmed by the evidence presented by the CIA asserting that Saddam was hoarding an arsenal of chemical and biological weapons—and that he was working at developing a nuclear capability—Bush himself, at a now-famous December 21, 2002, meeting in the Oval Office, asked George Tenet: "Is this the best we've got?" According to Woodward's account in *Plan of Attack,* Tenet leaped off a couch and replied, "It's a slam dunk case!"*

Tenet's assurances, and the sketchy evidence provided by the U.S. intelligence services, ultimately mollified Bush. It also satisfied Powell, who should have known better, and most of the American media as well. Powell's February 5, 2003, presentation to the United Nations earned him rave reviews for his poise and persuasiveness, but the hard evidence was thin, and Powell's performance depended too heavily for its credibility on the commanding presence of the man making the argument. Ironically,

---

*In his book *At the Center of the Storm: My Years at the CIA,* Tenet claimed that Woodward's context was slightly amiss and that Tenet had been referring to the ability to convince the American public that Saddam possessed a forbidden arsenal. Because this book appeared four years into the Iraq War and no such weapons had yet been found, this seems a quibble.

Powell was one of the few Americans in a position of authority who worried about this. Three months earlier, after the U.N. Security Council voted 15–0 to order Iraq to admit weapons inspectors—and the Bush administration was well on its way to war—a pensive Powell walked into the office of his top deputy, Larry Wilkerson. "I wonder what will happen," Powell mused aloud, "if we put half a million troops on the ground, and scour Iraq from one corner to the other, and find no weapons of mass destruction?"[46] Later, a friend of Powell's despondently told the authors that Powell and Wilkerson had made many corrections in drafting the U.N. speech. "They were trying to make chicken salad out of something you can't make chicken salad with," Powell's friend said. Despite the dubious evidence, Powell shared the near-consensus view that Saddam either had weapons of mass destruction or was in the process of acquiring them. This view was so widespread, as Richard Holbrooke observed in a later colloquy with Richard Perle, that Holbrooke believed it, Bill Clinton believed it, even Jacques Chirac believed it.[47]

Nonetheless, Powell's question about what would happen if no weapons of mass destruction were found was the sort of question Ronald Reagan asked of his aides in the run-up to much smaller proposed military incursions, including Grenada (which he approved) and Panama (which he didn't). By the end of 2002, however, George W. Bush was running on faith.

The invasion began on March 19, 2003, with the president telling the world that the people of the United States refused to "live at the mercy of an outlaw regime that threatens the peace with weapons of mass murder." He added that it would not be a campaign of half-measures, and that no outcome was acceptable other than victory. "We will defend our freedom," Bush said solemnly. "We will bring freedom to others and we will prevail."

Initially the Iraqi invasion lived up to its unfortunate "shock and awe" billing. A lean force of some 140,000 U.S. troops, maneuvering over great distances and aided by satellite navigation and precision-strike capabilities, raced to the outskirts of Baghdad in just three weeks. The U.S. 1st Marine Expedition Force swept up the country from the southeast, sealing off the city east of the Tigris River. The Army's 3rd Infantry Division closed the pincer from the southwest by crossing hundreds of miles of desert, through sandstorms and hostile forces, wreaking havoc in urban areas with its infamous "Thunder Run" tactics. After the second Thunder Run by U.S. armored forces deep into the center of Baghdad, Saddam Hussein's regime collapsed, and the city's stunned populace flooded into the streets welcoming the Americans. A huge statue of Saddam Hussein was torn down by U.S. troops and promptly defaced by Iraqis. Cheney and Wolfowitz had predicted that American troops would be greeted as liberators, and they were—until the pall of a security vacuum quickly settled over the capital. With too few troops and no viable plan for securing the city or stabilizing the country, U.S. commanders watched passively as looters took to the streets en masse, stripping government buildings and Baath Party palaces like locusts. Baghdad descended into a state of lawlessness, violence, and rampant criminality from which it has never recovered. At what seemed like the cusp of victory, the seeds of defeat were sown.

News accounts of the looting focused on priceless art and antiquities that were plundered; what was really being stolen was Iraq's future. Its very infrastructure was being ripped away. So was its optimism. Security, or rather the lack of it, was the key. Informed that people were living in the dark because of power shortages, Colin Powell told a friend that it is possible to be secure in the dark if people have a feeling of safety. If people aren't safe, he added, nothing else matters. The people weren't safe. Looting and insecurity began a litany of miscalculations and bloody calamities in Iraq, each accompanied by a corresponding reaction in Washington ranging from the inadequate to the inane. Rumsfeld, for example, sounded more annoyed by the media's questions about the vandalism and theft than the events themselves. "Stuff happens," he said at one Pentagon briefing. "Freedom's untidy."[48]

Looting helped perpetuate the power shortages, making life miserable for ordinary Iraqis just as Baghdad was heating to the temperature of an oven for the summer of 2003. Within weeks, Lt. Gen. Jay Garner, a Vietnam veteran who had commanded Army missile batteries during the Persian Gulf War, was replaced, without explanation, by career State Department official L. Paul (Jerry) Bremer III as administrator of the U.S. occupation. Bremer had a solid reputation in the diplomatic corps, but he was an odd choice. He lacked combat experience, he did not speak Arabic, and his posting as the senior American civilian in the war zone was the first time in his life he'd set foot in Iraq. Bremer promptly issued an order demobilizing the Iraqi army, a decree that put tens of thousands of armed young men out on the streets without any practical means of making a living. In the prewar planning, Garner had proposed reconstituting the Iraqi armed forces—and paying them with U.S. dollars to help stabilize the country. But when Garner left Iraq, so did the thinking behind that proposal. Bremer's directive disbanding the Iraqi armed forces went out on May 23, apparently with Rumsfeld's blessing. Five months later, when it was obvious that this had been imprudent, Rumsfeld was dismissive of questions about the Iraqi soldiers. "They just disbanded and went home," he told NBC. "There were conscripts, and they weren't paid very well, and they just left." Doug Feith disparaged the Iraqi armed forces as cruel and corrupt, "a pretty sick organization in a lot of respects." Be that as it may, without prospects for employment they made easy recruits into militias and the insurgency—when they could have been helping to secure the streets. By November 2003, General Zinni, then in retirement, pronounced disbanding the army the "worst mistake" the Bush administration made in post-invasion Iraq. An Iraqi respected by the Americans said the same thing. "This was a mistake, to dissolve the army and the police," said Ayad Alawi, head of the security committee of the Iraqi Governing Council. "The vacuum allowed our enemies to regroup and to infiltrate the country."[49]

Bremer also implemented a sweeping de-Baathification process that led to the dismissal of 30,000 Iraqis, most of them Sunnis, from their jobs in government or in the ministries. By April 2004, Bremer conceded that the plan had been "poorly implemented" and applied "unjustly," and about half of them were taken back on the job. By then, however, many Sunni tribal leaders had taken up arms against the Americans—and the Shia. By 2004, what had emerged in Iraq was a hydra-headed insurgency that featured remnants of the old regime, dueling Sunni and Shiite death squads, and a sadistic bin-Laden-confederated group calling itself "Al Qaeda in Iraq" that was led by Jordanian terrorist Abu Musab al-Zarqawi.

In January 2006, after he left the job, Bremer would concede, "We really didn't see the insurgency coming."[50] He should have—and so should the president of the United States. Two months before Bremer arrived in Iraq—a month before the United States and coalition forces even entered Baghdad—British intelligence agents told their American counterparts that Zarqawi was establishing terrorist cells in Baghdad to attack U.S.

forces after they occupied the city. In January 2004, the United States intercepted a letter from Zarqawi to bin Laden detailing his plans to foment sectarian hatred in the country, presumably by killing Shiites and bombing their most sacred mosques. He said that if an Iraqi government took hold, his insurgency would "wither." Bush administration officials released this letter publicly, and the president pointed to it frequently as a kind of vindication. But the American people had no doubts of Zarqawi's evil intentions; what they were beginning to doubt, amid endless news of roadside bombings, suicide attacks on police recruitment centers, televised beheadings, desecration of dead Americans, the torture by Americans of Iraqi prisoners at Abu Ghraib, and myriad other atrocities and bad news, was the U.S. government's ability to respond effectively to these events.

President Bush had pronounced an end to "major combat operations" in Iraq during his now-notorious appearance on the USS *Lincoln* on May 1, 2003. The soldiers who knew that part of the world the best, however, tended to be more circumspect. While the U.S. Army was still in Kuwait, Maj. Gen. David H. Petraeus began asking journalist and military historian Rick Atkinson, "Tell me how this ends."[51] Although Petraeus was not a household name in the United States at that time, he was no ordinary officer, either. Ambitious, bright, and in tip-top physical condition even by the standards of a professional soldier, Petraeus has an impressive record. He graduated from West Point in 1974, and in 1983 he earned the George C. Marshall award as the top graduate in his class at the U.S. Army Command and General Staff College in Fort Leavenworth, Kansas. The Army next sent him to Princeton, where he earned both master's and doctoral degrees at the Woodrow Wilson School of Public and International Affairs. He is, noted Steve Coll in *The New Yorker,* "perhaps the most scholarly American officer ever to wear four stars."[52] Petraeus's dissertation was a 337-page treatise called "The American Military and the Lessons of Vietnam." Although it includes George Marshall's cautionary advice: "Democracies cannot fight Seven Years' wars," the thrust of the dissertation is that sometimes democracies find themselves attempting to do that very thing. His view is that the "all or nothing" approach favored by the Army brass in response to Vietnam was understandable but unrealistic, and that because the United States will likely face numerous such small wars, knowledge of counterinsurgency tactics will be at a premium.[53]

Petraeus would oversee—in the middle of the Iraq War—the updating of the Army's manual on counterinsurgency. (He would also learn the truth of another Marshall dictum: "War in a democracy is no bed of roses.")[54] At the time he encountered Rick Atkinson in Kuwait, Petraeus was commanding the 101st Airborne Division. In Atkinson's account, the refrain Petraeus expressed was half-rhetorical, but by 2007 the question about how the Iraq War would end was Petraeus's to answer—to a skeptical Congress and a disillusioned nation. By then, Bremer and Rumsfeld had been shoved into retirement, along with Rumsfeld's handpicked field commanders. Petraeus had been named the top American general in Iraq at the beginning of 2007—and confirmed by the Senate in that position on a vote of 81–0. By then, he had convinced the administration to undertake counterinsurgency in a serious way. This new approach entailed a number of measures, chief among them holding towns and neighborhoods once they had been cleared of insurgents or terrorists and allying the U.S. military with various sheiks, tribal leaders, and the local populace, so that the Americans would seem less like an occupying force. Because the plan required 30,000 additional troops, it became known popularly as "the surge." The biggest question was whether this was too little, too late.

At the outset of this effort, President Bush forewarned the American people that the summer of 2007 in Iraq would be more violent, not less, as this new strategy was implemented. "We're going to expect heavy fighting in the weeks and months [ahead]—and we can expect more American and Iraqi casualties," Bush said in a Rose Garden press conference held on May 24, 2007, four years to the month after his appearance on the USS *Lincoln*. In his 2007 remarks, the president continued: "It could be a bloody—it could be a very difficult August."

On September 15, 2007, General Petraeus and Ryan Crocker, the U.S. ambassador to Iraq, came to Washington to deliver an interim report on the surge. In three days of testimony before both houses of Congress, Crocker conceded that the political situation in the country remained stalemated, and that Iraqis had met few of the benchmarks they'd agreed to in return for continued American support. Petraeus, in testimony Steve Coll described as "flinty and unrevealing," made the case that the surge had produced progress militarily, particularly in the previously ungovernable Anbar province in western Iraq and in Baghdad, where most of the additional U.S. resources had gone. Petraeus also offered his opinion that the military needed more time to make it work. Due to grandstanding by the members of the Senate Armed Services Committee, which counted no fewer than four 2008 presidential candidates among its ranks, the Senate sessions were particularly unenlightening, even by that institution's minimal standards of elucidating discourse.* One exchange, however, stood out.

That moment came when Senator John Warner, the ranking Republican on the committee, asked the general who had always wondered how it would turn out if he believed the Iraq War was "making America safer."

"I don't know, actually," he replied. "I have not sat down and sorted it out in my own mind."

A short time later, under probing from Democratic Senator Evan Bayh of Indiana, Petraeus amended his answer to "yes," although he provided the caveat that it was a question best left to others.

Long before then, many respected military writers had weighed in with their verdicts on the prosecution of this war, none kindly to the Bush administration. "President George W. Bush's decision to invade Iraq in 2003 ultimately may come to be seen as one of the most profligate actions in the history of American foreign policy." So begins *Fiasco: The American Military Adventure in Iraq,* by Thomas E. Ricks of *The Washington Post.* Dedicated to "the war dead," *Fiasco* is an angry book by a writer normally known for his dispassion. But Iraq is a polarizing war. "The U.S.-led invasion was launched recklessly, with a flawed plan for war and a worse approach to occupation," Ricks wrote. "Spooked by its own false conclusions about the threat, the Bush administration hurried its diplomacy, short-circuited its war planning, and assembled an agonizingly incompetent occupation." Ricks singled out for special disapprobation Rumsfeld, Wolfowitz, Bremer, and, of course, Bush, but he spread the blame around liberally.

In *Cobra II: The Inside Story of the Invasion and Occupation of Iraq,* Michael R. Gordon, the chief military correspondent for *The New York*

---

*Petraeus's tense dealings with a Senate that had confirmed him unanimously less than nine months earlier exemplified just what Marshall had in mind when opining that sometimes democracy's requirements were "hell" on the professional soldier.

Times, and retired Marine Lt. Gen. Bernard E. Trainor used more measured prose to reach similar conclusions. Gordon and Trainor identified
several "grievous errors" made by the president and his team: They underestimated their opponent by failing to comprehend the complexities
posed by Iraq's tribes and warring ethnic groups; they put too much faith
in high-tech weaponry; they ignored lessons in nation-building that
could have been readily borrowed from the Balkans and other war
zones; and they remained wedded to their prewar plans even after the
Iraqis turned to guerrilla tactics just days into the fight. "Instead of making plans to fight a counterinsurgency," they wrote, "the president and
his team drew up plans to bring the troops home and all but declared the
war won."

The poor execution of the war in time alienated neoconservatives; it
distressed traditional liberals who had supported the war despite their
misgivings about the administration even more. Such was the case with
liberal hawk George Packer, who wrote in support of the war and then
went and covered it with distinction for *The New Yorker.* Packer chronicled his own disillusionment in *The Assassin's Gate: America in Iraq,* a
withering critique of the Bush administration's actions in Iraq. "The administration's war was not my war—it was rushed, dishonest, unforgiv-
ably partisan, and destructive of alliances—but objecting to the authors
and their methods didn't seem reason enough to stand in the way," he
wrote. "One doesn't get one's choice of wars. I wanted Iraqis to be let out
of prison; I wanted to see a homicidal dictator removed from power before he committed mass murder again; I wanted to see if an open society
stood a chance of taking root in the heart of the Arab world."[55]

Packer saw some of these things, but not the last one. In a December
2005 interview with the *San Francisco Chronicle,* Packer said that he believed the Bush administration had put its energy into winning the debate
over the war, somehow thinking Iraq would take care of itself. "Over and
over again, while their backs were turned and they were focused on these
things, Iraq was slipping out of their control," he said. "It's really staggering to say it, but Bush rolled the dice in the biggest war of any president
in my lifetime and he didn't take it seriously."

The political discourse surrounding the war did indeed have an effect,
although not the intended one. While researching *Fiasco,* Tom Ricks discovered to his dismay that in the first days of the Iraq invasion, competent

American field commanders had discovered huge caches of conventional weapons on their way to Baghdad. The Americans didn't destroy those armaments because they feared that intermingled with them were chemical and biological weapons that could have unleashed deadly clouds over the populace. These officers made the mistake of believing their commander-in-chief. Two nights before launching the invasion, Bush had told the American people that "intelligence gathered by this and other governments leaves no doubt that the Iraq regime continues to possess and conceal some of the most lethal weapons ever devised."

And lacking the manpower to guard them, the American commanders simply left the weapons intact, thereby allowing insurgents of all types to arm themselves at will. Like so much else that has gone wrong in Iraq, from the abuses at Abu Ghraib prison and the inability to seal the Syrian border to the failure to bring electric power or physical security to Baghdad and the Iraqi outrage over the presence in their country of armed, unsupervised private security firms such as Blackwater USA, the inability to guard arsenals of abandoned weapons was a problem of numbers.

There were never enough U.S. troops on the ground.

In December 2001, Rumsfeld began pressuring his generals for their Iraq war plans. Tommy Franks, who had succeeded General Zinni as the ranking general of the U.S. Central Command, reached up on a shelf and pulled out the plans that Zinni had left behind. These envisioned sending 385,000 troops, the lowest number Pentagon planners believed would be needed to take and hold Iraq.[56] After Rumsfeld made it clear that this wasn't the order of magnitude he had in mind, Franks began paring. By December 19, when he presented a second plan to Rumsfeld, Franks was envisioning an initial invasion force of 145,000 troops—to be supplemented by reinforcements until the number reached some 275,000. This still wasn't lean enough for Rumsfeld. Three days after Christmas, Franks flew to Bush's Texas ranch to personally brief the president; the administration's war cabinet, including the vice president, was hooked up to the meeting via video conferencing. When Franks got to his 275,000 number, Rumsfeld's voice could be heard interjecting. "Mr. President," he said. "We are still working through the numbers. The number Tom is giving you is soft."[57] This interruption worried Powell, but raised no alarm bells with the president.

Rumsfeld's mania for transforming the U.S. military into a lighter, faster, more lethal, and technologically advanced fighting force was well known to all the principals in that meeting—and, it can be argued—was in the abstract long overdue. Rumsfeld had been making this argument for years, beginning when he was a congressman and later in his first tour as defense secretary. He (and Cheney) spared or attempted to spare the military from a number of costly and duplicative weapons systems, but he had no experience in the hard realities of insurgent war. Nor did the president. Bush, in his 1999 Citadel speech in which he set limits on nation-building, maintained that the military was still in a Cold War mind-set in a world in which "power is increasingly defined, not by mass or size, but by mobility and swiftness." In this speech, which the Vulcans had a hand in drafting, Bush specifically used the long, big buildup for the first Gulf War as an example of what he believed would *not* be effective in the future. "The Gulf War was a stunning victory," Bush said that day in 1999. "But it took six months of planning and transport to summon our fleets and divisions and position them for battle. In the future, we are unlikely to have that kind of time. . . . Our forces in the next century must be agile, lethal, readily deployable, and require a minimum of logistical support. We must be able to project our power over long distances, in days or weeks rather than months."

So Bush didn't blink when Rumsfeld calmly revealed that another, even lighter plan would soon be in the offing. This is what Bush expected, what he had let it be known before even coming to office that he wanted. But it was destined to undermine his efforts in Iraq before they began.

Rumsfeld and the generals he handpicked for the job—most notably Franks, John Abizaid (who succeeded Franks), and Army Chief of Staff George Casey—tended to look at the U.S. military as an "antibody" within Iraqi society, and they believed that the sooner they got out of there after toppling Saddam, the better. (General Petraeus, by contrast, believed that the U.S. military wasn't going to be able to leave until it insinuated itself into Iraqi society, built Iraq's army back up, and gained the confidence of the people—establishing a measure of security in the process.) Bush himself indicated that he shared both goals—a quick in-and-out war *and* setting up a lasting democracy in the Middle East—apparently not realizing that the two were inherently incompatible.

Thus did inadequate troop levels underscore a basic disconnect between a vision that was too grandiose and a battle plan that was too paltry.

Some of this friction was played out publicly from the beginning, although even vocal critics of the war didn't fully appreciate how dire were the implications of this confusion of mission. On February 25, 2003, less than a month before the invasion, Democratic Senator Carl Levin of Michigan asked Army Chief of Staff Gen. Eric K. Shinseki how many troops the administration was contemplating to assure the successful occupation of Iraq. "I would say that what's been mobilized to this point—something on the order of several hundred thousand soldiers—are probably, you know, a figure that would be required," the general replied. Shinseki was not a Rumsfeld guy; in April 2002, the Pentagon had leaked word of his replacement, rendering him a lame duck for a year and a half. Even so, what happened next was unusual: Rumsfeld flatly contradicted Shinseki publicly, and two days later, Wolfowitz told a House committee that the estimate was "wildly off the mark."

This was not how civilian leaders of the Pentagon usually talked publicly about four-star generals. It never happened in Reagan's presidency. That same day, February 27, 2003, Wolfowitz testified that he found it "hard to believe" more troops would be required to transition Iraq to democracy than to conquer it. He predicted that the French and other nations would send troops to assist in the reconstruction, and that increased Iraqi oil revenue would significantly offset the cost of the endeavor.

At this writing, nearly five years into the war, the fate of Iraq remains unknowable. "It is not too soon, however," wrote Gideon Rose, managing editor of *Foreign Affairs* magazine, "to return a judgment on those at the helm who took a difficult job and made it infinitely more so, dramatically undermining America's regional and global position in the process."[58] For one thing, it has long been obvious that General Shinseki was being prudent—and that those "wildly off the mark" were Bush, Cheney, Rumsfeld, and Wolfowitz. They reminded Gideon Rose of Tom and Daisy Buchanan, the "careless people" of F. Scott Fitzgerald's classic *The Great Gatsby,* who "smashed up things and creatures and then retreated back into their money or their vast carelessness, or whatever it was that kept them together, and let other people clean up the mess they had made."

Judging by the resentment they have expressed at inheriting Bush's handiwork if they assume office in 2009, the Democrats running for president concur with that sentiment. In the meantime, the neoconservatives have accounted for themselves in different ways. Some have turned

on Rumsfeld, some on the president, some on themselves. Francis
Fukuyama and Charles Krauthammer turned on each other. Fukuyama
formally resigned from neoconservatism, if one can do such a thing, and
announced this decision in a book, *America at the Crossroads: Democracy,
Power, and the Neoconservative Legacy.* In its opening scene, Krauthammer is speaking to an audience of enthralled neoconservatives in a large
hall. Their enthusiastic response is portrayed as the crystallizing moment in Fukuyama's disillusionment with his conservative brethren.
Iraq is the underlying source of his discontent, and he pines for the days
of Ronald Reagan. Comparing George W. Bush unfavorably to Reagan,
Fukuyama calls for a new U.S. foreign policy he describes as "realistic
Wilsonianism." (Krauthammer, none-too-pleased, fired back in a column called "Fukuyama's Fantasy," in which he said that in his 6,000-
word lecture he had said not one word about the "course or conduct of
the Iraq war.")

In 2006 British journalist David Rose, an associate editor for *Vanity
Fair,* went to several prominent neoconservatives and asked them if they
felt responsible for the debacle in Mesopotamia. The answer, in most
cases, was no. Sometimes, it was "hell no." "Huge mistakes were made,
and I want to be very clear on this: They were not made by neoconservatives, who had almost no voice in what happened, and certainly almost no
voice in what happened after the downfall of the regime in Baghdad,"
Richard Perle told Rose. "I'm getting damn tired of being described as an
architect of the war. I was in favor of bringing down Saddam. Nobody
said, 'Go design the campaign to do that.' I had no responsibility for
that."[59]

Former Bush speechwriter David Frum said the situation in Iraq was
ultimately traceable to "the failure at the center" of the White House, a
reference to the National Security Council and its head, Condoleezza
Rice, who, in his opinion, did not do enough to ensure that the president's
idealistic words were translated into action. This failure, he suggested,
undermined Bush's credibility. One didn't have to be a conservative to
concur with this point. Harvard professor Joseph S. Nye Jr., a veteran of
the State Department during the Clinton administration, agrees that the
discrepancy between Bush's words and his administration's deeds eroded
America's standing, particularly in the Arab world. Nye is the author of
Soft Power: The Means to Success in World Politics; indeed, he is the person

who coined the term "soft power," which he defined as "the ability to get what you want through attraction rather than coercion or payments." It can—and sometimes must—be supplemented by the threat of "hard power," Nye acknowledged. But in his view, Bush resorted to hard power too quickly because, despite the soaring words, he didn't understand the reach of soft power. "If you close your eyes and listen to the president discuss his 'freedom agenda,' it's true that those are clear attempts to cast world events in the light of soft power—especially in his second inaugural address," Nye said in his office in the John F. Kennedy School of Government in March 2007. Continuing, he said:

> Pete Wehner would say, "Of course he understands soft power. What's this rhetoric about if it's not soft power?" And yes, there are chunks of Truman, Wilson, Kennedy, in there. But when there's such a huge gap between your rhetoric and reality you undermine yourself. Truman coupled his vision with realism—and a Marshall Plan. Wilson coupled his vision with international institutions, JFK coupled his with the Alliance for Progress. This administration offers a truncated Wilsonian vision—the grandiose plans, but with no regard for international institutions. It's an abridged version of Trumanism—the rhetoric without the realism.[60]

Kenneth Adelman, an adviser to Reagan at his two summits with Gorbachev and a longtime friend of Don Rumsfeld, reluctantly came to the same conclusion. A year before the Iraq invasion, Adelman predicted that "demolishing Hussein's military power and liberating Iraq would be a cakewalk."[61] He had been right about that, but the administration's inability to maintain control in Iraq and give its citizens any semblance of democracy led to his almost immediate disillusionment. Adelman had worked for Rumsfeld three different times and stayed in vacation homes with him. The two men had traveled the world together with their wives. Yet, when he saw the U.S. military stand idle in the face of massive looting in Baghdad, while Rumsfeld shrugged it off as nothing, Adelman was appalled. "When he said, 'stuff happens,' and 'that's what free people do,' I couldn't understand what he was talking about—and I told him that in our last conversation," Adelman said. "That's not what free people do, it's what savages do."[62] Later, Adelman was incensed when Bush handed out Presidential Medal of Freedom awards to George Tenet, Tommy Franks, and Paul Bremer—the very people Adelman believed had failed Bush in Iraq.[63] Initially, Adelman had gone through channels, speaking to his old friend Don Rumsfeld directly, but after Rumsfeld booted him from the Defense Policy Board, he felt free to speak his mind. He began to speak with journalists, including David Rose, the authors of this book, and Jeffrey Goldberg, then a writer for *The New Yorker.*[65]

Inside the White House some Bush aides experienced the same doubts. In mid-2004 after the Abu Ghraib scandal broke and *The New York Times* called for Rumsfeld's resignation, one high-ranking White House aide complained, only half in jest, that now they were stuck with Rumsfeld indefinitely. "The president isn't going to let *The Times* pick his cabinet," the aide noted.[65] In *State of Denial,* the last book in his war trilogy, Bob Woodward revealed that after Bush won reelection in 2004, White House Chief of Staff Andrew Card tried to persuade Bush to replace Rumsfeld; he tried again a year later, this time with Laura Bush's approval. Cheney and Rove argued against it, Woodward wrote, swaying Bush with the reasoning that it might signal a lack of resolve. Michael Gerson told the authors that he gingerly raised the Rumsfeld issue with Bush himself. "I went to him about the need to replace Rumsfeld within days of the 2004 election," Gerson recalled after he left the White House. "Andy was doing the same thing. I was trying to be more subtle. My whole appeal was not to turn him against Rumsfeld, but to argue that the invasion—the way it was envisioned by the Pentagon—had been a success, but that the occupation was a different challenge, and it was time for a fresh set of eyes over there . . . [to] help us get a new start."[66] Gerson got nowhere.

Part of the problem, another high-ranking White House official told the authors, was that every time it looked as though the president was going to have to acknowledge that Iraq wasn't working, something would happen to give them hope: Saddam's capture in December 2003; Bush's own reelection in 2004; three successful Iraqi elections in January, October, and December 2005; the killing of Zarqawi in June 2006. "We kept wondering, 'Is this a tipping point?'" this official said privately in mid-2007. "But then that window would close. I haven't given up on the theory of the freedom agenda, but there's a real question: Even if this had been done right, was it cursed from the start?"[67]

The cruelest illusion of all came in a March 2005 moment—and in hindsight, that's all it was, little more than a moment—when the Lebanese Muslims and Christians marched together in the streets demanding freedom from Syria. Saudi Arabia held local elections, and Israelis and Palestinians were experiencing a lull in their long war. Commentators around the globe heralded the arrival of an "Arab spring"; they were joined in their enthusiasm by Arab leaders ranging from Libyan strongman Moammar Gadhafi to Lebanese Druze politician Walid Jumblatt. "It's strange for me to say it, but this process of change has started because of the American invasion of Iraq," Jumblatt told David Ignatius of *The Washington Post.* "I was cynical about Iraq. But when I saw the Iraqi people voting three weeks ago, eight million of them, it was the start of a new Arab world."[68] Jumblatt compared events in the Arab world to the collapse of the Berlin Wall. For a few weeks, Bush was Reagan. "It is time to set down in type the most difficult sentence in the English language," wrote *Toronto Star* columnist Richard Gwyn. "That sentence is short and simple. It is this: Bush was right."[69]

Herein lies a cautionary tale for those writing the history of George W. Bush contemporaneously—including the authors of this book: The world moves rapidly today, and public opinion changes rapidly with it. Bush's critics had eaten their humble pie prematurely. In the Arab world, and especially in Iraq, each good sign was trumped by a bad one: Saddam's trial devolved into an execution that had all the dignity of a gang murder. The Iraqi elections produced sectarian stalemate, and worse—ethnic cleansing by murderous militias that infiltrated the government. Zarqawi was dead, but al Qaeda in Iraq wasn't. The bombing of the al Askari Mosque, a revered Shia holy site in the city of Samarra, finally did ignite the sectarian civil war that the Jordanian terrorist had tried to set in motion. Doing Syria and Iran's bidding, Lebanon's anti-democratic Hezbollah militia provoked Israel into an attack, and Lebanon was aflame again, as it had been during Reagan's presidency. "Arab spring" quickly became but a memory.

In 2006, the American people sent a message to Washington, taking both houses of Congress away from Bush's party and putting them in the hands of the Democrats, who ran vocally against the president's foreign policy. A majority of American voters had tired of this war, which has now lasted longer than American involvement in World War II. Only then did Bush replace Don Rumsfeld, along with his top commanders on the ground in Iraq. The general given the implausibly difficult task of fixing things was Dave Petraeus, the same man who knew enough to ask a friend before it all started how it might end.

As Bush's presidency wound to a close, conservatives were left to ask themselves two related questions: First, is there any reason to believe Iraq ever could have worked even if it had been done right? Second, would Reagan have done this? Regarding the first question, the original accusation—that Bush had badly mismanaged the war—became the administration's defense. Invading Iraq was still a good idea, they insisted, but it had been poorly executed. The second question is even more speculative, and different answers to it have been put forth.

Edwin Meese, who served as a top Reagan adviser in Sacramento and Washington, where he was a White House aide and then attorney general, believes Reagan might have agreed to an invasion—but only with a much larger force. "My guess would be that if he were given the same intelligence that George W. Bush was given, about the probability of weapons of mass destruction . . . I think he would have gone in," said Meese. But Meese, who served on the Iraq Study Group, was confident that Reagan would have paid great attention to a four-star general who recommended drastically higher troop levels. Reagan's foreign policy team, he said, would have developed both a strategic plan for the occupation and contingency plans in case their pre-invasion assumptions proved incorrect. "So (Reagan) would have looked at worst-case scenarios, because that was what he generally tended to do," Meese said, contrasting the current administration's dismissive attitude toward General Shinseki with Reagan's solicitous inquiries of General Vessey about troop levels prior to the Grenada invasion. "I think that in the planning for the post-combat phase (for Iraq), Ronald Reagan would have insisted on more troops."[70] The counterargument—that Reagan wouldn't have seriously considered invading Iraq—is offered by Patrick J. Buchanan, who served as director of White House communications in Reagan's second term. Buchanan ridiculed the idea, and neoconservatives along with it, saying simply, "Reagan did not harbor some Wilsonian compulsion to remake the world in the image of Vermont."[71]

Craig Shirley, who wasn't inside the Reagan White House, but who has attempted to get inside Reagan's head while writing probing books about the 1976 and 1980 campaigns, said he wasn't certain, but leaned toward Buchanan's view. "I think that after September 11, every president in the history of America would have gone into Afghanistan," Shirley said. He continued:

> He had to go to the root of the Taliban. He had to get al Qaeda. On Iraq, I don't know. What is interesting is that Reagan only committed troops twice in his presidency, Grenada and Lebanon, and he really was shaken by Lebanon. And I think (Lebanon) made him start to think about a third way of doing things. Reagan was a student of history, and he knew that occupying armies of history usually fail, whether it was Alexander or Caesar or Napoleon. All failed as occupiers of countries, and that there was another way to do these. If you want to undermine the Warsaw Pact or the Soviet Union or if you wanted to undermine the Ortega government of Nicaragua, you didn't go in there with the U.S. Marines or the 82nd Airborne, you work from within, with an organic revolutionary movement. You worked with the contras or you worked with the Pope in Poland. And I'm wondering if he would have said, maybe there's a better way to take out Saddam.[72]

The authors' own answer to the question of whether Reagan would have invaded Iraq is that we have already shown to our satisfaction that Woodrow Wilson wouldn't have done it—and such an undertaking would be even more unlike Reagan. Wilson once said that "America has a spiritual energy in her which no other nation can contribute to the liberation of mankind." Modern Americans would be more likely to use the phrase "moral authority" than "spiritual energy," but the point is that both moral authority and spiritual energy are different from brute force—no matter how noble the intentions. So no, Reagan wouldn't have gone into Iraq. The cliché in political coverage is that George W. Bush is "incurious." Although the accuracy of that assessment may be open to question, it is reasonable to conclude that Bush did not ask enough tough questions about the limits of "hard" power before embarking on the course he pursued. The discussion between Bush and Tenet that led to Tenet's infamous "slam dunk" response is the only recorded instance of an expression of healthy skepticism on Bush's part before he made the decision to invade. But a successful president must regularly exhibit that kind of skepticism in the Oval Office in order to get at the truth of a situation. And the only known exclamation of self-doubt by those manning the top echelons of the Bush administration was heard not in the White House, but in Colin Powell's office at the State Department—a moment of private angst expressed to someone not in Bush's inner circle.

Larry Wilkerson, Powell's former aide, incidentally, has been vehement in his public criticism of Bush's decision to invade Iraq. He doesn't think any president in his right mind, let alone Reagan, would have gone there. "You're suddenly for this messianic spread of freedom and democracy around the world," he told *The Washington Post*. "You're suddenly an advocate of all things that John F. Kennedy was an advocate of: 'We will bear any burden, pay any price.' You've discarded John Quincy Adams, who said we're the friends of liberty everywhere, the custodians only of our own. And you've suddenly said, 'I'm the custodian of the whole world's liberty, and by God if you don't realize it I'm going to bring it to you—and if I have to bring it to you at the point of a gun, that's the way I'm going to bring it to you!'"[73]

By March 2003, it's fair to say that George W. Bush was no longer attempting to emulate Reagan as much as he was trying to avoid what he saw as the mistakes in Iraq and the greater Middle East made by his father and by Bill Clinton. No longer Reagan's disciple, he was his own man—for better or worse. The consequences of the decisions he made as commander-in-chief recalled the tenure of another Texan who served as president, Lyndon Baines Johnson. Reagan may have reminded his countrymen of the bravery and sacrifice of the young men who went to Vietnam for the "noble," if misguided, cause of confronting communism in Southeast Asia. But LBJ, and Bush, reminded Americans of the other half of the equation: how hard it is to impose democracy at the point of a gun, the danger of entering a faraway culture's civil war, and the cost to our own Republic of expending treasure and lives for a purpose that does not succeed.

Leo Strauss has not been the only conservative to admire Winston Churchill. Bush does, too. Along with busts of Lincoln and Eisenhower, a Jacob Epstein sculpture of Churchill was a prominent artwork in Bush's Oval Office. The bust of Sir Winston was loaned to the White House by the British government on July 16, 2001, after Bush mentioned to Tony

Blair that he admired Churchill. "He knew what he believed, and he really kind of went after it in a way that seemed like a Texan to me," Bush explained upon accepting custody of the artwork. Bush liked to josh visiting British journalists by saying he enjoyed "visiting with" Churchill's bust. "Sometimes he'll talk back, sometimes he won't, depending on the stress of the moment," Bush added.

Aware of this penchant, Brian Lamb, in his January 2005 interview with Bush, asked him, "The longer you're in this White House, with all those that have gone before you, do you see ghosts of past presidents?"

Bush parried this query with a quip. "Well, I quit drinking in '86."

Lamb tried again. "I mean, do you feel the history of the place?"

This time, Bush answered seriously, saying that he often wondered what it would be like to be Lincoln, "the country's greatest president," who served when the country was at war with itself. "He seemed to have a good spirit about him," Bush added. "But it's just really hard to project back into somebody else's shoes. So, no, I guess I don't see ghosts."[74]

They are there nonetheless. Ronald Reagan died on June 5, 2004, fifteen months into a war that was looking worse by the day. Without being overly opportunistic about it, conservatives sought to harness Reagan's memory to their own cause. "It was the vision and the will of Ronald Reagan that gave hope to the oppressed, shamed the oppressors, and ended an evil empire," said Dick Cheney in his eulogy.

GWB was in Paris when Reagan left this world; he was preparing to follow in Reagan's footsteps by speaking at the D-Day ceremonies overlooking the beaches at Normandy. At a press conference that afternoon, the tension between Bush and French president Jacques Chirac—a rift caused by the Iraq War—had been palpable. The following morning, Bush swept that mood aside, with help from the ghost of Reagan (whom he saluted as "a gallant leader in the cause of freedom"), in a speech that was evocative in the same way that Reagan's had been at the same place twenty years before. At a lectern from which he could see the English Channel, with World War II vintage ships anchored off the French coast, Bush told of the debris left on the beaches when the invasion ended and the guns were silent—miles upon miles of the belongings of the fallen.

"There were life belts and canteens and socks and K-rations and helmets and diaries and snapshots," Bush said. "And there were Bibles, many Bibles, mixed with the wreckage of war. Our boys had carried in their pockets the book that brought into the world this message: 'Greater love has no man than this, that a man lay down his life for his friends.' America honors all the liberators who fought here in the noblest of causes."

Turning toward Chirac, Bush added the final line. "And America would do it again for our friends." The French president, obviously moved, rose and went to Bush, clasping his right hand in both of his own and holding them for a moment. It was a reminder of what could have been.

More than six decades earlier, a young Austrian scholar had crossed that same body of water where Chirac and Bush stood together. His name was Peter Drucker, and he fled Nazism in time to survive the war, ending up in America where he carved out a reputation as the "father of management theory." Republican presidents, starting with Richard Nixon, have tended to like Drucker. Ronald Reagan quoted him approvingly. So did George W. Bush, who strived to follow Drucker's pioneering approach to management.

In the days after 9/11, Drucker had impressed the president by writing to his friends and telling them "not to abandon daily life and civil society," that this was "exactly what the terrorist wants." Soon thereafter, Drucker was chosen one of twelve recipients of the 2002 Presidential Medal of Freedom, the nation's highest civilian honor. This was the same award that would arouse Ken Adelman's anger when it was given to Tenet, Franks, and Bremer. (They were not present in 2002, but Nancy Reagan was—she was one of Drucker's fellow honorees.)

If a true Reagan disciple wouldn't have gone to war in Iraq, neither would a faithful follower of Drucker. Neither Reagan nor Drucker lived to see the end of the Iraq War. Drucker died the year after Reagan, in 2005. A year earlier, he'd spoken despairingly of the war, calling it the "tragedy of Iraq—a total disaster." Forty years before the invasion of Iraq, Drucker had laid down markers for chief executives that, if followed, might not have prevented the invasion of Iraq, but would certainly have prompted a much faster change of course in its prosecution. In a 1963 piece he wrote for *Harvard Business Review,* Drucker discussed business and products, not politics and war, but the management principles he espoused have a logic that is universal.

While the job to be done may look different in every individual company, one basic truth will always be present: Every product and every activity of business begins to obsolesce as soon as it is started. Every product, every operation, and every activity of a business should, therefore, be put on trial for its life every two or three years. Each should be considered the way we consider a proposal to go into a new product, a new operation or activity—complete with budget, capital appropriations request, and so on. One question should be asked of each: "If we were not in this already, would we now go into it?" And if the answer is "no," the next question should be: "How do we get out and how fast?"

This is the lesson George W. Bush forgot, or never knew.

Or perhaps the answer to the question about the American venture in Iraq—if we were not in this already, would we now go into it?—was simply too painful for the president to contemplate. Colin Powell's prediction about an Iraq occupation sucking the oxygen out of Bush's first term proved even truer in the second. All the while, Osama bin Laden remained at large, issuing threats the world had learned to take seriously. The Taliban began to slowly reconstitute itself and exert pressure on undermanned American and coalition forces in Afghanistan. And the U.S. military was led deeper and deeper into a merciless and multisided war in Iraq while the man at the top had all but exhausted his options.

8

M.B.A. PRESIDENT

In the last column he ever wrote,[1] Peter Drucker noted that the corporate CEO, like the presidency, is an American invention.* In George W. Bush, the nation found a man schooled in both traditions. His father had been president of the United States; GWB was the first resident of the Oval Office with a master's degree in business administration. Even before his 2001 inauguration, Bush was dubbed "America's CEO," a designation welcomed in his inner circle and by corporate America alike.[2] Peter Gebhard, a Rhode Island businessman—and Harvard Business School classmate of Bush—spoke for many executives when he said, "The lawyers and the generals have had their chance. Why not give an M.B.A. a shot?"[3]

---

*"The CEO is an American invention—designed first by Alexander Hamilton in the Constitution in the earliest years of the Republic, and then transferred into the private sector in the form of Hamilton's own Bank of New York and of the Second Bank of the United States in Philadelphia," Drucker wrote. "There is no real counterpart to the CEO in the management of any other country."

Teaching government how to function more "like a business" was a recurrent dream of Republicans of all stripes many years before Bush arrived in Washington. It was an oft-expressed desire of presidents, too, including some who were Democrats. As long ago as 1886, Grover Cleveland vetoed congressional pork-barrel spending using just that reasoning.[4] One hundred years later, Ronald Reagan repeatedly extolled the wisdom of applying "sound business practices" to the workings of the federal government.[5] Rudy Giuliani, a former Reagan administration official, prepared for his 1993 entrance into electoral politics in New York by scouring *Reinventing Government,* that year's hot book (also read by Bill Clinton), in which authors David Osborne and Ted Gaebler claimed that America's "entrepreneurial spirit" could revitalize the public sector as well.

At his first inaugural address as governor of California, Reagan described government as "the people's business." He amplified on this Lincolnesque imagery, adding that "every man, woman and child becomes a shareholder with the first penny of tax paid." As he was preparing to challenge Gerald Ford for the 1976 presidential nomination, one rationale Reagan offered Republicans for his candidacy was that he had as governor implemented the best practices of the private sector—and had the results to show for it. "When I went to Sacramento eight years ago, I had the belief that government was no deep, dark mystery, that it could be operated efficiently by using the same common sense practiced in our everyday life, in our homes, in business and private affairs," Reagan told a conservative convocation in 1975. "Two hundred and fifty experts in the various fields volunteered to serve on task forces at no cost to the taxpayers. They went into every department of state government and came back with 1,800 recommendations on how modern business practices could be used to make government more efficient. We adopted 1,600 of them."[6] The results were more modest than Reagan proclaimed. Many of the ideas were tiny or cosmetic, and a few cost more money than they saved. But some—such as collecting tolls in only one direction on San Francisco Bay area bridges—were commonsense measures that became standard practice in California. Even critics of the task forces acknowledged that they had encouraged some departments to find more efficient ways of operating.

Successful practitioners of private enterprise had fantasized about placing one of their own in the White House. This concept held appeal for the voting public as well. In Reagan's time, Chrysler chief Lee Iacocca attracted attention as a possible Reagan successor. That successor turned out to be George H. W. Bush, but his tenure in the White House was cut short, in part because of the third-party candidacy of billionaire spoiler Ross Perot, whose appeal was based on his pledge to bring sound business practices to Washington. In the first decade of the twenty-first century, public opinion polls revealed a reservoir of interest in successful computer-age entrepreneur (and New York mayor) Michael Bloomberg, also a Harvard Business School graduate, as a possible candidate to follow GWB to the presidency.

So what kind of chief executive did George W. Bush turn out to be—and where did his formative experiences in the field of leadership come from? Mostly, his business school professors tend not to remember Bush one way or the other.[7] His fellow students recall a confident, slightly older student who lived in a sparse Central Square apartment, rode his bike around campus, frequented beer-and-burgers joint Charlie's Kitchen, played intramural baseball and basketball, and talked politics as much as business.[8] Young Bush owned a 1970 Oldsmobile Cutlass, and some weekends he drove friends to the Bush family compound at Kennebunkport in that notoriously messy car. He was well enough liked that thirty classmates would attend his first inauguration in 2001. He was also a bit different from the stereotypical HBS student. Bush was not a "grade-grubber," the term for students who kissed up to their professors; he wore his old National Guard flight jacket around campus, and he chewed tobacco—in class.*An instructor at Harvard, Rudy Winston, who wasn't much older than the twenty-seven-year-old Bush, recalls coming into his classroom on the first day of school to find Bush idling the time away by folding paper airplanes and flying them around the room. "Plenty of students were scared out of their wits when they got there," Winston recalled dryly. "George felt that this environment was something he could handle."[9]

Bush was old-school, all right, but not as much as Harvard Business School itself, which since 1925 employed a method of instruction in

---

*"I was sitting in the front row, and I heard this strange noise coming from up behind me," Bush classmate Mitch Kurz later related to writer and fellow HBS alum John Solomon. "I remember thinking, 'What the heck is that?' I turned around and there was George spitting tobacco juice into a cup."

which the students are given case studies to read, and then called on, at the professor's discretion, in class. No student wants to be embarrassed either when cold-called by the professor or by an inability to keep pace in the ensuing discussion. This peer pressure generally works, as it did with Bush. When he ran for president, numerous journalists scoured the roster of Bush's classmates and professors for evidence he'd skated through school. Those in his Harvard study groups affirmed that young Bush did his work, even if he seemed to envision a destiny that did not entail life in a big corporation. Bush was particularly enamored of a class called Human Organization and Behavior. In another class, when a professor assigned a case study on the paper flow in Ted Kennedy's Senate office, some students questioned the value of the assignment to them as apprentices of the nation's boardrooms. "You never know," the instructor replied. "Don't count politics out. One of you could be president one day."[10] Bush, seated in "Sky Deck," the top row of the amphitheater classroom, got a laugh by smiling impishly and thrusting his arms in the air in victory, Richard Nixon–style. As far as having a future president in their midst, Bush's contemporaries were more likely to identify that person as the serious-minded Mormon student, Mitt Romney, who was already married with children and simultaneously earning a second diploma from Harvard Law School.[11]

If Bush didn't overly impress his Harvard peers and professors, the feeling became mutual. Fresh from his service in the National Guard, Bush was dropped in front of the school in 1973 by a taxi driver who told the young man he was "at the West Point of capitalism." That old adage, new to Bush's ears, impressed the young man. It also may have been his high-water mark at HBS. In his 1999 autobiography, the Harvard years are covered in three uninspired paragraphs that sound like something from a corporate brochure. (Sample sentence: "Harvard gave me the tools and the vocabulary of the business world.")[12] Little that happened after he left school endeared the place to Bush. He did not attend his class reunions, in contrast to Mitt Romney, who once stopped over in Boston for a two-hour reunion dinner with his study mates while en route from Salt Lake City to Europe.[13] Nor did Bush activate his Harvard Business School alumnus e-mail account, a favorite device for networking grads.[14] One Harvard instructor claimed, albeit long after the fact, to have had negative recollections of Bush. His name was Yoshihiro Tsurumi, and during the 2004 campaign he began giving interviews and speeches asserting that as a student Bush had sneered that *The Grapes of Wrath* was a "corny" movie (a remark that in some renditions of Tsurumi interviews came out "commie") and maintained that "people are poor because they are lazy."[15] The president never responded to Tsurumi, whose recollections are suspect. No one else remembers Bush talking this way, and while it's easy to imagine Bush making the "corny" or "commie" remark as a wisecrack, any assertion attributed to him that poor people are indolent does not square with the record of a young man who had come to Harvard after volunteering full-time the year before at Project P.U.L.L., a youth center in Houston's impoverished Third Ward. "He was a super, super guy," said Ernie Ladd, a 6-foot-9, 320-pound former pro football star affiliated with the center. "Everybody loved him so much. He had a way with people."[16] Bush bonded with a little boy at the youth center named Jimmy Dean, who eschewed the opportunity to pair off with a famous African-American athlete and instead gravitated to the scruffy white dude in the flight jacket. When Jimmy Dean lacked shoes, Bush bought them for him. Twenty-seven years later, when a reporter for *The Washington Post* asked Bush about Jimmy, he replied that as a teenager, the boy had been gunned down. "He was like my adopted little brother," Bush added quietly.[17]

His professors wouldn't have known any of that, although *Business Week* magazine, after examining Bush's HBS career, suspected that the Harvard admissions office did—and that it played a role in his acceptance. If antipathy to Bush's adult politics colored Tsurumi's objectivity, he had company. In the waning days of the 2004 campaign, more than fifty tenured and emeritus Harvard Business School professors circulated a letter excoriating Bush's economic policies. This time, the language wasn't unexpectedly personal, it was oddly banal, and included partisan clichés familiar to political writers. The upshot of this kind of disparagement was that even as his aides continued to tout his M.B.A. background, Bush grew nearly as estranged from Harvard as he was from Yale.[18]

Peter Drucker might have been able to relate. Drucker is commonly associated with Harvard, too, because so much of his work was published by the Harvard Business School press. Drucker never attended Harvard, however, didn't teach there, and most likely would not have been hired as a member of the business school faculty. Although his first book, *The End of Economic Man: The Origins of Totalitarianism,* was well received,*Drucker's breakthrough came when he was given free rein to roam around inside General Motors' headquarters at the time its CEO, Alfred Sloan, was creating the modern corporate management structure. Drucker's subsequent book, *Concept of the Corporation,* published in 1946, essentially launched the field of management theory. Drucker's original Big Idea was that workers should be considered assets. This concept struck a chord with people for the most intuitive of reasons— that working people want to value their work and be valued in return. Drucker had many other insights about the art of management over the course of his long career that became accepted wisdom,** and he made many prescient predictions. He pronounced "knowledge workers" (he invented the phrase) the wave of the future, said postwar Japan would become an economic powerhouse, and insisted that by using "management by objectives" (another phrase he coined), a business could administer for the long term by having corporate managers set a series of short-term goals. He is best known for his belief that the command-and-control model of management was less productive than decentralized decision-making. This theory became an organizing principle of American management and spread far beyond the corporate boardroom. In time, decades of Drucker's wisdom became distilled in a sentence or two, lines Drucker never actually uttered, but which can be summed up this way: *An effective manager hires good people, gives them specific goals to meet, delegates authority to them, backs them up while holding them accountable. And doesn't micromanage.*

Reagan, who invoked Drucker's wisdom on four separate occasions as president, was an apostle of business decentralization, largely because of his background as a "corporate ambassador" for General Electric from 1954–1962. He was hired for this job, which also put Reagan on national television screens as host of the popular Sunday night program *General Electric Theater,* by the company's visionary leader, Ralph Cordiner. Born in 1900, nine years before Drucker, in Walla Walla, Washington, Cordiner

---

*One of those friendly critics was Winston Churchill, who reviewed the book positively in the *Times (of London) Literary Supplement,* May 27, 1939.

***Concept of the Corporation* is a book about business," said Jack Beatty, author of a Drucker biography, "the way *Moby Dick* is a book about whaling."

was educated at tiny Whitman College, rose through the ranks of electric power companies in the Northwest, and from on-the-job observations learned to practice what Drucker subsequently preached. Before he was forty, Cordiner was president of the ailing Schick Company, which he put back on its feet.[19] In 1942 he went to Washington, D.C., as Charles Wilson's deputy on the War Production Board. He returned to General Electric as Wilson's assistant after the war and in 1950 succeeded Wilson as president of the company. Reagan revered Cordiner, calling him "the leader of decentralization of industry and business" in the United States.* Decentralization became Reagan's mantra, too. In his first campaign for governor, Reagan declared in a campaign speech, "Big business has already replaced autocratic rule from the top with decentralization, and government must do the same thing."[20] As president, Reagan neatly paraphrased Drucker—and inadvertently foreshadowed the Iran-contra scandal that would erupt two months later—in a 1986 interview about his management style: "Surround yourself with the best people you can find," Reagan said, "delegate authority, and don't interfere."[21]

Drucker's observations about business transferred easily enough to the public sector. In "The Sickness of Government," an article he penned in 1969 for *The Public Interest,* Drucker characterized modern governments as "ungovernable" bureaucratic behemoths that could do little more than inflate the currency or wage war. "There is mounting evidence that government is big rather than strong; that it is fat and flabby rather than powerful; that it costs a great deal but does not achieve much," he added in a book published the same year.[22] At the end of Reagan's first year in the Oval Office, Drucker proclaimed modern government to be "obese, muscle-bound, and having lost its capacity to perform."[23] A confirmed critic of Big Business and Big Government, Drucker became something of an all-purpose Populist, and Republicans, focusing on the half of his message they liked, began quoting him. (Of the last five GOP presidents, only Gerald Ford never mentioned Drucker in public.) Reagan did so

---

*In an interview with Lou Cannon on July 31, 1981, nearly twenty years after concluding his association with General Electric, Reagan waxed rhapsodic about Cordiner: "[General Electric] had 139 plants in 38 states, and he was the one that had the courage as the chief executive officer and chairman of the board to say to the managers of these plants, 'I want you to run them as if they were your plants.' They never had to get a ruling from the board of directors."

positively, whether drawing attention to gains in minority entrepreneur-ship or extolling the economic achievements of his own administration.

Drucker didn't always return the favor. Pontificating on Iran-contra in 1987, he wrote that those in the Reagan White House had made a com-mon but calamitous management mistake: They "confused delegation of authority with abdication of responsibility."

At Harvard, Bush passed muster in a two-year program in which students scrutinized and discussed several hundred case studies in a curriculum de-signed to inculcate in its young charges an effective, delegative manage-ment style. The idea was to take smart grad students and turn them into industry executives—and leaders of men and women—by emphasizing problem-solving techniques over rote memorization of facts. The illustri-ous roster of the school's alumni reveals a record of success, although what, exactly, these HBS grads have in common—or even what they absorbed— is hard to quantify. "I'm not exactly sure what I learned, but I use it every day," one Bush classmate told John Solomon, a freelance writer from New York who is also a Harvard Business School grad (class of 1991).[24] Solomon is one of the few writers who has closely examined Bush's management style in relation to the business school. His Harvard classmates weren't ex-actly sure how he did it, but Bush displayed natural leadership ability, whether as president of a mock company in the annual business school competition or as the marginally talented team captain of his intramural basketball team. "George showed he could herd cats," recalled team center Jim Schroer.[25] On the banks of the Charles River, Bush seamlessly estab-lished himself as a maverick—the Texas twang and tobacco tins were proof of that—and as the well-connected East Coast swell equally com-fortable on the tennis courts and golf courses of Kennebunkport. There is nothing intrinsically nefarious about such dualism; some of it is required in politics, as in life. Reagan, who once wondered aloud how someone who was *not* an actor could succeed at the presidency, won in 1980 while running as an outsider long after he was the undisputed champion of the Republican Party's rank and file. The "citizen-politician" of Reagan's first California gubernatorial campaign had evolved into a seasoned political professional—while retaining his gate-crasher's rhetoric. Bill Clinton promised in 1992 to be "a different kind of Democrat"—without chal-lenging Democratic orthodoxy in any significant way.

Bush traded Harvard's leafy confines for the oil fields of west Texas knowing that the risks of wildcatting were greatly softened by his surname and family connections. He set up a firm called Arbusto (Spanish for "bush") in 1977 with $13,000 left over from an education trust fund, then hung out a shingle in the storied Petroleum Building in Midland where his father had launched his west Texas oil career nearly three decades earlier. GWB's primary assets were his preternatural self-confidence (his Midland friends called him the "Bombastic Bushkin") and an influential last name, of which he took full advantage. An independent oilman needed investors, and Bush's primary rainmaker in rounding them up was Jonathan Bush, his uncle. "George was an easy sale," Jonathan Bush recalled many years later. "I mean, the people that met him would say, right away, 'I'd like to drill with this guy.' . . . He had run for Congress. He was an upstanding guy. They figured he knew what he was doing, but mostly they figured they'd get a fair shake with him. There were a lot of people bilking investors in the oil business in those days."[26]

The lure to invest in Arbusto was more than the opportunity to hang with the GOP's version of a made guy. The price of oil jumped from thirteen dollars a barrel in March 1979, when Arbusto got rolling, to around thirty dollars a barrel by the end of the year. There was money to be made in west Texas, if you knew where to look. Bush didn't know where to find it—he was not a geologist—nor was his company particularly lucky in the leases its drilling team chose to explore. Arbusto drilled nearly a hundred wells, half of which came up empty. That's not a bad average; the problem was that Bush's company never hit the big strike, the "elephant" that would have allowed his partners to recoup their investments. "I always felt bad I never found one for him," Arbusto geologist Tom Dickey said years later. "He was the best boss I ever had."[27] Despite Arbusto's limited success, Bush emerged with a solid reputation in the oil business—and a style of management he would carry into politics.

"He hires good men, and lets 'em do their job," Arbusto production manager James McAninch told *Time* magazine in June 1999.[28] "George was a good operator—very honest and straightforward," McAninch added in an interview with *The Washington Post*. "He had enough savvy to ask almost all the right questions, and [months later] he'd remember what the answers were. . . . He hired you for what you were qualified to do. He didn't interfere. He turned you loose. He'd say, 'Man, it's your responsibility. You do your job, no problem.' . . . He could make quick decisions too."[29]

Still, the company was failing until 1984 when Bush was rescued by two wealthy Cincinnati businessmen, Mercer Reynolds III and William DeWitt Jr., who essentially bought out Arbusto, rolled it into an existing company, Spectrum 7, and installed the Harvard M.B.A. as CEO. Although Bush's partners had deep pockets—and Reynolds possessed a genius for salesmanship—nothing could insulate Spectrum from the impending collapse in world oil prices. In mid-1986, Bush was once more on the financial brink. "I'm all name and no money," he'd tell friends.[30] Again, an angel appeared, this time in the form of Harken Oil and Gas, a Dallas firm gobbling up failing energy companies in the hope of recouping its investment when the price of oil rose again, as it invariably did. Harken assumed Spectrum's $3.1 million in debt, pumped in $2.2 million of its own stock, and took over Spectrum's oil and gas leases and its only other tangible asset—the son of a sitting U.S. vice president—and put him on its board.

By then, Bush had his sights set on the less precarious field of organized baseball. He sold his Harken stock for $835,000 and invested it in the Texas Rangers, which set him up as the public face of the team. It was a profitable alliance for Bush, the Rangers, and the American League. Bush and DeWitt lined up investors who gave the Rangers the infusion of cash needed to become a first-class franchise. Bush's political connections and soothing public persona also helped persuade the city of Arlington to put up $135 million (from a half-penny sales tax) for a new stadium. The Rangers were to put up $50 million, a goal they reached by allocating a one-dollar ticket surcharge for that purpose. Local liberals complained that the deal amounted to "corporate socialism," as indeed it did. Nonetheless, the upshot was a spanking new ballpark, increased fan interest in the team, and the emergence of a managing partner who earned the respect of baseball traditionalists. Bush attended between fifty and sixty games a year as the Rangers' managing partner, often with his wife or twin daughters.*

---

*In one of the better passages in *A Charge to Keep,* Bush wrote: "I always say if you're going to a baseball game, you had better go with someone you like, because you have ample time to talk. I went with someone I loved."

Bush was a familiar presence at the stadium, where he usually eschewed the owners' box in favor of his seats behind the home team dugout. As he watched the games, he willingly signed autographs for his fellow fans. He earned a reputation as an old-school baseball man who put principle and baseball tradition over profits, twice finding himself on the losing end of 27–1 votes among the owners. Bush's lone stands came in opposition to the addition of an extra ("wild card") playoff team, and to breaking longtime tradition by scheduling regular season games between the teams of the National and American leagues. Taking these stands earned Bush the admiration of baseball purists, including sports announcer Bob Costas, a Democrat. Costas told Bush weeks after he was inaugurated that if he showed the same level of courage and judgment as president that he did in baseball, he might be a candidate for Mount Rushmore.[31] Bush worked behind the scenes for the hiring and promotion of minorities in baseball's front offices, including the selection of Leonard Coleman, an African American, as league president. Bush made a point of speaking Spanish to the Latino players on his team, even doing a stint announcing—shades of "Dutch" Reagan—an inning or two for a Spanish-language radio station. Such efforts did not go unnoticed. The Hispanic players expressed respect for Bush, and he attended the wedding of veteran Rangers infielder Julio Franco.

If the family-oriented aspect of baseball appealed to Bush, so did its rough-and-tumble side. Like many Texans, Bush revered legendary Rangers pitcher Nolan Ryan, a native Texan and major league baseball's all-time strikeout king. Ryan wasn't averse to using his blazing fastball to intimidate hitters—or to punching in the face any hitter who objected by having the temerity to rush the mound. This appealed to Bush, too. When Ryan was inducted into the Hall of Fame, then-Governor Bush went with him to Cooperstown for the ceremony. "He's the toughest competitor I've ever seen," Bush said, adding, "Remember the Alamo!" Bush also enjoyed baseball's less-than-genteel ethic of verbal needling—bench-jockeying—and he excelled at it so much at Andover that his nickname was "The Lip."[32] His habit of bestowing nicknames on journalists, aides, and lawmakers after he entered politics was an outgrowth of this sensibility.

"Baseball is a great game because there's a needle factor, and George's quick wit and the bantering that goes on during games made him a natural fit for baseball," said Tom Schieffer, one of Bush's management partners.[33] Schieffer described Bush's management style in baseball as a "precursor" to his government service. "He was very good at delegating authority to other people," Schieffer said, echoing the testimonials from Bush's oil-patch colleagues. "He liked to participate in the strategic planning of the company, but hired people to implement that planning." Bush made the same observation about himself. When he decided to run for governor, he initially tapped a Texas political hand named Brian Berry to manage his campaign—and vowed not to micromanage things. "I run a baseball team," Bush told Berry. "I don't pick up a phone and criticize the players when they screw up in the outfield. That's my manager's job."

Baseball was good to George W. Bush. It got him out of the oil fields, prepared him for politics, and made him rich. Bush stepped away from an active role in the Rangers' front office before his 1994 gubernatorial campaign, putting his ownership stake in a trust. When the team was sold for $250 million in 1998, the new owners cut him a check for $14.9 million. Financially, Bush was set for life. ("Congratulations," boyhood friend Joseph J. O'Neill III told Bush. "Now you can run for president and you'll never have to depend on the rubber chicken circuit. . . . You hit the long ball.")[34]

Bush liked swinging for the fences, but the schooling in executive decision-making he received in organized baseball would prove a mixed bag. For one thing, Bush didn't absorb all the lessons he espoused. Baseball's orderliness appealed to him, as did the sport's unforgiving accountability. He emphasized this point as a candidate in 2000 while expounding on his support for mandatory testing of public school pupils, teacher-competency requirements, and other measures designed to make educators accountable for their students' academic performance. "I ran a baseball team," Bush wrote in his book. "The box scores are delivered in the driveway every morning, for everyone to read. Wins are right there in black and white."[35] In the summer of 2000, major league baseball spiced up its All-Star Game program with a series of questions and answers it put to both presidential candidates. In one answer, Bush equated the role of leading a baseball team to leading the United States. "The most important qualities for a manager are to plan for the season and foster a team spirit that encourages hard work and the desire to win," he said. "A good president must set clear goals, recruit the best, build a spirit of teamwork, and be willing to share credit and take the blame."

Joe DiMaggio biographer Richard Ben Cramer, reflecting on Bush's relationship with the sport, remarked, "There are no ties in baseball, and very little ambiguity. He's okay with that."[36] Still, baseball has a basic paradox: It is a sport in which prevailing in three out of ten at-bats constitutes success, a ratio that puts even the sport's stars in their place, yet playing it well requires a measure of cockiness. Bush was okay with that, too. In his first term, Americans learned that GWB was humble—from Bush himself, who kept telling them so. "Baseball gives you every chance to be great," observed broadcaster Joe Garagiola, formerly a major league catcher. "Then it puts every pressure on you to prove that you haven't got what it takes. It never takes away that chance, and it never takes away that pressure."[37] In *A Charge to Keep,* Bush quoted this passage, adding that this description applies to politics. "Baseball was a great training ground for politics and government," Bush wrote, adding once again: "The bottom line in baseball is results: wins and losses."[38]

As president, Bush too often forgot this lesson. It was crowded out by other personality traits, including stubbornness, an excessive sense of loyalty, a little-noticed passive streak, an odd indifference to public opinion, and a Pollyannaish view of the world that Bush and his team believed was a reflection of Ronald Reagan's sunny optimism. Actual Reaganites saw it as something else: a refusal to face hard facts. Appearing as an honored guest at the 2007 Aspen Ideas Festival, Colin Powell portrayed the president and his top advisers as letting their foreign policy be guided by "wishful thinking." Asked by PBS anchorman Jim Lehrer why there had been so many misconceptions by Bush and his war cabinet about Iraq, Powell replied, "I think it begins with not wanting to see things as they are."

When Bush ran the Rangers, the time came, as it inevitably does, to fire the manager. His name was Bobby Valentine, and he had held the job for seven and a half years—a long stint for a skipper who never won a division—and Valentine spoke well of Bush for years afterward. Bush rather enjoyed being called a stand-up guy; to him the moral of the story was his friendship with Valentine. But it was Bobby Valentine's 581 wins and 605 losses during eight middling seasons that got him sacked, not lack of loyalty. A manager's job is to win pennants, just as a secretary of defense's job is to win wars. This is what President Bush forgot, particularly when it came to Iraq. George W. Bush neglected his own lesson: He didn't keep reading the box scores.

Bush brought to the Oval Office another work of art that was quite different from the sunrise side of the mountain painting by Tom Lea. Lent to him in 1995 by Joe O'Neill, it was an oil painting by W. H. D. Koerner depicting a horseman in western garb leading his men up a rocky slope. It is impossible to say how many men are following him, but several are just visible on the trail behind, emerging over the hill. The lead horseman is hatless—it appears that he and his men have been struggling courageously, even desperately, to attain the mountaintop. But they are not finished, and they seem to be in a hurry: The rider has a determined expression on his face, and the horse appears to be at a gallop. The artist called this tableau *A Charge to Keep,* after a Methodist hymn by Charles Wesley.* Bush was so inspired by the imagery and the message that he borrowed the title for his autobiography. As governor, he had hung the portrait in his office in Austin, and he had urged his gubernatorial staff, in writing, to "take a look at the beautiful painting of a horseman determinedly charging up what appears to be a steep and rough trail."[39]

"This is us," Bush added. "What adds complete life to the painting for me is the message of Charles Wesley that we serve One greater than ourselves." This expression of the ideals behind government service was hardly alien to the political landscape of the Bible belt. In Austin, Bush fit in, establishing himself as one of the most popular Texas governors of the twentieth century. Even in a state trending Republican, this feat required support from the other party, and Bush earned the admiration of a healthy share of Texas Democrats. While Karl Rove plotted the Texas Democrats' demise, Bush played the role of good cop, and played it well. As Reagan had done in Sacramento, Bush willingly negotiated with Democrats. His Austin workday began early, when Bush would drop by the offices of Texas legislators unannounced, dispensing nicknames and good cheer. These lawmakers remembered Bush as being informal in a

---

*The full name of the hymn is "A Charge to Keep, I Have," and its lyrics are derived from the writings of Matthew Henry, a London-based Protestant pastor who wrote commentaries on the Old and New Testaments from 1704 to 1714.

typical Texas way, but respectful. "One of the first things he did after he got elected was he came by and saw people who you would think would be his natural opponents," recalled Robert Junell, a conservative Democrat who chaired the House Appropriations Committee. "He called me 'Mr. Chairman,' which is a title of deference, I suppose, and said, 'I want you to help me, and I want to help you. Here are some things I'm thinking about doing. What do you think about these?'"[40]

Reagan brought to Sacramento an ethic honed as president of the Screen Actors Guild; namely, that the goal of a negotiation is to get a deal. In Austin, Bush operated under the same principle—when he cared about the issue. As a candidate, he had promised action on four issues: tort reform, juvenile justice, education funding and accountability, and changes in the welfare system. To the annoyance of Governor Ann Richards, Bush would discuss little else. As governor, he didn't bother himself with much else either. In 1995, Bush wouldn't make a call in support of a bill designed to allow Texans to more easily obtain home equity loans. He favored it, he just wouldn't work for it—and it failed to pass that legislative session. "It wasn't one of his four," explained Dan Shelley, his first legislative director.[41]

Bush obtained results on his four priorities, each requiring significant compromise. Regarding civil lawsuits, for example, Bush had been seeking to cap punitive damages at $500,000. The Democrats wanted a $1 million ceiling. They met in the middle, at $750,000. "You don't get everything you want," Bush said, adding mischievously, "A dictatorship would be a lot easier."[42] Even stipulating that Bush was kidding, his record in Austin begs the question of what happened in the decade between Bush's first term as governor and his second term as president. These are two different chief executives. In Washington, compromise was seldom attempted and even more rarely achieved. Why?

Karl Rove's explanation is that it's the Democrats' fault. "I think there was a qualitative difference to the nature of political dialogue in the 1990s that is still corrupting the system," he said in an interview for this book. "If the Clinton administration had proposed a prescription drug benefit like ours, it would have gained enormous support among Democrats. And yet, it didn't in this administration. NAFTA was passed with substantial Democrat support. We've had to pass trade agreements like the Central American Free Trade Agreement, or [an]

Australia [trade pact]—deals that were clearly in the national interest economically, diplomatically, politically—we've had to pass with virtually no Democrat support. . . . And it's because they adopted, the moment he came in, in the aftermath of the contested 2000 election, a policy of deliberate obstructionism on things big and small that was unhealthy for the country."[43]

In the same interview, Rove outlined the ways he believed Bush was like Reagan, mainly in looking at the big picture and using the presidency to accomplish significant goals. Yet Rove, quoting William Shakespeare ("comparisons are odorous"),* also said he thought it unfair for the forty-third president of the United States to be compared to the fortieth. "Look, Reagan is a dominant political figure," Rove said. "It's like FDR."

Although he might have appreciated that analogy, Reagan was on record as being unimpressed with the excuse that Republican failures were the Democrats' fault, an alibi also employed by conservatives in his day. Two months into his presidency, at a dinner attended by conservatives, Reagan told a baseball story of his own to illustrate how futile he found partisan finger-pointing, even from his own side.

> We conservatives, if we mean to continue governing, must realize that it will not always be so easy to place the blame on the past for our national difficulties. You know, one day the great baseball manager Frankie Frisch sent a rookie out to play center field. The rookie promptly dropped the first fly ball that was hit to him. On the next play he let a grounder go between his feet and then threw the ball to the wrong base. Frankie stormed out of the dugout, took his glove away from him and said, "I'll show you how to play this position." And the next batter slammed a line drive right over second base. Frankie came in on it, missed it completely, fell down when he tried to chase it, threw down his glove, and yelled at the rookie, "You've got center field so screwed up nobody can play it!"

---

*This time, unlike when he botched the quotation on Reagan's desk, Rove's memory was correct: The line is in Shakespeare's *Much Ado about Nothing*.

The audience laughed at the punch line, but Reagan provided a kicker: "The point is we must lead a nation, and that means more than criticizing the past," Reagan said. "Indeed, as T.S. Eliot once said, 'Only by acceptance of the past will you alter its meaning.'"[44]

A close look at Bush's past—his tenure in Austin—finds evidence that the seeds of future failure, as well as future success, were taking root even as Bush was wowing his fellow Texans, the national media, and a coterie of Californians who believed they were seeing Reagan's heir at work. If Governor Bush demonstrated willingness to compromise, he also had a short attention span, an unnerving level of certitude, and a habit of hiring underlings based on personal loyalty. Bush generally did not seek a broad range of policy advice, and he didn't read enough on his own to be exposed to unconventional thinking—or, sometimes, the most up-to-date official news. He did not read the long-awaited 261-page report on the 1999 bonfire collapse at Texas A&M that killed twelve young people, for example. He did not read the 36-page executive summary, either. "I highlighted half a page," said Clay Johnson, Bush's gubernatorial chief-of-staff. "He read that."[45] Utilities commissioner Patrick Henry Wood III told the *Los Angeles Times* that Bush would offer witty rejoinders to queries about long-term goals or how to finesse a certain legislator, but when Wood sought to engage Bush on policy specifics, the governor sloughed him off. "Pat, I have you to do that," Bush would say.[46]

When Bush cared about an issue, he could get into the weeds with it. In 1995 when tort reform was languishing, the Republican author of the legislation, state senator David Sibley, went to the governor's mansion to tell Bush the bill was imperiled. Bush invited Sibley to stay for dinner, pressed him for details about the sticking points, then called Bob Bullock, the Democratic lieutenant governor. The two men forged a compromise in minutes. "He's like the guy at the pool party who sort of walks up to the diving board and does a double twist with a flip," Sibley recalled later. "He made it look easy."[47]

But when an issue didn't engage Bush, watch out. Four months after assuming office, Bush began devoting fifteen minutes to each death penalty review instead of thirty minutes. When he ran for president, he assured skeptical journalists that every one of the 152 executions carried out by the state of Texas when he was governor involved undeniably guilty convicts.* Bush believed this to be true, and he certainly hoped it was so, but the fact of the matter was that he had no real way of knowing—and there are obvious reasons for doubt. The State of Texas doesn't guarantee competent counsel for defendants in capital cases, and it imposes stringent time limits on appeals of criminal convictions, restrictive rules regarding introduction of new evidence, and cumbersome clemency procedures.

As far back as his Yale days, Bush's fraternity brother Lanny J. Davis was struck by how Bush cruised through school without ever seeming to crack a book, a quality that Neil Reagan had also observed about his brother, then known as Dutch Reagan, at Eureka College. Davis, a lawyer who worked on damage control in the Clinton White House, claims friendship with both Bill Clinton and George W. Bush and says they are more alike than is generally acknowledged. Bush, Davis said, displayed "analytical people skills," which he used to size people up quickly.[48] To be sure, this is a knack some people possess, although Bush's initial claim upon meeting Vladimir Putin that he'd gotten a sense of the Russian leader's "soul" revealed its limitations.

Bush's predilection for sailing above issues that didn't intrigue him was another kind of constraint. When Bush was campaigning in Milford, New Hampshire, in September 1999, a woman asked him how he planned to "promote peace in the Middle East." "I want to stand by Israel," Bush replied. "We're not gonna allow Israel to be pushed into the Red Sea. There's something called the Arrow missile system, which is an inter-ballistic, a short-range inter-ballistic missile system that intercepts missiles coming from [elsewhere]."[49] This was an unimpressive response.

---

*In contrast, only two executions were scheduled during Reagan's eight years as governor, first because the California Supreme Court struck down the death penalty (a decision Reagan criticized), and later because the U.S. Supreme Court imposed a moratorium while it debated the constitutionality of capital punishment. The high court eventually restored the death penalty, and voters did the same in California through a ballot initiative. Still, it is notable that Reagan granted clemency—after extensive investigation by his legal affairs secretary, Ed Meese—in one of the two capital cases that reached his desk. This spared the life of Calvin Thomas, convicted of killing the three-year-old son of his girlfriend by hurling a firebomb into her home. To the surprise of many, Meese and Reagan decided that a medical examination conducted after Thomas was convicted "revealed preexisting brain damage resulting in a chronic mental condition."

There is no such animal as an "inter-ballistic" missile, although Bush apparently had in mind an anti-ballistic missile system then in the testing stage, and the woman hadn't asked about missile defense, but about peace talks. "Bush is trying to turn his weakness into a virtue," University of Texas political scientist Bruce Buchanan remarked at the time. "He's not a policy wonk, so he has to rely on people who are." Buchanan, who admired the job Bush had done in Texas, added, "Bush's biggest weakness is that he might not be in a position to discern the credibility of the options his advisers lay out for him."[50]

Bush's answer was that his street sense had taken him pretty far, thank you very much. "I know what I can do," Bush told James Carney of *Time* magazine in 1999. "I've never held myself out to be any great genius, but I'm plenty smart. And I've got good common sense and good instincts. And that's what people want in their leader."[51] To Bob Woodward, Bush put it this way: "I'm not a textbook player. I'm a gut player."[52] Historian Richard Brookhiser, writing in the April 2003 *Atlantic Monthly,* suspected that this exalting of Bush's instinct had a whiff of rationalization to it, "a cover for his lack of more obvious qualifications, such as intellect conventionally measured." Bush saw it as cutting through jargon and excuses so he could get to an action point. Or, as Condoleezza Rice told Nicholas Lemann of *The New Yorker,* what Bush liked least was when she described some foreign policy problem as "complex."[53] At no point in his life, even after Iraq turned bad, did GWB publicly second-guess himself. Reagan said while running for governor of California in 1966, and later while running for president, that there were "simple answers, just not easy ones," a sentiment he repeated as president.* Bush took this notion and ran with it. Both Reagan and Bush were stubborn, but Reagan had a practical streak and a gift for euphemism that enabled him to distance himself from his rhetoric when it became a barrier to political success. As we have seen, Reagan described the forced withdrawal of Marines from Lebanon in 1984 as "redeployment." Similarly, Reagan acceded to several tax increases (without abandoning his overall goal of tax reduction) by explaining that they were "tax reforms." Bush, arguably more consistent

---

*"There are simple answers to a great many things that we've made unnecessarily complicated, but they're not easy," Reagan said at a February 10, 1986, session with regional reporters and editors.

than Reagan, but not his equal temperamentally, had a harder time discarding his catchwords.

Lanny Davis had taken notice of Bush's stubbornness many years earlier, calling it the "potential obstacle" to a successful Bush second term. Davis recalled a night of shooting pool in the Deke House at Yale. Bush had gotten it into his head that he had to make a double-bank shot in a side pocket before he could quit for the night—but he couldn't make the shot. "He wouldn't give up until we forced him to leave," Davis recalled, using the phrase "competitive stubbornness" to describe Bush.[54]

This trait intrigued—and ultimately repelled—David Gergen, a veteran of the White House under four presidents, including Reagan. Gergen spent GWB's presidency ensconced at Harvard University's John F. Kennedy School of Government as director of the Center for Public Leadership. In a 2003 essay penned for the school's journal, Gergen gave Bush high marks for being decisive, daring, and more effective in enacting his agenda than was thought possible after the 2000 election. Gergen's primary focus, however, was Bush's hardheadedness, insularity, and "top-down, macho" style of governance.[55] "We have seen this kind of tough, decisive leadership before—in Jack Welch at General Electric, George Patton on the battlefield, Bobby Knight on the basketball court," Gergen wrote. "But we don't often see this brand of leadership in the presidency, and it very much runs against the grain of current leadership studies." Gergen made two other provocative observations. The first was that Harvard Business School had changed its emphasis (though not its teaching methods) since Bush was a student there. "The command-and-control approach was still in vogue for CEOs when Bush studied at the Harvard Business School . . . and there is little doubt that as the first M.B.A. president, he reflects its training," Gergen wrote.[56]

Lawrence H. Summers, who served as treasury secretary in the Clinton administration and as Harvard's president during the first five years of Bush's administration, made the same point in an interview for this book. Summers spoke of an "inbox-outbox" culture of management in which the premium is on decisiveness—the culture of Jack Welch and George Bush—that had given way to a less hierarchical generation of executives, such as Microsoft founder Bill Gates and Goldman Sachs CEO Lloyd Blankfein. "This style of management is more deliberative," said Summers. "They think it is better to be right, and take a little more time deciding, than to be decisive and wrong." He named two American presidents as epitomizing this modern style. The first was Clinton, the man for whom Summers had worked. The second was Reagan. "I think he had a deeper kind of security than you normally see," Summers said.[57]

Summers, like many of Bush's critics, assigns feelings of insecurity to GWB. It seems just as likely that Bush's problem is excessive self-confidence, a tendency that might be said to flow naturally out of the Bush family's famously averse attitude toward introspection or excessive cogitation. This is a trait GWB shares with his father. (As president, George H. W. Bush invoked Peter Drucker only one time. "Peter Drucker said, quote, 'Leadership is action,'" said Forty-One, on September 9, 1992, at a campaign rally in Middletown, New Jersey. "But you know, nowhere have I seen leadership defined as, 'Hey, I'll get back to you later.' You can't do that when you're in the Oval Office. You've got to make a decision.")

Gergen also focused on the painting of the horseman by W. H. D. Koerner in Bush's Oval Office. Gergen noted that Bush's fans see him as that horseman—the fearless leader riding bravely up the mountain, against unseen enemies, fulfilling the admonishment of Charles Wesley's hymn to do God's will. "His critics can look at the same painting and see something very different: a lone, arrogant cowboy plunging recklessly ahead, paying little heed to danger, looking neither left nor right, listening to no voice other than his own," Gergen wrote. "That he believes he is doing the Lord's work only increases their apprehension. He's not taking us up a mountain, they fear, but over a cliff."

The fact that the horseman charging up the mountain has lost his hat could be viewed as a sign of his dedication and sacrifice, but it could also be disquieting. Being hatless doesn't make the rider more dashing; it makes him seem imprudent, reckless. It seems that he is rushing headlong into danger, taking his men with him. This interpretation escaped Bush. Discussing the painting at a 2004 session at Constitutional Hall with senior members of the executive agencies, he said, "You know that at least two horsemen are coming with him. There may be three or four, or a thousand—you just don't know. But you know it's a tough hill to climb."

There also may be a thousand enemy horsemen—or four thousand—on the other side of the mountain. That's something else you don't know.

In 1999, presidential candidate George W. Bush visited the Connecticut home of supporter Thomas C. Foley for a meeting of the Young Presidents Organization. Among those attending was Ned Lamont, a politically moderate business leader and a Greenwich selectman, the same job held by Prescott Bush before he ran for the Senate. (Distressed over Iraq, Lamont would run for the Senate, too, defeating Senator Joe Lieberman in the 2006 Democratic primary. He lost a three-way race in the general election to Lieberman, however, who had refiled as an Independent.) Lamont recalled later that during the question-and-answer period that night, Bush was asked about his lack of foreign policy experience, and what he would do if violence erupted again in the Middle East.

"I'd call Brent Scowcroft," Bush replied.[58]

This pithy deflection satisfied his audience, who inferred that in invoking the man who had served as his father's White House national security adviser, Bush was saying he'd reach out to the best foreign policy minds in the Republican Party—and that because of his connections, he'd know just where to find them. Yet, when just such a thing did occur, Bush did not consult with Scowcroft, who would have advised him not to invade Iraq. Although Condi Rice, Scowcroft's former protégée, was aware of his misgivings, Scowcroft still feared that GWB had not been apprised of them, so he penned an op-ed (it ran in the *Wall Street Journal*) warning of dire consequences if the United States went on the attack.[59] This is what old Washington hands do when they believe their advice is no longer being heeded. It is not, however, what those who want to remain in the good graces of George W. Bush and his top aides do, and Scowcroft received an incensed phone call from Rice. "How could you do this to us?" she asked.[60] Scowcroft believed he had simply been trying to help Bush by offering a viewpoint Bush had insulated himself from hearing. But in December 2001, GWB virtually boasted to Bob Woodward that he didn't go beyond the White House walls for counsel on such issues. ("I have no outside advice," Bush said. "Anybody who says they're an outside adviser of this administration on this particular matter is not telling the truth.")[61]

Scowcroft wasn't the only person close to Bush's father who worried that the son was isolated from opinions cutting against the prevailing neoconservative grain. "We always made sure the President was hearing all the possibilities," John Sununu, who served as chief of staff to George H. W. Bush, told Jeffrey Goldberg of *The New Yorker*. "That's one of the differences between the first Bush Administration and this Bush Admin-istration."[62] There was a hint of score-settling in this dig: It was First Son George W. Bush who had told Sununu it was time to move on when the chief of staff had outlived his usefulness to Forty-One.

It has long been known that the Bushes place an uncommon premium on loyalty to their kinsmen: They delineate in an almost caste fashion be-tween family and staff. George W. Bush added a couple of wrinkles of his own. The first was his Texas-centric view of life; another his convic-tion that loyalty is a two-way street. Bush feels entitled to return the loy-alty he demands from his crew. This is admirable; it also undermines his inner Drucker, because, like his love of Texas, it blurs the lines of ac-countability.

"Texas is a state of mind," John Steinbeck wrote after touring the United States in 1960 and ending up in Abilene for Thanksgiving. "Texas is an obsession."[63] Native Texans love quoting Steinbeck on that point; transplanted Texans have an even more concise epigram to describe their love of place. It's "G.T.T.," which means "Gone to Texas," a sign that be-gan showing up on abandoned cabins in the southeastern states in the 1880s. It appeared on the office doors of Matt Dowd and Mark McKin-non at Bush/Cheney 2004 headquarters after the November victory, sig-nifying a return to their Austin homes. The real migration after the reelection went the other way as Bush sent for Lone Staters to staff his ad-ministration. Newly elected presidents invariably bring their local aides-de-camp with them to Washington, whether it's John Kennedy's "Boston mafia" or Ronald Reagan's cadre of Californians. Typically, a weeding-out process ensues, particularly for second-term presidents. Among Rea-gan's Californians and Bill Clinton's Arkansans, aides were let go, reassigned, or simply opted out. The dynamic with Bush was the reverse. In his second term, he promoted the men and women he had brought from his home state to ever higher positions—and brought in more of them.

Some were Texas transplants, such as Rove, who moved from the sec-ond floor in the White House to the first, down a short hall from the Oval Office, as deputy chief of staff. ("Is Rove a Texan?" mused Texas-born press secretary Scott McClellan. "Absolutely!")[64] Most were Texas natives, including McClellan; Clay Johnson, Bush's Yale roommate who helped him staff the administration with fellow Texans, and then moved to the

Office of Management and Budget; Karen Hughes, who returned from her Austin hiatus for a high-level State Department job; Dina Powell, who manned the White House personnel office, then joined Hughes at State; Margaret Spellings, who became secretary of education; Dan Bartlett, elevated from director of communications to counselor to the president; Harriet Miers, Bush's personal lawyer from Dallas, promoted from staff secretary to White House counsel—and nominated for the Supreme Court; and Alberto Gonzales, attorney general. Condi Rice, who was not a Texan—more like honorary family—was elevated from national security adviser to secretary of state. This was the milieu in which Don Rumsfeld chose Tommy Franks, another Texan, to lead the U.S. forces in Iraq. Bush publicly expressed pride in Franks's promotion, noting for reporters at his ranch in Crawford on December 28, 2001, that Franks had attended the same Midland school as Laura. "He's a down-to-earth, no-nonsense guy—precisely the kind of man we need to lead a complex mission such as this," Bush added.

"Naturally, there's a bond we share because we come from Texas," McClellan explained as Bush's second term began three years later. "There are a number of Texans in the White House who've worked for him for a long time, who believe in his agenda and his leadership, and who understand his tone and philosophy. They are people he has complete trust in; they are also people he considers to be friends."[65] That's a highfalutin way of saying Bush picked these people for his comfort level. For a Texan this is logical. "What Texans can dream, Texans can do," Bush said in his first inaugural address as governor. McKinnon expounded on this attitude days before Bush's second inaugural as president. "Texans are, by their nature, tough, loyal and think really big," he said. "No small ball. Always going for the fences. The best way to get a Texan to do something is tell 'em they can't."[66]

This was a fitting maxim for Bush and helps explain his most controversial personnel move—the selection of Dick Cheney as vice president.

Initially, Cheney was viewed as an inspired choice. He had served as President Ford's chief of staff, had been a member of Congress from his home state of Wyoming, and was defense secretary when Bush's father was president. He had the experience and gravitas that many observers found wanting in Bush, although political commentators had fun with the Bush vice presidential selection process: Cheney was tapped by Bush to head the search, and the name that came out on top was . . . Dick Cheney. That was never the whole story, of course. Bush wanted Cheney all along. In the summer of 2004, Clay Johnson told journalist Nicholas Lemann that Bush had offered Cheney the vice presidential nomination before he headed up the search committee.[67] Cheney had told the authors the same thing at a lunch in his office in 2002, recounting a call he received from Austin in the spring of 2000 when Bush had locked up the nomination. Cheney was living in Texas, serving as CEO of Halliburton. Bush was probing Cheney's willingness to run on the GOP ticket. When he demurred, Bush asked him to run the search committee that vetted the potential running mates. Cheney agreed. He soon noticed that when he'd call to report on a prospective nominee, Bush would sign off by saying, jocularly, "You could make my problem go away," or, "You could make my life a whole lot easier."[68]

Cheney was merely flattered until the day he called Bush to tell him he had a list of finalists, and Bush replied, "Fine, but I want your name on that list, too."* Realizing Bush was serious, Cheney drove to Austin and put it to the governor straight: He'd had heart trouble since his thirties, had a record that included two drunk driving convictions, lacked the kind of charisma associated with national campaigns, and hailed from a state with only three electoral votes that Bush would carry anyway. Bush was undeterred, although he did meet with the other finalist, former Missouri Senator John Danforth, a tall, well-spoken patrician from St. Louis. Danforth, who had gone through prep school, Princeton, Yale Law School, and Yale Divinity School, is an ordained Episcopal priest. Nick Lemann conjectures that Bush rejected Danforth because he was taller than Bush, more intellectually imposing, and a creature of Washington. This seems uncharitable, but Danforth and his wife, Sally, had dinner with Bush in Chicago on July 18, 2000, and Cheney made the introductions, then excused himself. If this was a courtship dinner, it didn't go well.[69] Within days, Cheney had been offered the slot, and he accepted.

---

*Cheney subsequently provided a similar account to his biographer, Stephen F. Hayes, to whom the vice president gave extensive access. So, too, did President Bush in his interviews with Robert Draper, author of *Dead Certain: The Presidency of George W. Bush*.

Two summers later, when the authors dined with Cheney in his White House office, the vice presidency had been redefined. Most people in politics have their favorite quotation about the ignominious nature of the vice presidency, many of which were uttered by the actual holders of that office. John Adams, for example, noted drolly, "I am vice president. In this, I am nothing. But I may be everything."[70] Over time, the duties of the office evolved, particularly after an unprepared Harry Truman took over for Franklin Roosevelt. Truman knew almost nothing about the atomic bomb or what Roosevelt had promised Stalin at Yalta, and he had met alone with FDR only three times. ("I don't know if you boys pray," Truman told the White House press corps the day after Roosevelt died, "but if you do, please pray God to help me carry this load.")[71] Partly because of his own experience, Truman assisted in the upgrading of the vice president's official duties. The National Security Act of 1947, which Truman supported and signed, made the vice president a member of the National Security Council; Truman's vice president, Alben Barkley, regularly attended NSC meetings. Over time, the vice presidency steadily grew in power and prestige. Walter Mondale was the first to be given office space in the West Wing. George H. W. Bush enjoyed weekly lunches with Reagan. (On his last full day in office, Reagan wrote his vice president a note that ended, "I'll miss our Thursday lunches. Ron.")[72] Al Gore set the bar even higher, producing administration initiatives, particularly on environmental policy, from his own staff, and he was consulted on most important policy questions. At the time of our lunch with him, Cheney was well aware of this evolution in the powers of his office—he mentioned the dearth of Truman meetings with Roosevelt on his own—and he was prepared for the perspicuous question: How many times have you met privately with Bush?

"Let me see," Cheney said, reaching into the breast pocket of his suit coat. "Three, four, five, six, seven," he said going slowly over the schedule in his hand. "Seven times," he said, pausing for effect, "today."[73]

Cheney is conventionally recognized as the most powerful of modern vice presidents. He is also the only vice president since Charles Curtis, Herbert Hoover's second in command, who was not prospectively a candidate for president.* In this Cheney conspicuously differed from Mon-

---

*Some would put Spiro T. Agnew, Richard Nixon's first vice president, in this category, but Agnew was a conservative favorite, and he might have been a contender had he not been forced to resign in 1974 after pleading no contest to charges of tax evasion and

dale and Gore, his two most influential predecessors in the vice presidency. "Those guys wanted to run (for president)," top Cheney aide Mary Matalin explained in 2002. "That changes everything."[74] Cheney amplified on this point in our interview. "I'm not running in 2008," he said. "I looked at running in '96, and decided against it. That was my time. In this job, I'm not spending my time figuring out how to do a side deal for a county chairman in New Hampshire or raising money for some guy in Colorado so he'll owe me a personal favor. One hundred percent of my time is spent doing the work of the Bush administration."

Cheney's notion of his job, described in an article published in *National Journal,* was received by many longtime students of the executive branch as a good-government approach that would spare the president some of the internal political machinations that had caused rifts in previous administrations. That reaction turned out to be too sanguine. Cheney, with Bush's consent, had really done two things that produced adverse consequences:

First, the vice president is *supposed* to want to succeed the president. That ambition facilitates one of the important checks and balances of modern politics by providing the White House with a crucial link to the grassroots. If Bush had had a vice president with ambitions of his own, making calls around the nation to keep in touch with potential supporters, then someone in the GOP, working as a county chairman or a fundraiser, might have told him what Republican voters were thinking about Bush's job performance and policy goals. One of those workers might have said that people were getting damned nervous about all the talk of war in Iraq.

Second, in redefining the role of the vice president (without bothering to cue in the American people), Bush and Cheney upended the traditional management structure of the White House in a way that complicated lines of authority, as either Peter Drucker or Ronald Reagan could have told them it would. The changes were carried out deliberately. "Dick's major concern, one of them, was . . . that there needs to be a greater and more effective role for the vice president," former Army chief of staff

---

money laundering. In all, seven vice presidents became president during the twentieth century, five of them because they inherited the job after the president died in office or (in Nixon's case) resigned. Three others—Hubert Humphrey, Walter Mondale, and Al Gore—were Democratic presidential nominees. Henry Wallace, Franklin Roosevelt's second of three vice presidents, became a third-party nominee.

John O. Marsh Jr. told *The Washington Post.* "He holds the view, as I do, that the vice president should be the chief of staff in effect, that everything should run through his office."[75] This system churned up everything, as *The Post* observed in its eye-opening four-part series on Cheney published in June 2007. If Cheney was the de facto chief of staff, what did that make Andy Card? Colin Powell was confronted with this dilemma in August 2002 while attempting to slow the rush to war. After giving the president his go-slow pitch, and receiving a follow-up call from Condi Rice, Powell wondered about the utility of such a presentation. "That's why I wanted to talk to the president without those other guys," he said in a 2007 interview. Those "other guys" included Cheney.[76] But a vice president is a constitutional officer, not a paid employee who serves at the discretion of the president. In the management structure that took shape, Cheney became an *über* chief of staff, the functional equivalent of a very hands-on CEO. In effect, this made Bush a kind of White House chairman of the board, although it's unclear why the president acquiesced to such an arrangement. Mondale, the first truly modern vice president, wondered the same thing. In a July 29, 2007, op-ed in *The Washington Post,* Walter Mondale wrote, "Somehow, not only has Cheney been given vast authority by President Bush—including, apparently, the entire intelligence portfolio—but he also pursues his own agenda. The real question is why the president allows this to happen."

Before he became vice president, Cheney typically earned respectful testimonials from insiders in both political parties as well as from veteran Washington journalists. The taciturn figure who came to be associated with undisclosed locations, the stonewalling of Congress, and the invisible hand behind an unpopular war had been a popular and public fixture on Capitol Hill, lauded widely for his candor and sense of humor. Political professionals, however, soon began to wonder what had happened to the Cheney they knew. Cheney's erstwhile friend Brent Scowcroft told journalist Jeffrey Goldberg, "Dick Cheney I don't know anymore," and former Illinois congressman Bob Michel said much the same about the man he had handpicked to succeed him as the Republicans' leader in the House. "I never thought of him as being a hothead with respect to going to war," Michel told Stephen Hayes, author of a book on Cheney. "He was a mediator, I thought."[77] In Washington, "What happened to Dick Cheney?" became something of a parlor game, although it was one

Cheney and his closest friends refused to play. When asked how his long-time friend and fellow Wyoming Republican had changed, Alan Simpson blurted out, "I'm not going to put him on the couch for you!"[78]

Bush expressed a similar reluctance to analyze Cheney—or himself. "Look, we don't sit around psychoanalyzing each other," he told Hayes.[79] Questions remain, however, especially about how the decision was made to invade Iraq. Why didn't Bush and Cheney listen to officials in the Democratic Party (Ted Kennedy, for instance) with whom they had worked before? Why didn't they defer to John McCain, a senator from their own party, on the question of torture—hadn't McCain's horrific experiences as POW earned him that much? For that matter, why did Cheney not listen to himself on Iraq? In 1994, while defending the first Bush administration's decision to halt the victorious U.S. forces at the Kuwait border, Cheney explained that occupying Iraq would have alienated the Arab nations in the large coalition stitched together by Bush's father; entwined the United States in factional fighting among Iraqi Kurds, Sunnis, and Shiites; and cost considerable American lives. "It's a quagmire if you go that far and try to take over Iraq," Cheney concluded.

Nevertheless, having Cheney aboard suited Bush's temperament. Never a detail man, Bush can also be maddeningly and improbably passive. This trait fits neither the image of liberal critics, who see him as a reckless cowboy, nor that of his own followers, who consider him a resolute decision-maker. Bush's passive streak manifested itself in the decision-making surrounding Iraq, which suffered from a relentless barrage of bad intelligence work, faulty predictions by his military defense team, and an increasingly untenable situation on the ground. Bush greeted these mistakes not with tantrums, wholesale firings, or radical new war plans, but with a refusal to cashier generals, change strategy, or remove cabinet secretaries.

"The irony is that he's the only president with an M.B.A., but the fact is he's not a good manager," Joseph S. Nye Jr. said in an interview. "The system just didn't work," Nye added. "They froze out Colin Powell. Condi Rice didn't manage the barons, Cheney and Rumsfeld. They disregarded the State Department's Arabist experts. Jay Garner—Woodward has this in his book—comes back from Iraq and goes to the White House—and he and the president talk football! The president didn't understand the climate of fear that Rumsfeld had created. He'd ask them, 'Do you have the troops you need?' And they'd say, 'Yes sir.' Leadership involves a degree of management, particularly managing flows of information. If you don't ask the tough questions, and don't get answers, you become part of the cheerleading."[80]

A better listener might have deduced the stranglehold Rumsfeld exerted on his generals; after all, when Rumsfeld dismissively interrupted Tommy Franks to say the 275,000 troop level Franks anticipated for the Iraq invasion was a "soft" number, Bush was sitting right there with Franks in the president's Crawford home. Late into his tenure in office, Bush seemed oblivious to the buck-passing aspect of his answers on the inadequacy of troop levels. At a July 12, 2007, White House press conference, Wendell Goler of Fox News zeroed in on the president's perceived shortcomings in the Iraq war planning, only to have the president toss it back on Franks and the brass. Here is the exchange:

GOLER: You have spoken passionately about the consequences of failure in Iraq. Your critics say you failed to send enough troops there at the start, failed to keep al Qaeda from stepping into the void created by the collapse of Saddam's army, failed to put enough pressure on Iraq's government to make the political reconciliation necessary to keep the sectarian violence the country is suffering from now from occurring. So why should the American people feel you have the vision for victory in Iraq, sir?

THE PRESIDENT: . . . Should we have sent more in the beginning? Well, I asked that question—"Do you need more?"—to General Tommy Franks. In the first phase of this operation, General Franks was obviously in charge, and . . . my primary question to General Franks was: "Do you have what it takes to succeed? And do you have what it takes to succeed after you succeed in removing Saddam Hussein?" And his answer was, "Yes." Now, history is going to look back to determine whether or not there might have been a different decision made. But at the time, the only thing I can tell you, Wendell, is that I relied upon our military commander to make the proper decision about troop strength. And I can remember a meeting with the Joint Chiefs, who said, we've reviewed the plan . . . and seemed satisfied with it. I remember sitting in the PEOC, or the Situation Room, downstairs here at the White House, and I went [from] commander to commander. . . . I said to each one of them, "Do you have what it takes? Are you satisfied with the strategy?" And the answer was, "Yes."

"Reagan in his first term was very successful. Reagan in his first half of his second term was a disaster," said Nye. "But Reagan had the sense to recover in his last two years. He did that because he listened to people who were telling him what was wrong. Nobody's done for Bush what Howard Baker, David Abshire, and Ken Duberstein did for Reagan. Replacing Rumsfeld with Gates was a good idea, but it was two years too late."[81]

Nye's views were shared by many inside the Bush White House. Aside from Cheney, Rumsfeld is the administration official who most engendered animosity among Bush aides. Mike Gerson seethed when Rumsfeld personally crossed David Petraeus's name out of speeches he had drafted for the president. In a June 2007 interview, another top West Wing aide mentioned this while twice referring to Rumsfeld as "a jerk" over breakfast at the Hay Adams Hotel. "Rumsfeld is an ideologue in the worst way—he's impervious to new information," the aide said. "Don Rumsfeld did more to hurt this president than anyone on the planet." By way of example, this official cited something unrelated to Iraq: Rumsfeld's resistance to Andy Card's suggestion that U.S. troops be dispatched to New Orleans while people were on rooftops needing to be rescued in the aftermath of Hurricane Katrina.[82]

After he left the White House, Gerson confirmed this account as well. He recalled being in the White House Situation Room on Wednesday, August 31, 2005, as it became clear that Louisiana officials and the Federal Emergency Management Agency (FEMA) were in over their heads. Card made his recommendation: send in the Army. "Rumsfeld adamantly refused to use the military," Gerson recalled. "The local authorities were overwhelmed, FEMA couldn't do the job, but he wouldn't budge."[83] Gerson had gone to the president within days of the 2004 reelection and urged him to replace Rumsfeld, to no avail, and the Pentagon chief's intransigence, coupled with the president's passivity, created an impasse that nettled Gerson, but did not mystify him. "Look, I saw it early and I benefited by it, but [Bush] believes that a chief executive should stand by his team and empower people by showing confidence in them," Gerson recalled. "It frustrated me to no end. I'd think, 'Why don't you fire *everybody?*"[84]

Until Katrina, even Bush's critics tended to give his administration high marks for competence—or, at the least, ruthless efficiency. That reputation was left in the storm's wreckage along with a large portion of the Gulf Coast. Some of the criticism directed at the White House was over the top. The leadership exerted by New Orleans' mayor and Louisiana's governor was halting; much of the New Orleans police department simply abandoned the city. But George W. Bush's own response was tardy and tepid. On Monday, August 29, 2005, as New Orleans filled with water, Bush abruptly cut short a California trip only to return to his ranch in Crawford, Texas, for two nights and a day. Meanwhile, the magnitude of the calamity overwhelmed the capacity of local, state, and federal authorities to cope with it. On Wednesday, August 31, Bush flew east—but to Andrews Air Force Base. Adding to the infelicitous symbolism, the president directed Air Force One to fly *over* the flooded area at a low altitude so he could see the damage. Then, at precisely 10:38 A.M. on Friday, September 2, 2005, in Mobile, Alabama, Bush, having gone to the stricken area, tried to buck up his beleaguered FEMA director, Michael Brown, by blurting out, "Brownie, you're doing a heckuva job."

What made this slow response so inexplicable was that nine months earlier Bush had had a dress rehearsal for just this sort of calamity when a tsunami slammed into Indian Ocean coastal areas with a horrific loss of life. The killer wave struck on Sunday, December 26, 2004, while Bush was in Crawford for Christmas. The White House press office issued a statement of condolence that day, but Bush did not appear. On Monday, Deputy White House Press Secretary Trent Duffy announced $15 million in American assistance. Duffy upped the amount to $35 million on Tuesday, even as Bush directed U.S. C-130s from Pacific Command to airlift relief supplies into the region. Still, no Bush. Not until Wednesday, December 29, as criticism mounted, did the president make a personal appearance. Conservatives pointed out that U.N. Secretary General Kofi Annan, frolicking in Jackson Hole, Wyoming, with jet-setting American friends, took longer to surface. Their complaint about anti-Bush bias in news coverage has merit, but Americans don't particularly care what U.N.

bureaucrats have to say; in an international crisis of that magnitude, they want to hear from their president. This was the lesson of the tsunami, a lesson Bush should have learned in time for Katrina. When he did engage, Bush did positive things for the situation in Indonesia. When he urged Americans to donate, they did, to the tune of hundreds of millions of dollars. Appointing his father and Bill Clinton to spearhead the U.S. relief efforts was also appropriate. The upshot was improved standing for America in the Muslim nation of Indonesia, a fact not lost on the White House—all of which makes the slow response to Katrina so baffling.

Part of this riddle, ironically enough, related to Clinton. White House officials put on the defensive about Bush's delayed appearance maintained that when he was president, Clinton was too quick to milk every tragedy for political gain by heading straight for the cameras. "The president wanted to be fully briefed on our efforts. He didn't want to make a symbolic statement about 'We feel your pain,'" a Bush aide in Crawford said. "Actions speak louder than words."[85]

This was more than a throwaway line issued for temporary partisan gain. It was a glimpse into the mind of George W. Bush and the way his team worked. Team Bush believed Clinton squandered his political gifts in his quest for high approval ratings, a goal they considered less a holy grail than a mythical pot of gold at the end of a rainbow. In Bush-world, nothing was more pathetic than reports of Dick Morris doing polls for Clinton on whether he should vacation at Martha's Vineyard. (The American public thought not; Clinton headed that year to Wyoming.) Yet Bush's experiences in his second term proved something that Ronald Reagan never doubted: A president can get a lot more done with high job approval ratings than with low ones.

Opinion surveys can be a crude yardstick, particularly when trying to measure the public's mood on complex issues. The media almost certainly put too much stock in them. Yet, precisely because they drive news coverage, and because Congress pays them so much heed, it is essential that a leader not be too dismissive of polls. "The job of the president of the United States is not the job of a chairman of the board of any corporation, nor is it the CEO of a business," said Kenneth Duberstein, Reagan's last chief of staff. "You can't govern by polls, but you need the American people with you to govern effectively. Ronald Reagan understood with all his fiber that he needed the American people on his side."

Duberstein said that when calling members of Congress for their support on legislation, Reagan would tell them, disarmingly, that he knew he
wasn't the most effective lobbyist—it was the people of their districts and
states who mattered. "My job," Reagan would say, "is to convince them to
convince you I'm right." It was both a veiled threat and a charming expo-
sition on the vagaries of a representative democracy. "If you have the
people, you can get Congress to work with you, not against you," Duberstein explained. "The same is true of foreign leaders, who sense when a
president is vulnerable."[86]

Reagan also knew the corollary to this postulate, which is that foreign
leaders look for guidance from a popular American president. In December 1988, as Reagan prepared to leave office with an approval rating in
the 60 percent range, he met one last time as president with Soviet General Secretary Mikhail Gorbachev—and President-elect George H. W.
Bush—on Governor's Island, New York. Duberstein recalls Gorbachev
being pessimistic about perestroika and glasnost, unsure whether his
country would be able to continue making strides toward reform. His
doubts weren't about the new American president, but about the Soviet
nomenklatura—his own bureaucracy. "It was almost like he was looking
for insight from an older brother," Duberstein related. "Ronald Reagan
replied, gently, 'The bureaucracy, as I have told you, is the same the world
over. The only way to get the bureaucracy on your side is to get the people
on your side.'"[87]

The approach of George W. Bush, Dick Cheney, and the neoconservatives they put in power was quite different: It seemed their goal was to
marginalize the bureaucrats of the State Department and the CIA,
steamroll Congress on party-line votes, ignore public opinion—and hope
the ambitious agenda they had launched would come to fruition. If Iraq
had turned out the way Bush had predicted it would, this book might be
hailing the genius of a bold new type of presidential leadership. But it
didn't, and one reason it didn't is that no one heeded the voices of some of
those who were sidelined by the administration.

Sean Wilentz, the Princeton historian who had written approvingly of
Bush's decisive decapitation of the Taliban after 9/11 and his "simple, unflinching eloquence" as he rallied the nation, believed that Bush—and the
United States—suffered greatly because of Bush's reluctance to solicit advice he might not want to hear. "Bush wasted his chance (after 9/11) by

quickly choosing partisanship over leadership," Wilentz wrote. "No other president—Lincoln in the Civil War, FDR in World War II, John F. Kennedy at critical moments of the Cold War—faced with such a monumental set of military and political circumstances failed to embrace the opposing political party to help wage a truly national struggle. But Bush shut out and even demonized the Democrats."[88]

Even when he did listen to dissenting voices, Bush managed to convey an impression that he didn't. One of the most specious criticisms leveled against Bush was that he wouldn't meet with families of soldiers who'd been killed or wounded in Iraq, or with the soldiers themselves returning from duty in Iraq. In truth, Bush met hundreds of such soldiers and their families, and while most of them were grateful to the president for his time, some wanted to vent against the war. The commander-in-chief did not cut them off. One Gold Star mother, Cindy Sheehan, met with Bush, then decided that she hadn't really said what was on her mind. Sheehan desired a second audience with Bush; when she didn't get one she became an unlikely symbol for the peace movement. Her vigil outside Bush's ranch in Crawford went on for months, adding to the image of an insulated, stubborn president hiding behind his compound. Finally, even some Bush aides began to wonder what the president was thinking. Even if the Sheehan charade could be chalked up to poor White House public relations, it is not a mistake Ronald Reagan would have made. In February 1983, at the height of the nuclear freeze movement—a cause aimed squarely at Reagan's policies—he met privately, at his youngest daughter's behest, with two of the anti-nuclear movement's most ardent leaders. The first was Helen Caldicott, head of Physicians for Social Responsibility; the second was wealthy Southern California liberal Harold Willens. Reagan and these disarmament activists exchanged diametrically opposed viewpoints, cordially, in the Oval Office. "Thanks for not chopping off the messenger's head," Willens told Reagan as he left.[89]

The ripple effects of the Iraq quagmire were not insignificant. Bush vowed to use his "political capital" to effect fundamental change in Social Security. Yet when his popularity dropped, a phenomenon that began *before* Hurricane Katrina, Bush found the opposite to be true. Features of his proposed reform, notably private accounts, enjoyed broad public support until they were paired with the name Bush—then the bottom fell out. Even as the situation in Iraq deteriorated, Bush spent much of the first half of 2005 on a sixty-city tour stumping for Social Security reform. His coattails were so frayed by then that the White House did not produce a bill. Democrats wouldn't meet the administration at the bargaining table, and Congress declined to act, never knowing precisely what it decided not to act upon.

Asked why the Bush administration hadn't emulated the Reagan model for a Social Security fix, Rove pooh-poohed the 1983 deal shepherded though Congress and signed by Reagan as a temporary fix. The deal had raised taxes but didn't solve the underlying structural problems of the system, Rove said.[90] Reagan's approach in fact accomplished more than Rove gave it credit for. The compromise rescued Reagan politically, bought the government twenty years of solvency, and led to relative peace between Democrats and Republicans on an issue sometimes described as the "third rail of politics." Rove, in being dismissive of Reagan's accomplishment, was channeling the "big ball" inclinations of his boss. And indeed, Bush seems to have believed a better solution could be achieved: "I'm asking the Congress to reform Social Security," he cheerfully told Brian Lamb on January 27, 2005. "There are some big things ahead. I think it may be in my DNA, though, that I believe in trying to solve big problems."

It was this attitude that prompted essayist Jonathan Rauch, writing in the July 26, 2003, edition of *National Journal,* to label Bush an "accidental radical." By that token, perhaps Reagan was an accidental realist. "All presidents surprise you," said Roger Porter, a Harvard professor of business and government who worked for both Reagan and George H. W. Bush. Reagan, Porter said, "was a lot more pragmatic than I thought he'd be. He had a talent for knowing what he could get, and the good judgment to tell us, 'We can live with this.'"[91]

Tip O'Neill once said that the problem in compromising with Reagan was that Reagan generally got 80 percent of what he wanted. This amused Reagan, who told his staff he'd take 80 percent every time. "In the last two years, he told us to take 60 percent," Duberstein said. "Reagan always told us that in a negotiation you've got to leave the other side with their clothes on. . . . His idea was to keep moving the ball down the field. You get the feeling with this [Bush] crowd, it's 100 percent or nothing. That's not the way it works. It should have been called the 'Reagan

Evolution,' not the 'Reagan Revolution.' Americans like their change in bite-sized chunks, not all at once—ask Hillary Clinton how it worked on health care. Reagan knew that instinctively."[92]

Bush had a grander notion. He wanted to swing for the fences even when batting against Reagan. In that pre–9/11 damage-control interview Bush granted Peggy Noonan, he suggested that in his meetings with Vladimir Putin, he was trying to go Reagan one better. "I just didn't complete the Reagan sentence," Bush said. "Reagan said, 'trust and verify.' My attitude was, I said, 'Trust.'"[93] Trusting Putin turned out to be a precarious proposition; Bush discovered that Ronald Reagan is a hard act to improve upon.

Peter Drucker could have explained that to George W. Bush and may have actually tried. Eleven months before he died, in an interview with *Forbes* magazine, Drucker offered the opinion that the two most effective U.S. presidents he had observed were Harry Truman and Ronald Reagan. Truman's great strength, according to Drucker, was that those who worked for him believed he was "absolutely trustworthy." Regarding the fortieth president, Drucker echoed the opinion of Roger Porter and so many others who saw Reagan up close. "His great strength was not charisma, as is commonly thought," Drucker said, setting aside his misgivings about Iran-contra, "but his awareness and acceptance of exactly what he could do and what he could not do."[94]

That characteristic turns out to be one of the most important, if little discussed, aspects of corporate and presidential governance. The missing element in George W. Bush's bold assertions about transformative leadership, refusing to play "small-ball," and charging valiantly up hills as his hat flies off his head is this: To be effective, let alone great, the chief executive of the United States must convince the American people that the president's hopes for their future are not just noble, but attainable. In his 2006 reassessment of Reagan, author Richard Reeves concluded that "Reagan was not a man of vision, he was a man of imagination."[95] They are not mutually exclusive traits, for Reagan could be both visionary and imaginative. Above all, however, he was practical, in ways that George W. Bush was not.

9

REAGAN'S DISCIPLE

I n his first debate with Al Gore during the 2000 presidential election
campaign, George W. Bush said he did "not believe in liberal activist
judges" and would appoint "strict constructionists" to the federal
bench. Gore responded that "strict constructionists" was code for conservative judges.[1] If this is so, President Bush has kept his promise to the
American people in his judicial appointments. He has appointed two conservatives, Chief Justice John G. Roberts Jr. and Samuel A. Alito, to the
Supreme Court. Refining a system developed by President Reagan, Bush
has also left his mark on the appellate and district courts. "His appointments have been as good as Ronald Reagan's at all levels," said Edwin
Meese, the former attorney general and longtime Reagan adviser, who
also gives Bush high marks for a tax-reduction policy on the Reagan
model.[2]

As his presidency wound to a close, Bush's approval ratings were in
Jimmy Carter territory. A spate of anti-Bush conservative books appeared in bookstores alongside the anti-Bush liberal reading list, and the
2008 Republican presidential candidates sounded as if they were trying
to succeed Ronald Reagan instead of George W. Bush, whom they didn't

mention if they could help it. In two matters of long-standing concern to conservatives, however, Bush's fealty to the vision of America's fortieth president is not in dispute. These two matters are taxes and judicial appointments—with the latter by far the more important. (Tax policies can be repealed. Federal judges are appointed for life.) In both these matters, Bush validated the high hopes of those who had believed he would be Reagan's torchbearer more than his own father's.

This view on judicial appointments is echoed by Terry Eastland, who served in the Reagan Justice Department and became publisher of *The Weekly Standard,* a Washington-based conservative magazine, who said: "George W. Bush's strongest achievement is the judiciary, particularly the Supreme Court."[3] Liberals, although more apt to describe Bush's appointments as "extremist" than as his "strongest achievement," offer a similar evaluation. Senator Patrick Leahy, Democrat of Vermont, complained that the president has sought to make the judiciary "an arm of the Republican Party."[4] Be that as it may, Bush will have appointed roughly one in three members of the federal bench by the time he leaves office, and it is undisputed that he has made the federal judiciary more conservative than he found it. A non-partisan study on George W. Bush's judicial legacy by University of Connecticut scholar David A. Yalof found that his appointees to the lower federal courts have been slightly more conservative than Reagan's. "Bush 43 borrowed far more from the playbook of President Ronald Reagan than he did from Bush 41," Yalof wrote."[5]

Courts—and particularly the Supreme Court—matter in the United States of America. In George W. Bush's lifetime the Supreme Court has outlawed racial discrimination in schools; decreed that all Americans have the right to a lawyer in a criminal case; imposed and then lifted a moratorium on the death penalty and later narrowed its scope; legalized abortion, homosexuality, and the burning of the American flag; and directed the Environmental Protection Agency to assess the impact of global warming. Most of these decisions dismayed conservatives. The original arch-villain in their eyes was Earl Warren, chief justice from 1953–1969, but conservatives became even more frustrated when the Court did not, as anticipated, move right under Warren's successor, Warren Burger. The Burger Court discovered hitherto undetected privacy rights in the Constitution and in 1973 issued the landmark abortion-rights ruling in *Roe v. Wade.* Between the time Earl Warren retired and

George W. Bush took office, Republican presidents named eight of ten Supreme Court justices without having much to show for it. The Reagan years were especially discouraging to conservatives. Reagan used his first appointment in 1981 to honor what he believed to be a campaign promise by appointing the first woman to the high court.* Sandra Day O'Connor charmed Reagan and voted with the Court's conservatives in her early years on the bench, but gradually she moderated her views. She refused to provide a fifth vote to strike down *Roe,* the principal target of social conservatives. Reagan did not have another Supreme Court appointment until 1986, when Burger retired. At the urging of Meese, he then elevated the conservative justice William Rehnquist to chief justice and appointed the even more conservative Antonin Scalia to fill the vacancy. It seemed a smart move at the time; liberal Democrats in the Senate challenged Rehnquist, but he was ultimately confirmed. Scalia sailed through. Since he was the first Italian-American nominee to the Court, even the liberal champion, Senator Edward M. Kennedy of Massachusetts, where Italian Americans are a potent constituency, had good words for him.

Conservatives were now in their strongest position on the Court in decades, but Rehnquist was respectful of precedent and moved incrementally. With O'Connor unwilling to make sweeping changes in constitutional law, Rehnquist still lacked a fifth vote on *Roe* and other issues of import to social conservatives. Then, on June 26, 1987, Justice Lewis Powell resigned, giving Reagan another chance to create a working conservative majority on the Court. On July 1, Reagan nominated Robert H. Bork, a brilliant jurist who had been a colleague of Scalia's on the U.S. Court of Appeals for the District of Columbia and had received a rating of "exceptionally well qualified" from the American Bar Association. Unfortunately for Bork, he also had a quarter-century trail of

---

*What Reagan actually promised—on October 14, 1980—was to name a woman to "one of the first vacancies in my administration." This promise came out of a conversation between Reagan and his political adviser, Stuart Spencer. Sensing that the campaign had gone "flat," Spencer urged Reagan to propose something new. They discussed various ideas; the one Reagan liked best was putting a woman on the Supreme Court. When the vacancy arose, President Reagan decided immediately to name a woman. Attorney General William French Smith sent him a list of twenty names, including twelve women, but when it became clear that Reagan wouldn't even consider a man, he narrowed the list to four women.

provocative writings that made him an easy target for liberals. Banded together in an umbrella organization known as the Leadership Conference on Civil Rights, Bork's adversaries portrayed him as a foe of civil rights and demonized him so effectively in the court of public opinion that it was easy for the senators who opposed him to vote against his confirmation. Kennedy, instead of supporting him as he did Scalia, was particularly outspoken in opposing Bork.*

The White House, which had been expecting a more traditional confirmation battle, did not respond effectively. But even if the White House had not been politically asleep at the switch, Bork would have been a difficult sell after the 1986 elections, in which the Democrats won control of the Senate. Bork made matters worse with his testimony to the Senate Judiciary Committee, in which he came across as cold and disengaged. He was voted down 58–42, the largest margin by which any Supreme Court nominee has ever been rejected. Fuming Senate Republicans blamed Bork less than they did their Democratic colleagues. Senator Gordon Humphrey, a New Hampshire Republican, decried the "demagogic, irresponsible, unfair (and) unfounded"[6] attacks on Bork. Republican Senator Alan Simpson, a high-profile member of the Senate Judiciary Committee, made two predictions. First, he said, the Democrats' "scorched earth" tactics would set the tone for future nomination fights. It was, Simpson feared, a precedent that would "jade and gall us for years to come."[7] Simpson also began talking of the logical replacement for Bork, an imagined lawyer named Jerome P. Sturdley, "who has written very little that was either thoughtful, challenging or provocative"—and who would tell his Senate inquisitors "nothing" about his true views of constitutional law.[8] Although Simpson's warnings would prove prescient, conservatives

---

*Kennedy set the tone of the debate with this statement the day Bork was nominated: "Robert Bork's America is a land in which women would be forced into back alley abortions, blacks would sit at segregated lunch counters, rogue police could break down citizens' doors in midnight raids, school children could not be taught about evolution, writers and artists would be censured at the whim of government, and the doors of the federal courts would be shut on the fingers of millions of citizens for whom the judiciary is—and is often the only—protector of the individual rights that are the heart of democracy." Ethan Bronner wrote in *Battle for Justice: How the Bork Nomination Shook America* (p. 99), the authoritative book on the Bork confirmation battle, that Kennedy's words "shamelessly twisted Bork's world view."

gained little from the Bork debacle except a new verb—"to bork"—and a determination to make life difficult for liberal nominees when the opportunity arose.

In retrospect, it was obvious that the White House had erred strategically in putting Scalia ahead of Bork—a decision made in large part because Bork, who was then a smoker, was perceived as having health habits that were inferior to Scalia's. Even with the liberal alliance mobilized against him, Bork would have had a reasonable chance to be confirmed in 1986 when Republicans controlled the Senate; it would have been difficult for Democrats to have blocked Scalia at any time. But neither Meese, who preferred Scalia to Bork, nor Reagan possessed second sight. There was no way for them to know that the Democrats would control the Senate the next time Reagan had the opportunity to make a Supreme Court nomination. (Indeed, the Democrats improbably captured the Senate in 1986, as the Republicans had in 1980—and the Democrats would again in 2006—by winning every closely contested seat.)

Bork's rejection spurred another intramural battle, commonplace in the Reagan administration, between conservatives and pragmatists. The conservatives, represented by Attorney General Meese and one of his most confrontational Justice Department assistants, William Bradford Reynolds, favored Douglas H. Ginsburg, a forty-one-year-old former Harvard professor and Justice Department official who had spent a year on the U.S. Court of Appeals for the District of Columbia. The pragmatists, in this case White House Chief of Staff Howard Baker and White House Counsel A. B. Culvahouse, preferred Anthony Kennedy, an appointee of President Gerald Ford to the Ninth Circuit Court of Appeals in California. They thought he would be easier to confirm. Meese did not disagree with their perception, but he had read some of Kennedy's appellate opinions and suspected that he would not be a dependable conservative vote on the high court. Meese made this argument to Reagan—also pointing out that Ginsburg was ten years younger—and enlisted Reagan's first attorney general and longtime legal adviser, William French Smith, now back home in California, to lobby the president. Reagan picked Ginsburg. It soon became apparent that Meese and Reynolds had been more successful in discovering Kennedy's supposed shortcomings than in researching their man Ginsburg. Social conservatives cooled on Ginsburg when they learned that his wife, an obstetrician, had performed abortions. Then it came out that Ginsburg, during a time when he was developing the Justice Department's position on a Supreme Court case involving the First Amendment rights of cable television, had been an investor in a cable company. The final blow was the revelation that Ginsburg had used marijuana when he was a law professor at Harvard. This didn't bother Reagan, who said in his diary that it was "a brief thing back when everybody experimented with it,"[9] but Ginsburg soon withdrew. (Reagan in 1986 appointed Ginsburg to the U.S. Court of Appeals for the District of Columbia; he became chief judge of this important court in 1991.) In his practical way Reagan then nominated Kennedy to the Supreme Court and became his cheerleader. After Kennedy had finished testifying before the Senate Judiciary Committee, Reagan wrote in his diary: "They didn't lay a glove on him."[10]

Viewed politically, Tony Kennedy was a blessing for Reagan after the Bork and Ginsburg fiascos. He was a Roman Catholic who had never expressed his views in writing outside his appellate court opinions. A few of these opinions hinted at Kennedy's flexibility, as Meese and the Justice Department lawyers had noticed when they were preparing their brief for Ginsburg. In one particularly prescient ruling, Kennedy had reluctantly upheld Navy regulations barring homosexuals but said he approved of privacy rights and would not bar homosexual conduct except in a military context. This was little remarked on at the time of Kennedy's confirmation hearings. The 1987 *Almanac of the Federal Judiciary* described the way lawyers viewed Judge Kennedy: "Courteous, stern on the bench, somewhat conservative, bright, well prepared, filled with nervous energy, asks many questions, good analytical mind, not afraid to break new ground, open minded, good business lawyer, hard to peg, an enigma, tends to agonize over opinions." This complimentary evaluation was on the mark, but hardly descriptive of a justice who would provide a fifth vote to carry out a social revolution on the high court. Senate liberals, recognizing that Kennedy was the best justice they were likely to get out of Reagan, did not put up a fight. Nominated by Reagan on November 11, 1987, Kennedy was confirmed unanimously by the Senate on February 3, 1988.

Meese's worry that the new justice would prove insufficiently conservative seemed misplaced during Kennedy's first three years on the Court, when he voted regularly with Rehnquist and Scalia. Justice Kennedy infuriated liberals in 1988 by providing the fifth vote for striking down a racial-harassment claim. (A civil rights law passed by Congress in 1991 nullified this decision.) But Kennedy, broad-gauged in the Earl Warren mold and responsive to the shifting tides of political opinion, was having second thoughts about his more conservative positions. In 1991, Rehnquist assigned Kennedy to write the opinion in a Rhode Island case in which a litigant named Daniel Weisman contested a public school graduation prayer required of his daughter Deborah on grounds it violated the First Amendment, which prohibits government making laws "respecting an establishment of religion." Based on an earlier dissent by Kennedy in which he had upbraided the majority for displaying "hostility" toward religion, Rehnquist was confident that Kennedy would uphold the Rhode Island prayer. Instead, Kennedy wrote what became the 5–4 decision upholding Weisman's claim. This was the start of an odyssey in which Kennedy would change his position on abortion, the death penalty, and other issues and move from the right margins of the Court to its center. In time, after O'Connor retired, Kennedy would become *the* center of the Court, determinative of the outcome on every contested issue. Kennedy's slide to the middle would change the conservatives' evaluation of Reagan's appointments to the Supreme Court. As Eastland put it, only Scalia was a "home run."[11] O'Connor and eventually Kennedy were disappointments.

The disappointments did not end with Reagan's presidency. George H. W. Bush had two appointments to the Supreme Court during his single term as president. His first came when William Brennan, the celebrated leader of the Court's liberal bloc, retired. Bush chose an obscure New Hampshire state judge named David Souter, who was the candidate of that state's senior senator, Warren Rudman. White House Chief of Staff John Sununu believed that Rudman's support had been decisive when Sununu was elected governor of New Hampshire; in effect, he allowed Rudman to cash this campaign debt by endorsing Souter. In many respects, Souter was the anti-Bork. He had not expressed himself in outside writings. He was also the anti–Tony Kennedy, in that his opinions on the state court had not wrestled with constitutional issues as had Kennedy's on the Ninth Circuit. The jurist he most resembled was Alan Simpson's mythical Joseph P. Sturdley. Souter said little and volunteered less at his confirmation hearings, and was easily approved on a 90–9 vote. After a brief conservative flirtation he became a reliably liberal justice. Bush's second appointment, Clarence Thomas, an African American, was chosen to fill the vacancy of the Court's first African American, Justice Thurgood Marshall. One leading feminist lawyer said of Thomas, "We're going to bork him," and they almost did.[12] After tawdry confirmation hearings in which Thomas was accused of sexual harassment and lying and in which he fought back by claiming his opponents were racially biased, Thomas scraped through and was confirmed on a 52–48 vote, the closest for a Supreme Court appointment in the twentieth century. But George H. W. Bush, like Reagan, had missed his chance to make the Supreme Court dependably conservative. Brennan and Marshall were two of the Court's three most liberal members, and Bush had replaced them with one liberal and one conservative. This scorecard was even worse than it looked on the surface. In her absorbing book *Supreme Conflict: The Inside Story of the Struggle for Control of the United States Supreme Court,* Jan Crawford Greenburg observed that other justices reacted negatively to Thomas's proclivity for writing sweeping assertions in opinions in which consensus might have been possible on narrower grounds. "His arrival on the Court actually pushed moderates like O'-Connor further to the left," she wrote.[13] At the end of the twelve Reagan-Bush years and five appointments, the Court was only slightly more conservative than when Reagan took office.

President Bill Clinton had two Supreme Court appointments in as many terms. He chose high-quality appellate judges, both of them liberal, Jewish, well respected by their colleagues, and temperamentally suited for the high court. When Byron White retired, Clinton appointed the Brooklyn-born Ruth Bader Ginsburg, replacing a conservative with a liberal. She had been a litigator for the American Civil Liberties Union, a professor at three law schools, and an appellate judge on the D.C. Circuit, to which President Carter appointed her in 1980. When Harry Blackmun retired, Clinton replaced him with Stephen G. Breyer, a San Francisco native and popular Harvard Law School professor. Breyer, the last Carter judicial appointee confirmed by the Senate, had spent fourteen years on the U.S. Court of Appeals for the First Circuit and was well known to senators because of his prior service as counsel to the Senate Judiciary Committee. Although often described as a moderate Democrat, Breyer was a liberal in terms of the Court's politics. His appointment exchanged one liberal for another, but Breyer was more collegial and less touchy than Blackmun. The two Clinton appointments gave the Court's liberal bloc the upper hand. Although the Court remained closely divided, the liberals needed the votes of either O'Connor or Kennedy to prevail, while the conservatives needed the votes of both of them. Rehnquist and his allies on the Court were now on the defensive, fighting rearguard actions against the expansion of civil rights and civil liberties. The liberal ascendancy would be of special consequence for gays and lesbians.

In 1992, Colorado voters amended the state constitution to prevent municipalities from enacting laws that outlawed discrimination against "homosexual citizens." The measure, known as Amendment 2, would have struck down ordinances in Denver, Boulder, and Aspen that outlawed such discrimination. Gay rights groups challenged the constitutionality of the amendment, which was sponsored by Colorado Citizens for Family Values. A federal district judge held that the amendment was unconstitutional, as did the Colorado Supreme Court. The case was appealed to the U.S. Supreme Court. On May 20, 1996, writing for a 6–3 majority that included John Paul Stevens, O'Connor, Souter, Ginsburg, and Breyer, Justice Kennedy scathingly rejected the state's argument that the amendment blocked gays from receiving "special rights." He wrote: "To the contrary, the amendment imposes a special disability upon those persons alone. Homosexuals are forbidden the safeguards that others enjoy or may seek without constraint."

Kennedy wasn't done. Gays and lesbians remained legal outcasts in many states, where "anti-sodomy" statutes outlawed homosexual sex between consenting adults. In a 1986 Georgia case, *Bowers v. Hardwick*, the Court had upheld an anti-sodomy law by a 5–4 vote; O'Connor had voted with the majority. But on the last day of the 2003 session, an opinion by Kennedy dramatically and explicitly repudiated *Bowers*, which had referred to the notion of gay rights as "facetious." The case, *Lawrence v. Texas*, involved two men who on the night of September 18, 1998, were having consensual sex in an unlocked apartment when a sheriff's deputy, responding to a false report of a "weapons disturbance," entered with gun drawn. The two men were arrested, spent the night in jail, and were fined. They appealed to a panel of a Texas appellate court, which ruled in their favor; the full court then ruled against them. In time, the case arrived at the Supreme Court, where Kennedy expanded on the view he had expressed as a member of the Ninth Circuit about the privacy rights of homosexuals. As attorneys for the plaintiffs wept openly, Kennedy found that "the intimate, adult consensual conduct at issue here was part of the liberty protected" by the Fourteenth Amendment. It was for gays and lesbians a liberating and sweeping victory that invalidated similar anti-sodomy statutes across the nation. For social conservatives, however, it was the last straw. Appearing on the *Larry King Show* on CNN, the influential evangelist James Dobson, founder of Focus on the Family, called Kennedy "one of the most dangerous men in America."[14]

Would Kennedy's decision in *Lawrence* have been similarly disconcerting to Reagan? We can't be certain—Reagan was at this point lost to Alzheimer's disease—but Reagan's past behavior suggests that it is unlikely that he would have considered *Lawrence* a repudiation of conservatism.* Reagan had spent much of his adult life in Hollywood, where gays are part of the culture. Early in Reagan's governorship, several of his closest aides (Meese among them) concluded that the chief of staff, whom they were trying to displace for other reasons, was homosexual.[15] The aides didn't tell Reagan because they didn't believe it would matter to him.[16] Eventually, many of these aides confronted Reagan and told him that the chief of staff had taken unauthorized actions in his name and was indeed homosexual. Faced with what amounted to a revolt of his aides, Reagan asked for the chief of staff's resignation. But he never quite understood why it was such a big deal. Years later, Reagan told an aide, "Let me tell you something about homosexuals. There are a lot of them." Reagan did not romanticize homosexuality, but gay people were never "the other" to him. In 1978, when he was out of office and preparing to run for president, Reagan ignored strategists who wanted him to sidestep a California ballot initiative that would have barred homosexuals from teaching in the state's public schools. Instead, he opposed the initiative and was

---

*Homosexual rights aside, Reagan had very general standards for what constituted a conservative judge. His most frequent statement in California and in his early campaigns was that he wanted judges who would interpret the law, not make it. As president he expressed satisfaction with O'Connor's performance on the Supreme Court. When, on October 11, 1984, a reporter told Reagan that Jerry Falwell was boasting he would convince the president to put two conservatives on the Court in his second term, Reagan replied that he had already made "one appointment, and I give that as a pattern as to the criteria that will be employed."

widely credited for defeating it. In his statement against the initiative, Reagan said: "Whatever it is, homosexuality is not a contagious disease like the measles. Prevailing scientific opinion is that an individual's sexuality is determined at a very early age and that a child's teachers do not really influence this."

Measles was a reference point for Reagan. As president in 1984 and 1985, when the mysterious acquired immune deficiency syndrome (AIDS) was beginning to take a deadly toll of homosexual men in San Francisco, Los Angeles, and New York, Reagan, according to his White House physician, Brig. Gen. John Hutton, thought of AIDS as if "it was measles and it would go away."[17] What changed Reagan's view was the illness of his friend, the actor Rock Hudson. Reagan, told that Hudson had inoperable cancer, telephoned him in a Paris hospital on July 24, 1985, to offer condolences. Later that day, Reagan noted in his diary, he learned from a television report that Hudson had AIDS. The Reagans invited Hudson to a White House state dinner in August, where Nancy Reagan noticed that he had lost weight. Hudson died on October 2. The Reagans issued a statement praising Hudson for his "dynamic impact on the film industry," but made no mention of AIDS. By now, however, Dr. Hutton had convinced Reagan that this new disease was quite unlike the measles. "I always thought the world would end in a flash, but this sounds worse," Reagan said.[18]

Nonetheless, the Reagan administration moved more slowly in the battle against AIDS than gay activists and the nation's health officials wanted—although more swiftly than liberals recalled afterward. Two decades later, California congressman Henry Waxman, a leading Democrat from Los Angeles, maintained on his House of Representatives website that "the Reagan Administration consistently refused to commit the resources and effort necessary to provide urgently needed research, health care and preventive services. Indeed, President Ronald Reagan refused to mention AIDS publicly until 1987, after 19,000 Americans had already died of AIDS." This second and inaccurate assertion has been repeated so often that it has acquired the power of truth and found its way into the accounts of media outlets with contrary evidence in their files. A docudrama produced by CBS in 2003 showed Reagan, played by Barbra Streisand's husband James Brolin, responding to the AIDS crisis by refusing his wife's entreaties to address the issue. Brolin says, "Those who live in sin shall die in sin." This exchange is invented. Waxman's assertions are not, but they are much exaggerated.

In the early 1980s, Waxman was one of the voices urging the Reagan administration to respond to the epidemic with more urgency; apparently, he and other early prophets have forgotten their successes at galvanizing the Reagan administration into action. In 1983, Reagan sought—and with congressional blessing was granted—authority to transfer funds within the Health and Human Services (HHS) budget to meet the AIDS challenge. That same year, Margaret Heckler, Reagan's HHS secretary, repeatedly declared AIDS her agency's "number one priority."[19] In June, while appearing at the U.S. Conference of Mayors, Heckler alienated leaders in the gay community by saying that "panic" over the disease was unwarranted and that the epidemic was confined to those already "at high risk." But her promise to spend $26.5 million on AIDS—up from $8 million in 1982—was welcomed by activists and public officials from hard-hit areas. San Francisco Mayor (and future U.S. Senator) Dianne Feinstein told reporters she was satisfied that Heckler was "fully committed to putting all available resources" behind the fight against AIDS.[20]

Even so, neither the administration's spending nor its rhetorical response kept pace with the spread of the disease. As the summer of 1983 wore on, Heckler realized this. She appeared in August, with Mayor Ed Koch, at the bedside of a forty-year-old AIDS patient named Peter Justice who was hospitalized at Cabrini Medical Center in New York. Heckler took Justice by the hand as a way of allaying the public's fears about transmission. "The person with AIDS is bearing a very heavy burden," she explained. "We ought to be comforting the sick rather than inflicting them and making them a class of outcasts."[21]

In fiscal year 1983, the Reagan administration, again prodded by congressional Democrats, spent $44 million fighting AIDS, a number that essentially doubled each year of Reagan's presidency and reached $2.3 billion in the fiscal year ending in 1989. As the magnitude of AIDS became apparent, those on the front lines fighting the disease wanted more from the White House than funding, however. They wanted Reagan to speak out about AIDS, both for educational purposes and to mitigate the prejudice attendant to an epidemic that had initially struck gay men. Reagan finally did so at a September 17, 1985, press conference in which he said that fighting the disease was one of his administration's "top priorities." This was two years earlier than Waxman claimed on his website, but two years *after* his health secretary had personally held the hand of an AIDS patient. By this time, battle lines had formed within Reagan's own White House over how visible the president should be in discussing the plague. As the 1986 State of the Union address approached, a mention of AIDS would appear in drafts of the speech and then disappear. When the final draft was delivered to Reagan on February 4, AIDS was not mentioned. Reagan, who resented being criticized for his inattention to the epidemic, paid a surprise visit to HHS headquarters the following day and spoke for the first time about AIDS without being prompted.[22]

"One of our highest public health priorities is going to be continuing to find a cure for AIDS," Reagan said that morning. He also announced that he was asking Surgeon General C. Everett Koop to prepare a major report on AIDS and said, "We're going to focus on prevention." The report, which did not come out until October, stressed prevention, monogamy, and condoms. It divided Reagan's conservative constituency, with the Religious Right (including Jerry Falwell) largely supportive, and secular conservatives (such as Phyllis Schafly) opposing Koop's suggestion to teach teenagers the dangers of unsafe sex. As happened so often in the Reagan administration, on issues ranging from Central America to the Supreme Court, Reagan was now pulled in different directions. Koop and Nancy Reagan wanted Reagan to use the powerful bully pulpit of his presidency to speak out about AIDS. A trio of conservative administration figures—domestic policy adviser Gary Bauer, Secretary of Education William Bennett, and White House communications director Patrick Buchanan—urged Reagan to keep his distance from AIDS and gays. Buchanan had sarcastically expressed a characteristic view in a 1983 column he wrote before joining the White House staff: "The poor homosexuals. They have declared war on nature and now nature is exacting an awful retribution."[23] Bauer seemed distressed at the thought that the president of the United States might utter the word "condom."[24]

Reagan typically tried to find a middle ground and took too much time to do so. He did not give a speech on AIDS until May 31, 1987, and the draft had been somewhat watered down by Bauer.* (This is the occasion most Reagan critics apparently have in mind when they inaccurately assert that it was the first time he had discussed the subject.) Still, Reagan disputed the view of Bauer and his allies that AIDS could be casually transmitted "from telephones or swimming pools or drinking fountains." In a widely quoted line from his speech, Reagan said, "There's no reason for those who carry the AIDS virus to wear a scarlet A." The speech, delivered in a hot, steamy tent along the Potomac River, also called for routine testing for AIDS. As Reagan noted in his diary, "a block of the Gay community in the tent booed me enthusiastically" at this passage.[25] Overall, Reagan added in his diary entry, the speech went well. It would have gone over even better if he had given it earlier, as Koop and Nancy Reagan wanted him to do. But although Reagan can certainly be faulted for waiting too long to address the issue, he did not share the fearful views of homosexuality expressed by Dobson, Bauer, and Buchanan—or that often are attributed to him now by liberal critics. Reagan's record suggests that he would have agreed with Justice Kennedy that gays and lesbians have the right to be treated like everyone else.

George W. Bush believed this when he became president, too, and had for a long while. Lanny Davis, the Clintonite and former Bush fraternity brother who was so struck by Bush's youthful stubbornness, was equally impressed by his tolerance for gay people. Davis said that one of his "most vivid memories" of Bush as a young person occurred one day in 1965—he was a junior at Yale, Bush a sophomore—when a group of Dekes were hanging out in the common room of a dorm, making their typically "snarky" comments about passersby. When a student they believed to be gay came into the room, someone muttered the word "queer" as he walked by.

"George heard it and, most uncharacteristically, snapped: 'Shut up!'" Davis recalled, adding: "Then he said, in words I can remember almost

---

*It would have been watered down even more but for Nancy Reagan, who wanted her husband to make a strong statement about AIDS. She brought in Landon Parvin, who had left the White House in 1983, to write the speech draft. Parvin battled throughout with Bauer, finally retaining the strongest passages of the speech by telling Bauer, in reference to Nancy: "Look, this is the way she wants it" (Interview with Bauer by LC, May 15, 1990).

verbatim: 'Why don't you try walking in his shoes for a while and see how it feels before you make a comment like that?'"[26]

For liberals, the emergence of gay marriage as an issue in the 2004 re-election campaign cycle would reveal the limits of Bush's willingness to stick his neck out in the cause of tolerance. That's a fair criticism. Yet as a presidential candidate four years earlier, Bush consciously tried to move the Republican Party to higher ground in the culture wars, while also invoking the inclusive side of Reaganism. Sometimes he tried to do this in the same breath. "Too often, on social issues, my party has painted an image of America slouching toward Gomorrah," Bush said. "But many of our problems—particularly education, crime and welfare dependence—are yielding to good sense and strength and idealism."

The "slouching toward Gomorrah" reference was no accident—it was the title of a book written by Robert Bork. Traveling with Bush that day was another apostle of the dangers of cultural decay, William Bennett. Asked by conservative journalist Bill Sammon whether Bush was trying to distance himself from the right wing of the GOP, Bennett replied, "I think he is trying to distance himself from the pessimists of the party, from people who say the country is irretrievably damned."[27]

Candidate Bush, his dig at Bork aside, was mindful long before he became president of the conservative lament about the paucity of "strict constructionist" appointments to the Supreme Court during past Republican administrations. When Meese gave a speech in Austin in the late 1990s, one of his hosts asked him if he would like to meet Governor Bush. Meese replied affirmatively, assuming it would be a brief courtesy call. Instead, Bush engaged him in a forty-five-minute discussion of Reagan's criteria for judicial selection. Bush asked Meese a number of questions and told him that he wanted justices on the model of justices Scalia and Thomas.[28] What Bush didn't want, as he subsequently made clear, was another appointment on the model of Justice Souter, his father's first appointment to the Court. President George W. Bush's judicial selection team saw Souter as an example of inadequate preparation and poor research, and Bush was determined not to repeat these mistakes. But Bush went through his first term without an appointment to the Supreme Court. Many of his appointments to appellate courts, several of them women, were meanwhile bottled up in committee or denied hearings on the ostensible grounds that they were unacceptably conservative.

It was another chapter in the saga that began with Bork. Presidents were once presumed to have an almost absolute right to their choice of judges. All of the appellate court nominees of Presidents Truman and Eisenhower were confirmed. Even President Nixon, who lost two of his Supreme Court nominations, won confirmation of 96 percent of his appellate choices. For Reagan, the figure was 89 percent. After Bork, however, both sides were spoiling for a fight, and the Senate, in the words of former U.S. Solicitor General Theodore Olson, abandoned its role of "advise and consent" for a policy of "search and destroy."[29] This happened on both sides, as Olson said, but Senate Democrats went to greater lengths than their Republican counterparts to discredit legitimate nominations. Republican senators were also generally more willing than Democratic senators to vote for meritorious Supreme Court nominees with whom they disagreed philosophically. Ruth Bader Ginsburg, for instance, was confirmed on a 96–3 vote, and Stephen Breyer by an 87–9 vote. Republican partisans saved their fire for some of Clinton's more liberal nominees to lower courts. In Clinton's first two years in office, eleven of his district court nominees were withdrawn, returned, or rejected, as were three of his appellate court nominees. Overall, Clinton won confirmation of 59 percent of his appellate court nominees.

Democratic reaction against George W. Bush's judicial appointments was both more extreme and more effective than Republican retaliation had been against Clinton. In Bush's first two years in office, forty-four of his appellate nominees and thirty-five of his district court nominees were withdrawn, returned, or rejected. During most of these two years, thanks to the defection of Senator Jim Jeffords of Vermont to the Democratic Party, Democrats controlled the Senate. After Republicans regained control of the Senate in the 2002 mid-term elections, Senate Democrats continued to block Bush's judicial appointments through use (and threat) of the filibuster, once the preferred tool of Dixie senators to maintain racial segregation in the South. Through 2005, only 53 percent of Bush's appellate nominees had been confirmed. Use of the filibuster in this way undermined the president's power to name judges of his own choosing, but Attorney General Alberto Gonzales did not challenge it, and Senate majority leader Bill Frist, new to his post when Democrats began using the filibuster tactic, was ineffectual. As a result, Bush's judicial nominations began piling up in the Senate, and several of the nominees withdrew. Beginning in 2004 and again in 2005, Republican senators belatedly fought back with a proposal to abolish the filibuster for judicial nominations. A bipartisan group of fourteen senators forged a compromise: The filibuster stayed, and Democrats allowed a vote that confirmed two of Bush's conservative appointments, both women, to the appellate courts. But the compromise had the ironic impact of making the nomination of a conservative woman to the high court less likely. Nearly all of the best choices among women were conservatives with appellate records that the Democrats could pick apart. Neither Bush nor the Republican Senate wanted another such battle.

Bush finally got his chance to name a Supreme Court justice in his second term, when Sandra Day O'Connor announced her retirement on July 1, 2005, so she could care for her husband, John, who had Alzheimer's disease. Chief Justice Rehnquist was by now mortally ill with thyroid cancer, but he didn't want to leave the Court. So President Bush and his legal team set about finding a replacement for O'Connor. Bush, like Clinton before him, took this work with great seriousness, all the more so since it had been eleven years since the last Supreme Court vacancy. He interviewed J. Harvey Wilkinson and Michael J. Luttig, both highly regarded, conservative appellate judges, but was most impressed by John G. Roberts Jr., a judge on the U.S. Court of Appeals for the District of Columbia. Roberts, a Roman Catholic and only fifty years old, seemed a dream candidate, combining an impressive legal resume with an easygoing manner and an attractive family. He had been editor of the *Harvard Law Review* in college, clerked for Rehnquist when he was an associate justice, worked in the Reagan White House, and served as principal deputy solicitor general in the administration of President George H. W. Bush, who nominated him to the D.C. Court of Appeals in 1991. Democrats had bottled up that nomination in the Judiciary Committee, where it died after Clinton became president. Roberts had gone into private practice with a prestigious Washington law firm and argued thirty-nine cases before the Supreme Court. In 2001, President George W. Bush nominated Roberts to the same D.C. appellate court; once more the nomination was buried, this time with twenty-nine others, in the Senate Judiciary Committee. After Republicans took control of the Senate, Bush renominated Roberts in 2003; he was approved and made his mark on the appellate court as a low-key conservative. Roberts's confirmation hearings for the O'Connor vacancy were pending when Rehnquist died on September 3, 2005. Three days later, Bush withdrew Roberts as a replacement for O'Connor and nominated him as chief justice. Within the month (September 29), Roberts had cleared the Judiciary Committee and, by a 78–22 vote, was confirmed as the seventeenth chief justice of the United States.

Bush needed this victory. The president was reeling from public disapproval of the federal response to Hurricane Katrina, which in turn had a megaphone effect on growing criticisms of the Iraq War. But Bush soon raised new questions about his competence with his surprising nomination of White House counsel Harriet Miers to fill the O'Connor vacancy. In naming a woman, Bush was responding to the only sour note of the Roberts appointment. It had been sounded backhandedly by O'Connor, who said when Roberts was chosen as her replacement that he was "good in every way except that he's not a woman." This objection diminished when Roberts was named to replace Rehnquist, who was a reliable conservative. Replacing him with Roberts would not change the balance of the Court and left open the possibility that a woman might be chosen for the O'Connor vacancy. But since O'Connor was a fifth vote for *Roe* and a moderate on many other issues, ideology became more crucial than gender in filling her vacancy. Bush should have realized this, but in his weakened political condition was unable to ignore what soon became a widespread clamor for a woman. First Lady Laura Bush was part of the clamor. Miers was a friend of the Bushes and had gone to college and law school at Southern Methodist University, the first lady's alma mater. She was the first woman president of the Texas Bar Association and managing partner of a Dallas law firm with more than 400 employees. If Miers had ever entertained any thought of becoming a Supreme Court justice, there is no record of it. Indeed, she recommended to the president that he fill the O'Connor vacancy with Samuel Alito. But George W. Bush was listening to the call for diversity. Conservatives had already made it clear to him that Attorney General Gonzales was unacceptable—"Gonzales is Spanish for Souter" went a familiar line—but no one had passed judgment on Miers for the simple reason that no one, including Miers herself, had thought she was in the running. In this context, White House Chief of Staff Andy Card took Miers's loyal deputy, Bill Kelley, aside and asked him to vet Miers for the O'Connor seat. As Jan Crawford Greenburg observed, "Card's decision to ask the trusted Kelley to vet his own boss was an egregious managerial mistake."[30] To Kelley's credit, he told Bush that Alito was the best choice, but he also found Miers acceptable. On October 3, Bush appointed her to fill the O'Connor vacancy.

Miers's honeymoon as a Supreme Court nominee was nasty, brutish, and short. In interviews with friendly Republican senators, she failed to demonstrate a grasp of constitutional law. A questionnaire she filled out for the Senate Judiciary Committee was woefully incomplete. Conservative pundits were withering in their criticism of Miers.* Liberals, content to let Bush sink in a quagmire of his own making, did not come to her defense, despite the fact that Democratic Majority Leader Harry Reid had signaled to the White House that Miers was an acceptable choice. Soon she became a punch line on late-night talk shows. On October 27, she withdrew. She had lasted fourteen days as a nominee, five more than Douglas Ginsburg did when Reagan named him to the high court. Ginsburg's collapse after the Bork debacle had reduced the pressure on Reagan to name a dyed-in-the-wool conservative to the Court; Miers's meltdown silenced the clamor for a woman. Bush did what Miers had suggested he do in the first place and nominated Alito for the O'Connor vacancy.

Alito was no shoo-in. By the second week of January 2006, when the Alito confirmation hearings were held, the liberal alliance that had defeated Bork and almost taken down Thomas was mobilized to defeat him. Alito was depicted as a right-wing zealot in the Bork mold, even a closet bigot. But when it came his turn to testify before the Senate Judiciary Committee, Alito was no Bork. Instead of discussing abstractions, Alito told a compelling story of his life, recounting how his father was a poor Italian immigrant and his mother a first-generation American whose father had worked in a steel mill. He talked with pride of going to Princeton and becoming a lawyer. Judges are different from lawyers, he said. "The judge's only obligation—and it's a solemn obligation—is to the

---

*"Let me just say," wrote Ann Coulter, "if the top male lawyer in the country is John Roberts and the top female lawyer is Harriet Miers, we may as well stop allowing girls to go to law school."

rule of law." At the end, wrote Jan Crawford Greenburg, he "was so understated that he never gave Democrats a chance to spark a fight. It was like lighting a match on a smooth surface. They couldn't do it."[31] That Alito, a graduate of Yale Law School, was a conservative was undeniable. He had demonstrated as much during his fifteen years on the U.S. Court of Appeals for the Third Circuit (where he had been placed by the first President Bush), although some of his opinions on First Amendment issues showed a libertarian streak. But his judicial capability was similarly evident. After a filibuster attempt by Senator John Kerry collapsed, the Senate on January 31 confirmed Alito by a 58–42 vote, nearly on party lines. (Four Democrats voted for confirmation, and one Republican and one independent voted against.) Bush was fortunate to have fought this crucial battle for control of the Court in 2006, when Republicans had a majority in the Senate.

More than in any other arena of his presidency, and the Miers fiasco notwithstanding, Bush's judicial appointments—many of them "strict constructionists," as he promised—stamped him as Reagan's disciple. The president's legal team thoroughly vetted most of his judicial nominees, and Bush himself was actively involved in their selection and in lobbying for their confirmation. The Bush team can be faulted for waiting too long to challenge the partisanship that bottled up some of his most qualified (and most conservative) appellate nominees. This arguably cost Bush the appointment of the brilliant Miguel Estrada, a bootstraps success story who was blocked by Democrats, ostensibly because of his conservatism, but also because of the possibility that he might become the first Hispanic justice. Overall, however, Bush did what Reagan and his father had failed to do: put two authentic conservatives on the Supreme Court.

After so many false dawns, conservatives were slow to proclaim the sunrise, a caution that seemed warranted as 2006 passed without a startling change in direction. In 2007, however, the Court's new conservative majority asserted itself. On April 18, in a 5–4 opinion by Justice Kennedy, with Roberts and Alito in the majority, the Court upheld the constitutionality of the Partial Birth Abortion Law that Congress had passed and Bush signed in 2003. The measure banned a late-term abortion procedure that Kennedy called "brutal and inhumane" and which his opinion described in clinical detail. Seven years earlier, a decision written by Justice

O'Connor had struck down a similar Nebraska law. Kennedy, consistent on this issue, was then in the minority. The Court had changed its position because of O'Connor's replacement by Alito.

By the time the Roberts Court ended its first full term on June 28, 2007, its direction was no longer in doubt. A series of rulings, all by 5–4 margins, had made it more difficult for workers alleging job discrimination to sue their employers, had declared unconstitutional on free speech grounds a section of the 2002 McCain-Feingold campaign finance law that had restricted political advertising, and had limited the power of school boards to use race as a tool for maintaining or achieving diversity. As Joan Biskupic, the Supreme Court reporter for *USA Today,* summarized the term: "Roberts, fulfilling the conservatism inspired by his personal hero, Ronald Reagan, [took] command of the bench in a way that eluded his predecessor, the late William Rehnquist."[32] For the first time in more than half a century, conservatives had a Court they could call their own.

Whether this signifies a Reagan revolution (or a Roberts revolution) remains to be seen. Certainly, that is what the Court's liberal minority fears. Several of the 5–4 decisions produced heated dissents, which on some occasions were read from the bench to emphasize the concerns of the dissenters. Particularly notable was Justice Breyer's declaration from the bench on the last day of the 2007 session: "It is not often in the law that so few have so quickly changed so much." Perhaps, but what the Roberts Court has actually accomplished to date falls short of the rhetorical claims on either side. For one thing, as Ted Olson noted, the change in judicial direction has been less than uniform and is arguably liberal on some issues.[33] Olson's Exhibit A is an April 2, 2007, ruling in which the Court, in an opinion written by Justice Stevens, held that the Environmental Protection Agency has the authority to regulate carbon dioxide and other emissions under the Clean Air Act. The post–Christine Todd Whitman EPA had absolutely no interest in undertaking this task and responded to a lawsuit brought by Massachusetts and joined by eleven other states by saying it had no such authority. The Court, in a 5–4 decision hailed by environmentalists and deplored by the Bush administration, said motor-vehicle emissions make a "meaningful contribution to greenhouse gas emissions" and therefore global warming. Roberts and Alito were in the minority. Tony Kennedy was not.

Another reason for skepticism about the reach of the Roberts revolution is that some of the Court's most important decisions come with qualifications attached. The decision upholding the Partial Birth Abortion Act, for instance, did not even ban all late-term abortions, let alone reverse *Roe*. The 5–4 decision invalidating school district integration plans in Seattle and Louisville did not live up to a sound-bite summary of it saying that the Court had prohibited school boards from using race as any kind of factor in drawing up diversity plans. Certainly, this is what Chief Justice Roberts sought to do in his majority opinion. But Justice Kennedy refused to sign it. The other four members of the majority, he said, were "too dismissive" of the values of diversity and the "important work of bringing together students of different racial, ethnic, and economic backgrounds." Kennedy concurred with the majority but wrote a separate opinion in which he said that school boards did not have to accept "the status quo of racial isolation in schools." He went on to suggest ways in which boards might take race into account. One of Kennedy's suggestions was that schools could draw attendance zones that took racial demographics into account, leaving open the possibility that creative school boards may find a way to use race as a factor in future diversity plans. Seattle school officials immediately praised Kennedy and said they would come up with a new plan to promote racial diversity.[34]

Despite the limited practical effect of the school integration ruling, it resonated symbolically with liberals and conservatives alike. Although the Warren Court's famous 1954 decision in *Brown v. Board of Education* had been unanimous, its larger meaning had always been subject to conflicting interpretations. Liberals tended to view *Brown* as a clarion call for integration, while conservatives looked at it as a declaration of color-blindness. Neither of these competing interpretations has been realized, but the ruling that the Seattle and Louisville plans violated the constitutional guarantee of equal protection came down on the conservative side. Still, a 5–4 majority on a court composed of mortals, especially when one of the five wrote an opinion that indulged both interpretations, hardly qualifies as total victory. The issue will come before the Court again.

As this is written in the aftermath of the high court's 2006–2007 term, it is impossible to know if the conservative judicial revolution is at high tide or just beginning. Time is ostensibly on the conservatives' side, as the average age of the four conservative justices is thirteen years less than the average age of the four liberal justices. Roberts, the youngest, is fifty-two at this writing, Stevens, the oldest, is eighty-seven. (Kennedy, midway as usual, is seventy-one.) But age is not the only guide to the health of the justices, as the seizure that Roberts suffered on July 31, 2007, attests. The bigger reason for judicial conservatives to be bullish, at least in the short run, is that they hold a tactical advantage over the liberals. Unlike the situation on the Rehnquist Court, where conservatives needed the votes of both O'Connor and Kennedy to prevail, they now need only Kennedy's. In the nineteen cases decided along ideological lines in the first full term of the Roberts Court, Kennedy was always in the majority. He sided with the conservatives in thirteen of these cases and with the liberals in six. But this scorecard does not tell the full story. As the school integration decision demonstrated, Kennedy is reluctant to put all his eggs in any ideological basket, adding an element of uncertainty to forecasts of the Court's direction.

The high court's unpredictability is highest on an issue of great importance: the power of the executive branch to hold and try prisoners taken captive as part of the Bush administration's "war on terror." At the times of their confirmations, Roberts and Alito were expected on the basis of their judicial records to be deferential to executive authority in terrorism cases; they have fulfilled expectations but have yet to carry the Court with them on this issue. In *Hamadan v. Rumsfeld,* Justice John Paul Stevens wrote for a 5–3 majority on June 29, 2006, that the military commissions in which the Bush administration planned to try the prisoners detained at Guantanamo Bay were unauthorized by federal law.* Congress responded three months later by passing the Military Commissions Act, which authorized the trials. On February 20, 2007, in *Boudmediene v. Bush,* a federal appeals court upheld the law. In April, the Supreme Court refused to hear an appeal from this decision. This would have been the end of it, but in a rare action on the last day of the 2006–2007 term, the Supreme Court reversed itself and agreed to hear the case. The action required at least five votes, prompting speculation that Kennedy had sided with the liberals, who believe that the Constitution's guarantee of habeas

---

*Roberts, who had ruled in favor of the government on the appellate court, did not participate. Alito voted with the minority. Kennedy joined the majority.

corpus gives the detainees the right to contest in court the government's reason for holding them.

As Justice Kennedy goes, so goes the Court. This was the lesson of the Court's last term, so much so that the Roberts Court is now sometimes called "the Kennedy Court." Robert Barnes of *The Washington Post* called Kennedy "the decider,"[35] President Bush's description of himself. This is one of the kinder descriptions of the centrist justice, who in 2007 drew withering fire from the Left on a scale almost matching the earlier attacks from the Right. Writing in *The New Republic,* George Washington law school professor Jeffrey Rosen accused Kennedy of arrogance, of "self-dramatizing utopianism," and of "forcing legislators to respect a series of moralistic abstractions about liberty, equality, and dignity."[36] Kennedy has been as undeterred by such criticism as he was by Dobson's characterization of him as one of America's most dangerous men. In the manner of his hero Earl Warren, he is unconstrained by the narrow walls of constitutional jurisprudence: Kennedy's opinions take into account what the Founders called a decent respect for the opinion of mankind, and he does not shrink from invoking national values. "At the heart of liberty is the right to define one's own concept of existence, of meaning, of the universe, and of the mystery of human life," Kennedy wrote in a widely quoted opinion.* It is not a view that endears him either to legal scholars or ideologues, but Kennedy is healthy and has no known retirement plans. Any conservative revolution—or any liberal counter-revolution—will have to come through him.

On the same day the Supreme Court concluded its term by striking down the Seattle and Louisville school integration plans, the Senate decisively rejected George W. Bush's bipartisan attempt to overhaul the nation's immigration laws. The action was described in the media as a bitter loss for

---

*Justice Kennedy expressed this view in *Planned Parenthood v. Casey,* a 1992 opinion he wrote with Justices O'Connor and Souter. This decision upheld *Roe* but allowed states, in this case Pennsylvania, to place various restrictions on abortion, as long as they did not put an "undue burden" on women. Kennedy used a similar formulation in his historic 2003 opinion in *Lawrence* upholding the right of homosexuals to have consensual sex. In his dissent Justice Antonin Scalia referred sarcastically to this language as the "famed sweet-mystery-of-life passage."

Bush, but it was equally a defeat for liberal forces of reform that were try-ing to establish a path to citizenship for two-thirds of an estimated 12 mil-lion illegals living in the United States and for business groups that wanted a reliable supply of guest workers. Ted Kennedy, who on immi-gration issues puts policy above partisan politics, warned fellow Demo-crats that they were passing up a rare opportunity to pass constructive immigration legislation. They were unmoved; on a procedural maneuver to move the legislation forward, the normally influential Kennedy lost nearly a third of the Democratic senators. Bush, with his approval ratings hovering around 30 percent, did worse. Despite the president's pleas, only a dozen of forty-nine Senate Republicans supported the motion, which fell fourteen votes short of the sixty required to keep the bill alive. Senator Kennedy said that senators had "voted their fears, not their hopes." Re-publican leader Mitch McConnell said he had hoped for a bipartisan vic-tory and instead settled for a bipartisan defeat. But McConnell himself voted against keeping the bill alive. With talk radio on the warpath against a measure routinely described as "amnesty for illegal aliens," Sen-ate Republicans listened to grassroots conservatives and ignored the White House.

The immigration vote demonstrated Bush's impotence. By 2007, he had become the Rodney Dangerfield of presidents, ignored or spurned by fellow Republicans even when he was faithful to his campaign promises and the premises of Reaganism. For what Bush was trying to do in 2007 was not all that different from what Ronald Reagan had done in 1986. Under the Immigration Reform and Control Act that Reagan signed into law that year, 2.7 million illegal aliens became citizens. In signing it, Rea-gan said his objective was "to establish a reasonable, fair, orderly, and se-cure system of immigration into this country and not to discriminate in any way against participating nations or people." Although Reagan did not describe this bipartisan legislation as "amnesty," the result of this law was amnesty by any other name.

The similarities between Reagan's and George W. Bush's approaches to immigration issues underscore their common experience as Republican governors of western states. There are many differences between Califor-nia and Texas, but they share a long border with Mexico, a significant im-migrant population, a world outlook, and a brisk international trade. When Reagan ran for governor in 1966, he made a conscious appeal to

Mexican Americans, then only a small segment of the California electorate. In the final days of the campaign, he toured the state with mari-
achi bands and finished his speeches with the words, *"Ya basta?,"* the
Spanish-language equivalent of "Had enough?" Reagan won an estimated 40 percent of the vote in Mexican-American communities, better
than any Republican had ever done, and also ran strongly in many Mexican-American areas in his presidential races. In Texas, Bush garnered
similar percentages of Latino votes—in a state where things had historically been more difficult for the GOP. The estimated 40 percent of the
Latino vote Bush attracted in 1998 was the first time any Anglo Republican had achieved that level of support in a statewide race in Texas. Taking advantage of an easy rapport with Mexican Americans that Texas
political observers likened to Bill Clinton's harmony with African-American voters, Bush pursued a *"Tejano"* strategy in which he campaigned
both in Latino areas (always speaking a few words in Spanish) and on
Spanish-language radio and television outlets while stressing the values of
work, pride, and devotion to family that are cherished in both the Anglo
and Latino communities.

Bush also characterized the border region as an asset, not a liability,
and was dismissive of the hoary image of the border region "as a haven
for crime, drugs and pollution," noted Gregory Rodriguez, a scholar at
the Pepperdine Institute for Public Policy.[37] "Because in Texas parlance
the border is synonymous with Mexican Americans, this economic message has ethnic implications," he added.*

The political appeals of Reagan and Bush to Latinos dovetailed with
their approach to trade and hemispheric issues. Reagan began his 1980
campaign for the presidency by calling for a "North American accord,"
an undefined alliance with Canada and Mexico that during his presidency foreshadowed a "framework agreement." This in turn became the
basis of the North American Free Trade Agreement signed into law by
President Clinton. Using the "fast-track" authority granted the president

---

*"When you say the border is good, you're saying Mexicans are good," Thomas Lon-
goria, a political science professor at the University of Texas at El Paso, told Rodriguez.
"When you say the border is worth investing in, you're saying that Mexicans are worth
investing in."

by Congress, George W. Bush expanded NAFTA to Chile, the Dominican Republic, and the six nations of Central America; implemented a series of free trade agreements with Africa designed to encourage manufacturing on that continent; and negotiated trade agreements with Australia, Peru, and Panama.

Bush has also generally followed Reagan precepts on tax policy. The 2001 tax cuts briefly examined in Chapter 3 of this book amount to an estimated $1.3 trillion to $1.4 trillion over ten years. Some analysts question the permanence of these reductions because of sunset provisions that will cause taxes to revert to higher rates unless Congress preserves them. Nonetheless, despite bold talk by Democratic presidential candidates on the campaign trail about repealing the tax reductions to pay for health care, the Democratic-controlled Congress in 2007 made no move to get rid of any of them. Even so, Bush's tax policy gets little respect. Despite the progressive nature of most of the Bush tax cuts, liberals invariably characterize them as a giveaway to the rich. Conservatives such as supply-side economist Bruce Bartlett take the cuts for granted and assail Bush for failing to use his veto power to restrain lavish congressional spending. To Bartlett, who worked in the Reagan White House, Bush is a "pretend conservative" who has abandoned Reaganite principles.[38] Bush also disappointed Alan Greenspan, the former chairman of the Federal Reserve Board and a self-described "libertarian Republican." Glossing over the important role he had played in giving his imprimatur to Bush's economic policies, Greenspan assailed the Republican Congress for passing excessive spending bills and President Bush for signing them. "My biggest frustration remained the president's unwillingness to wield his veto against out-of-control spending," Greenspan wrote in his memoirs.[39] A few days after these memoirs were published, Bush finally responded to the concerns of deficit hawks by threatening to veto pending appropriations measures that he deemed excessive.[40]

In sum, Bush's "big government conservatism" (in Fred Barnes' memorable phrase) was often said to be at odds with Reaganism. On some issues, notably education policy, this was true, but Reagan also allowed spending to get out of hand and for much the same reason—he anticipated that Republican members of Congress would show a spending restraint that they failed to exercise. The difference—and it is a big one—was that there wasn't much that Reagan could have done about it since the Democrats in his day had firm control of the House. Bush had a Republican majority in the House during the first six years of his presidency.

These objections to Bush's domestic problems are more than quibbles, but on his core domestic policies Bush has pursued and substantially achieved the Reaganite agenda he espoused when seeking the White House. He has appointed conservative judges and transformed the Supreme Court. He cut taxes. He has followed Reagan's example—and his own—in pressing for free trade and enlightened immigration laws. He has, arguably for better and for worse, demonstrated on these significant issues that he truly deserves to be called Ronald Reagan's disciple.

10

LEGACY

Heeding the lessons of his tardy response to the Indian Ocean tsunami and to Hurricane Katrina, George W. Bush reacted efficiently and sympathetically on April 16, 2007, when informed of the horror unfolding among the picturesque limestone buildings of Virginia Tech.

At 12:35 P.M. on that grim Monday, before the full magnitude of the tragedy was known, Bush was apprised of events by deputy White House press secretary Dana Perino. Aware only of the early news accounts that two students had been killed, Bush was having lunch with Secretary of Treasury Henry M. Paulson Jr. in his private dining room adjacent to the Oval Office. Perino interrupted them to inform Bush that at least twenty people were dead in Blacksburg at the hands of a gunman, and that the toll would probably go higher. "His face fell," she recalled later.[1] This time, Bush did not waste time ruminating about whether anyone would think he was grandstanding. He did what Americans have come to expect of their presidents. He assumed the role of comforter-in-chief.

Twenty-three minutes after her conversation with Bush, Perino informed reporters in the White House briefing room that the president was "horrified," had expressed his "deep concern" for the families of the victims, and was monitoring the situation. Meanwhile, Bush phoned Virginia Tech President Charles W. Steger and Virginia Governor Tim Kaine to offer any federal assistance they might need in coping with the massacre. Just after 4 P.M., Bush spoke publicly about the tragedy. The following day, at Steger's invitation, he flew with First Lady Laura Bush to Blacksburg, where he delivered moving remarks at a memorial service on the Virginia Tech campus. "As a dad, I can assure you a parent's love is never far from their child's heart," Bush said. "And as you draw closer to your own families in the coming days, I ask you to reach out to those who ache for sons and daughters who will never come home."

Bush reacted similarly after the August 1, 2007, collapse of a Minneapolis bridge spanning the Mississippi River during the evening rush hour. The following morning, he was in the Rose Garden giving voice to Minnesotans' grief and the nation's fear—and vowing to increase spending for transportation infrastructure. Once again, he made timely phone calls, this time to Minnesota Governor Tim Pawlenty and Minneapolis mayor R. T. Rybak. Two days later, Bush toured the scene in person, where he met and publicly praised Gary Babineau, a twenty-four-year-old construction worker who was on the bridge when it collapsed. The section in front of him disappeared, and his pickup truck fell thirty feet. After scrambling to higher ground, Babineau rushed toward a dangling school bus and helped ferry more than fifty children to safety. "We have an amazing country, where people's instinct, first instinct, is to help save life," Bush said. Bush reacted quickly again in October after the devastating California fires.

On the surface, it seemed that in his seventh year in office Bush had learned how to be president, or at least had become versed in a crucial aspect of the job so mastered in times of crisis by Reagan and other successful communicators, from Franklin Roosevelt to Bill Clinton. In truth, George W. Bush was *remembering* what he had already known—and not just in the days following September 11, 2001. Articulating Americans' fears, and demonstrating grace and competence in confronting them, is not an incidental part of a president's job description.

How was it possible to have forgotten such a lesson? This turns out to be a key question of the Bush presidency. One answer is that Bush and his advisers seemed unable to remember the past—even the immediate past—including their own previous words or deeds.

This was a president who vigorously resisted comparisons between Iraq and Vietnam—right up until he began using them himself. At an April 13, 2004, prime-time press conference, when asked about the "Vietnam comparison," Bush brushed it aside. "I think the analogy is false," he replied. Three years later, in an August 22, 2007, speech, the president drew just such an analogy. Addressing the Veterans of Foreign Wars convention in Cincinnati, Bush said that critics of the war who'd maintained that a U.S. departure from Vietnam would not precipitate a bloodbath had been proven wrong—adding that violent retribution would be meted out to America's allies in Iraq if U.S. forces departed prematurely. Bush made front-page news with this speech, but White House aides and the neoconservative press had been invoking Vietnam comparisons for months, without irony, or even a passing acknowledgment of their intellectual about-face. For years, neoconservatives in and out of the administration had upbraided liberals (and journalists) who had the temerity to mention Vietnam or the dreaded word "quagmire."

"Iraq isn't Vietnam, it's Guadalcanal," the influential neoconservative magazine *The Weekly Standard* argued in 2004.[2] Three years later, as congressional Democrats debated cutting off funding for the Iraq War, *The Standard* decided Iraq was Vietnam after all. But, like Bush, the Vietnam that *The Standard* editors invoked was the nation the United States had supposedly abandoned prematurely because the political will had been lost in the United States just as the tide was turning in the U.S. military's favor on the battlefield.[3] This revisionist view had gained currency among a set of military historians in the years since the fall of Saigon—one of its adherents was Ronald Reagan—and it now became the neocons' mantra regarding Iraq. Bush joined this off-key chorus even though such reasoning contradicted his earlier rationale—apparently not comprehending that by invoking Vietnam he only confirmed what his critics had been saying for years. Many of them, most prominently Ted Kennedy, had argued that America had exhibited the same kind of recklessness by entering Iraq as it had by entering Vietnam— but this time it was worse, really, because it meant Bush had learned nothing from history. "As I have said since April of 2004, Iraq is George Bush's Vietnam. It is a quagmire," Kennedy said in response to Bush's VFW speech, adding, "As in Vietnam, truth was the first casualty of the Iraq War."

This perception became a majority view in the United States during Bush's presidency. This always surprised Bush and his aides, who considered the president an inveterate truth-teller. They never seemed to weigh the consequences of Bush's expressions of cockeyed optimism on a public growing disillusioned with what they were reading and seeing of Iraq on their own. Moreover, if the White House rebuttal to every criticism involved a kind of situational logic, there could be no lessons learned from failures, whether they were mistakes of communication or deeds. White House aides marveled at Bush's ability to make a decision and stick with it, never fretting or second-guessing himself, so he could move on to the next issue.[4] Even on his staff, however, there was a hint of unease in these testimonials. Decisiveness, so often demonstrated by Ronald Reagan,* is a prized quality in a leader, but so is willingness to learn from human error. Bush was not as quick to learn as Reagan had been. In the winter of 2004, Bush reacted slowly to the Indian Ocean earthquake partly out of concern for being seeing as a leader who exploited the calamity of others for his own political gain, à la Bill Clinton. Bush successfully atoned for this misjudgment by pairing Clinton with his own father to undo the perception that he didn't care about the tsunami victims. Yet, less than a year later, it took him five days to get himself to the Gulf Coast after Katrina struck. Once there, Bush discovered dazed stragglers who walked up to him and gave him hugs of gratitude. These would have been heartwarming images had they not followed days of television footage of stranded Americans on the rooftops around New Orleans. And it was in stark contrast to Lyndon Johnson, who was pressured to visit New Orleans after it was hit by Hurricane Betsy in 1965. Johnson resisted such entreaties—for about an hour. (The pressure came from Johnson's former Senate colleague, Russell Long, and was captured for posterity by LBJ's taping device. The tapes pick up Long saying, "Mr. President, aside from the Great Lakes, the biggest lake in America is Lake Pontchartrain. It is now drained dry. That Hurricane Betsy picked the lake up and put it inside

---

*An oft-cited example of Reagan's decisiveness was his action on August 3, 1981, when 13,000 members of the Professional Air Traffic Controllers Organization (PATCO) walked off their jobs. PATCO had been one of the few unions to support Reagan for president, but he immediately told them they would be fired unless they returned to work within forty-eight hours.

New Orleans and Jefferson Parish and the 3rd [congressional] district. . . . It's like my home—the whole damn home's been destroyed, but that's all right. My wife and kids are still alive, so it's OK. Mr. President, we have really had it down there, and we need your help." After initially attempting, unsuccessfully, to dissuade Long, Johnson replied, "All right. You got it." At that time, Betsy had claimed but one life.) The next thing White House officials knew, LBJ was barking out orders to fuel Air Force One.[5] By that evening, he was shining flashlights in the faces of startled New Orleans residents—power had not yet been restored—and telling them, "This is your president. I'm here to help you!"

Although it was always ad hoc with him, Bush could rise to the occasion, too. When he did so, he could come across like Johnson—or sometimes sound even Reaganesque. On February 1, 2003, sixteen months after the 9/11 attacks, the president and senior members of his staff were ensconced at Camp David when another kind of tragedy took place. Shortly before 9 A.M. White House Chief of Staff Andrew Card was flipping through channels on the television in his cabin when he saw on the NASA channel that the landing of Space Shuttle *Columbia* was imminent. Mesmerized, he sat down to watch. As it became apparent that a catastrophe had occurred instead, Card called the White House Situation Room, and then NASA headquarters. The man who had handed Bush a note informing him of the attacks on the World Trade Center braced himself once again and walked to the president's cabin to tell him that NASA had lost contact with the shuttle's crew.[6]

Since Thomas Jefferson's day, presidents have expressed special affinity for America's explorers. The bond between president and astronauts is especially strong, rivaled perhaps only by the responsibility felt by a commander-in-chief for combat troops. But astronauts are not warriors; they are pilgrims, and defenseless ones at that. Lyndon Johnson considered the treaty he negotiated with the Soviet Union and Great Britain barring nuclear weapons from space one of the three great accomplishments of his presidency, and signing ceremonies were held in Moscow, London, and Washington. The U.S. ceremony took place in the East Room on January 27, 1967, but what LBJ would later remember about that night was the conflagration on the runway at Cape Kennedy that took the lives of Apollo 1 astronauts Virgil I. (Gus) Grissom, Edward H. White II, and Roger Chaffee.

"The shock," Johnson recalled later, "hit me like a physical blow."[7]

Nineteen years later, on January 28, 1986, disaster struck the United States space program again, this time after liftoff and with a schoolteacher, Christa McAuliffe, aboard—along with six astronauts. Reagan would later describe that time as "one of the hardest days I ever had to spend in the Oval Office."[8] He had called the parents and wives of many American servicemen, but he said a president never gets used to these calls, which he described as weighing on his shoulders "like a ton of iron."[9] McAuliffe had been to the White House with the other teachers vying for the honor of going to space. Reagan had personally announced her as the winner.

Setting aside his private grief, Ronald Reagan addressed the nation— something Lyndon Johnson had not done. His 649-word talk lasted less than five minutes, yet was acclaimed as one of the most stirring of his presidency.* "The future doesn't belong to the fainthearted," Reagan told the nation. "It belongs to the brave." He ended his speech by borrowing the words of a World War II–era sonnet. "We will never forget them, nor the last time we saw them, this morning," Reagan said, "as they prepared for their journey and waved goodbye and 'slipped the surly bonds of Earth' to 'touch the face of God.'"

Seventeen years after Reagan said these words, George W. Bush was riding in his motorcade from Camp David to the White House to address the nation shocked by the loss of the Space Shuttle *Columbia*. His speech that day, little remembered in the din of his second term, was quite worthy of Reagan's example. Bush began simply, as Reagan had done. "The *Columbia* is lost," he said. "There are no survivors." Bush also emulated Reagan in addressing the families of the astronauts directly, and he ended with a poignant quote, too, this one an Old Testament passage, from Isaiah, in which the prophet says the Lord knows all the stars in the heavens and calls them by name.

---

*On the day the *Challenger* exploded, Reagan was to give the State of the Union address, which was postponed. House Speaker Tip O'Neill, who had squared off with Reagan in the Oval Office earlier in the day over the budget, wrote in his autobiography, *Man of the House* (p. 363), that he had seen Reagan at his worst and at his best in the same day. "It was a trying day for all Americans," O'Neill recalled, "and Ronald Reagan spoke to our highest ideals."

"The same Creator who names the stars also knows the names of the seven souls we mourn today," Bush said. "The crew of the shuttle *Columbia* did not return safely to Earth; yet we can pray that all are safely home."

All presidents, no matter how much they know or think they know, gain from experience in the White House, and Bush's learning curve continued well into his second term. Humbled somewhat by the realities of governance and by the deadly impasse in Iraq, Bush became more willing to concede misjudgments. Most of these admissions were at the margins and behind the scenes in discreet conversations with friends, aides, or sympathetic journalists. Privately, for example, Bush expressed a change of heart about Vladimir Putin. The "sense of his soul" that Bush had detected in Putin during the summer of 2001 gave way to a more realistic view of a former KGB functionary whose spirituality was buried under layers of paranoia and authoritarianism.[10]

Bush, albeit belatedly, changed defense secretaries, easing Don Rumsfeld out in favor of the more conciliatory Robert Gates. While Bush never publicly acknowledged that he'd stayed too long with Rumsfeld, Gates's approach to the job suggested that his commander-in-chief had been harboring second thoughts not only about his defense secretary but about his entire military team. One of Gates's first moves was to decline to reappoint Marine Corps General Peter Pace as chairman of the Joint Chiefs of Staff. Instead, Gates tapped Admiral Mike Mullen, then chief of naval operations, for the post. In written answers to questions posed by the Senate Armed Services Committee, Mullen promptly listed seven mistakes the United States had made in Iraq, including disbanding the Iraqi army.[11]

That acknowledgment was consistent with other belated actions taken by the Bush administration. Although he never publicly embraced the Iraq Study Group report, the president began implementing some of its previously ignored recommendations, including sending diplomatic feelers to Iran and Syria. As commander-in-chief with troops in combat, Bush found it difficult to admit fault about Iraq, but he began speaking of the war in a more nuanced way. Without precisely saying so, the president began leaving the impression that he realized in hindsight that invading Iraq might not have been a smart move, but still believed that quitting that country—as an increasing number of Democrats and some Republicans were demanding—was a terrible idea with grievous potential consequences for the American and Iraqi people. The view that it had been a mistake to invade Iraq in 2003—*and* that it would be a mistake to precipitously leave Iraq in 2007—became a majority perspective in the United States, according to public opinion surveys.*

Bush received little credit for his subtle shift in position. For one thing, voters found it difficult to overlook what they considered a mistake of Iraq's magnitude. During the Vietnam War, blame was shared by three presidents, but this was Bush's war alone. The same public opinion polls that showed Americans turning against the war by the end of 2007 also found that a majority had lost confidence in Bush or any affinity for him. They were so alienated, in fact, that they didn't want to hold the same positions Bush held on the major issues of the day. One manifestation of this trend was that various policy solutions, such as private accounts for Social Security, would poll reasonably well—until Bush's name was attached to them. Then the bottom would fall out. Asked, for example, if "people should have the choice to invest privately up to five percent of their Social Security contributions," 60 percent of those surveyed said yes, with only 27 percent saying no.[12] When the question was asked this way: "President Bush favors changing the Social Security system to allow people to invest part of their Social Security payroll tax in stocks and bonds," Americans disapproved of the idea by a margin of 47–44 percent.[13]

Partly this phenomenon was a result of the increased partisan polarization that occurred in American public life before Bush was on the scene. It was present during all eight years of Bill Clinton's presidency, and it left the forty-second and forty-third presidents with political challenges more obdurate than those faced by President Reagan. Other factors contributing to Bush's second-term unpopularity were of his own making—pushing so hard in 2005 for Social Security reform while Iraq was going south, for example. In using some of the same overheated rhetoric (no-

---

*And not only in the United States. One leader in the Muslim world expressed the concern succinctly to conservative writer Jay Nordlinger in 2007 at the World Economic Forum on the Middle East, held in Jordan: "The thing is, if you leave Iraq too soon, you may find that you have to come back."

tably the word "crisis") to describe a problem that wouldn't come to a head until 2018,[14] Bush undermined his plans for Social Security, his stated rationale for invading Iraq, and his own credibility—all at the same time. His unwillingness to face the deteriorating situation in Iraq undermined the president most of all. Eventually, Americans just stopped listening to George W. Bush.

"Whatever he's selling, they aren't buying," former Reagan chief of staff Ken Duberstein said in a mid-summer 2007 interview. "When George W. Bush comes on television, people either change the channel or hit the mute button. The last time this happened was during the final months of Jimmy Carter's presidency."[15] Even in the days before mute buttons existed, the American people stopped listening to various embattled presidents, inevitably with unhappy results for their administrations. Herbert Hoover was one such president. One of Franklin Roosevelt's signature lines as president—used most famously in his 1933 inaugural address—was that in confronting the Great Depression, "the only thing we have to fear is fear itself." Hoover had spent the better part of 1932 making this same point, and in similar language, urging countrymen to replace their "unjustifiable fear" with "confidence."[16] By that time, as presidential historian Richard Norton Smith has noted, Americans had long stopped listening to Herbert Hoover. ("He's not the last president to be tuned out," Smith said, "before he was turned out.")[17]

This phenomenon is most true of presidents who preside over unpopular wars, a description that applies most directly in modern American history to Lyndon Johnson and Harry Truman. These are the presidents, not Ronald Reagan or his own father, to whom George W. Bush found himself most frequently compared as his time in office came to a close—often unfavorably. "I am constantly asked to compare [Bush] with Lyndon Johnson. But with Lyndon Johnson the scale has two sides," Pulitzer Prize–winning Johnson biographer Robert Caro wrote in *Texas Monthly* in March 2007. "Certainly on one side you have his mighty domestic achievements. . . . On the other side you have Vietnam. You have a balance. So far, I do not see any comparable domestic accomplishments in George Bush's presidency. As of now, Iraq is going to be his legacy. All the weight is on the foreign policy half of the scale."[18]

The comparison preferred by Bush is with Truman, who left office widely scorned as a mule-headed bumpkin who put cronyism ahead of competence, and who led his nation into his own deadly military morass—in this case in Korea. In February 1952, his last year in office, Truman earned the lowest job approval rating (22 percent) of any president before or since in the Gallup Poll. "To err is Truman," went a quip of the day. Bush has seized on this example to make the point that presidents' reputations are unknowable in their own time. When Karl Rove would wring his hands over Bush's declining approval ratings, Bush reassured his top political aide that snapshots of public opinion eventually give way to the weightier and wiser judgments of time. "History will get it right," Bush would tell Rove, adding lightheartedly, "but it will be fifty or a hundred years from now, and we'll both be dead, so don't worry about it."[19]

In another context, discussing whether investment decisions should be based on short-term or long-term factors, British economist John Maynard Keynes notably quipped, "In the long run, we'll all be dead." And while the long run certainly altered some presidential reputations, most of the nation's greatest presidents were revered in their own time— Washington, Lincoln, and Franklin Roosevelt come to mind. When presidential reputations are reevaluated, it is usually because of something that happens after they leave office. Reagan is illustrative of this point. The Soviet Union disappeared on George H. W. Bush's watch, flowing from events that occurred in the Reagan presidency. Viewed with this knowledge, Reagan's decision to launch a military buildup that enabled him to bargain with the Soviets from a position of strength seemed a wise course of action, even to many who had criticized the buildup when it began. Similarly, the enormous budget deficits of the Reagan years, regarded as a blot on his presidency when he left office, became less consequential when a reduction in military spending made possible by the end of the Cold War enabled a Democratic president and a Republican Congress to balance the budget in the mid-1990s.

In George W. Bush's case, historians tend to be intrigued, even impressed, by his sanguinity and willingness to take the long view. That is not the same thing as agreeing that his confidence is well placed, however, as many scholars find the Truman analogy strained. "What's interesting with Bush is how he believes he'll be viewed by historians," noted presidential biographer Robert Dallek, in the same issue of *Texas Monthly* in which Robert Caro weighed in. "When asked about his legacy, he says it's too soon to tell, that we'll have to wait thirty, forty, fifty years. And he points to Truman. Bush is banking on the fact that he'll get credit for putting in place the strategy for winning this larger war against terrorists even if Iraq looks like a stumbling affair at the end of his term, in January 2009." Dallek is unconvinced. "What I think historians will ask is, 'What is Bush's strategy?' There isn't a containment strategy," Dallek wrote. In a mid-2007 interview with *U.S. News & World Report,* he amplified his skepticism of the Bush-Truman comparison. "He may come across to some people as a man of principle, but a great majority see him as stubborn and unyielding," Dallek said. "And everything he touches turns to dust."[20]

Historian Douglas Brinkley has noted that in spite of Korea, Truman was also the president who successfully oversaw the conclusion of World War II. Brinkley compared Bush to a poker player "who bet all his chips on Iraq, and it hasn't come out the way he wanted."[21] When Brinkley made this observation, in early 2007, he was editing Reagan's diaries. "Nancy Reagan gave them to me, and they're extraordinary," he wrote. "When terrorists blew up the Marine barracks in Lebanon, Reagan was frustrated and furious, as Bush was after 9/11. But he didn't stick us in a war in the Middle East with no exit."[22]

Throughout the history of the republic, war has made and ruined the reputations of U.S. presidents. George Washington was first in war before becoming first in peace. The statecraft that as president made Washington first in the heart of his countrymen was a bonus. President James Madison was widely reviled, especially after the burning of Washington, D.C., in 1814, for taking the nation into what historians know as the second U.S. war for independence and is more popularly called the War of 1812. When this war ended in a stalemate that Americans perceived as victory, the tide of public opinion turned in Madison's favor. More than three decades later, war hawks acclaimed James K. Polk as a great president after he seized Texas from Mexico in the U.S.-Mexican War. A Whig member of the House from Illinois named Abraham Lincoln voted against this war, which Ulysses S. Grant, who fought in it as a second lieutenant, called "one of the most unjust ever waged by a stronger against a weaker nation."[23] Nonetheless, President Polk's reputation was enhanced by victory, and he was hailed as a strong president who had made the United States a continental power.

Victory has been the touchstone for every U.S. president who led the nation in military conflict, with the possible (and ironic) exception of George W. Bush's father. Lincoln's great achievements—the preservation of the Union and the freeing of the slaves—were made possible by his military leadership, which included the sacking of several top generals until Lincoln found the one he needed in the person of Grant. President William McKinley, Karl Rove's unlikely hero, was elected on a domestic platform and was partly prodded into the Spanish-American War in 1898 by his vice president, Theodore Roosevelt, who became an enduring American hero in that conflict. McKinley fared less well. The United States won an easy victory over Spain in Cuba but in an eerie anticipation of Iraq was dragged into an ugly decade-long insurgency in the Philippines, which Spain had ceded to the United States. Americans have never had much appetite for the costly wars of empire. We have in this book reviewed how President Woodrow Wilson, after a brief flirtation with intervention in Mexico, repudiated imperialism and resisted entreaties to enter World War I until his hand was forced by the terror weapon of his day: the German submarine-launched torpedoes that sank the *Lusitania* and many other ships. Reelected for keeping the United States out of war, Wilson dispatched U.S. troops, thereby assuring an Allied victory. The pattern was repeated a generation later when President Franklin D. Roosevelt won a third term after promising voters: "I have said this before, but I shall say it again and again and again. Your boys are not going to be sent into any foreign wars."[24]* But after the Japanese attack on Pearl Harbor, on December 7, 1941, FDR sent more American "boys" into foreign wars than any U.S. president in history. Allied forces defeated Nazi Germany and Imperial Japan, and Roosevelt earned a reputation as a highly effective wartime leader.

World War II was the last major American conflict in which "victory" could be defined as the complete and unconditional defeat of a military

---

*This pledge was a plank in the 1940 Democratic platform, which qualified it by saying "except in case of attack." In *Roosevelt and Hopkins: An Intimate History,* p. 191, FDR biographer Robert Sherwood wrote that Roosevelt's speechwriter Sam Rosenman suggested the addition of these words to the president's speeches. But Roosevelt, who was besieged with telegrams urging him to make an unqualified promise, would have none of it. "Of course, we'll fight if attacked," Sherwood quoted FDR as saying. "If someone attacks us, then it isn't a foreign war, is it?"

adversary. The atomic bombs that the United States dropped on Hiroshima and Nagasaki in 1945 forever changed the equation of victory, which in the long twilight struggle of the Cold War came to mean avoiding "total" war altogether. Wars that could not be avoided—or that could have been avoided but were not—were ruinous to the reputations of the presidents who conducted them. American young men (and now young women) were sent to fight and die in conflicts in which their leaders were not committed to victory. Americans initially supported Truman when he sent in U.S. troops under United Nations auspices after North Korea invaded South Korea in June 1950. But the Korean War, which Truman called a "police action," quickly became so destructive and unproductive that public opinion turned against him. Two years into the war, Truman was too unpopular to stand for reelection, and Democratic candidates did not want to appear with him or in some cases even receive a presidential endorsement. After 54,000 U.S. military fatalities, the war ended in a stalemate in July 1953, with both sides holding the territory they had at the beginning of the war. The best that could be said about the Korean War is that it preserved an independent South Korea that in time evolved into a democracy. President Lyndon Johnson could not take even this limited comfort from the Vietnam War, which cost more than 58,000 American lives. Like Truman, Johnson's reputation was too tarnished for him to seek reelection. The Iraq War drove George W. Bush's approval ratings below Johnson's in 1968 toward Truman territory, circa 1952.

Truman's return from his political purgatory inspired Bush, whose expectations regarding his own legacy went from hoping to be the next Ronald Reagan to hoping *not* to be the next Herbert Hoover, the name often on the lips of liberal critics as Bush's presidency wound down. Bush wasn't the first to invoke Harry Truman as a fallback position; in the last half of the twentieth century, Truman became the patron saint of beleaguered presidents. In his harrowing final two years in office, Bill Clinton used Truman as a kind of talisman, mentioning him constantly in public appearances. And as Bush's father prepared to run for reelection against Clinton in 1992, he invited Truman biographer David McCullough to the White House for a history lesson on how Truman managed to pull out his unlikely 1948 campaign win.[25]

Harry Truman's biggest comeback occurred posthumously, two decades after he left office, and it is this resurrection that captivates Bush and his loyalists. The nation's reconsideration of Truman was gradual, but it gained momentum after his death, which occurred the day after Christmas in 1972. Richard Nixon was president, and the crude content of the tape recordings made public during the Watergate scandal exposed Nixon as a paranoid, duplicitous, and insecure chief executive. A nation recoiling from the unplugged Nixon embraced Truman's refreshing directness just in time to make a runaway best-seller of a 1974 book called *Plain Speaking,* Merle Miller's oral history of Truman based on interviews taped in 1962.* The end of the Cold War brought another round of pro-Truman revisionism. Many conservatives heaped praise on Reagan for ending the Cold War "without firing a shot" (to use Margaret Thatcher's phrase), but an honest appraisal of the fall of the Iron Curtain entailed spreading the credit around to most of America's postwar leaders—starting with Truman, the first U.S. president to confront Soviet expansionism.

Reagan himself wouldn't have minded. Truman was the last Democrat he voted for, and his affection for "Little Harry" remained after Reagan won national office. Reagan (with help from his speechwriters) invoked Truman's name more than 130 times as president. Many of these were passing references. Others came from the heart, including a warm May 8, 1984, tribute at a White House luncheon commemorating the centennial of Truman's birth. Reagan was especially fond of invoking the Truman line about giving people hell ("I don't give 'em hell, I just tell the truth and they think it's hell"), which Reagan paraphrased to describe his own attitude about everything from resisting Democrats on tax policy to calling out Soviet leaders. Most of Reagan's Truman references, in fact, concerned Truman's recognition of the threat of international communism and his willingness to confront it. The day after the Truman centennial lunch, Reagan delivered a nationally televised speech in which he sought to bolster public support for his policies in Nicaragua and El Salvador. He said that if the nation rallied behind Truman's vision in a non-partisan way, "Soviet- and Cuban-supported aggression can be defeated" in Central America. "On this, the centennial anniversary of President Harry

---

*An odd irony—that Miller apparently fabricated some of the saltiest quotes he attributed to Truman—wasn't revealed until 1995, when Truman historian Robert Ferrell documented Miller's embellishments in *American Heritage.*

Truman's birth," Reagan added, "it's fitting to recall his words, spoken to a Joint Session of the Congress in a similar situation: 'The free peoples of the world look to us for support in maintaining their freedoms. If we falter . . . we may endanger the peace of the world, and we shall surely endanger the welfare of this nation.'"

To Bush, the threat posed by militant Islam in his time is similar to the challenge posed by world communism a generation earlier. In Bush's telling, he may not be Reagan, but he sure as hell can be Truman. This is the context in which Bush seeks to use Truman's new and improved reputation to bolster his own. "As we advance the cause of freedom in Iraq, our nation can proceed with confidence because we have done this kind of work before," Bush said in a second-term speech to the scholars of the Woodrow Wilson Center in a December 14, 2005, speech at the Ronald Reagan Building. He continued:

> After World War II, President Harry Truman believed that the way to help bring peace and prosperity to Asia was to plant the seeds of freedom and democracy in Japan. Like today, there were many skeptics and pessimists who said that the Japanese were not ready for democracy. Fortunately, President Harry Truman stuck to his guns. He believed, as I do, in freedom's power to transform an adversary into an ally. And because he stayed true to his convictions, today Japan is one of the world's freest and most prosperous nations, and one of America's closest allies in keeping the peace. The spread of freedom to Iraq and the Middle East requires the same confidence and persistence, and it will lead to the same results.

Leading Truman scholar Alonzo L. Hamby, one of the most prominent of the revisionists, observed that Truman was "magnificently right on what may have been the two most important issues of his time: civil rights and the Soviet challenge."[26] These were huge achievements with political corollaries: In the 1948 election, Truman's stand on civil rights drove the segregationist southern wing out of the Democratic Party; his policy of containing the Soviet Union similarly prompted the desertion of the party's far left wing, which supported Henry Wallace. But these political accomplishments were subsequently overshadowed by the Korean War, which even the revisionists find as dubious an undertaking in retrospect as it seemed to Truman's contemporaries. "The frustrating Korean stalemate, which delivered the fatal blow to [Truman's] presidency, was ultimately the result of a serious disparity between expanding ends and contracting means that characterized the first five years of his presidency," Hamby wrote. "Well into his second term, Truman pursued a policy of ever-widening and sometimes unclear commitments while enforcing a rigid, budget-driven contraction of American capability. Korea laid bare the inadequacies of these moves, alienating large segments of the American population and alarming the Western allies. The heavy military buildup that followed inflicted economic pain at home while doing nothing to relieve the ongoing blood-letting in Korea."[27]

These words could be written with nearly equal force about George W. Bush's war in Iraq, yet Bush and his loyalists saw what they wanted to see when looking back at the Truman presidency. The most ambitious Bush/Truman comparison was probably made by Vice President Dick Cheney, in a 2004 address to the World Affairs Council in Los Angeles. Noting that 9/11 had been frequently compared to December 7, 1941—Pearl Harbor Day—Cheney suggested that the more salient analogy could be drawn "not to the days of Franklin Roosevelt and World War II, but to the decisions that faced Harry Truman at the outset of the Cold War."

"President Truman made clear at the outset that the United States recognized the danger, and that—for the sake of future generations—we would face it squarely," Cheney said that day. "In a short time, our government created the architecture of national security we know today: the Department of Defense, the Central Intelligence Agency, the National Security Council. To defend ourselves and free Europe, the United States helped to found NATO. To build and strengthen new democracies, our government led in the reconstruction of Japan, and devoted the present-day equivalent of over $100 billion to European assistance through the Marshall Plan. And when aggression occurred on the Korean Peninsula, it was President Truman's decision and America's sacrifice that saved South Korea."

This, Cheney concluded, was the kind of danger America was facing in the twenty-first century; fortunately, the nation had a modern version of Harry Truman—George W. Bush—to handle things. It was a claim Cheney and others would make on the campaign trail throughout 2004, and one Bush made on his own behalf throughout his second term. Sometimes he did it implicitly, such as when he told the graduating cadets at the U.S. Military Academy at West Point in May 2006 (in a speech in which Bush mentioned Truman seventeen times): "By the actions he took, the institutions he built, the alliances he forged and the doctrines he set down, President Truman laid the foundations for America's victory in the Cold War." At other times he staked his claim to Truman's mantle directly, such as in 2006 on Pearl Harbor Day, after inviting Democratic congressional leaders to the White House in a gesture of magnanimity following the opposition party's mid-term victories. The topic on the table that day: the Iraq Study Group report, which had delivered its recommendations the day before. "He drew an interesting parallel," Senator Dick Durbin of Illinois recounted after the meeting. "He said Harry Truman, with the Truman Doctrine, came up with the right doctrine, the right approach, to fight communism. It wasn't popular. He left office not as popular as he once was, but history showed he was right. He's trying to position himself in history."[28]

Durbin took issue with the Truman analogy, telling the president, "Aren't there a couple of significant differences here? Harry Truman had allies. NATO was behind him. When Great Britain leaves next year, we're going to be virtually alone in Iraq."* Dick Durbin is a partisan Democrat. In this case he was also well-grounded. Bush's comparison ignores a central fact of the historical revisionism that has polished the luster of the Truman presidency. That fact is that the revised, positive view of Truman has come about not because of the Korean War but despite it.

This lesson seemed to elude Bush, who was so enamored of the Truman comparison that he took it to odd lengths: At a September 13, 2007, White House luncheon where he hosted network anchors on the day of a prime-time speech on Iraq,** Bush discussed his likely successor. The

---

*Durbin related the gist of this conversation to his hometown newspaper, *The Chicago Tribune,* from which these quotes are taken. Asked for confirmation, White House spokesman Tony Snow conceded that the exchange occurred, without vouching for the exact quotes in the *Tribune.*

**Drawing from his Harvard Business School days, Bush used a term only an M.B.A. could love: In explaining how American troops might be withdrawn from Iraq, he spoke of a "return on success"—as though the Iraq theater were a money market. Political scientist Sherry Jeffe Bebitch wrote in her column on the KNBC–Los Angeles website that Bush's new slogan sounded "like an investment firm slogan," and added: "Try draping that on an aircraft carrier."

identity of the person Bush had in mind fascinated the anchors: The president speculated openly that it was likely to be Hillary Clinton. They were even more surprised to hear Bush, drawing the Truman comparison to its ultimate conclusion, compare Mrs. Clinton to Truman's successor, Dwight D. Eisenhower.[29]

The essential claim made on behalf of Truman is the following: first, that he possessed the foresight to recognize the Soviet threat early on; second, that he had the judgment and political skill to construct a host of policy prescriptions designed to meet the challenge posed by worldwide communism; and third, that he had the courage to commit U.S. troops to the Korean peninsula, the initial (but not only) combat phase of the Cold War.

Even if one stipulates to the validity of the analogy between international communism and international jihad, and even if one grants Bush credit for his willingness to face up to the danger he perceives, something fundamental is missing from the equation (beyond the fact that Iraq was not attacked by this new enemy, as Korea had been). Where is Step 2 in the Truman analogy? What, in Bush's approach, is the equivalent of the Marshall Plan, or NATO, or the U.S. intervention in Greece, or the Berlin airlift, or the president's insistence that the Korean response be ratified by the United Nations? These examples were cited not only by Democratic politicians and liberal historians, but by Vice President Cheney himself. Yet they were missing in the years 2001–2008. That is the structural weakness in the comparisons between George W. Bush and other past presidents who were internationalists. In this way, he is not the equal of Hoover or LBJ—let alone Wilson, Truman, or Reagan.

Historical analogies sometimes distract from the record. In the last article he wrote before his untimely death, David Halberstam took aim at what he called the "History Boys" of the Bush administration, singling out Bush, Cheney, Rumsfeld, and Condoleezza Rice. "In one of [Bush's] appearances in March 2006, in Cleveland," wrote Halberstam, "I counted four references to history, and what it meant for today, as if [Bush] had dinner the night before with Arnold Toynbee, or at the very least Barbara Tuchman, and then gone for a few hours to read his Gibbon."[30] Halberstam, who had spent five years researching a book published posthumously on the Korean War, became convinced that the circumstances surrounding it were so utterly different from those in Iraq that the comparison made little sense.

Suppose, however, that the analogy is accepted, for the purpose of argument, as a serious comparison. If Bush truly saw himself as Truman, would he have kept Don Rumsfeld as long as he did? Louis A. Johnson was secretary of defense in the Truman administration when North Korea invaded South Korea in 1950. He was capable, wealthy, successful, and opinionated, adjectives that also describe Rumsfeld. But Johnson was a bust as secretary of defense. He alienated members of Congress, conspired against the secretary of state (Dean Acheson in this case), and, in the words of Truman biographer David McCullough, "had a basic distrust of generals and admirals when it came to spending money."[31] Truman had supported Johnson in a vigorous effort to reduce military spending, an achievement that left the United States even more unprepared for the Korean War than the Bush administration would be for the Iraq insurgency. On September 11, 1950, less than three months into the Korean War, Truman fired Johnson and replaced him with George Marshall. Seven months later, Truman more famously fired General Douglas MacArthur for his insubordination in sending U.S. troops to the Chinese border. There is no analogue for the MacArthur dismissal in the Bush administration (or in any administration, except perhaps Lincoln's), but suppose for a moment that Bush *had* fired Rumsfeld when the Iraq War went bad. In that case, it is likely that David Petraeus, whom Rumsfeld had tried to marginalize, would have been given command of U.S. forces in Iraq when the insurgency was in its infancy. This was at a time when there was bipartisan support at home for a troop surge. It isn't clear what would have happened if General Petraeus had been given this chance—except this: Bush's claim to Truman's legacy would have made more sense.

The purpose of this book, however, was to compare George W. Bush to Ronald Reagan, not to Harry Truman. Colin Powell, among others, told the authors that he considered such a comparison a stretch because Reagan and Bush are dissimilar in so many ways. But we did not conjure up this analogy ourselves. As a presidential candidate in 2000, Bush explicitly and implicitly compared himself to Reagan, and he sought to emulate him once he was elected. On January 26, 2003, as noted in the preface to this book, a cover story in *The New York Times Magazine* called "Reagan's Son" made the case that Bush was modeling his presidency after Reagan's. That article quoted members of both administrations to make the point. At that time, Bush was a popular president who had risen to the terrible occasion of September 11, 2001, with grace and firmness. The

Iraq War that Bush would launch eighteen months later ultimately dampened these comparisons while simultaneously making it more imperative to understand how and why Bush deviated from the Reagan model he had earlier proclaimed.

The most problematic aspect of the comparison is that it is often made in a restrictive, ideological way, using Reagan's conservative advocacies as a template for examining what Bush has done. In this sort of comparison, Bush measures up fairly well—better than many conservatives acknowledge. He has, as we have seen, proven to be Reagan's disciple on tax and trade policies, immigration issues, and judicial appointments. (Deficit hawks would observe that Bush has also patterned himself after Reagan in his almost casual acceptance of enormous budget deficits.) A more pertinent comparison is between the two men as effective national and international leaders, a standard on which the iconic Reagan set a high bar. Nonetheless, when Bush took office, it seemed a standard within reach; Reagan, like all presidents, made his share of mistakes and misjudgments. On the whole, he was less disciplined than Bush, in part because his circle of advisers and his cabinet were more diverse, and Reagan tended to split the difference when principal subordinates were in disagreement. At its worst, in Lebanon, this difference-splitting strategy produced a muddled policy that ended in catastrophe. At its best, in dealing with the Soviet Union, it produced a desirable outcome: The cacophony of advisers helped Reagan develop a nuanced approach that mixed military calculation with common sense. This outcome rarely happened easily, and even Reagan's most successful policy ventures sometimes stumbled. As Walter Lippmann once said of Charles de Gaulle, Reagan resembled a nearsighted man who bumped over the furniture up close but could see across the room. Reagan's military buildup, combined with blunt descriptions of the Soviets, alarmed both the national security community and congressional liberals, but his overall approach to the Soviet Union was visionary. Later in his presidency, Reagan distressed conservatives when he sought to cash in the benefits of the buildup by bargaining freely to reduce U.S. and Soviet nuclear arsenals. But Reagan's actions in dealing with the Soviets were of a piece. On this most crucial issue, history suggests that he did indeed see across the room.

Other aspects of the Reagan presidency were more experimental. Lenin, promoting communism while tolerating private production in the nascent Soviet Union, famously called for one step backward and two steps forward. That would fairly describe Reagan's fiscal policy, which included a spate of tax increases after an early tax reduction but ended up significantly lowering the marginal tax rate. When the supply-side tax cuts Reagan had embraced failed to produce a quick turnaround and the economy plunged into recession, Reagan turned to the more traditional remedy advocated by Federal Reserve chief Paul Volcker, a Wall Street Democrat appointed by President Carter, who proposed to hobble runaway inflation with high interest rates. After Volcker succeeded, his policy retrospectively had many champions, but Reagan's original decision to back Volcker worried Republican congressional leaders and some of his own White House advisers. On a host of other issues, foreign and domestic, Reagan tried one thing and then another, as his first political idol, Franklin Roosevelt, had been wont to do, before opting for a practical solution that contradicted bolder goals. The withdrawal from Lebanon and the refusal to invade Panama were paramount examples. So was Social Security reform. After failing utterly in a frontal assault on Social Security, Reagan worked with Democratic House Speaker Tip O'Neill to produce a time-buying compromise that none of his successors has emulated.* On other issues where his goals were unrealistic or unattainable, Reagan simply abandoned them. On the 1980 campaign trail, he dropped hints about stripping the Department of Education and other federal agencies of their cabinet-level status. Instead, Reagan kept Education and acceded to giving cabinet designation to the Department of Veterans Affairs. Bush could do this on occasion himself, with positive results. As we saw in Chapter 3, Bush's willingness to forgo private school vouchers smoothed passage of a sweeping education bill, No Child Left

---

*The instrument for this compromise was the bipartisan National Commission on Social Security Reform. Reagan appointed Alan Greenspan as chairman of the commission. O'Neill and Senate Majority Leader Howard Baker also had appointments to the commission; O'Neill's most notable choice was Robert Ball, a respected former Social Security commissioner. Greenspan, Ball, and their fellow commissioners recognized that politics is the art of the possible. Their compromise proposal, which bought Social Security a quarter century of solvency, raised the retirement age and delayed a cost-of-living payment (which Republicans wanted) and taxed high-income recipients for the first time (a Democratic goal). Reagan signed the Social Security amendments into law on April 20, 1983, with O'Neill at his side. "This is a happy day for America," O'Neill said.

Behind. This example is so notable because compromises of this sort were so rare for Bush.

Reagan's practical streak showed itself with particular force in the dismissal or reassignment of advisers whom he found an impediment to his presidency. As a Hollywood movie actor, Reagan had been accustomed to changing casts and different directors, and he assumed from the first that similar practices would prevail in politics. In Martin Anderson's useful phrase, Reagan could be "warmly ruthless"[32] in ridding himself of aides whom he no longer needed. This was a recurrent tendency throughout his political career: Reagan fired chiefs of staff both as governor and as president. He fired his campaign manager, the brilliant but moody John Sears, during the 1980 presidential race. He fired Secretary of State Al Haig in 1982. He also rid himself of an Environmental Protection Agency administrator, a secretary of interior, a secretary of labor, and a veteran affairs director who had become embarrassments. Even his most cherished aides were not immune. Reagan quietly eased out Attorney General Ed Meese in 1988 for ethics charges that paled in comparison to the litany of complaints about Bush's second attorney general, Alberto Gonzales, who finally resigned under pressure on August 27, 2007. In dismissing officials who had become a burden, Reagan was usually less than forthright about the reasons for his actions. Along with Harry Truman and George W. Bush, Reagan believed that attacks on members of his administration were disguised attacks on him.* But he nonetheless discarded subordinates who were no longer of use to him, a practice that throughout his presidency served the purpose of bringing new blood into his inner circle. It is true that many of the resignations or dismissals were orchestrated by aides who had a greater sense of urgency than Reagan, or by Nancy Reagan, who was quicker to perceive and slower to excuse incompetence or corruption than her husband. In this respect, she was an incomparable asset. But although the lineups differ, successful presidents always have good teams, as Reagan did during most of his political career. When on occasion the team was poorly managed, as it was when Donald Regan

---

*"I have the feeling that I'm really the target they would like to get at, and they are doing it by going after these other people," Reagan told Lou Cannon in an interview for *The Washington Post* on February 25, 1988. Truman more colorfully said his critics had made "a fraudulent build-up of flyspecks on our Washington window into a big blot or mess" (Harry S. Truman, *Memoirs of Trial and Hope,* p. 498).

was White House chief of staff, Nancy Reagan often took the lead in changing managers.

By far the most important personnel change Reagan made as president was the replacement of Haig with George Shultz as secretary of state. Firing Haig was the equivalent of the Truman firing of Johnson or Bush's dismissal of Rumsfeld, but it was done much earlier in the game. Johnson lasted five years and Rumsfeld six, while Haig was gone less than a year and a half into the Reagan presidency. Haig had a distinguished record of public service, but he did not fit Reagan's carrot-and-stick approach to the Soviet Union. Shultz did. The arch-conservatives of the Reagan administration, from first to last, distrusted Shultz, whom they considered too willing to negotiate with Communists, but Shultz mirrored Reagan's impulses and was doing what Reagan wanted him to do. For all his talents, Shultz had a petulant streak, but he was so important to Reagan that the usual rules did not apply to him. In truth, Reagan coddled him. He was one member of the cast whom Reagan was determined not to replace, and he never did. In time, this reliance on Shultz paid substantial dividends, especially in the negotiations with Soviet leader Mikhail Gorbachev during the last years of the Reagan presidency. By this time Reagan had surrounded himself with a bevy of practical moderates in the Shultz mold: Howard Baker and after him Ken Duberstein as White House chiefs of staff, Colin Powell as national security adviser, and Jack Matlock as U.S. ambassador to the Soviet Union. Reagan never lost touch with the right wing of his administration—indeed, neoconservatives Ken Adelman and Richard Perle made useful contributions in the negotiations with the Soviets—but the dominant impulse of the Reagan endgame was practical and realistic.

George W. Bush was not similarly blessed with a diverse and sometimes quarrelsome circle of advisers. When members of his Texas-centric cast left the White House, as so many did in 2007, it was usually of their own volition. In the rare instance when dissenters, such as Colin Powell, made a case contrary to the general flow of administration opinion, Bush tended to hear them out respectfully—and then ignore them. The personnel style of the Bush White House might be characterized as: no hard feelings, no agonized choices, and not too much introspection.

"Good judgment in politics . . . depends on being a critical judge of yourself," wrote political scientist Michael Ignatieff in a reflection on the

Iraq War. "It was not merely that [Bush] did not take the care to understand Iraq. He also did not take the care to understand himself."[33] In Ignatieff's view, Bush was so convinced that his good intentions would yield
positive results that he did not listen sufficiently to those who questioned
his course of action in Iraq. "The sense of reality that might have saved
him from catastrophe would have taken the form of some warning bell
sounding inside, alerting him that he did not know what he was doing,"
Ignatieff wrote.[34] Unlike many of Bush's detractors, Ignatieff, who left a
Harvard professorship to become a member of Parliament in his native
Canada, is self-critical. He supported the war, and he also did not hear
any warning bells.

The question of why Bush didn't hear them is not easy to answer. Popular theories abound regarding Bush's habit of willfully ignoring unpleasant news; three, in particular, gained currency during his second term.
The first is that Bush is an intellectually incurious man who lacked
enough good information to make informed decisions. The second is that
Bush's mid-life embrace of Christianity provided a healthy dose of inner
peace, but an unhealthy dose of certitude. The third is that the premium
he put on loyalty discouraged dissent in his inner councils. There are holes
in all these explanations. For starters, in the penultimate year of his presidency, Bush embarked on a book-reading contest with Karl Rove—who
left the administration just before Labor Day 2007—and the two men
were on pace to read a hundred books apiece before year's end. These
books weren't pulp fiction. They were books about history, power, politics, and the presidency.* Second, if religious faith were a barrier to unpleasant news, Lincoln and FDR would have been lousy wartime
presidents. Finally, those who worked for Bush say flatly that he simply
never punished aides for bringing him contrary opinions. "I was never in-
timidated," Michael Gerson said in 2006.[35] Former press secretary Ari

---

*The president's eclectic reading list included baseball books, such as Leigh
Montville's biography of Babe Ruth and David Maraniss's examination of Roberto
Clemente—both written in 2006—as well as two recent Lincoln biographies, one about
Mao Tse-tung, and a couple of riveting medical narratives: *Polio: An American Story,* by
David M. Oshinsky, and *The Great Influenza: The Epic Story of the Deadliest Plague in
History,* by John M. Barry. The most surprising entry on the list? Perhaps *The Stranger* by
Albert Camus.

Fleischer echoed this view and related specific examples. On July 2, 2003, when Bush made his infamous "Bring 'em on" taunt, Fleischer told Bush on their way out of the Roosevelt Room that this remark would offend a military mom with a child serving in Iraq. Fleischer said there were no repercussions, and Bush never used that language again.[36]

Yet it is also a matter of record that Bush was continually surprised by the events of the world, even those of his own making. One constant claim of his critics was that faith trumped facts in Bush's world—especially when it came to Iraq. In other words, as Colin Powell suggested at the Aspen conference, Bush believed what he wanted to believe. Bush's penchant for giving voice to expressions of wishful thinking had been present in Texas—evident in his sanguine confidence in his capital punishment policies—and it became more pronounced in Washington as the war on terror and the war in Iraq took unpleasant turns. In 2004, Bush conveyed revulsion and shame in response to the revelations regarding the degrading treatment of prisoners at Abu Ghraib prison by U.S. forces, but he treated it as an isolated event. The following year, in response to a *Washington Post* exposé revealing the existence of secret U.S. military prisons around the world, where terrorism suspects are detained without benefit of counsel or under the protection of the international rules of warfare, Bush blithely told reporters traveling with him in Panama, "We do not torture." The next month, in a December 18, 2005, Oval Office address, Bush insisted, "We are winning the war in Iraq." In a September 6, 2006, East Room speech, he responded to questions about the treatment of presumed enemy combatants held in a U.S. military prison in Cuba by saying, "We have in place a rigorous process to ensure those held at Guantanamo Bay belong at Guantanamo." (It was soon evident even to military lawyers who had no partiality to the Guantanamo defendants that the process was in shambles. By the following June, the Supreme Court, in a rare reversal of its own decision, decided to hear an appeal from detainees claiming a right to challenge their detention in federal court. On July 20, 2007, in a body blow to the administration's case, a federal appeals court ordered the government to turn over virtually all of the information to the detainees. The opinion was written by the conservative Douglas H. Ginsburg, chief judge of the U.S. Court of Appeals for the District of Columbia circuit—the man Ronald Reagan had once attempted to appoint to the Supreme Court.)

In mid-2007, at a time when many Washington policy-makers were losing confidence in the ability of Prime Minister Nouri al-Maliki to lead Iraq anywhere other than into full-scale civil war, Bush expressed no doubts at all. Speaking at the VFW convention in the same speech in which he invoked Vietnam, Bush said, "Prime Minister Maliki is a good guy, a good man with a difficult job, and I support him." This comment was illustrative of Bush's habit of happily framing the question—in this case, the makeup of al-Maliki's character—as though it were the answer. To Bush, such upbeat expressions were all but required of a commander-in-chief, and he and his aides indicated that he believed he was following Reagan's example. Bush's growing chorus of critics found such blasé buoyancy in the face of the grim news from Iraq unsettling; it so exaggerated the famous Reagan optimism as to render it something unrecognizable. To paraphrase Stanford professor David Kennedy (who called the Bush doctrine of preemption "Wilsonianisn on steroids"), Bush's relentless rosiness in the face of bad news was optimism on steroids.

Peter W. Galbraith, author of a book critical of Bush's prosecution of the war, concluded that this sanguine attitude came to define the administration's entire foreign policy. "With regard to Iraq, President Bush and his top advisers have consistently substituted wishful thinking for analysis and hope for strategy."[37] Bob Woodward's *State of Denial* ends with the same point. "The strategy was denial," Woodward wrote. "With all Bush's upbeat talk and optimism, he had not told the American public the truth about what Iraq had become."

If it was never clear that Bush told himself the full truth about Iraq, he was hardly the first chief executive who demonstrated a reluctance to admit fault. This is an all-too-human trait, seemingly commonplace in politicians and especially pronounced among presidents. Yet, the manner in which Bush employed selective historical memory to justify his policies had a quality of willful stubbornness to it. Bush often pointed out privately (and occasionally publicly) that journalists and critics who demanded he "apologize" for invading Iraq were asking him to do something that no commander-in-chief with troops in the field had ever done—or should do. Think of the morale of the troops, Bush would say. He was right about that, but he would use the same argument—troop morale—to justify remaining in Iraq long after the fighting there had devolved into a depressing stalemate. "It is important for every American to understand the consequences of pulling out of Iraq before our work is done," he said in a December 18, 2005, Oval Office address to the nation. "We would abandon our Iraqi friends and signal to the world that America cannot be trusted to keep its word. We would undermine the morale of our troops by betraying the cause for which they have sacrificed."

If Bush realized how much this sounded like former presidents during the Vietnam War, he never let on. This was the real irony of Bush's mention of Vietnam in his September 13, 2007, speech on Iraq: He'd been invoking Vietnam unintentionally for years. Bush did not exactly say, as President Kennedy did in 1962, that he saw the "light at the end of the tunnel." But he came close. "The progress in the past year has been significant," Bush said in a 2005 speech at Fort Bragg, North Carolina, "and we have a clear path forward." In his 2003 State of the Union address, Bush said in the context of Iraq that Americans "exercise power without conquest, and we sacrifice for the liberty of strangers." This was an (unattributed) echo of Lyndon Johnson's assurances in February 1966 that "our purpose in Vietnam is to prevent the success of aggression. It is not conquest, it is not empire, it is not foreign bases, it is not domination." And so it went. Richard Nixon had promised Americans in his "Vietnamization" speech of November 3, 1969, that "as South Vietnamese forces become stronger, the rate of American withdrawal can become greater." This was strikingly similar both to Bush's September 13, 2007, reference to a "return on success" and to his June 28, 2005, vow, "Our strategy can be summed up this way: As the Iraqis stand up, we will stand down." Bush also sounded very much like Nixon on the subject of setting deadlines for bringing the troops home:

NIXON: "I have not and do not intend to announce the timetable for our program. And there are obvious reasons for this decision, which I am sure you will understand. . . . The enemy . . . would simply wait until our forces had withdrawn and then move in."

BUSH: "Setting an artificial timetable would send the wrong message to the Iraqis. . . . It would send the wrong message to our troops . . . and it would send the wrong message to the enemy, who would know that all they have to do is to wait us out."

That George W. Bush could echo the hollow promises of recent wartime presidents without knowing it wasn't a good sign. Worse still was the underlying inference that could be drawn from such rhetoric: that Bush and his speechwriters and war council didn't understand enough about recent American history to avoid repeating it. When Colin Powell came to Bush and urged him to go slow in Iraq, he wasn't merely speaking as a secretary of state representing the diplomatic corps of the U.S. foreign service officers—or even as a former junior officer who fought in Vietnam and who experienced the shortcomings of American foreign policy firsthand. Powell was also representing the accumulated wisdom of the U.S. armed forces and its civilian leadership during the past two generations. Ignoring Powell meant ignoring the hard-earned lessons learned from Korea through Lebanon.

Somewhere along the line, the "Powell Doctrine" began being portrayed in the mass media as a set of principles for going to war. These purportedly consisted of two main criteria: First, the United States should only go into battle with an overwhelming advantage in military force; and, second, policy-makers should have a clear "exit strategy" in mind before committing troops. Actually, neither of those requirements—however desirable—were part of Colin Powell's formulation. The Powell Doctrine was, as earlier noted, a recasting of the Weinberger Doctrine, spelled out clearly in Caspar Weinberger's National Press Club speech a year after the deadly bombing of the Marine Barracks in Lebanon. Both an exit strategy and a qualitative advantage in forces can be inferred from Weinberger's criteria in his November 23, 1984, speech. Moreover, if taken to heart, those aspects of Weinberger's doctrine might well have stopped an Iraq invasion before it began—and certainly would have required a rethinking of strategy and tactics two or three years before General Petraeus was given the green light to launch the surge.

Weinberger was a San Francisco native who attended Harvard for both his undergraduate studies and his law degree. He received an Army commission in World War II and served in the Pacific, where he became a captain on Gen. Douglas MacArthur's intelligence staff. Back home in California after the war, he worked his way through Republican politics; he was serving in the first Reagan administration in Sacramento when he was brought to Washington by Richard Nixon. In 1968, Nixon had campaigned on a pledge to end the Vietnam War—and involuntary conscription along with it. As president, Nixon neutralized opposition to his continuation of the war (as well as the impending advent of the eighteen-year-old vote) by pushing successfully to end the draft. The all-volunteer military would result, although before it did the Nixon administration wrestled with the impact such a move would have on military readiness. On August 21, 1970, Nixon defense secretary Melvin Laird sent a two-page memorandum to the Joint Chiefs envisioning a system in which National Guard and reserve units would "be prepared to be the initial and primary source for augmentation of the active forces in any future emergency requiring a rapid and substantial expansion of the active forces."[38]

This "astonishing directive," in the words of National Guard historian Bruce Jacobs, planted the seed for a system that would result in the troop deployment patterns in Iraq. It soon became known as the Total Force Policy, after being embraced and codified by Creighton W. Abrams, the last army chief of staff to serve under Nixon. Abrams was a West Point graduate and decorated World War II officer so respected as a tank commander that George Patton pronounced Abrams his equal.[39] In Vietnam, however, Abrams was tasked with overseeing the gradual withdrawal of half a million men from a theater in which America had not prevailed in either its political or its military objectives. Partly necessitated by an end of the draft and the military budget cuts of the 1970s, the Total Force doctrine was embraced by Abrams because he saw it as a way of protecting his beloved U.S. Army from future Vietnams. "Its deeper logic," wrote historian David M. Kennedy, "was to structure the armed force in such a way that they could not easily be deployed in the absence of strong and sustainable public support—something that had gone fatally missing in Vietnam."[40]

The idea here was that the reserves and guard units were typically composed of men (and now women) with deeper roots and more established ties in their communities than conventional soldiers, and that civilian leaders would therefore be more hesitant to deploy them to some faraway theater of war than they would be to dispatch rootless nineteen-year-olds with no sense of their own mortality. Conversely, a popular deployment of such older civilian-soldiers implied a network of community support for the endeavor. At the time these plans were adopted, Weinberger was serving in the Nixon administration, and Governor Reagan was in Sacramento, beginning to attract the favorable attention of the military community as far away as Hanoi, which is where John McCain was imprisoned. George W. Bush and Dan Quayle were serving in the National Guard under the pre–Total Force regulations, which all but insulated them from combat.

This, then, was the context of Weinberger's momentous 1984 speech when, as defense secretary, he oversaw an all-volunteer force. "Once it is clear our troops are required, because our vital interests are at stake, then we must have the firm national resolve to commit every ounce of strength necessary to win the fight to achieve our objectives," he said that day. "In Grenada we did just that. Just as clearly, there are other situations where United States combat forces should not be used. I believe the postwar period has taught us several lessons, and from them I have developed six major tests to be applied when we are weighing the use of U.S. combat forces abroad." Weinberger said the United States should commit forces only in situations vital to the national interest, fight to win, have clearly defined political and military objectives, reassess the role and composition of the combat forces and readjust accordingly, have in advance a "reasonable assurance" of public support, and commit troops only as a last resort. (This "Weinberger Doctrine," as it became known, was cited in an abridged form in Chapter 6.) Colin Powell believed that the sum of Weinberger's tests was overly restrictive, but he, too, believed that the United States should err on the side of caution in its military commitments—which is why he tried without success to dissuade Bush from going to war in Iraq. As a military man, Powell worried about the corrosive effect of unpopular commitments on the armed forces, particularly on an Army that was stretched too thin. Writing in *Foreign Affairs* eight years after Weinberger's speech, Powell issued a simultaneous call for leadership and prudence. "The 'last best hope on Earth,'" Powell said, using Lincoln's words to describe America, "has no other choice. We must lead." But he added, "We cannot lead without our armed forces."[41]

Powell was at that time the chairman of the Joint Chiefs of Staff under George H. W. Bush, a position he would retain for seven months under President Clinton. Powell made it clear that as he considered how and when the United States should commit military forces, Lebanon was still very much on his mind. He had another, grander frame of reference than

Weinberger did when he invoked Grenada in 1984: He had the example of the Persian Gulf War. "When the political objective is important, clearly defined, and understood, when the risks are acceptable, and when the use of force can be effectively combined with diplomatic and economic priorities, then clear and unambiguous objectives must be given to the armed forces," Powell wrote. "These objectives must be firmly linked with the political objectives."[42] Expelling Iraqi forces from Kuwait in 1991 met these standards, Powell stated; injecting the Marines into Lebanon in 1983 did not.

Powell did not have a problem with "limited" war. ("All wars are limited," he wrote, noting that mankind has yet to annihilate itself.) He added that he believed "peacekeeping and humanitarian operations are a given." The dilemma, then, is figuring out what is attainable—and worth the cost. "The Gulf War was a limited-objective war," maintained Powell. "If it had not been, we would be ruling Baghdad today—at unpardonable expenses in terms of money, lives lost and ruined regional relationships."[43]

Unlike Dick Cheney, Powell never really deviated from this view after 9/11. While working for President George H. W. Bush's son, Powell did, however, defer to the commander-in-chief, telling George W. Bush that if he persisted in going into Iraq, he—Powell—would stand by his side. The attacks of September 11, 2001, altered many judgments. Weinberger himself argued strongly in favor of the Iraq invasion, citing all of the reasons Bush did. In testimony to the Senate Foreign Relations Committee on July 31 and August 1, 2002, Weinberger also downplayed the notion that invading Iraq could destabilize that country. "People say there will be chaos," he said in his written testimony. "I disagree, but I must confess frankly that even chaos would be better than Saddam." During an exchange with the senators on the committee, Weinberger added: "I think you're dealing with a very unpredictable person who has no civilized restraints and that argues even more strongly for getting rid of him as quickly as possible. Frankly, I wished we'd done it at the end of the Gulf War."

This was an understandable impulse; and although he never said so directly, Cheney shared Weinberger's sentiment. Moreover, both the president and the vice president also seem to have shared Weinberger's view that "chaos" was preferable to Saddam. In this they had plenty of company, although they wound up with more chaos than they bargained for. The nation would have been better served if George W. Bush had been able to step back from the moment and reflect not on Weinberger's testimony in 2002 but the earlier wisdom of the Powell and Weinberger doctrines. The battle plan that George W. Bush approved for Iraq did not come close to meeting these useful criteria, especially the one about having clearly defined political and military objectives. And once the war started, Bush certainly did not follow the Weinberger precept stipulating that civilian and military leaders should continually reassess their policies based on conditions on the battle-field. That particular failure, in turn, led to an abrogation of another Wein-berger rule: that the administration should maintain public and congressional support for the mission. George W. Bush didn't need the Weinberger rules to tell him that—or he shouldn't have. In allowing the war in Iraq to drag on for most of his presidency, Bush was violating his own first principles, enunciated repeatedly in the 2000 campaign—namely, that the most effective military interventions are of short duration and that the American people have little appetite for long wars. As the 2008 presidential campaign gathered steam, even the leading Democratic candidates acknowledged that the next president would face the realities of a continuing U.S. military deployment in Iraq.

New presidents can be ambushed by such foreign policy entanglements whether or not they are prepared for them. In 2000, the Center for the Study of the Presidency produced a study called "In Harm's Way" and presented it to the Bush transition team. The paper examined what made for successful—and unsuccessful—foreign military interventions. The center is headed by David M. Abshire, a Tennessee native and West Point graduate who served in the Korean War as an Army platoon leader, company commander, and division intelligence officer. He was awarded a Bronze Star for valor in Korea, went on to earn his doctorate (in history) at Georgetown University, and served in both the Nixon and Reagan administrations. Under Reagan he was ambassador to NATO (1983–1987) until tapped directly by Reagan to serve as a cabinet-level special counsel looking into Iran-contra. He later wrote a book about the experience, *Saving the Reagan Presidency: Trust Is the Coin of the Realm.* After the contentious 2000 recount between Bush and Al Gore, and during the truncated Bush transition, Abshire personally made sure that Condoleezza Rice saw the work on military interventions done by his center. He later recalled with dismay her good-natured, yet dismissive response: "Well, David, if your fellow Tennessean had won, this would be important because there would have been a lot of nation-building going on. We're not going to be involved in any of that."[44] As the Iraq War passed the four-and-a-half-year mark with no end in sight, Abshire ruefully expressed hope that the next administration would be more prescient—and more prepared.

Along with heeding the warnings of the Center for the Study of the Presidency and brushing up on the Weinberger-Powell guidelines, George W. Bush might also profitably have consulted the League of Nations report of July 16, 1925, which warned of the tenuous nature of the new country that the British had created from remnants of the Ottoman Empire. The report predicted that "serious difficulties" would arise from differences among the Sunni, Shia, and Kurds, and—doing something George W. Bush and his advisers never did—questioned whether Iraq was a viable country.[45]

As the clamor against the war increased, it was often said by Bush's growing legion of opponents that he had misled the country about the nature of the conflict. If so, it was because he had misled himself. Self-delusion can be particularly damaging, and Bush's unwillingness to recognize that Iraq was falling apart on his watch had deleterious consequences for the military he commanded, the nation he was elected to lead, and his own legacy. What the rest of his legacy will ultimately be, as Bush has said, is a mystery that will be unraveled only in the fullness of time. ("I'm reading about George Washington still," Bush said at an end-of-the-year press conference on December 20, 2006. "My attitude is, if they're still analyzing No. 1, Forty-Three ought not to worry about it.") This point is not necessarily wrong, and it can be made about Ronald Reagan, too. In our time, however, a direct comparison of the aftermath of the Bush and Reagan presidencies does not flatter "Forty-Three."

In Ronald Reagan's last year in office, his job approval rating fluctuated in the low to mid-fifties, ticking up to 63 percent in a Gallup Poll (with only 29 percent disapproval) the month after the public had chosen Reagan's vice president as his successor. Americans, it seemed, missed Reagan even before he was gone. Why wouldn't they? When President Reagan returned home to California, the U.S. unemployment rate was at a fourteen-year low, inflation barely above 4 percent. True, the national debt had tripled to $2.8 trillion, making it more difficult for George H. W. Bush to imbue his "kindler, gentler" pledge with much in the way of increased federal spending, but George H. W. Bush was bequeathed something of value by Reagan: The military buildup that had helped run up that deficit had left the Soviet Union on the verge of collapse. Reagan seemed aware of this and confident in the man left in charge to deal with it. When a friend remarked to Reagan after the campaign that it would be sad to see him leave the White House, Reagan replied that he was leaving the presidency "in good hands."[46]

Reagan left a nation at peace, and one more confident of its place in the world than it had been when he began his first term, as even his political adversaries conceded. Democratic presidential nominee Michael Dukakis, speaking before he was bested by Bush 41, gave credit to the man he was trying to replace. "Thanks to President Reagan and General Secretary Gorbachev, we may have the best opportunity in our lifetime to build a safer world," Dukakis had said.[47] Commenting in the magazine of the Council on Foreign Affairs, historian Paul Johnson predicted that the decade of the 1980s would come to be called simply, "The Reagan Years."[48]

This lesson was not lost on future presidential candidates—of either party. After defeating George H. W. Bush in 1992, the first trip made by President-elect Bill Clinton was to Southern California, where he paid his respects to Reagan.* This was only the beginning of Clinton's efforts to embrace a man already fading into mythic status. In 1994, as Clinton prepared to go to Normandy for the fiftieth anniversary of the Normandy invasion, Clinton aides borrowed from the Reagan Library tapes of Reagan's D-Day performance at the fortieth anniversary. They continued this practice of borrowing footage of Reagan speeches, and in 1996 Clinton's political advisers admitted to emulating Reagan's successful 1984 "Morning Again in America" reelection campaign.[49] Some Reaganites were flattered, others annoyed. Aides to doomed Republican presidential nominee Bob Dole could only throw up their hands. "I guess when we see (Clinton) take out an axe and start clearing the brush behind the White

---

*Demonstrating a habit that would typify the next eight years, Clinton was fifteen minutes late for the meeting. Reagan presented the president-elect with a jar of jelly beans and some unsolicited advice: Escape when you can to Camp David for the solitude. This suggestion underscored the difference between the older and younger man: The gregarious Clinton wasn't much interested in seclusion.

House, we'll see that the transformation is complete," groused one Dole adviser.[50]* Dole was so flustered trying to escape the dual shadows cast by Reagan and Clinton that as he commenced his presidential run, he told the Republican National Committee, in desperation, "Well, I'm willing to be another Ronald Reagan, if that's what you want. I'll be another Ronald Reagan."[51]

Notwithstanding the Clinton victories of 1992 and 1996, Reagan had changed the political calculus of the Republican Party. Under the banner of Newt Gingrich's "Contract with America" (largely a collection of old Reagan ideas), Republicans took control of the House in 1994 and set their sights on a political realignment that would make their party a lasting majority. The GOP had been pursuing this fantasy up hill and down dale for more than three decades, beginning in 1968 when the remnants of the New Deal coalition fell apart under the dual pressures of urban riots and the Vietnam War. In an election in which George C. Wallace ran as an independent and carried five southern states, Richard Nixon was elected president. But realignment was scuttled by Nixon, who, in Michael Barone's words, "squandered the chance to campaign for the ideas and policies he professed privately" and in 1972 waged a negative reelection campaign that "enraged" his opponents.[52] Nixon won an empty landslide in which the Republicans lost ground in the Senate. Watergate soon swept him into the dustbin of history.

Reagan's decisive victory in 1980 and his landslide reelection in 1984 gave Republicans another chance. As he always did throughout his life, no matter which party he belonged to, Reagan campaigned for the entire ticket. He was pleasantly surprised (along with GOP strategists) in 1980 when Republicans won twelve Senate seats and took control of the Senate for the first time since 1952. Reagan also improved the GOP's prospects at the grassroots. In 1980, Reagan's coattails resulted in a net gain of 300 Republican seats in state legislatures around the country, a feat repeated in 1984. Bush 41 nearly held these gains in 1988. Moreover, a CBS/*New York Times* poll found that in eight years of Reagan rule, from 1980 to 1988,

---

*"Actually," quipped Clinton White House political director Rahm Emanuel, "that's what we've got him doing for Father's Day."

Republican identification grew from 33 percent to 42 percent, while the percentage of self-identified Democrats fell from 54 percent to 48 percent.[53] These were the trends that enabled Republicans to capture both houses of Congress in 1994 and hold them until 2006, when the trifecta of Iraq, congressional corruption, and Bush's unpopularity cost them their ruling majority in Congress. Once more, political realignment had become a will-o'-the-wisp.

Political commentators have assigned responsibility for the Republican downturn in varying degrees to President Bush and to lax congressional leaders who failed to deliver on promised reforms and who proved even more ethically challenged than the Democrats they had replaced. It can also be argued, however, that Reagan's success contained within it the germ of the GOP downfall. Truth may be the glue that holds government together, as Gerald Ford said in his inaugural speech, but anti-communism was the glue that bound the disparate elements of the Republican Party together throughout the Cold War. To the degree that Reagan's policies brought about the demise of the Soviet Union, which passed into history on Christmas Day 1991, he also removed the essential element of Republican unity. After September 11, 2001, George W. Bush attempted to substitute for anti-Soviet unity the unity of the "war on terrorism." It worked for a while, and it might have worked longer if Bush had not attacked a country that was peripheral to that "war."

As the Bush presidency drew to a close, Republicans faced the prospect of the 2008 elections at a distinct disadvantage. By mid-2007, only 28 percent of Americans expressed a "positive" view of the Republican Party, compared to 42 percent for the Democrats—with the GOP trailing Democrats on the generic ballot badly in both presidential and congressional ballots.[54] By autumn of 2007, some eighteen Republican incumbent members of Congress—four of them senators—had decided not to run for reelection, with more defections expected. The GOP presidential candidates were able to generate far less in the way of campaign contributions than their Democratic counterparts. In public opinion polls, Democrats kept pronouncing themselves pleased with their field of 2008 presidential candidates, while Republican voters revealed angst and dissatisfaction with their own slate of contenders. Partly, this was because the Republican candidates running for office were caught between having to defend Bush's war, so as to not alienate the conservative base voters who show up in primary elections—and who regard Bush as a good president—and their inner desire to forget all about Bush and strut their own credentials, such as they were, as the true heir to Ronald Reagan.

"It took thirty years to build the Reagan coalition," political scientist John Kenneth White wrote on the eve of the 2006 mid-term elections. "It has taken George W. Bush just two years to destroy it."[55] According to White, a professor at Catholic University in Washington, D.C., even the attainment of a president's stated policy goals ultimately undermines political coalitions. Thus, he believes that the Roosevelt coalition that was eventually replaced by the Reagan coalition was a victim of the New Deal's economic *successes* as much as the Democratic Party's cultural *excesses*. This comports with our view that Reagan's success in dealing with the Soviet Union undermined the Republican raison d'être. But outright failure is even more harmful than success. Failure kills coalitions immediately rather than gradually, and Bush has been widely perceived as a failure in the second half of his second term. "George W. Bush sought to revive the Reagan coalition," White wrote. "But this year the public has reached the following conclusions: Iraq is a disaster; change is required; Bush and the Republican Congress are unable to effect change."[56]

If this was a near-consensus among academics, many conservatives came to the same conclusion as Bush's presidency entered its final phase. These anti-Bush conversions often had both a wrenching personal aspect and a whiff of betrayal about them. Matthew Dowd, an Austin Democrat before converting to Republican and supporting George W. Bush, took a swipe at Bush in the same March 2007 issue of *Texas Monthly* devoted to Bush's legacy in which Robert Caro, Robert Dallek, and Douglas Brinkley all criticized the president. But Dowd was a key member of Bush's inner circle on the 2000 and 2004 campaigns. In *Texas Monthly,* Dowd lamented that Bush had "missed some real opportunities" after 9/11 to bring the country together by calling for "some shared sacrifice."[57] A month later, Dowd, whose only son was soon to be deployed to Iraq as an army intelligence specialist, sought out reporter Jim Rutenberg of *The New York Times* to make his break from Bush complete. In the *Times* article, Dowd criticized the president directly, saying that on the war in Iraq, he now agreed with John Kerry, the candidate he had helped (with numerous assists from Kerry himself) to undermine.[58]

That same weekend, Republican speechwriter Vic Gold, a friend and former office-mate of Lynne Cheney's who coauthored George H. W. Bush's autobiography, sat for an interview with *The Washington Post* while hawking a much different kind of book, a bitter screed called *Invasion of the Party Snatchers: How the Holy-Rollers and the Neo-Cons Destroyed the GOP.* Seven years earlier, Gold had written glowing bios of the Bushes and Cheneys for the official inauguration program. Of Cheney, Gold had written for the 2001 program: "A man of gravitas with a quick and easy wit; a conservative who'll see a road less traveled; a political realist who sees his country and the world around him not in terms of leaden problems but golden opportunities."[59] In his 2007 book, Gold's view changes to this: "A vice president in control is bad enough. Worse yet is a vice president out of control."[60]

Meanwhile, the April 2 issue of *National Review* published a caricature on its cover of Bush as Casey Stengel, complete with a New York Mets uniform with the famous Stengel lament: "Can't Anyone Here Play This Game?" These words appeared in huge type over a cover story by *NR* editor Richard Lowry entitled, "The Roots of Bush's Competence Problem." Two weeks earlier, *Time* magazine put a picture of Reagan on its cover with a digitally created tear running down his cheek. The headline said: "What Would Ronnie Do? And Why the Republican Candidates Need to Reclaim the Reagan Legacy."

The 2008 GOP presidential candidates would like nothing better than to recapture the Reagan magic. They have been doing their best, swimming upstream against the numerous polls that suggest that the 2008 Republican presidential nomination is a passport to political oblivion. "We must return to the commonsense Reagan Republican ideals," Mitt Romney said in a campaign statement.[61] Stumping in Florida in August 2007, Romney was asked to rate himself on a scale of conservatism from one to ten—if Reagan were a ten. "Probably a 10 as well," he replied. "I'm trying to think in what places we would differ. As I've gotten older, Reagan keeps getting smarter and smarter."[62]

"I am a conservative Republican and remain so in the school of Ronald Reagan," John McCain assured a national television audience.[63] "I took the exact same path Ronald Reagan took," Arkansas Governor Mike

Huckabee said on the *Today* show in August 2007, while explaining his pro-life credentials. An Illinois congressman introduced Rudy Giuliani, the former New York mayor, as "the Ronald Reagan of the 2008 election."[64] Fans of former Tennessee Senator Fred Thompson insisted with a straight face that their man was the most Reaganesque of the lot. Presumably, this was because of Thompson's acting background, as though being a character actor in a television series was equivalent to being a leading man on the big screen—and as if either one qualifies someone to be president. Another Republican candidate named Thompson, also-ran Tommy Thompson, a former Wisconsin governor and member of George W. Bush's cabinet, made sure to quote Reagan the day he quit the race.[65]

As this all began to sound a bit desperate for the Republicans, a handful of conservative writers, including David Frum, who once wrote speeches for Bush, and George F. Will, who once helped Reagan's campaign team prepare for his debate with Jimmy Carter, began to say "enough already." Will lamented that the Republican activists of the 2008 cycle were attempting, in the name of Reaganism, to hold the GOP presidential candidates to a standard of conservative purity that Reagan never would have passed.[66] Frum went further, saying flatly that new times require new solutions and that, in any event, the things Reagan cared most about, including a less invasive tax code, a lower crime rate, and an end to Soviet-style communism, are now facts of life. Republicans who simply pine for another Reagan, he said, are no more persuasive than Tip O'Neill was in the 1980s, when he was berating middle-class voters to show unqualified gratitude to the New Deal. "The Democrats lost election after election looking first for the next Franklin Roosevelt, then for the next John F. Kennedy," Frum wrote. "Republicans in these frustrating days feel the tug of Reagan nostalgia. We feel: If only we had another Reagan! . . . And so we demand from our candidates ever-more fervent declarations of fealty to an ideology that interests an ever-dwindling proportion of the public. It gives me no pleasure to say this, but these hopes are delusions. In every way we can measure, the voting public is moving away from the kind of conservatism we know as Reaganism."[67]

As for the legacy of George W. Bush, his most eloquent advocate remains Mike Gerson. In *Heroic Conservatism,* which Gerson wrote after leaving the White House, Bush's former senior speechwriter draws a straight line between Reagan's anti-communism and Bush's determination to confront radical Islam, and he does so on the thread of human rights. Gerson certainly doesn't believe Reaganism has lost its potency. It will remain a dynamic political force, he maintains, as long as there are places in the world where human rights are a distant dream. "President Ronald Reagan repudiated a tired policy of détente, and determined to seek victory, not a stalemate in the Cold War," Gerson wrote. "And he symbolized this shift by calling the Soviet Union an 'evil empire.'"[68]

Natan Sharansky, in a book read by Bush, related what occurred next among the invisibles hidden in the gulag. "Tapping on walls and talking through toilets, word of Reagan's 'provocation' quickly spread through the prison," Sharansky wrote. "The dissidents were ecstatic. Finally, the leader of the free world had spoken the truth—a truth that burned inside the heart of each and every one of us."[69]

In this telling of the story, George W. Bush, with his insistence that "freedom is not America's gift to the world. . . . [It] is the almighty God's gift to each man and woman in this world,"[70] is very much Ronald Reagan's disciple. He is also Harry Truman's disciple (and Franklin Roosevelt's and John F. Kennedy's). Gerson's implication is that Bush's foresight and heroism have not been recognized for the same reason that Truman's wasn't for a very long time—because the United States is not yet winning on this new front in the age-old war against tyranny. When the argument is framed this way, the prospect of Bush's future rehabilitation is linked to the eventual success of U.S. foreign policy in a dangerous world. If one depends upon the other, it is hard to root against Bush, and the authors—despite persistent misgivings about the wisdom of the Iraq War—are not doing so.

We do believe, however, that George W. Bush's legacy will have to stand on its own feet, without the historical helping hand of Roosevelt or Truman or Kennedy—or even Ronald Reagan. "Men make history and not the other way around," wrote Harry Truman,[71] who made much history, for better and for worse. Bush was Reagan's disciple, to be sure, but he did not face the seminal crises of his administration—especially the Iraq War—with the blend of principle and pragmatism that was the hallmark of Reagan's dealings with the Soviet Union. We do not fault Bush's intentions, but noble intentions do not excuse his performance in Iraq or the domestic failures of his second term. Nor do they explain his refusal to learn from his mistakes.

On the last day of his presidency, as he inspected the white laminated card that carried the launching codes for U.S. nuclear missiles, Ronald Reagan turned to his national security adviser, Colin Powell, for a final report on world crises. "The world is quiet today," Powell told Reagan.[72]

It is doubtful that George W. Bush's national security adviser will be able to say the same.

Acknowledgments

This book was conceived in March 2006 at Stanford University, when, as media fellows at the Hoover Institution on War, Revolution and Peace, we gave a joint presentation on the presidencies of Ronald Reagan and George W. Bush. The audience response was positive, and we decided to expand the idea into a book. We were encouraged to do so and helped in various ways by David Brady, director of the media fellows program, and by his assistant Mandy MacCalla, to whom we are indebted. Our friends, economists Annelise Anderson and Martin Anderson, who held important posts during the Reagan administration and are now Reagan scholars, were consistently helpful. So were others at Hoover, especially George P. Shultz, a towering figure in the Reagan administration, and John Cogan, Morris Fiorina, and Peter Robinson. John Raisian, director of the Hoover Institution, made it possible for us to return to Stanford in June 2007 and work together on the concluding chapters of this book. We thank them all.

Mary Cannon, the researcher on three of Lou Cannon's earlier books, carefully read the manuscript of this book several times. We thank her for many corrections and patient counsel.

Jack F. Matlock Jr., the author of a definitive book on the collapse of the Soviet Union and a valuable book on Reagan and Mikhail Gorbachev, made constructive suggestions that improved Chapter 2. John Milton Cooper Jr., a distinguished biographer of Woodrow Wilson, contributed a helpful interview that enlightened Chapter 4.

Delia M. Rios, a C-SPAN history producer, edited Carl's chapters with her customary insight and eye for detail. Special thanks also to Alexander I. Burns, editor of the *Harvard Political Review* and fact-checker extraordinaire. This project is also obligated to Steve Gettinger and Charlie Green, Carl's editors at *National Journal,* for their forbearance while this book was being written, and to *NJ* chief executive John Fox Sullivan and owner David Bradley for, among other things, allowing Carl to spend three months in 2007 at the John F. Kennedy School of Government as a resident fellow at the Institute of Politics. Among those who helped facilitate Carl's work on this book during the semester he spent at Harvard are Eric Andersen, fellows coordinator for Institute of Politics; then-director of the I.O.P. Jeanne Shaheen; Senator Edward M. Kennedy; and Carl's "fellow fellow" Ned Lamont. Faculty members at the Kennedy School and the rest of the Harvard community were generous with interviews and insights; foremost among them were David Gergen, Roger Porter, Lawrence H. Summers, and Joseph S. Nye Jr.

We are beholden to many other scholars for their writings, comments, or advice—sometimes it was all three. The historians and political scientists we wish to thank include David M. Abshire, Douglas Brinkley, George Colburn, George C. Edwards III, Alvin Felzenburg, Morris Fiorina, Fred I. Greenstein, David M. Kennedy, Martha Joynt Kumar, Frederick Logevall, the late Richard E. Neustadt, James P. Pfiffner, Richard Norton Smith, Timothy Walch, Shirley Anne Warshaw, John Kenneth White, Sean Wilentz, and Andrew J. Bacevich. A word about Andy Bacevich: A West Point graduate, Vietnam veteran, and history professor at Boston University, he expressed deep misgivings to the authors—and to anyone else who would listen—about the war in Iraq, and antipathy for the civilian and military leaders who brought it about. On May 13, 2007, his most personal fears were realized when his son and namesake, Andrew J. Bacevich Jr., a first lieutenant in the United States Army, was killed in Iraq. This loss was a sober reminder to the authors of the stakes involved when presidents commit American troops to battle.

Several important figures in the Reagan administration shared their insights with the authors. Particularly helpful, in addition to Shultz and the Andersons, were former attorney general Edwin Meese III, who served Reagan in many capacities; James A. Baker III, who was Reagan's chief of staff and treasury secretary and later secretary of state under

President George H. W. Bush; Kenneth Adelman, who under Reagan headed the Arms Control and Disarmament Agency and has been an important commentator on the Iraq War; and Kenneth Duberstein, who has helped many presidents and was Reagan's final chief of staff. The late Michael Deaver, the closest of Reagan aides, was helpful on several occasions, as was Stuart K. Spencer, the longtime political consultant. So was Landon Parvin, who served Ronald and Nancy Reagan as a speechwriter, and has become a friend.

We appreciate the insights of Colin L. Powell, acknowledging that he raised questions about the sagacity of comparing George W. Bush to Ronald Reagan in the first place—and hoping that he finds some usefulness in this book. John W. Vessey, chief of the Joint Chiefs of Staff under President Reagan, contributed a useful interview, as did several advisers to America's forty-third president, including Mark McKinnon, Peter H. Wehner, Michael J. Gerson, Scott McClellan, and Karl Rove. Other current or former White House aides who generously answered the authors' queries are John McConnell, David Frum, Dana Perino, Noelia Rodriguez, and Ari Fleischer.

David Russell, an oral historian at the University of California at Santa Barbara, tracked down quotations that eluded both of us and helped in various other ways. He also enlisted the repeated assistance of the staff of the Davidson Library at UCSB, and we appreciate his assistance very much. The archivist and researchers at the Harry S. Truman Presidential Library and the Miller Center of Public Affairs at the University of Virginia were always willing to look up a presidential record or help locate an elusive fact. The same is true of Princeton University archivist Dan Linke.

The Ronald Reagan Presidential Library in Simi Valley, California, was most accommodating, as it has been on other books. Jenny Mandel and Steve Branch deserve special thanks. We also want to thank Gregory Cumming, a National Archives researcher at the Nixon Library, for his assistance.

Various fellow journalists and writers also helped, among them Michael Barone, William Beaman, Adam Clymer, James Gibney, Ken Herman, Ronald Kessler, Michael Kranish, Stryker McGuire, John Micklethwait, Jay Nordlinger, Kathleen Parker, Peter Schweizer, Craig Shirley, Alexis Simendinger, and George Wilson.

Chapter 7 benefited from the sage counsel of James Kitfield, a defense writer and war correspondent who was with the U.S. Army as it raced into Baghdad.

In writing about the judiciary in Chapter 9, we received valuable assistance from Terry Eastland, who held an important post in the Reagan Justice Department; from the eminent attorney Theodore Olson; and, again, from Ed Meese. Joan Biskupic, the Supreme Court correspondent for *USA Today* and author of a biography of Sandra Day O'Connor, shared her files and insights. David A. Yalof, a University of Connecticut scholar, shared his useful study of George W. Bush's judicial legacy. Harland Braun, a noted Los Angeles criminal attorney, read this chapter (and others) and made useful suggestions.

Amanda Searles was always helpful when Lou Cannon's computer faltered. Al Hyam helped obtain needed books.

Kristine Dahl of ICM, our nonpareil agent, was supportive, as she has been to the Cannon family for twenty-seven years. We have many people to thank at PublicAffairs, beginning with our able and resourceful editor Robert Kimzey. We also thank project editor Meredith Smith; patient and keen-eyed copyeditor Katherine H. Streckfus; publicists Gene Taft and Whitney Peeling; and page designer Jeff Williams.

It goes without saying, but we will say it anyway: While the efforts of many people made this book possible, any errors or misperceptions are the fault of the authors.

LOU AND CARL CANNON

October 10, 2007

Notes

Reagan's Disciple: George W. Bush's Troubled Quest for a Presidential Legacy is based upon manifold source material, including the reporting we have done over the years, by Lou Cannon for *The Washington Post* and the *San Jose Mercury-News* and by Carl Cannon for *National Journal, The Atlantic,* and *The Baltimore Sun.* The book also draws on earlier books by the authors, especially *President Reagan: The Role of a Lifetime,* by Lou Cannon.

We have identified sources whenever possible. On those occasions where a source has insisted on confidentiality, we have followed our usual journalistic practice of holding anonymous information to a higher standard of verification.

Quotations from Ronald Reagan, George W. Bush, and other presidents during their presidencies, unless otherwise specified, are from *The Public Papers of the Presidents of the United States* (abbreviated PPP), which are available from the U.S. Government Printing Office or various websites. In our notes, Carl M. Cannon has been abbreviated as CMC and Lou Cannon as LC.

PREFACE

1. Tony Harnden, "Two Men, One Ambition. How Will They Put Their Stamp on the White House?" *The Daily Telegraph* (London), November 7, 2000.

2. "Jack Kemp Tribute Dinner to the Reagan Revolution and Supply Side Economics," Federal News Service transcript, December 1, 1988.

3. Jeffrey Hart, "Conservative Crackup; He's a Right-Wing Ideologue, Not a True Conservative," *Los Angeles Times,* March 12, 2006.

CHAPTER 1: THREE GENERATIONS

1. Robin Abcarian, "The Race to the White House; the Candidates Strive to Overcome Privilege," *Los Angeles Times,* June 20, 2004.

2. Lou Cannon, "Actor, Governor, President, Icon," *The Washington Post,* June 6, 2004.

3. Nicholas Lemann, "Remember the Alamo," *The New Yorker,* October 18, 2004.

4. Peter Schweizer and Rochelle Schweizer, *The Bushes: Portrait of a Dynasty,* p. 52.

5. Doro Bush Koch, *My Father, My President: A Personal Account of the Life of George H. W. Bush,* pp. 5–6.

6. Michael Duffy and Nancy Gibbs, "The Quiet Dynasty," *Time*, July 31, 2000.

7. Interview with Albert Hunt by CMC, June 2006.

8. Barbara Bush, *Barbara Bush: A Memoir,* pp. 39–49.

9. Ibid.

10. Conversation with George W. Bush by CMC at White House Correspondents' Association dinner, May 1, 2004.

11. Peter Dreier, "Presidential Legacy," *American Prospect* (online version), January 27, 2003.

12. Jane Mayer and Alexandra Robbins, "Dept. of Aptitude: How George W. Made the Grade," *The New Yorker,* November 8, 1999.

13. John Wark, "The Spring That Lurks in the Fall," *Tampa Tribune,* November 21, 1998.

14. Schweizer and Schweizer, *The Bushes,* p. 257.

15. David S. Broder, "Texas Runoff Strains GOP Relations; Some Sour Feelings in the Bush Camp over Reagan's Role," *The Washington Post,* June 3, 1978.

16. Bill Minutaglio, *First Son: George W. Bush and the Bush Family Dynasty,* p. 189.

17. Ibid., p. 188.

18. Michael Kranish, "An American Dynasty," *Boston Globe,* April 23, 2001.

19. Ibid.

20. Ibid.

21. Robert Draper, *Dead Certain: The Presidency of George W. Bush,* p. 110.

22. Kranish, "An American Dynasty."

23. George H. W. Bush, with Victor Gold, *Looking Forward,* p. 30.

24. Bob Woodward, "To Bones Men, Bush Is a Solid Moderate," *The Washington Post,* August 7, 1988.

25. Hanna Rosin, "The Seeds of a Philosophy," *The Washington Post,* July 23, 2000.

26. Carl M. Cannon, "Family Tree, Party Roots," *National Journal,* July 21, 2001.

27. Minutaglio, *First Son,* p. 135.

28. David Maraniss, "The Bush Bunch," *The Washington Post Magazine,* January 22, 1989.

29. Schweizer and Schweizer, *The Bushes,* p. 259.

30. Interview with Molly Ivins by CMC, January 2004.

31. "So Now You Know: George Bush," *The Economist,* October 9, 2004.

32. Minutaglio, *First Son,* p. 191.

33. Walter Isaacson, "My Heritage Is Part of Who I Am," *Time,* August 7, 2000.

34. Minutaglio, *First Son,* pp. 196–197.

35. Lana Cunningham, "Bush Cites Reagan Stamina, Class," *Midland-Reporter Telegram,* February 15, 1981.

36. Interview with Gerald R. Ford by CMC, August 20, 2004.

CHAPTER TWO: WHAT REAGAN WROUGHT

1. James MacGregor Burns, "Risks of the Middle," *The Washington Post,* October 24, 1999.

2. Howell Raines, "The 'Dumb' Factor," *The Washington Post,* August 27, 2004.

3. David A. Andelman, "Life after the Times," *Forbes* (online edition), May 17, 2006.

4. Fox News/Opinion Dynamics poll of 900 adults, conducted May 15–16, 2007, with a plus-minus error rate of 3 percent. Reagan was the preference among Republicans and independents, Kennedy among Democrats.

5. Dick Wirthlin, with Wynton C. Hall, *The Greatest Communicator: What Ronald Reagan Taught Me about Politics, Leadership and Life,* p. 12.

6. Harold L. Ickes, *The Harold Ickes Diaries, 1933–1951*, pp. 9394–9395, manuscript at Library of Congress, Washington D.C. Ickes, in a diary entry of December 16, 1944, wrote that Senator Owen Brewster of Maine was his guest at lunch after recently seeing Truman. According to the diary, Brewster told Ickes that Truman "had one objection to the President and that was 'he lies.'" This information was provided to the authors by James Hafner, rare book cataloger for the Library of Congress. Truman and Brewster, both of them World War I combat veterans, were friends from Truman's days in the Senate.

7. Interview with Landon Parvin by LC, April 17, 1989.

8. Speech by Douglas Brinkley to Channel City Club, Santa Barbara, California, October 5, 2006.

9. David S. Broder, "End of a Dream," *The Washington Post,* April 1, 1981.

10. Ward Sinclair and Peter Behr, "Reagan Triumphs in House Budget Vote, Horse Trading," *The Washington Post,* June 27, 1981.

11. Quoted by Lou Cannon, *President Reagan: The Role of a Lifetime,* p. 7.

12. Message to Lou Cannon from Jack Matlock, January 20, 2007. For a more extended discussion of Dobrynin's role, see Jack Matlock, *Reagan and Gorbachev: How the Cold War Ended,* pp. 17–23.

13. Reagan often made this remark. In his autobiography, *An American Life,* p. 611, he attributed this comment to himself after the death of Chernenko. "How am I supposed to get anyplace with the Russians," I asked Nancy, "if they keep dying on me?"

14. Declassified memo of discussion between Prime Minister Thatcher and President Reagan at Camp David, December 28, 1984, The Thatcher Foundation.

15. Ibid.

16. Reagan, *An American Life,* p. 612.

17. William C. Wohlforth, ed., *Witnesses to the End of the Cold War,* p. 19. This book, which includes additional commentary, is based upon the transcripts of the Princeton Conference on the End of the Cold War, held at Princeton University, February 25–27, 1993.

18. Wohlforth, *Witnesses,* p. 18.

19. David Hoffman, "I Had a Funny Feeling in My Gut; Soviet Officer Faced Nuclear Armageddon," *The Washington Post,* February 10, 1999.

20. Martin Anderson, *Revolution,* p. 83.

21. Undated interview with Reagan by LC. Quoted in Lou Cannon, *Ronald Reagan: The Presidential Portfolio,* p. 27.

22. Ibid., p. 402n. The students were overheard by Gary Lee, a Russian-speaking correspondent for *The Washington Post.*

23. Interview with Condoleezza Rice by LC, November 8, 1999.

24. Quoted by Don Oberdorfer, *The Turn: From the Cold War to a New Era. The United States and the Soviet Union, 1983–1990,* p. 14.

25. Wohlforth, *Witnesses,* pp. 107–108.

26. Reagan, *An American Life,* p. 715.

27. Margaret Thatcher, "Reagan's Leadership, America's Recovery," *National Review,* December 30, 1988.

28. "Meet the Press," with Tim Russert, November 12, 2006.

29. Harold Meyerson, "The Most Dangerous President Ever," *The American Prospect,* May 2003.

CHAPTER THREE:
THE THREE PRESIDENCIES OF GEORGE W. BUSH

1. George W. Bush, speech at Great American Ballpark, Cincinnati, Ohio, October 31, 2004.

2. Conversation between Mark McKinnon and CMC, February 13, 2007.

3. Roosevelt used this "little allegory," as he called it, during a press conference on December 28, 1943.

4. George W. Bush, speech at a GOP fundraiser in Washington, D.C., April 26, 2000.

5. Interview with George W. Bush by Steve Cooper of WMUR of Manchester, New Hampshire, February 2, 1999.

6. George W. Bush, acceptance speech at the Republican National Convention, First Union Center, Philadelphia, August 3, 2000.

7. Interview with Noelia Rodriguez, First Lady Laura Bush's former press secretary, by CMC, July 2002.

8. Fred I. Greenstein, "Terror and Transformation: The Making of Bush's Leadership Style," *Compass: A Journal of Leadership,* published by Harvard's John F. Kennedy School of Government, Fall 2003.

9. Bill Sammon, *Fighting Back: The War on Terrorism from Inside the Bush White House,* pp. 53–81.

10. Sean Wilentz, "The Worst President in History?" *Rolling Stone,* April 21, 2006.

11. Interview with Ari Fleischer by CMC, July 2002.

12. "The President's Story," CBS News, 60 Minutes II, September 11, 2002.

13. Carl M. Cannon, "America's Challenge," *National Journal,* September 15, 2001.

14. Condoleezza Rice's recollection to the National Commission on Terrorist Attacks upon the United States, as related in the 9/11 Independent Commission Report, p. 326.

15. Interview with Mark McKinnon by CMC, March 19, 2007.

16. Burt Solomon, "National Security: All Leadership, All the Time," *National Journal,* December 1, 2001.

17. Kweisi Mfume, comment to Hazel Trice Edney, a writer for the National Newspaper Publishers Association, a news service for African-American newspapers. The dispatch appeared July 9, 2004. Julian Bond's remarks were made in Washington at a public forum called Take Back America, June 2, 2004.

18. Susan Page, "Bush Is Opening Doors with a Diverse Cabinet," *USA Today,* December 9, 2004.

19. Eleanor Clift, "Racial Icons," *Newsweek*, February 10, 2006.

20. Tim Bonfield, "Rock Star Bono Praises Bush for AIDS Plan," *The Cincinnati Enquirer,* July 8, 2003.

21. Walter Shapiro, "MBA President's Success Leaves Dems Out in Cold," *USA Today,* December 5, 2002.

22. Stephen Hess and James P. Pfiffner, *Organizing the Presidency*, p. 169.

23. David Frum, *The Right Man: The Surprise Presidency of George W. Bush,* p. 20.

24. Ibid., p. 34.

25. Arthur M. Schlesinger Jr., *The Imperial Presidency,* p. 139.

26. Carl M. Cannon attended both presidential conferences; the accompanying quotations are from his notes.

27. Karl Rove lecture, November 13, 2002, at the University of Utah's Rocco C. Siciliano Forum. Transcript furnished by the College of Social and Behavioral Science.

28. PBS *Frontline* interview with Matthew Dowd, aired April 12, 2005, for "Karl Rove: The Architect." Dowd interview conducted January 4, 2005.

29. PBS *Frontline* interview with Ken Mehlman, conducted December 21, 2004.

30. Interview with Karl Rove by CMC at the White House, June 6, 2007.

31. Interview with James A. Baker III by LC at Reagan Presidential Library, March 20, 2007.

32. Interview with Karl Rove by CMC, June 6, 2007.

33. Interview with Grover Norquist by CMC, May 1, 2007.

34. Senator Edward Kennedy's comments were to the *Associated Press,* September 18, 2003.

35. Jeffrey Goldberg, "Party Unfaithful: The Republican Implosion," *The New Yorker,* June 4, 2007.

36. Christine Todd Whitman, testimony before the Senate Subcommittee on Superfund, Waste Control, and Risk Assessment, February 27, 2001.

37. Jake Tapper, "Bush's EPA Chief Seeks Greener Pastures," *Salon*, May 22, 2003.

38. PBS *Frontline* interview with Christine Todd Whitman, conducted January 31, 2005.

39. President Bush made this comment for the first time in Trenton, New Jersey, on September 23, 2002. The second occurrence was in Cedar Rapids, Iowa, November 4, 2002.

40. Lou Cannon, *President Reagan: The Role of a Lifetime,* p. 89.

41. Paul Begala, "Vengeance Is His," *Washington Monthly,* September 2004.

42. Interview with Les Francis by CMC, June 2006.

43. President Bush posed this question to Carl Cannon at the head table of the White House Correspondents' Association annual dinner, May 1, 2004.

44. Burt Solomon, "National Security: All Leadership, All the Time," *National Journal,* December 1, 2001.

45. Philander Chase made these observations in September 2001 to Delia M. Rios of Newhouse Newspapers.

46. Interview with George W. Edwards III by CMC, May 15, 2007.

47. Interview with Louis Gould by CMC, December 13, 2005.

CHAPTER FOUR: SAFE FOR DEMOCRACY

1. Cited by Jonathan Sikorsky, "From British Cassandra to American Hero: The Churchill Legend in the World War II American Media," Churchill Centre website. Sikorsky said that Churchill first used this quote in an article for *Collier's* magazine, for which he often wrote, "three months before World War II."

2. Interview with Michael Gerson by CMC, May 3, 2005.

3. Interview with John McConnell by CMC, May 6, 2005.

4. Ibid.

5. William Bundy, *A Tangled Web: The Making of Foreign Policy in the Nixon Presidency,* p. 291.

6. James Chace, *Acheson: The Secretary of State Who Created the American World,* p. 108.

7. Stanley Karnow, *Vietnam: A History,* p. 121.

8. Fred Barnes, *Rebel-in-Chief: Inside the Bold and Controversial Presidency of George W. Bush,* p. 101.

9. Ibid., p. 158.

10. OpenDemocracy.net, a London-based online magazine, April 21, 2004. Mearsheimer said that the Bush Doctrine "is essentially Wilsonianism with teeth. The theory has an idealist strand and a power strand: Wilsonianism provides the idealism, an emphasis on military power provides the teeth."

11. Interview with David Kennedy by CMC, June 19, 2006.

12. John B. Judis, *The Folly of Empire: What George W. Bush Could Learn from Theodore Roosevelt and Woodrow Wilson,* p. 201.

13. Joseph S. Nye Jr., "Transformational Leadership and U.S. Grand Strategy," *Foreign Affairs,* July/August 2006.

14. Karnow, *Vietnam,* p. 13.

15. Interview with John Milton Cooper by LC, August 3, 2006.

16. Communication from John Milton Cooper to LC, July 2, 2007.

17. Judis, *The Folly of Empire,* p. 92.

18. John Milton Cooper Jr., *Breaking the Heart of the World: Woodrow Wilson and the Fight for the League of Nations,* p. 342, n. 21.

19. Nye, "Transformational Leadership."

20. Cooper, *Breaking the Heart of the World,* p. 422. For a discussion of the effects of Wilson's stroke on his ability to compromise, see chapter 10 in this book and chapter 21 in *Woodrow Wilson: A Medical and Psychological Biography* by Edwin A. Weinstein.

21. Nye, "Transformational Leadership."

22. Ronald Reagan, "Killed in Action, May 7, 1931." The short story is reprinted on pp. 430–433 of *Reagan In His Own Hand: The Writings of Ronald Reagan That Reveal His Revolutionary Vision for America,* by Kiron K. Skinner, Annelise Anderson, and Martin Anderson. It is noted to the pre-presidential papers, special collection, Ronald Reagan Presidential Library.

CHAPTER FIVE: NOBLE CAUSES

1. Stephen Vaughn, *Ronald Reagan in Hollywood: Movies and Politics,* p. 112.

2. Ibid., p. 113.

3. Ronald Reagan and Richard C. Hubler, *Where's the Rest of Me? Ronald Reagan Tells His Own Story,* p. 160.

4. Conversation with Frank Mankiewicz by LC, January 1990.

5. Ronald Reagan article in *Fortnight* magazine, January 22, 1951.

6. Quoted by Alonzo L. Hamby, *Man of the People: A Life of Harry S. Truman,* p. 557.

7. Ronald Reagan, *An American Life,* p. 133.

8. Barry Goldwater, *The Conscience of a Conservative,* p. 87.

9. Goldwater speech, March 19, 1964. Barry M. Goldwater Papers, Arizona Historical Foundation, Arizona State University, Tempe, Arizona. In this speech at the Los Angeles Sports Arena, Goldwater expressed astonishment at the Johnson administration's expressed goal of bringing the situation in Vietnam "under control." Said Goldwater: "Why in heaven's name isn't it under control? It isn't under control because it remains just what it has been for three years—an aimless, leaderless war."

10. Fredrik Logevall, *Choosing War: The Lost Chance for Peace and the Escalation of War in Vietnam,* p. 244.

11. Arthur M. Schlesinger Jr., *A Thousand Days: John F. Kennedy in the White House,* p. 339. The words are Schlesinger's. In a later book, *Robert Kennedy and His Times,* pp. 703–705, Schlesinger quoted from what he said was a "rare *aide-memoire,*" dictated by President Kennedy after a meeting with MacArthur. In this document MacArthur is quoted as saying "that we would be foolish to fight on the Asiatic continent and that the future of Southeast Asia should be determined at the diplomatic table."

12. Garry Wills, "The Hostage," *New York Review of Books,* August 13, 1992.

13. Barry Bearak, "His Great Gift, to Blend In; Team Player Bush: A Yearning to Serve," *Los Angeles Times,* November 22, 1987.

14. Reagan interview with *Fresno Bee,* October 10, 1965.

15. Chesly Manly, "Reagan Calls for U.S. Drive to Victory in Vietnam," *Chicago Tribune,* March 5, 1968.

16. Ken Sheets, "Reagan Blasts U.S. Tactics in War," *Houston Chronicle,* October 10, 1968.

17. Letter by Ronald Reagan to Holmes Alexander, c. December 1979, reprinted in *Reagan: A Life in Letters,* by Kiron K. Skinner, Annelise Anderson, and Martin Anderson, pp. 589–591.

18. George W. Bush, with Karen Hughes, *A Charge to Keep,* p. 55.

19. George Washington, letter to his troops from New York, August 1, 1776. George Washington Papers, Library of Congress.

20. Speech by Harry S. Truman to Jackson Day dinner at Mayflower Hotel in Washington, D.C., March 23, 1946.

21. Interview of John McCain by CMC and William Beaman, January 4, 2007.

22. Ibid.

23. Lou Cannon, *President Reagan: The Role of a Lifetime,* p. 163.

24. Ibid.

25. Ibid.

26. Reagan, *An American Life,* p. 361.

27. Roy Gutman, *Banana Diplomacy: The Making of American Policy in Nicaragua, 1981–1987,* pp. 80–81.

28. Lou Cannon, "Hang the Polls, Conviction Is What Counts on Latin Policy," *The Washington Post,* May 14, 1984.

29. Interview with Jeane Kirkpatrick by LC, March 7, 1990.

30. Cannon, *President Reagan,* p. 311.

31. George P. Shultz, *Turmoil and Triumph, My Years as Secretary of State,* p. 964.

32. Ibid., p. 960.

CHAPTER SIX:

THE SHORT WARS OF RONALD REAGAN

1. Dwight D. Eisenhower, Message to the U.S. forces withdrawing from Lebanon, October 18, 1958, PPP.

2. Dwight D. Eisenhower, *Mandate for Change: The White House Years, 1953–1956. A Personal Account,* vol. 2, p. 275.

3. Emmet John Hughes, *The Ordeal of Power: A Political Memoir of the Eisenhower Years,* p. 263. Hughes wrote that Eisenhower "moved as fast as the clock." At 9:45 A.M. he "reviewed with the National Security Council his decision to deploy on the eastern shore of the Mediterranean the largest peacetime concentration of American military power ever assembled." At 2:30 P.M. he met with ranking members of Congress. At 4:30 P.M. he told General Nathan Twining, chairman of the Joint Chiefs, to "send 'em in."

4. Laurence I. Barrett, *Gambling with History: Reagan in the White House,* p. 275.

5. Ibid., p. 271.

6. Ronald Reagan, *An American Life,* p. 270.

7. Alexander M. Haig, Jr., *Caveat: Realism, Reagan, and Foreign Policy,* p. 312.

8. Lou Cannon, *President Reagan: The Role of a Lifetime,* pp. 168–171.

9. Ronald Reagan, *Reagan Diaries,* entry for June 25, 1982, p. 91.

10. Caspar W. Weinberger, with Gretchen Roberts, *In the Arena: A Memoir of the 20th Century,* p. 259.

11. Interview with Frank Carlucci by LC, March 22, 1989.

12. For a more detailed account of the Shultz-Weinberger conflict, see Cannon, *President Reagan,* pp. 350–354.

13. Michael K. Deaver, with Mickey Herskowitz, *Behind the Scenes,* p. 166.

14. Interview with Geoffrey Kemp by LC, February 1, 1990. Kemp, who headed the Near East and South Asian affairs office on the National Security Council staff from 1981–1984, monitored the Reagan-Begin conversation.

15. Ibid.

16. Deaver, *Behind the Scenes,* p. 166.

17. Cannon, *President Reagan,* p. 356.

18. David C. Martin and John Walcott, *Best Laid Plans: The Inside Story of America's War against Terrorism,* p. 98.

19. Ibid.

20. Interview with Caspar Weinberger by LC, March 29, 1990.

21. Lou Cannon reported this for *The Washington Post;* Chris Wallace for NBC News.

22. Lou Cannon, "Reagan Appoints McFarlane Adviser on U.S. Security," *The Washington Post,* October 18, 1983.

23. Report of the Department of Defense Commission on Beirut International Terrorist Act, October 23, 1983, hereinafter Long Report, December 29, 1983, pp. 32–33.

24. Reagan, *An American Life,* p. 437.

25. Interview with Ronald Reagan by LC, May 5, 1989.

26. Martin and Walcott, *Best Laid Plans,* p. 148.

27. Remarks by Ronald Reagan to reporters at the south portico of the White House, October 23, 1983, PPP, p. 1498.

28. Conversation with Colin Powell by LC, April 17, 1990. Weinberger twice expressed the same sentiment in a March 17, 1989, interview with LC. He said it was "a source of enormous pain and unhappiness to me that I was not persuasive enough to have the force withdrawn before that tragedy happened."

29. Martin and Walcott, *Best Laid Plans,* p. 147.

30. Long Report, pp. 39, 44.

31. Interview with Robert McFarlane by LC, February 21, 1989.

32. George P. Shultz, *Turmoil and Triumph: My Years as Secretary of State,* p. 230.

33. Interview with Robert McFarlane by LC, February 21, 1989.

34. Cannon, *President Reagan,* p. 392. Mike Deaver, in an interview with LC the same day, said that Reagan was "a tired and unhappy man."

35. Shultz, *Turmoil and Triumph,* p. 331.

36. Caspar Weinberger, *Fighting for Peace: Seven Critical Years in the Pentagon,* p. 113. Weinberger said in his book that Vessey "reminded" him he had said these words. Vessey confirmed this when LC interviewed him on February 26, 2007.

37. Margaret Thatcher, *The Downing Street Years,* p. 331.

38. Ibid.

39. Interview with John Vessey by LC, February 26, 2007.

40. Ibid.

41. Richard Harwood, "Tidy U.S. War Ends: 'We Blew Them Away,'" *The Washington Post,* November 6, 1983.

42. *Reagan Diaries,* entry for October 27, 1983, p. 191.

43. Cannon, *President Reagan,* p. 390. O'Neill's suspicions were unfounded but understandable. He had patriotically supported Reagan's actions in Lebanon despite the grumbling of some Democrats.

44. Colin Powell, with Joseph E. Persico, *My American Journey,* p. 292.

45. Lou Cannon, "What Happened to Reagan the Gunslinger?" *The Washington Post,* July 7, 1985.

46. *Reagan Diaries,* entry for April 14, 1986, p. 405.

47. Thatcher, *The Downing Street Years,* p. 449.

48. Conversation with Kenneth Duberstein by LC, October 19, 1989.

49. Interview with Ronald Reagan by LC, May 5, 1989.

50. Shultz, *Turmoil and Triumph,* p. 1073. Shultz told LC that the comments he attributed to Reagan and government officials in the Noriega discussion were from contemporaneous notes.

51. Ibid., p. 1072.

52. Ibid.

53. Ibid.

54. Ibid., p. 1052.

55. Interview with Ronald Reagan by LC, May 5, 1989.

56. Ibid.

CHAPTER SEVEN:
THE LONG WARS OF GEORGE W. BUSH

1. Bill Clinton, *My Life*, p. 592.

2. Interview with Karl Rove by CMC in the White House, June 6, 2007.

3. Stephen Grey, et al., "The Road to Ground Zero," *The Sunday Times* (London), January 6, 2002.

4. The 9/11 Commission Report, p. 71.

5. Ibid., p. 60.

6. Ibid.

7. Robert Fisk interview with Osama bin Laden, *The Independent,* July 10, 1996.

8. Steve Coll, *Ghost Wars: The Secret History of the CIA, Afghanistan, and Bin Laden, from the Soviet Invasion to September 10, 2001,* p. 10.

9. The text was faxed to *Al Quds Al Ababi,* an Arabic-language newspaper in London, which reprinted it.

10. John Miller, "A Conversation with the Most Dangerous Man in the World," *Esquire,* February 1999.

11. Ibid.

12. David C. Martin and John Walcott, *Best Laid Plans: The Inside Story of America's War against Terrorism,* p. 113.

13. 9/11 Commission Report, p. 119.

14. "Republicans Skeptical of Iraq Attack on Eve of Impeachment Vote," CNN, December 16, 1998.

15. John McWethy, *ABC World News Tonight,* August 25, 1998.

16. William S. Cohen, "Operation Desert Fox Briefing," U.S. Department of Defense News Transcript, December 21, 1998.

17. Mark J. Conversino, "Operation Desert Fox: Effectiveness with Unintended Effects," *Air & Space Power Journal,* July 13, 2005.

18. Ibid.

19. William Drozdiak, "Dissent Heard in Some Foreign Capitals," *The Washington Post,* December 17, 1998.

20. Bob Woodward, *Bush at War,* p. 15.

21. Ibid., p. 41.

22. Howard Fineman, "A President Finds His True Voice," *Newsweek,* September 24, 2001.

23. Michael R. Gordon and Gen. Bernard E. Trainor, *Cobra II: The Inside Story of the Invasion and Occupation of Iraq,* p. 15.

24. Ibid., p. 16.

25. Woodward, *Bush at War,* p. 155.

26. Peggy Noonan, "A Chat in the Oval Office," *Wall Street Journal,* June 25, 2001.

27. David Frum, *The Right Man: The Surprising Presidency of George W. Bush,* p. 265.

28. C-SPAN, "Q&A" with President Bush, White House Map Room, January 27, 2005.

29. Bob Woodward, *Plan of Attack,* pp. 1–8.

30. Bryan Burrough, Evgenia Peretz, David Rose, and David Wise, "The Path to War," *Vanity Fair,* May 1, 2004.

31. John Judis, *The Folly of Empire: What George W. Bush Could Learn from Theodore Roosevelt and Woodrow Wilson,* pp. 167–168.

32. The article was "Dictatorships and Double Standards" in the November 1979 issue of *Commentary.*

33. Jeane J. Kirkpatrick, *Making War to Keep Peace,* p. 281.

34. Matlock used this phrase in answering a question from the audience after a joint discussion with Lou Cannon at Princeton University on November 30, 2005.

35. Francis Fukuyama, *America at the Crossroads: Democracy, Power, and the Neoconservative Legacy,* p. 31.

36. Quoted in James Mann, *Rise of the Vulcans: The History of Bush's War Cabinet,* p. 27.

37. PBS, *Frontline,* "The Case for War," April 17, 2007.

38. George W. Bush, State of the Union address, January 29, 2003.

39. Carl M. Cannon, "The Presidency: What Bush Said," *National Journal,* July 26, 2003.

40. "A Conversation with General Colin Powell," Jim Lehrer, interviewer, Aspen Institute, July 5, 2007.

41. Interview with Colin Powell in Aspen, Colorado, by CMC, July 6, 2007.

42. William Safire, "If You Break It . . . ," *The New York Times,* October 17, 2004.

43. Woodward, *Plan of Attack,* p. 150.

44. Ibid.

45. Jane Mayer, "The Manipulator," *The New Yorker,* June 7, 2004.

46. Richard Leiby, "Breaking Ranks," *The Washington Post,* January 19, 2006.

47. PBS, *Frontline,* "The Case for War," April 17, 2007.

48. Department of Defense briefing with Secretary Donald Rumsfeld and Richard B. Myers, chairman of the Joint Chiefs of Staff, April 11, 2003.

49. Peter Slevin, "Wrong Turn and Postwar Crossroads?" *The Washington Post,* November 20, 2003.

50. NBC, *Dateline,* "Bremer on Iraq," interview with Brian Williams, January 8, 2006.

51. Rick Atkinson, interviewed by Soledad O'Brien of CNN, March 23, 2004.

52. Steve Coll, "General Accounting," *The New Yorker,* September 24, 2007.

53. Ibid.

54. Jack Uldrich, *Soldier, Statesman, Peacemaker: Leadership Lessons from George C. Marshall,* p. 199.

55. George Packer, *The Assassin's Gate: America in Iraq,* p. 87.

56. Gordon and Trainor, *Cobra II,* p. 28.

57. Ibid.

58. Gideon Rose, "Welcome to the Occupation," *The Washington Post,* October 9, 2005.

59. David Rose, "Neo Culpa," *Vanity Fair,* November 3, 2006 (online edition).

60. Interview with Joseph S. Nye Jr. by CMC, March 6, 2007.

61. Kenneth Adelman, "Cakewalk in Iraq," *The Washington Post,* February 13, 2002.

62. Interview with Kenneth Adelman by CMC, July 6, 2006.

63. Interview with Kenneth Adelman by CMC, July 8, 2007.

64. Jeffrey Goldberg, "The End of the Affair," *The New Yorker,* November 20, 2006.

65. Interview with unnamed White House official by CMC, May 7, 2004.

66. Interview with Michael Gerson by CMC, March 19, 2007.

67. Interview with presidential adviser, who agreed to be identified as "high-ranking White House official," by CMC, June 7, 2007.

68. David Ignatius, "Beirut's Berlin Wall," *The Washington Post,* February 23, 2005.

69. Richard Gwyn, "Admit It: Bush Was Right on Iraq," *Toronto Star,* February 1, 2005.

70. Interview with Edwin Meese by LC, September 20, 2006.

71. Patrick J. Buchanan, "Was Reagan the First Neoconservative?" Creators Syndicate Inc., June 14, 2004.

72. Interview with Craig Shirley by LC, June 9, 2006.

73. Richard Leiby, "Breaking Ranks: Larry Wilkerson Attacked the Iraq War. In the Process, He Lost the Friendship of Colin Powell," *The Washington Post,* January 19, 2006.

74. Brian Lamb interview with President Bush, January 30, 2005, C-SPAN.

CHAPTER EIGHT: M.B.A. PRESIDENT

1. Peter F. Drucker, "The American CEO," *Wall Street Journal,* December 30, 2004.

2. Abraham McLaughlin, "The Bush Team Brings Very Corporate Values," *The Christian Science Monitor,* January 9, 2001.

3. John Solomon, "Bush, Harvard Business School and the Makings of a President," *The New York Times,* June 18, 2000.

4. Grover Cleveland, "Veto Message," June 19, 1886, PPP.

5. Ronald Reagan, "Message to the Congress Outlining Proposals for Improving the Organization of the Defense Establishment," April 24, 1986, PPP.

6. Ronald Reagan, "Let Them Go Their Way," speech at Conservative Political Action Conference, Washington, D.C., March 1, 1975.

7. Interview with William George, professor of management and practice at Harvard Business School, by CMC, July 6, 2007.

8. Mica Schneider and Douglas Harbrecht, "George W's B-School Days," *Business Week,* February 15, 2001.

9. Solomon, "Bush, Harvard Business School and the Makings of a President."

10. Michael Kranish, "Hallmarks of Bush Style Were Seen at Harvard," *Boston Globe,* December 28, 1999.

11. Ibid.

12. George W. Bush, *A Charge to Keep,* p. 60.

13. Interview with Howard C. Serkin, HBS class of 1974, by CMC, June 19, 2007.

14. Schneider and Harbrecht, "George W's B-School Days."

15. Simon W. Vozick-Levinson, "Former HBS Prof Blasts Bush," *The Harvard Crimson,* July 16, 2004.

16. George Lardner Jr. and Lois Romano, "At Height of Vietnam, Bush Picks Guard," *The Washington Post,* July 28, 1999.

17. Ibid.

18. Conversation between George W. Bush and CMC at a reception before the White House Correspondents' Association dinner, April 17, 2007.

19. Cited in *Our Company,* a General Electric online report, which attributes Cordiner's rescuing of the Schick Company to an undated article in *Time.*

20. Ronald Reagan, "The Creative Society," speech at the University of Southern California, April 19, 1966.

21. Marshall Loeb, Lee Smith, and Ann Reilly Dowd, "Reagan on Decision-Making, Planning, Gorbachev, and More," *Fortune,* September 15, 1986.

22. Peter F. Drucker, *The Age of Discontinuity: Guidelines to Our Changing Society,* p. 212.

23. Alvin P. Sanoff, "Nobody Believes Any More That Government Delivers: A Conversation with Peter F. Drucker," *U.S. News & World Report,* December 21, 1981.

24. John Solomon, "Managing USA Inc. Takes a Little More Drive," *The Washington Post,* July 28, 2002.

25. Ibid.

26. George Lardner Jr. and Lois Romano, "Bush Name Helps Fuel Oil Dealings," *The Washington Post,* July 30, 1999.

27. Eric Pooley, with S. C. Gwynne, "How George Got His Groove," *Time,* June 14, 1999.

28. Ibid.

29. Lardner and Romano, "Bush Name Helps Fuel Oil Dealings."

30. Ibid.

31. "On the Record with Bob Costas," HBO, February 22, 2001.

32. Carl M. Cannon, "For the Love of the Game," *National Journal,* March 24, 2001.

33. Chris Casteel, "Bush Runs on Honesty, Charisma," *Daily Oklahoman,* January 30, 2000.

34. Lois Romano and George Lardner Jr., "Bush's Move Up to the Majors," *The Washington Post,* July 31, 1999.

35. Bush, *A Charge to Keep,* p. 70.

36. Interview with Richard Ben Cramer by CMC, March 2001.

37. Bush, *A Charge to Keep,* p. 207.

38. Ibid.

39. George W. Bush, memo, "To Hard-Working Staff Members," office of the governor, April 3, 1995.

40. *CNN Insight,* January 19, 2001.

41. Alan C. Miller and Judy Pasternak, "Records Show Bush's Focus on Big Picture," *Los Angeles Times,* August 2, 2000.

42. Jonathan Walters, "The Taming of Texas," *Governing,* July 1998.

43. Interview with Karl Rove by CMC, June 6, 2007.

44. Ronald Reagan, "Remarks at the Conservative Political Action Conference Dinner," March 20, 1981, PPP.

45. Miller and Pasternak, "Records Show Bush's Focus on Big Picture."

46. Ibid.

47. James Carney, "Why Bush Doesn't Like Homework," *Time,* November 15, 1999.

48. Interview with Lanny J. Davis by CMC, April 25, 2007.

49. Carney, "Why Bush Doesn't Like Homework."

50. Ibid.

51. Ibid.

52. Bob Woodward, *Bush at War,* p. 144.

53. Nicholas Lemann, "Without a Doubt," *The New Yorker,* October 14, 2002.

54. Lanny J. Davis, "True Confessions: A Democrat Likes George," *Los Angeles Times,* January 20, 2005.

55. David Gergen, "Stubborn Kind of Fellow," *Compass: A Journal of Leadership,* Fall 2003.

56. Ibid.

57. Interview with Lawrence H. Summers by CMC, May 1, 2007.

58. Interview with Ned Lamont by CMC, April 17, 2007.

59. Brent Scowcroft, "Don't Attack Saddam," *Wall Street Journal,* August 15, 2002.

60. Jeffrey Goldberg, "Breaking Ranks: What Turned Brent Scowcroft against the Bush Administration," *The New Yorker,* October 31, 2005.

61. Conversation between CMC and Bob Woodward researcher Brady Dennis, November 14, 2007.

62. Goldberg, "Breaking Ranks."

63. John Steinbeck, *Travels with Charley,* p. 228.

64. Carl M. Cannon and Alexis Simendinger, "Team Texas," *National Journal,* January 15, 2005.

65. Interview with Scott McClellan by CMC, January 9, 2005.

66. Interview with Mark McKinnon by CMC, January 10, 2005.

67. Nicholas Lemann, "Remember the Alamo," *The New Yorker,* October 18, 2004.

68. Interview over lunch with Vice President Dick Cheney in his White House office, CMC and LC, May 15, 2002.

69. Ibid.

70. David G. McCullough, *John Adams,* p. 389.

71. "The Thirty-Second," *Time,* April 23, 1945.

72. Lou Cannon, *President Reagan: The Role of a Lifetime,* p. 2.

73. Carl M. Cannon, "The Point Man," *National Journal,* October 12, 2002.

74. Interview with Mary Matalin by CMC, October 2002.

75. Jo Becker and Barton Gellman, "Angler, the Cheney Vice Presidency: A Strong Push from Backstage," *The Washington Post,* June 26, 2007.

76. Conversation between Colin Powell and CMC, July 6, 2007.

77. Stephen F. Hayes, *Cheney: The Untold Story of America's Most Powerful and Controversial Vice President,* p. 506.

78. Conversation between Alan Simpson and CMC at Harvard's Institute of Politics, March 2007.

79. Ibid.

80. Interview with Joseph S. Nye Jr. by CMC, March 6, 2007.

81. Ibid.

82. Interview with confidential White House source by CMC, June 7, 2007.

83. Interview with Michael Gerson by CMC, March 19, 2007.

84. Ibid.

85. John F. Harris and Robin Wright, "Aid Grows amid Remarks about President's Absence," *The Washington Post,* December 29, 2004.

86. Interview with Kenneth Duberstein by CMC, July 18, 2007.

87. Ibid.

88. Sean Wilentz, "The Worst President in History? One of America's Leading Historians Assesses George W. Bush," *Rolling Stone,* April 21, 2006.

89. Lou Cannon, "At Daughter's Request, the President Hears Out a Peace Activist," *The Washington Post,* February 14, 1983.

90. Interview with Karl Rove by CMC, June 6, 2007.

91. Interview with Roger Porter by CMC, April 16, 2007.

92. Interview with Kenneth Duberstein by CMC, July 18, 2007.

93. Peggy Noonan, "A Chat in the Oval Office," *Wall Street Journal,* June 25, 2001.

94. Rich Karlgaard, "Peter Drucker on Leadership," *Forbes,* November 19, 2004.

95. Richard Reeves, *President Reagan: The Triumph of Imagination,* p. 8.

CHAPTER NINE: REAGAN'S DISCIPLE

1. Debate between George W. Bush and Al Gore, University of Massachusetts, October 3, 2000.

2. Interview with Edwin Meese by LC, September 20, 2006.

3. Conversation with Terry Eastland by LC, June 14, 2007.

4. "Democracy Now," radio and television interview with Senator Patrick Leahy by Amy Goodman, March 2, 2005.

5. David A. Yalof, *The George W. Bush Legacy.*

6. John Hanrahan, "Senate Rejects Bork," United Press International, October 23, 1987.

7. Alan Simpson on *The McNeil-Lehrer NewsHour,* October 6, 1987.

8. Charles Truehart, "In Bork's Corner: Alan Simpson's Angry Defense," *The Washington Post,* October 2, 1987.

9. Ronald Reagan, *The Reagan Diaries,* p. 545.

10. Ibid., p. 558.

11. Conversation with Terry Eastland by LC, June 14, 2007.

12. Beth J. Harpaz, "Feminists Say Clarence Thomas Must Be Rejected," Associated Press, July 5, 1991.

13. Jan Crawford Greenburg, *Supreme Conflict: The Inside Story of the Conflict for Control of the United States Supreme Court,* p. 166.

14. CNN, *Larry King Live,* interview with James Dobson, September 5, 2003.

15. For a complete account of this incident, see Lou Cannon, *Governor Reagan: His Rise to Power,* pp. 238–255.

16. Lyn Nofziger, *Nofziger,* p. 74. Nofziger wrote that the Reagans had lived in Hollywood "where dwell and work a significant number of homosexuals. As a result, both were tolerant of this sort of aberrant sexual behavior."

17. Warren King, "Reagan Regarded AIDS 'Like It Was Measles,'" *Seattle Times,* August 31, 1989.

18. Ibid.

19. Don McLeod, "Domestic News," Associated Press, June 14, 1983.

20. William E. Schmidt, "Mrs. Heckler Lists Added Funds," *The New York Times,* June 15, 1983.

21. Jerry Schwarz, "Secretary Announces Doubling of AIDS Funding Requests," Associated Press, August 17, 1983.

22. Fuller accounts of this jockeying on AIDS policy inside the Reagan White House can be found in Lou Cannon's *President Reagan: The Role of a Lifetime,* pp.

731–736, and Richard Reeve's *President Reagan: The Triumph of Imagination*, pp. 306–308.

23. Randy Shilts, *And the Band Played On: Politics, People, and the AIDS Epidemic*, p. 311.

24. Interview with Gary Bauer by CMC, October 1986.

25. *Reagan Diaries*, p. 502.

26. Interview with Lanny Davis by CMC, summer of 2000. (Davis repeated this account in an op-ed he wrote in the *Los Angeles Times*, January 20, 2005.)

27. Bill Sammon, "Bush Fires Another Salvo at GOP," *The Washington Times*, October 6, 1999.

28. Interview with Edwin Meese by LC, September 20, 2006.

29. Interview with Theodore Olson by LC, June 20, 2007.

30. Greenburg, *Supreme Conflict*, p. 248.

31. Ibid., p. 310.

32. Joan Biskupic, "Roberts Steers Court Right Back to Reagan," *USA Today*, June 29, 2007.

33. Interview with Theodore Olson by LC, June 20, 2007.

34. William Yardley, "Seattle Schools Take Stock after Justices Issue Ruling," *The New York Times*, July 1, 2007.

35. Robert Barnes, "Justice Kennedy: The Highly Influential Man in the Middle," *The Washington Post*, May 13, 2007.

36. Jeffrey Rosen, "The Arrogance of Justice Anthony Kennedy," *The New Republic*, June 18, 2007.

37. Gregory Rodriguez, "The GOP's High Hispanic Hopes," *Salon*, December 7, 1999.

38. Bruce Bartlett, *Imposter: How George W. Bush Bankrupted America and Betrayed the Reagan Legacy*, p. 1.

39. Alan Greenspan, *The Age of Turbulence: Adventures in a New World*, p. 242. Greenspan reserved his harshest words for the Republican Congress that passed the spending bills. In his memoirs (p. 243), he wrote: "The Republicans in Congress lost their way. They swapped principle for power. They ended up with neither."

40. Sheryl Gay Stolberg, "Suddenly, Bush Speaks of Controlling Spending," *The New York Times*, September 22, 2007.

CHAPTER TEN: LEGACY

1. Interview with Dana Perino by CMC, August 18, 2007.

2. Powl Smith, "Iraq Is Not Vietnam, It's Guadalcanal: Learning the Real Lessons History Has for Today's War on Terror," *The Weekly Standard*, September 24, 2004.

3. Fred Barnes, "Not This Time: Don't Give Up When Victory Is at Hand," *The Weekly Standard*, February 5, 2007.

4. Carl M. Cannon, "Untruth and Consequences," *The Atlantic Monthly*, January 2007.

5. Carl M. Cannon, "Life Is Politics," *National Journal*, September 17, 2005.

6. Carl M. Cannon, "The Mourner-in-Chief," *National Journal,* February 8, 2003.

7. Lyndon Baines Johnson, *The Vantage Point: Perspectives of the Presidency, 1963–1969,* p. 270.

8. Ronald Reagan, *An American Life,* p. 403.

9. Ibid., p. 402.

10. Interview with Washington Post Writers' Group columnist Kathleen Parker by CMC, August 14, 2007, about her July 13, 2007, meeting with President Bush at the White House.

11. Richard Lardner, "Admiral Cites Problems Undermining Iraq," Associated Press, July 30, 2007.

12. Fox News/Opinion Dynamics poll, December 14–15, 2004.

13. Time/SRBI poll, January 12–13, 2005.

14. George W. Bush, State of the Union address, February 2, 2005.

15. Interview with Kenneth Duberstein by CMC, July 18, 2007.

16. Herbert Hoover, "Special Message to the Congress on the Economic Recovery Program," January 4, 1932, PPP.

17. Interview with Richard Norton Smith by CMC, August 21, 2007.

18. Robert Caro, "The Test of Time," *Texas Monthly,* March 2007.

19. Interview with Karl Rove by CMC, June 6, 2007.

20. Kenneth T. Walsh, "A Sinking Presidency," *U.S. News & World Report,* May 14, 2007.

21. Douglas Brinkley, "The Test of Time," *Texas Monthly,* March 2007.

22. Ibid.

23. Ulysses S. Grant, *Personal Memoirs of U.S. Grant: Selected Letters, 1839–1865,* p. 41.

24. Franklin D. Roosevelt, speech at Boston Garden, October 30, 1940.

25. Holly Bailey, Richard Wolffe, and Evan Thomas, "Bush's Truman Show," *Newsweek,* February 12, 2007.

26. Alonzo L. Hamby, *Man of the People: A Life of Harry S. Truman,* p. 640.

27. Ibid.

28. Christi Parsons, "Durbin Questions Bush on Comparisons to Truman," *Chicago Tribune,* December 8, 2006.

29. Peter Baker, "Off-the-Record Bush Wonders if She Likes Ike," *The Washington Post,* September 22, 2007.

30. David Halberstam, "The History Boys," *Vanity Fair,* August 2007.

31. David McCullough, *Truman,* p. 741.

32. Martin Anderson, *Revolution,* p. 288.

33. Michael Ignatieff, "Getting Iraq Wrong: What the War Has Taught Me about Political Judgment," *The New York Times Magazine,* August 5, 2007.

34. Ibid.

35. Interview with Michael Gerson by CMC, March 19, 2007.

36. Interview with Ari Fleischer by CMC, July 25, 2006.

37. Peter W. Galbraith: *The End of Iraq: How American Incompetence Created a War without End,* p. 5.

38. Bruce Jacobs, *National Guard,* March 2003.

39. Arlington National Cemetery burial citation, "Creighton Williams Abrams Jr., U.S. Army General."

40. David M. Kennedy, "The Wages of a Mercenary Army: Issues of Civil-Military Relations," *Bulletin of the American Academy,* Spring 2006.

41. Colin L. Powell, "U.S. Forces: Challenges Ahead," *Foreign Affairs,* Winter 1992/1993.

42. Ibid.

43. Ibid.

44. Interview with David M. Abshire by CMC, September 26, 2007.

45. Roger Cohen, "The Ottoman Swede," *The New York Times,* September 11, 2007.

46. Lou Cannon, "Hard Shoes to Fill," *The Washington Post,* January 20, 1989.

47. Editorial, "Reagan's Legacy for America," *Christian Science Monitor,* January 19, 1989.

48. Paul Johnson, "Europe and the Reagan Years," *Foreign Affairs,* January 1989.

49. Carl M. Cannon, "Clinton Staff Annoys Republicans by Tapping Successful Reagan Style," *The Baltimore Sun,* June 2, 1996.

50. Ibid.

51. Paul West, "Dole Exploits His Lead as His Rivals Tread Gingerly," *The Baltimore Sun,* July 16, 1995.

52. Michael Barone, *Our Country: The Shaping of America from Roosevelt to Reagan,* p. 509.

53. Thomas B. Edsall, "Bush Ascends Minus Solid Base," *The Washington Post,* January 20, 1989.

54. NBC News/Wall Street Journal Poll, "President Bush, White House 2008," June 18, 2007.

55. John Kenneth White, "The Death of the Reagan Coalition," Special Report for Zogby International, October 31, 2006.

56. Ibid.

57. Matthew Dowd, "The Test of Time," *Texas Monthly,* March 2007.

58. Jim Rutenberg, "Ex-Aide Details a Loss of Faith in the President," *New York Times,* April 1, 2007.

59. Michael Abramowitz, "Rightist Indignation: GOP Insider Vic Gold Launches a Broadside at the State of the Party," *The Washington Post,* April 2, 2007.

60. Ibid.

61. Susan Milligan, "Hastert Won't Seek Leadership Post in GOP," *Boston Globe,* November 9, 2006.

62. Brendan Farrington, "Romney: Conservative Like Reagan," Associated Press, August 6, 2007.

63. John McCain on *Meet the Press,* November 12, 2006.

64. Eric Krol, "Biggert Favors Rudy Giuliani," *Chicago Daily Herald,* July 31, 2007.

65. Katherine M. Skiba, "Romney Notches First Win in Iowa; Thompson Is 6th," *Milwaukee Journal Sentinel,* August 12, 2007.

66. George F. Will, "Three Good Options for the Right," *The Washington Post,* March 8, 2007.

67. David Frum, "Memo to GOP: Get a Grip," *National Review,* June 11, 2007.

68. Michael J. Gerson, *Heroic Conservatism,* p. 21.

69. Natan Sharansky, *The Case for Democracy: The Power of Freedom to Overcome Tyranny and Terror,* p. 138.

70. George W. Bush, "Remarks by the President in a Conversation on the USA Patriot Act," April 20, 2004.

71. Harry S. Truman, *This Week,* February 22, 1959.

72. Lee May and Laurie Becklund, "Citizen Reagans Are Home after Bittersweet Farewell," *Los Angeles Times,* January 21, 1989.

Bibliography

BOOKS AND MANUSCRIPTS

Abshire, David M. *Saving the Reagan Presidency: Trust Is the Coin of the Realm.* College Station: Texas A&M University Press, 2005.

Anderson, John Lee. *The Fall of Baghdad.* New York: Penguin, 2004.

Anderson, Martin. *Revolution.* New York: Harcourt, Brace Jovanovich, 1988.

Bacevich, Andrew J. *The New American Militarism: How Americans Are Seduced by War.* New York: Oxford University Press, 2005.

Barnes, Fred. *Rebel-in-Chief: Inside the Bold and Controversial Presidency of George W. Bush.* New York: Crown Forum, 2006.

Barone, Michael. *Our Country: The Shaping of America from Roosevelt to Reagan.* New York: The Free Press, 1990.

Barrett, Laurence I. *Gambling with History: Reagan in the White House.* Garden City, N.Y.: Doubleday, 1983.

Bartlett, Bruce. *Imposter: How George W. Bush Bankrupted America and Betrayed the Reagan Legacy.* New York: Doubleday, 2006.

Beatty, Jack. *The World according to Peter Drucker.* New York: The Free Press, 1998.

Beinart, Peter. *The Good Fight: Why Liberals—and Only Liberals—Can Win the War on Terror and Make America Great Again.* New York: HarperCollins, 2006.

Broder, David S., and Stephen Hess. *The Republican Establishment.* New York: Harper & Row, 1967.

Bronner, Ethan. *Battle for Justice: How the Bork Nomination Shook America.* New York: W. W. Norton, 1989.

Bundy, William. *A Tangled Web: The Making of Foreign Policy in the Nixon Presidency.* New York: Hill and Wang, 1998.

Bush, Barbara. *Barbara Bush: A Memoir.* New York: Lisa Drew Books, 1994.

Bush, George H. W., with Victor Gold. *Looking Forward.* New York: Random House, 1988.

Bush, George W., with Karen Hughes. *A Charge to Keep.* New York: William Morrow, 1999.

Cannon, Carl M. *The Pursuit of Happiness in Times of War.* Lanham, Md.: Rowman and Littlefield, 2004.

Cannon, Carl M., Lou Dubose, and Jan Reid. *Boy Genius: Karl Rove, the Architect of George W. Bush's Remarkable Political Triumphs.* New York: PublicAffairs, 2005.

Cannon, Lou. *Governor Reagan: His Rise to Power.* New York: PublicAffairs, 2003.

———. *President Reagan: The Role of a Lifetime.* New York: Simon and Schuster, 1991; 2d ed., New York: PublicAffairs, 2000.

———. *Reagan.* New York: G. P. Putnam's Sons, 1982.

———. *Ronald Reagan: The Presidential Portfolio.* New York: PublicAffairs, 2001.

———. *Ronnie and Jesse: A Political Odyssey.* Garden City, N.Y.: Doubleday, 1969.

Chace, James. *Acheson: The Secretary of State Who Created the American World.* New York: Simon and Schuster, 1998.

Clinton, William Jefferson. *My Life.* New York: Knopf, 2004.

Coll, Steve. *Ghost Wars: The Secret History of the CIA, Afghanistan, and Bin Laden, from the Soviet Invasion to September 10, 2001.* New York: Penguin, 2004.

Cooper, John Milton, Jr. *Breaking the Heart of the World: Woodrow Wilson and the Fight for the League of Nations.* Cambridge: Cambridge University Press, 2001.

Corwin, Edward S. *The President: Office and Powers.* New York: New York University Press, 1940.

Crile, George. *Charlie Wilson's War: The Extraordinary Story of the Largest Covert Operation in History.* New York: Atlantic Monthly Press, 2003.

Daalder, Ivo H., and James M. Lindsay. *America Unbound: The Bush Revolution in Foreign Policy.* Washington, D.C.: The Brookings Institution Press, 2003.

Deaver, Michael K. *A Different Drummer: My Thirty Years with Ronald Reagan.* New York: HarperCollins, 2001.

Deaver, Michael K., with Mickey Herskowitz. *Behind the Scenes.* New York: William Morrow, 1987.

DeYoung, Karen. *Soldier: The Life of Colin Powell.* New York: Alfred A. Knopf, 2006.

Diggins, John Patrick. *Ronald Reagan: Fate, Freedom, and the Making of History.* New York: W. W. Norton, 2007.

Doder, Dusko, and Louise Branson. *Gorbachev: Heretic in the Kremlin.* New York: Viking Penguin, 2000.

Draper, Robert. *Dead Certain: The Presidency of George W. Bush.* New York: The Free Press, 2007.

Drucker, Peter F. *The Age of Discontinuity: Guidelines to Our Changing Society.* New York: Harper and Row, 1992.

———. *Concept of the Corporation.* New York: John Day, 1946.

———. *The Essential Drucker.* New York: HarperCollins, 2001.

Eisenhower, Dwight D. *Mandate for Change: The White House Years, 1953–1956. A Personal Account,* vol. 2. New York: Doubleday, 1963.

Evans, Rowland, and Robert Novak. *The Reagan Revolution.* New York: E. P. Dutton, 1980.

Farrell, John A. *Tip O'Neill and the Democratic Century.* Boston: Little, Brown, 2001.

Frum, David. *The Right Man: The Surprising Presidency of George W. Bush.* New York: Random House, 2003.

Fukuyama, Francis. *America at the Crossroads: Democracy, Power, and the Neoconservative Legacy.* New Haven, Conn.: Yale University Press, 2006.

Galbraith, Peter W. *The End of Iraq: How American Incompetence Created a War without End.* New York: Simon and Schuster, 2006.

Garagiola, Joe. *Baseball Is a Funny Game.* New York: J. B. Lippincott, 1960.

Gergen, David. *Eyewitness to Power, the Essence of Leadership: Nixon to Clinton.* New York: Simon and Schuster, 2000.

Gerson, Michael J. *Heroic Conservatism.* New York: HarperCollins, 2007.

Goldwater, Barry. *The Conscience of a Conservative.* Shepardsville, Ky.: Victor, 1960.

Gorbachev, Mikhail. *At the Summit.* New York: Richardson, Steirman and Black, 1988.

_____. *Gorbachev: On My Country and the World.* New York: Columbia University Press, 2000.

Gordon, Michael R., and Bernard E. Trainor. *Cobra II: The Inside Story of the Invasion and Occupation of Iraq.* New York: Random House, 2006.

Gould, Louis L. *The Modern American Presidency.* Lawrence: University Press of Kansas, 2004.

Grant, Ulysses S. *Personal Memoirs of U.S. Grant: Selected Letters, 1839–1865.* New York: Library of America, 1990.

Greenburg, Jan Crawford. *Supreme Conflict: The Inside Story of the Struggle for Control of the United States Supreme Court.* New York: Penguin, 2007.

Greenspan, Alan. *The Age of Turbulence: Adventures in a New World.* New York: Penguin, 2007.

Greenstein, Fred I., ed. *The George W. Bush Presidency: An Early Assessment.* Baltimore: Johns Hopkins University Press, 2003.

_____. *The Hidden Hand Presidency: Eisenhower as Leader.* New York: Basic Books, 1982.

Gutman, Roy. *Banana Diplomacy: The Making of American Policy in Nicaragua, 1981–1987.* New York: Simon and Schuster, 1988.

Haig, Alexander M., Jr. *Caveat: Realism, Reagan, and Foreign Policy.* New York: Macmillan, 1984.

Halper, Stefan, and Jonathan Clarke. *America Alone: The Neo-Conservatives and Global Order.* Cambridge: Cambridge University Press, 2004.

Hamby, Alonzo L. *Man of the People: A Life of Harry S. Truman.* New York: Oxford University Press, 1995.

Hart, Jeffrey. *The Making of the American Conservative Mind:* National Review *and Its Times.* Wilmington, Del.: ISI Books, 2005.

Hayes, Stephen F. *Cheney: The Untold Story of America's Most Powerful and Controversial Vice President.* New York: HarperCollins, 2007.

Hess, Stephen, and James P. Pfiffner. *Organizing the Presidency.* Washington, D.C.: The Brookings Institution Press, 2002.

Hughes, Emmet John. *The Ordeal of Power: A Political Memoir of the Eisenhower Years.* New York: Atheneum, 1963.

Hughes, Karen. *Ten Minutes from Normal.* New York: Viking, 2004.

Jefferson, Thomas. *The Writings of Thomas Jefferson.* Vol. 1, *1760–1775.* Collected and edited by Paul Leicester Ford. New York: G. P. Putnam's Sons, 1892.

Johnson, Lyndon Baines. *The Vantage Point: Perspectives of the Presidency, 1963–1969.* New York: Holt, Reinhart and Winston, 1971.

Judis, John B. *The Folly of Empire: What George W. Bush Could Learn from Theodore Roosevelt and Woodrow Wilson.* Oxford: Oxford University Press, 2004.

Karnow, Stanley. *Vietnam: A History.* New York: Viking Penguin, 1983.

Kennedy, David M. *Freedom from Fear: The American People in Depression and War, 1929–1945.* New York: The American Oxford University Press, 1999.

Kirkpatrick, Jeane J. *Making War to Keep Peace.* New York: HarperCollins, 2007.

Kitfield, James. *War and Destiny: How the Bush Revolution in Foreign and Military Affairs Redefined American Power.* Dulles, Va.: Potomac Books, 2005.

Koch, Doro Bush. *My Father, My President: A Personal Account of the Life of George H. W. Bush.* New York: Warner Books, 2006.

Levy, Frank. *What Ronald Reagan Can Teach the U.S. about Welfare Reform.* Washington, D.C.: Urban Institute, 1977.

Logevall, Fredrik. *Choosing War: The Lost Chance for Peace and the Escalation of War in Vietnam.* Berkeley: University of California Press, 1999.

Mann, James. *Rise of the Vulcans: The History of Bush's War Cabinet.* New York: Viking, 2004.

Martin, David C., and John Walcott. *Best Laid Plans: The Inside Story of America's War against Terrorism.* New York: Harper and Row, 1988.

Matlock, Jack F., Jr. *Autopsy on an Empire: The American Ambassador's Account of the Collapse of the Soviet Union.* New York: Random House, 1983.

_____. *Reagan and Gorbachev: How the Cold War Ended.* New York: Random House, 1994.

McCullough, David. *John Adams.* New York: Simon and Schuster, 2002.

_____. *Truman.* New York: Simon and Schuster, 1992.

Meese, Edwin, III. *With Reagan: The Inside Story.* Washington, D.C.: Regnery, 1992.

Minutaglio, Bill. *First Son: George W. Bush and the Bush Family Dynasty.* New York: Times Books, 1999.

Neustadt, Richard E. *Presidential Power.* New York: John Wiley and Sons, 1960.

9/11 Commission. *Final Report of the National Commission on Terrorist Attacks upon the United States.* New York: W. W. Norton, 2004.

Nofziger, Lyn. *Nofziger.* Washington, D.C.: Regnery Gateway, 1992.

Noonan, Peggy. *What I Saw at the Revolution: A Political Life in the Reagan Era.* New York: Random House, 1990.

Nye, Joseph S., Jr. *Soft Power: The Means to Success in World Politics.* New York: PublicAffairs, 2004.

Oberdorfer, Don. *The Turn: From the Cold War to a New Era. The United States and the Soviet Union, 1983–1990*. New York: Poseidon Press, 1991.

Osborne, David, and Ted Gaebler. *Reinventing Government: How the Entrepreneurial Spirit Is Transforming the Public Sector*. New York: Penguin, 1993.

Packer, George. *The Assassins' Gate: America in Iraq*. New York: Farrar, Straus and Giroux, 2005.

Podhoretz, John. *Bush Country: How Dubya Became a Great President while Driving Liberals Insane*. New York: St. Martin's Press, 2005.

Powell, Colin, with Joseph E. Persico. *My American Journey*. New York: Random House, 1995.

Reagan, Ronald. *A Life in Letters*. Edited and with an introduction and commentary by Kiron K. Skinner, Annelise Anderson, and Martin Anderson. New York: The Free Press, 2003.

———. *Reagan: An American Life*. New York: Simon and Schuster, 1990.

———. *Reagan, In His Own Hand: The Writings of Ronald Reagan That Reveal His Revolutionary Vision for America*. Edited by Kiron K. Skinner, Annelise Anderson, and Martin Anderson. New York: The Free Press, 2001.

———. *The Reagan Diaries*. Edited by Douglas Brinkley. New York: HarperCollins, 2007.

Reagan, Ronald, and Richard C. Hubler. *Where's the Rest of Me? Ronald Reagan Tells His Own Story*. New York: Dell, 1965.

Reeves, Richard. *President Reagan: The Triumph of Imagination*. New York: Simon and Schuster, 2005.

Ricks, Thomas E. *Fiasco: The American Military Adventure in Iraq*. New York: Penguin, 2006.

Sammon, Bill. *Fighting Back: The War on Terrorism from Inside the Bush White House*. Washington, D.C.: Regnery, 2002.

Schlesinger, Arthur M., Jr. *The Imperial Presidency*. Boston: Houghton Mifflin, 1973.

———. *Robert Kennedy and His Times*. Boston: Houghton Mifflin, 1978.

———. *A Thousand Days: John F. Kennedy in the White House*. Boston: Houghton Mifflin, 1965.

Schweizer, Peter, and Rochelle Schweizer. *The Bushes: Portrait of a Dynasty*. New York: Doubleday, 2004.

Sharansky, Natan. *The Case for Democracy: The Power of Freedom to Overcome Tyranny and Terror*. New York: PublicAffairs, 2004.

Sherwood, Robert E. *Roosevelt and Hopkins: An Intimate History*. New York: Harper and Brothers, 1948.

Shilts, Randy. *And the Band Played On: Politics, People, and the AIDS Epidemic*. New York: St. Martin's Press, 1987.

Shultz, George P. *Turmoil and Triumph: My Years as Secretary of State*. New York: Charles Scribner's Sons, 1993.

Steinbeck, John. *Travels with Charley*. New York: Viking, 1962.

Thatcher, Margaret. *The Downing Street Years*. New York: HarperCollins, 1993.

Uldrich, Jack. *Soldier, Statesman, Peacemaker: Leadership Lessons from George C. Marshall*. New York: AMACOM Books, 2005.

Vaughn, Stephen. *Ronald Reagan in Hollywood: Movies and Politics.* Cambridge: Cambridge University Press, 1994.

Walsh, Lawrence E. *Iran-Contra: The Final Report.* New York: Times Books, 1994.

Wead, Doug. *All the President's Children.* New York: Atria Books, 2003.

Weinberger, Caspar. *Fighting for Peace: Seven Critical Years in the Pentagon.* New York: Warner Books, 1990.

Weinberger, Caspar W., with Gretchen Roberts. *In the Arena: A Memoir of the 20th Century.* Washington, D.C.: Regnery, 2001.

Whitman, Christine Todd. *It's My Party, Too: The Battle for the Heart of the GOP and the Future of America.* New York: Penguin, 2005.

Wills, Garry. *Reagan's America: Innocents at Home.* New York: Doubleday, 1987.

Wirthlin, Dick, with Wynton C. Hall. *The Greatest Communicator: What Ronald Reagan Taught Me about Politics, Leadership, and Life.* Hoboken, N.J.: John Wiley and Sons, 2004.

Wohlforth, William C., ed. *Witnesses to the End of the Cold War.* Baltimore: Johns Hopkins University Press, 1996.

Woodward, Bob. *Bush at War.* New York: Simon and Schuster, 2002.

_____. *Plan of Attack.* New York: Simon and Schuster, 2004.

_____. *State of Denial: Bush at War, Part III.* New York: Simon and Schuster, 2006.

Yalof, David A. "In Search of a Means to an End: George W. Bush and the Federal Judiciary." In *The George Bush Legacy,* edited by Colin Campbell, Bert A. Rockman, and Andrew Rudalevige. Washington, D.C.: Congressional Quarterly, 2007.

ARTICLES AND DOCUMENTS

Abcarian, Robin. "The Race to the White House; the Candidates Strive to Overcome Privilege," *Los Angeles Times,* June 20, 2004.

Abramowitz, Michael. "Rightist Indignation: GOP Insider Vic Gold Launches a Broadside at the State of the Party," *The Washington Post,* April 2, 2007.

Adelman, Kenneth. "Cakewalk in Iraq," *The Washington Post,* February 13, 2002.

Bailey, Holly, Richard Wolffe, and Evan Thomas. "Bush's Truman Show," *Newsweek,* February 12, 2007.

Baker, Peter. "Off-the-Record Bush Wonders if She Likes Ike," *The Washington Post,* September 22, 2007.

Barnes, Fred. "Not This Time: Don't Give Up When Victory Is at Hand," *The Weekly Standard,* February 5, 2007.

Barnes, Robert. "Justice Kennedy: The Highly Influential Man in the Middle," *The Washington Post,* May 13, 2007.

Bearak, Barry. "His Great Gift, to Blend In; Team Player Bush: A Yearning to Serve," *Los Angeles Times,* November 22, 1987.

Beatty, Jack. "The Education of Peter Drucker," *The Atlantic Monthly,* December 15, 2005.

Becker, Jo, and Barton Gellman. "Angler, the Cheney Vice Presidency: A Strong Push from Backstage," *The Washington Post,* June 26, 2007.

Begala, Paul. "Vengeance Is His," *Washington Monthly,* September 2004.

Biskupic, Joan. "Roberts Steers Court Right Back to Reagan," *USA Today,* June 29, 2007.

Bonfield, Tim. "Rock Star Bono Praises Bush for AIDS Plan," *The Cincinnati Enquirer,* July 8, 2003.

Brinkley, Douglas. "The Test of Time," *Texas Monthly,* March 2007.

Broder, David S. "End of a Dream," *The Washington Post,* April 1, 1981.

_____. "Texas Runoff Strains GOP Relations; Some Sour Feelings in the Bush Camp over Reagan's Role," *The Washington Post,* June 3, 1978.

Buchanan, Patrick J. "Was Reagan the First Neoconservative?" Creators Syndicate, June 14, 2004.

Burns, James MacGregor. "Risks of the Middle," *The Washington Post,* October 24, 1999.

Burrough, Bryan, Eugenia Peretz, David Rose, and David Wise. "The Path to War," *Vanity Fair,* May 1, 2004.

Byrne, John A., and Lindsey Gerdes. "The Man Who Invented Management," *Business Week,* November 28, 2005.

Cannon, Carl M. "America's Challenge," *National Journal,* September 15, 2001.

_____. "Clinton Staff Annoys Republicans by Tapping Successful Reagan Styles," *The Baltimore Sun,* June 2, 1996.

_____. "Family Tree, Party Roots," *National Journal,* July 21, 2001.

_____. "For the Love of the Game," *National Journal,* March 24, 2001.

_____. "Life Is Politics," *National Journal,* September 17, 2005.

_____. "The Mourner-in-Chief," *National Journal,* February 8, 2003.

_____. "The Point Man," *National Journal,* October 12, 2002.

_____. "The Presidency: What Bush Said," *National Journal,* July 26, 2003.

_____. "Untruth and Consequences," *The Atlantic Monthly,* January 2007.

Cannon, Carl M., and Alexis Simendinger. "Team Texas," *National Journal,* January 15, 2005.

Cannon, Lou. "Actor, Governor, President, Icon," *The Washington Post,* June 6, 2004.

_____. "At Daughter's Request, the President Hears Out a Peace Activist," *The Washington Post,* February 14, 1983.

_____. "Hang the Polls, Conviction Is What Counts on Latin Policy," *The Washington Post,* May 14, 1984.

_____. "Hard Shoes to Fill," *The Washington Post,* January 20, 1989.

_____. "More Than Teflon and Tinsel," *The Washington Post,* December 7, 1987.

_____. "Reagan Appoints McFarlane Adviser on U.S. Security," *The Washington Post,* October 18, 1983.

_____. "Reagan Defends Nicaraguan Role," *The Washington Post,* October 18, 1983.

_____. "What Happened to Reagan the Gunslinger?" *The Washington Post,* July 7, 1985.

Cannon, Lou, and Don Oberdorfer. "The Scripting of the Moscow Summit," *The Washington Post,* June 3, 1988.

_____. "Standing Fast: 'Vital Interests' of U.S. at Stake," *The Washington Post,* October 25, 1983.

_____. "The Superpowers' Struggle over 'Peaceful Coexistence,'" *The Washington Post,* June 3, 1988.

Cannon, Lou, and Juan Williams. "161 Marines Killed in Beirut; U.S. May Station Many Offshore," *The Washington Post,* October 24, 1983.

Carney, James. "Why Bush Doesn't Like Homework," *Time,* November 15, 1999.

Caro, Robert. "The Test of Time," *Texas Monthly,* March 2007.

Casteel, Chris. "Bush Runs on Honesty, Charisma," *Daily Oklahoman,* January 30, 2000.

Churchill, Winston. "Commentaries," *Times Literary Supplement,* May 27, 1939.

Clift, Eleanor. "Racial Icons," *Newsweek,* February 10, 2006.

Cohen, Roger. "The Ottoman Swede," *The New York Times,* September 13, 2007.

Coll, Steve. "General Accounting," *The New Yorker,* September 24, 2007.

Conversino, Mark J. "Operation Desert Fox: Effectiveness with Unintended Effects," *Air & Space Power Journal,* July 13, 2005.

Cunningham, Lana. "Bush Cites Reagan Stamina, Class," *Midland-Reporter Telegram,* February 15, 1981.

Davis, Lanny J. "True Confessions: A Democrat Likes George," *Los Angeles Times,* January 20, 2005.

Denton, Herbert H. "Israelis Begin Pulling Back Troops to Southern Lebanon," *The Washington Post,* September 4, 1983.

Department of Defense Commission (Long Commission) Report on Beirut International Airport Terrorist Attack, October 23, 1983.

Dowd, Matthew, et al. "The Test of Time," *Texas Monthly,* March 2007.

Drucker, Peter F. "The American CEO," *Wall Street Journal,* December 30, 2004.

_____. "Management Lessons of Irangate," *Wall Street Journal,* March 24, 1987.

Duffy, Michael, and Nancy Gibbs. "The Quiet Dynasty," *Time,* July 31, 2000.

Economist, The. "So Now You Know: George Bush," October 9, 2004.

Edsall, Thomas B. "Bush Ascends Minus Solid Base," *The Washington Post,* January 20, 1989.

Farrington, Brendan. "Romney: Conservative Like Reagan," Associated Press, August 6, 2007.

Fineman, Howard. "A President Finds His True Voice," *Newsweek,* September 24, 2001.

Frum, David. "Memo to GOP: Get a Grip," *National Review,* June 11, 2007.

Gergen, David. "Stubborn Kind of Fellow," *Compass: A Journal of Leadership,* Fall 2003.

Goldberg, Jeffrey. "Breaking Ranks: What Turned Brent Scowcroft against the Bush Administration," *The New Yorker,* October 31, 2005.

_____. "The End of the Affair," *The New Yorker,* November 20, 2006.

_____. "Party Unfaithful: The Republican Implosion," *The New Yorker,* June 4, 2007.

Greenstein, Fred. "Terror and Transformation: The Making of Bush's Leadership Style," *Compass: A Journal of Leadership,* Fall 2003.

Grey, Stephen, et al. "The Road to Ground Zero," *The Sunday Times* (London), January 6, 2002.

Gwyn, Richard. "Admit It: Bush Was Right on Iraq," *Toronto Star,* February 1, 2005.

Halberstam, David. "The History Boys," *Vanity Fair,* August 2007.

Hanrahan, John. "Senate Rejects Bork," United Press International, October 23, 1987.

Harpaz, Beth J. "Feminists Say Clarence Thomas Must Be Rejected," Associated Press, July 5, 1991.

Harris, John F., and Robin Wright. "Aid Grows amid Remarks about President's Absence," *The Washington Post,* December 29, 2004.

Harwood, Richard. "Tidy U.S. War Ends: 'We Blew Them Away,'" *The Washington Post,* November 6, 1983.

Hoffman, David. "Administration Credibility under Strain: Plans, Pronouncements on Mideast Contradictory," *The Washington Post,* February 12, 1984.

_____. "Day of Grief: President Mourns Dead," *The Washington Post,* September 5, 1983.

_____. "I Had a Funny Feeling in My Gut; Soviet Officer Faced Nuclear Armageddon," *The Washington Post,* February 10, 1999.

Ignatieff, Michael. "Getting Iraq Wrong: What the War Has Taught Me about Political Judgment," *The New York Times Magazine,* August 5, 2007.

Isaacson, Walter. "My Heritage Is Part of Who I Am," *Time,* August 7, 2000.

Johnson, Paul. "Europe and the Reagan Years," *Foreign Affairs,* January 1989.

Karlgaard, Rich. "Peter Drucker on Leadership," *Forbes,* November 19, 2004.

Kennedy, David M. "The Wages of a Mercenary Army: Issues of Civil-Military Relations," *Bulletin of the American Academy,* Spring 2006.

King, Warren. "Reagan Regarded AIDS 'Like It Was Measles,'" *Seattle Times,* August 31, 1989.

Kranish, Michael. "An American Dynasty," *Boston Globe,* April 23, 2001.

_____. "Hallmarks of Bush Style Were Seen at Harvard," *Boston Globe,* December 28, 1999.

Krauthammer, Charles. "Fukuyama's Fantasy," *The Washington Post,* March 28, 2006.

Krol, Eric. "Biggert Favors Rudy Giuliani," *Chicago Daily Herald,* July 3, 2007.

Lardner, George, Jr., and Lois Romano. "At Height of Vietnam, Bush Picks Guard," *The Washington Post,* July 28, 1999.

_____. "Bush Name Helps Fuel Oil Dealings," *The Washington Post,* July 30, 1999.

Lardner, Richard. "Admiral Cites Problems Undermining Iraq," Associated Press, July 30, 2007.

Leiby, Richard. "Breaking Ranks: Larry Wilkerson Attacked the Iraq War. In the Process, He Lost the Friendship of Colin Powell," *The Washington Post,* January 19, 2006.

Lemann, Nicholas. "Remember the Alamo," *The New Yorker,* October 18, 2004.

_____. "Without a Doubt," *The New Yorker,* October 14, 2002.

Loeb, Marshall, Lee Smith, and Ann Reilly Dowd. "Reagan on Decision-Making, Planning, Gorbachev, and More," *Fortune,* September 15, 1986.

Manly, Chesly. "Reagan Calls for U.S. Drive to Victory in Vietnam," *Chicago Tribune,* March 5, 1968.

Maraniss, David. "The Bush Bunch," *The Washington Post Magazine,* January 22, 1989.

May, Lee, and Laurie Becklund. "Citizen Reagans Are Home after Bittersweet Farewell," *Los Angeles Times,* January 21, 1989.

Mayer, Jane. "The Manipulator," *The New Yorker,* June 7, 2004.

Mayer, Jane, and Alexandra Robbins. "Dept. of Aptitude: How George W. Made the Grade," *The New Yorker,* November 8, 1999.

McLaughlin, Abraham. "The Bush Team Brings Very Corporate Values," *The Christian Science Monitor,* January 9, 2001.

McLeod, Don. "Domestic News," Associated Press, June 14, 1983.

Meyerson, Harold. "The Most Dangerous President Ever," *The American Prospect,* May 2003.

Miller, Alan C., and Judy Pasternak. "Records Show Bush's Focus on Big Picture," *Los Angeles Times,* August 2, 2000.

Milligan, Susan. "Hastert Won't Seek Leadership Post in GOP," *Boston Globe,* November 9, 2006.

Noonan, Peggy. "A Chat in the Oval Office," *Wall Street Journal,* June 25, 2001.

Nye, Joseph S., Jr. "The Decline of America's Soft Power," *Foreign Affairs,* May/June 2004.

_____. "Transformational Leadership and U.S. Grand Strategy," *Foreign Affairs,* July/August 2006.

Page, Susan. "Bush Is Opening Doors with a Diverse Cabinet," *USA Today,* December 9, 2004.

Parsons, Christi. "Durbin Questions Bush on Comparisons to Truman," *Chicago Tribune,* December 8, 2006.

Pfiffner, James P. "The First MBA President: George W. Bush as Public Administrator," *Public Administration Review,* January/February 2007.

Pooley, Eric, with S. C. Gwynne. "How George Got His Groove," *Time,* June 14, 1999.

Powell, Colin L. "U.S. Forces: Challenges Ahead," *Foreign Affairs,* Winter 1992–1993.

Raines, Howell. "The 'Dumb' Factor," *The Washington Post,* August 27, 2004.

Rodriguez, Gregory. "The GOP's High Hispanic Hopes," *Salon,* December 7, 1999.

Romano, Lois, and George Lardner Jr. "Bush's Move Up to the Majors," *The Washington Post,* July 31, 1999.

Rose, David. "Neo Culpa," *Vanity Fair,* November 3, 1966, online edition.

Rose, Gideon. "Welcome to the Occupation," *The Washington Post,* October 9, 2005.

Rosen, Jeffrey. "The Arrogance of Justice Anthony Kennedy," *The New Republic,* June 18, 2007.

Rosin, Hanna. "The Seeds of a Philosophy," *The Washington Post,* July 23, 2000.

Rutenberg, Jim. "Ex-Aide Details a Loss of Faith in the President," *The New York Times,* April 1, 2007.

Safire, William. "If You Break It . . . ," *The New York Times,* October 17, 2004.

Sammon, Bill. "Bush Fires Another Salvo at GOP," *The Washington Times,* October 6, 1999.

Sanoff, Alvin P. "Nobody Believes Any More That Government Delivers: A Conversation with Peter F. Drucker," *U.S. News & World Report,* December 21, 1981.

Schmidt, William E. "Mrs. Heckler Lists Added Funds," *The New York Times,* June 15, 1983.

Schneider, Mica, and Douglas Harbrecht. "George W's B-School Days," *Business Week,* February 15, 2001.

Schwartz, Peter, and Kevin Kelly. "The Relentless Contrarian," *Wired,* August 1996.

Schwarz, Jerry. "Secretary Announces Doubling of AIDS Funding Requests," Associated Press, August 17, 1983.

Scowcroft, Brent. "Don't Attack Saddam," *Wall Street Journal,* August 15, 2002.

Shapiro, Walter. "MBA President's Success Leaves Dems Out in Cold," *USA Today,* December 5, 2002.

Sheets, Ken. "Reagan Blasts U.S. Tactics in War," *Houston Chronicle,* October 10, 1968.

Sikorsky, Jonathan. "From British Cassandra to American Hero: The Churchill Legend in the World War II American Media," The Churchill Centre website, July 26, 2007.

Sinclair, Ward, and Peter Behr. "Reagan Triumphs in House Budget Vote, Horse Trading," *The Washington Post,* June 27, 1981.

Skiba, Katherine M. "Romney Notches First Win in Iowa; Thompson Is 6th," *Milwaukee Journal Sentinel,* August 12, 2007.

Slevin, Peter. "Wrong Turn and Postwar Crossroads?" *The Washington Post,* November 20, 2003.

Smith, Powl. "Iraq Is Not Vietnam, It's Guadalcanal: Learning the Real Lessons History Has for Today's War on Terror," *The Weekly Standard,* September 24, 2004.

Solomon, Burt. "National Security: All Leadership, All the Time," *National Journal,* December 1, 2001.

Solomon, John. "Bush, Harvard Business School and the Makings of a President," *The New York Times,* June 18, 2000.

———. "Managing USA Inc. Takes a Little More Drive," *The Washington Post,* July 28, 2002.

Stolberg, Sheryl Gay. "Suddenly, Bush Speaks of Controlling Spending," *The New York Times,* September 22, 2007.

Tapper, Jake. "Bush's EPA Chief Seeks Greener Pastures," *Salon,* May 22, 2003.

Thatcher, Margaret. "Reagan's Leadership, America's Recovery," *National Review,* December 30, 1988.

Time, "The Thirty-Second," April 23, 1945.

Truehart, Charles. "In Bork's Corner: Alan Simpson's Angry Defense," *The Washington Post,* October 2, 1987.

Truman, Harry S., *This Week,* February 22, 1959.

Vozick-Levinson, Simon W. "Former HBS Prof Blasts Bush," *The Harvard Crimson,* July 16, 2004.

Walsh, Kenneth T. "A Sinking Presidency," *U.S. News & World Report,* May 14, 2007.

Walters, Jonathan. "The Taming of Texas," *Governing,* July 1998.

Wark, John. "The Spring That Lurks in the Fall," *Tampa Tribune,* November 21, 1998.

White, John Kenneth. "The Death of the Reagan Coalition," Special Report for Zogby International, October 31, 2006.

Wilentz, Sean. "The Worst President in History? One of America's Leading Historians Assesses George W. Bush," *Rolling Stone,* April 21, 2006.

Will, George F. "Three Good Options for the Right," *The Washington Post,* March 8, 2007.

Wills, Garry. "The Hostage," *New York Review of Books,* August 13, 1992.

Woodward, Bob. "To Bones Men, Bush Is a Solid Moderate," *The Washington Post,* August 7, 1988.

Yardley, William. "Seattle Schools Take Stock after Justices Issue Ruling," *The New York Times,* July 1, 2007.

Index

About the Authors

Lou Cannon is the author of five previous books about Ronald Reagan and has been writing about Reagan for more than four decades. He covered Reagan's first term as governor of California for the *San Jose Mercury News,* and his later campaigns and the Reagan presidency for *The Washington Post.* Lou's White House coverage earned him the two most prestigious honors conferred on journalists who cover the presidency: the Aldo Beckman Award for "overall excellence in presidential coverage" (1984) and the Gerald R. Ford Prize for "distinguished reporting on the presidency" (1988). Lou has been described as the preeminent biographer of Reagan; his books include *President Reagan: The Role of a Lifetime* and *Governor Reagan: His Rise to Power.* He also wrote the critically acclaimed *Official Negligence: How Rodney King and the Riots Changed Los Angeles and the LAPD* (1998). A native of New York City, Lou was raised in Reno and Fallon, Nevada. He attended the University of Nevada and San Francisco State University and in 1983 was named a Distinguished Nevadan. He lives in Summerland, California.

Carl M. Cannon is White House correspondent for *National Journal*, the authoritative Washington magazine on government and politics. He has covered the Bill Clinton and George W. Bush presidencies in their entirety—the first five years of the Clinton White House for *The Baltimore Sun.* Carl worked at newspapers in Virginia, Georgia, and California before coming to Washington in 1982 as a regional correspondent for the *San Jose Mercury News.* It was not the last time Carl followed in his father's footsteps. He, too, won the Ford Prize (1999) and the Beckman Award (2006). In 1989, Carl was a member of the *Mercury News* staff that was awarded a Pulitzer Prize for coverage of the Loma Prieta earthquake. Carl has written for numerous magazines, including *The Atlantic Monthly*, *Forbes*, *Washington Monthly*, and *Reader's Digest*. He is a past president of the White House Correspondents' Association, author of *The Pursuit of Happiness in Times of War*, and co-author of *Boy Genius: Karl Rove, The Architect of George W. Bush's Remarkable Political Triumphs*. He was born in San Francisco, graduated from journalism school at the University of Colorado, and lives in Arlington, Virginia.

PublicAffairs is a publishing house founded in 1997. It is a tribute to the standards, values, and flair of three persons who have served as mentors to countless reporters, writers, editors, and book people of all kinds, including me.

I. F. STONE, proprietor of *I. F. Stone's Weekly*, combined a commitment to the First Amendment with entrepreneurial zeal and reporting skill and became one of the great independent journalists in American history. At the age of eighty, Izzy published *The Trial of Socrates*, which was a national bestseller. He wrote the book after he taught himself ancient Greek.

BENJAMIN C. BRADLEE was for nearly thirty years the charismatic editorial leader of *The Washington Post*. It was Ben who gave the *Post* the range and courage to pursue such historic issues as Watergate. He supported his reporters with a tenacity that made them fearless and it is no accident that so many became authors of influential, best-selling books.

ROBERT L. BERNSTEIN, the chief executive of Random House for more than a quarter century, guided one of the nation's premier publishing houses. Bob was personally responsible for many books of political dissent and argument that challenged tyranny around the globe. He is also the founder and longtime chair of Human Rights Watch, one of the most respected human rights organizations in the world.

.   .   .

For fifty years, the banner of Public Affairs Press was carried by its owner Morris B. Schnapper, who published Gandhi, Nasser, Toynbee, Truman, and about 1,500 other authors. In 1983, Schnapper was described by *The Washington Post* as "a redoubtable gadfly." His legacy will endure in the books to come.

Peter Osnos, *Founder and Editor-at-Large*

$1\frac{1}{2}$

2

$1\frac{1}{2}$

3 —

3 —

$1\frac{1}{2}$

4 x   8 : 8

$$\frac{\begin{array}{r} 11 \\ 6 \end{array}}{17}$$